1–2 CORINTHIANS

This commentary explains *1 and 2 Corinthians* passage by passage, following Paul's argument. It uses a variety of ancient sources to show how Paul's argument would have made sense to first-century readers, drawing from ancient letter-writing, speaking, and social conventions.

The commentary will be of interest to pastors, teachers, and others who read Paul's letters, because of its readability, firm grasp of the background and scholarship on the Corinthian correspondence, and its sensitivity to the sorts of questions asked by those wishing to apply Paul's letters today. It also will be of interest to scholars because of its exploration of ancient sources, often providing sources not previously cited in commentaries.

Craig S. Keener is a professor of New Testament at Eastern Seminary, a division of Eastern University. His previous twelve books include three award-winning commentaries: *The Gospel of John: A Commentary, A Commentary on the Gospel of Matthew*, and *The IVP Bible Background Commentary: New Testament*.

NEW CAMBRIDGE BIBLE COMMENTARY

GENERAL EDITOR: Ben Witherington III

HEBREW BIBLE/OLD TESTAMENT EDITOR: Bill T. Arnold

EDITORIAL BOARD
Bill T. Arnold, *Asbury Theological Seminary*
James D. G. Dunn, *University of Durham*
Michael V. Fox, *University of Wisconsin-Madison*
Robert P. Gordon, *University of Cambridge*
Judith Gundry-Volf, *Yale University*
Ben Witherington III, *Asbury Theological Seminary*

The New Cambridge Bible Commentary (NCBC) aims to elucidate the Hebrew and Christian Scriptures for a wide range of intellectually curious individuals. While building on the work and reputation of the Cambridge Bible Commentary popular in the 1960s and 1970s, the NCBC takes advantage of many of the rewards provided by scholarly research over the last four decades. Volumes utilize recent gains in rhetorical criticism, social scientific study of the Scriptures, narrative criticism, and other developing disciplines to exploit the growing edges in biblical studies. Accessible, jargon-free commentary, an annotated "Suggested Reading" list, and the entire New Revised Standard Version (NRSV) text under discussion are the hallmarks of all volumes in the series.

PUBLISHED VOLUMES IN THE SERIES
Exodus, Carol Meyers
Judges and Ruth, Victor H. Matthews
1–2 Corinthians, Craig S. Keener
The Letters of James and Jude, William F. Brosend II
Revelation, Ben Witherington III

FORTHCOMING VOLUMES
Genesis, Bill T. Arnold
Deuteronomy, Brent Strawn
Joshua, Douglas A. Knight
1–2 Chronicles, William M. Schniedewind
Psalms 1–72, Walter Brueggemann and Patrick D. Miller
Psalms 73–150, Walter Brueggemann and Patrick D. Miller
Isaiah 1–39, David Baer
Jeremiah, Baruch Halpern
Hosea, Joel, and Amos, J. J. M. Roberts
The Gospel of Matthew, Craig A. Evans
The Gospel of Luke, Amy-Jill Levine and Ben Witherington III
The Gospel of John, Jerome H. Neyrey
The Letters of John, Duane F. Watson

1–2 *Corinthians*

Craig S. Keener

Eastern Seminary

CAMBRIDGE UNIVERSITY PRESS
Cambridge, New York, Melbourne, Madrid, Cape Town, Singapore,
São Paulo, Delhi, Dubai, Tokyo, Mexico City

Cambridge University Press
32 Avenue of the Americas, New York, NY 10013-2473, USA

www.cambridge.org
Information on this title: www.cambridge.org/9780521542432

First published 2005

A catalog record for this publication is available from the British Library

Library of Congress Cataloging in Publication data

Keener, Craig S., 1960–
1–2 Corinthians / Craig S. Keener.
    p. cm. – (New Cambridge Bible commentary)
Includes bibliographical references and index.
ISBN 0-521-83462-7 (hardcover) – ISBN 0-521-54243-X (pbk.)
1. Bible. N.T. Corinthians – Commentaries.   I. Title: First–Second Corinthians.
II. Title.   III. Series.
BS2675.53.K44   2005
227′.2077 – dc22   2004024994

ISBN 978-0-521-83462-9 Hardback
ISBN 978-0-521-54243-2 Paperback

Contents

Abbreviations

AB	Anchor Bible
AGAJU	Arbeiten zur Geschichte des antiken Judentums und des Urchristentums 18
ANRW	*Aufstieg und Niedergang der Römischen Welt*
BA	*Biblical Archaeologist*
BAFCS	The Book of Acts in Its First Century Setting, 6 vols., ed. B. W. Winter (Grand Rapids, MI: Eerdmans; Carlisle: Paternoster Press, 1993–1996)
BDAG	*A Greek-English Lexicon of the NT and Other Early Christian Lierature*, by W. Bauer, rev. and ed. F. W. Danker, 3rd ed. (Chicago: University of Chicago, 2000)
BZ	*Biblische Zeitschrift*
CAH	*Cambridge Ancient History* (1966)
DNTB	*Dictionary of New Testament Background*, ed. Craig A. Evans and Stanley E. Porter (Leicester; Downers Grove, IL: Inter-Varsity, 2000)
ExpT	*Expository Times*
GRBS	*Greek, Roman and Byzantine Studies*
HTR	*Harvard Theological Review*
JBL	*Journal of Biblical Literature*
JETS	*Journal of the Evangelical Theological Society*
JPFC	*The Jewish People in the First Century*, 2 vols., ed. S. Safrai and M. Stern (Assen: Van Gorcum; Philadelphia: Fortress, 1974–1976)
JSNT	*Journal for the Study of the NT*
JSNTSS	Journal for the Study of the NT Supplement Series
JTS	*Journal of Theological Studies*
LEC	Library of Early Christianity, ed. W. A. Meeks
NASB	New American Standard Bible
NCB	New Century Bible

NICNT	New International Commentary on the New Testament
NIGTC	New International Greek Testament Commentaries
NovT	*Novum Testamentum*
NovTSup	Novum Testamentum Supplements
NRSV	New Revised Standard Version
NT	New Testament
NTS	*New Testament Studies*
OCD	*Oxford Classical Dictionary* (2003 ed.)
OJRS	*Ohio Journal of Religious Studies*
OT	Old Testament
RB	*Revue Biblique*
SBLDS	Society of Biblical Literature Dissertation Series
SBLRBS	Society of Biblical Literature Resources for Biblical Study
SBT	Studies in Biblical Theology
SJTOP	Scottish Journal of Theology Occasional Papers
SNTSMS	Society for New Testament Studies Monograph Series
TynB	*Tyndale Bulletin*
VigC	*Vigiliae Christianae*
WTWB	*The Westminster Theological Wordbook of the Bible*, ed. Donald E. Gowan (Louisville, KY: Westminster John Knox, 2003)

I. Introduction to Corinth and 1 Corinthians

I am happy to dedicate this commentary to two of my colleagues at the Palmer (formerly Eastern) Seminary of Eastern University: Ronald J. Sider and Samuel Escobar.

This commentary is meant to serve the needs of pastors and other students of the Bible. Although I include documentation for interested students to follow up, especially on otherwise difficult-to-trace claims about the ancient world, the focus is Paul's message and its value for readers today. I currently am organizing my research for a scholarly commentary on 1 Corinthians, but even my background notes for it already run to over seven times the space available for this commentary. Space constraints thus permit only cursory treatments of passages and documentation. (Nevertheless, although this is not the "scholarly" version, I hope that even scholars will find points of value here, especially ancient parallels to Paul's argumentation.)

We hear in Paul's correspondence his intimate and sometimes difficult pastoral relationship with the Corinthians. But whereas some principles he articulates seem straightforward, much sounds foreign to modern ears. Paul affirms the value of singleness in part because the end is near (1 Cor 7:26, 29); head coverings in part because of the angels (11:10) or because nature supports them (11:14); and the resurrection body in part on the analogy of heavenly "bodies" like the stars or moon. All of these arguments made sense for Paul's contemporaries, but modern readers find them difficult to apply directly. Yet if some readers' approach of simplistic, direct application is problematic, so is an approach that judges Paul unfit for modern readers based on modern criteria. Both approaches are anachronistic and culturally insensitive.

What is the value of two-thousand-year-old letters for today? Ancient writings in general reveal the underpinnings of much of modern intellectual thought, and often provide surprisingly contemporary critiques of analogous intellectual options available in our own era. Although their science is outdated, readers can profit from the ethical reflections of ancient philosophers and rabbis.

For those in the Christian tradition (presumably those most commonly interested in New Testament (NT) commentaries), we also stand in a tradition that claims to hear in a particular canon of texts God's message to the church. The NT canon includes not only biographic narratives about a salvation event, but other works, including samples of apostolic teaching to churches, such as Paul's letters. On these premises Christians may grant that God gave Paul wisdom to address the issues of his day. Yet even granting this, how do we translate his message in a manner relevant for our sometimes different issues today? Understanding the issues Paul addressed helps us better grasp the broader narrative of his conflict with the Corinthians, a narrative that, in addition to elements particular to ancient Corinth, reveals the sort of human interaction faced by most churches today. Observing how he applies his gospel to concrete situations provides us a model for how to reapply this gospel to other situations.

Although complete understanding of the particulars of Paul's advice to the Corinthians may elude us, much of the message of this apostle to the Gentiles challenges contemporary churches today. We could learn from him in matters such as mutual support versus competition; humility and sacrifice versus pursuit of status; marital fidelity; caring for the needy and rejecting materialism; spiritual gifts and their appropriate use for serving others; the value and sanctity of the body; and future accountability for present actions. In these letters we glimpse traces of Paul's ecstatic encounters with Jesus and an experience of the Spirit in early Christianity that is at once both strange and inviting to most modern Christians. Least often noted in "doctrinal" approaches but perhaps most characteristic of Paul (and some other ancient letter writers) is an intimate relationship between Paul and his churches that (once we account for different cultural approaches) offers some pastoral models today.

Some are tempted to read Paul's missionary enterprise in light of later colonialism. This is, however, a serious and anachronistic misreading of the first-century Paul. He advanced the cause of a tiny, persecuted minority; like many majority world ministers a half century ago, he belonged to a people subjugated by a colonial empire. It was largely through Paul's efforts that ethical monotheism became deeply grounded in, and eventually supplanted the polytheism of, much of the Western world. But monotheism was a largely Jewish notion, and Paul, following the lead of Diaspora Jews before him, had to strike the right balance between his ancient prophetic message, on the one hand, and, on the other, pastoral sensitivity to his Gentile converts. His synthesis offers a useful pastoral model today, especially if we understand the cultural setting he addressed.

PROPOSED BACKGROUNDS

Most proposed backgrounds for understanding the Corinthian correspondence contribute to our broader picture of the milieu, although some are more relevant than others.

Because mystery cults were by definition secretive and would hardly have been intimately known by Paul or all of his converts, the early-twentieth-century emphasis on mystery religions seems misplaced; they are one component among many constituting the religious milieu of the city. Corinth's status as a city with ports naturally invited a mixture of foreign religious elements, from Judaism to Egyptian cults (the latter increasing in the second century). But local Greco-Roman religion remained dominant, and the local Christians could not miss the temples and statues that filled their public places.

Although philosophic and other currents in Paul's day developed into Christian Gnosticism less than a century afterward, we lack secure evidence for Christian Gnosticism (in contrast to even many minor philosophers and orators) before the second century.[1] "Gnostic" elements and even the more commonly proposed emphasis on "overrealized eschatology" can be explained more simply by philosophic notions already prevalent in Greece. (Paul mentions eschatology in nearly every section, climaxing in Chapter 15, but this might counter Corinthians' Greek discomfort with eschatology rather than their emphasis on its realization.) Rabbinic Judaism provides a portrait of later developments in one strand of Palestinian Judaism (perhaps relevant to Paul's own background), but the Judaism of the Corinthian synagogue (cf. Acts 18:5–8) probably shared more in common with the Diaspora Judaism known from Asia Minor, Rome, and Egypt.[2]

Readings of the Corinthian correspondence today often stress social and rhetorical approaches. These are extremely valuable insofar as they follow concrete evidence. Sociological models must be used heuristically, hence adapted according to ancient Mediterranean evidence, but social history focuses on many questions that prove paramount in 1 Corinthians, especially the conflict between low- and high-status members.[3]

Because letters were not speeches and even later rhetorical handbooks treat them differently, rhetorical outlines of Paul's letters (as if they were handbook model speeches) are suspect.[4] But because Paul's letters, unlike most letters,

---

[1] For the most thoroughly "Gnostic" reading of 1 Corinthians, see W. Schmithals in the bibliography; one thorough refutation of pre-Christian Gnosticism is E. M. Yamauchi, *Pre-Christian Gnosticism: A Survey of the Proposed Evidences* (Grand Rapids, MI: Eerdmans, 1973).

[2] For Judaism in Asia Minor and Rome, see P. R. Trebilco, *Jewish Communities in Asia Minor*, SNTSMS 69 (Cambridge: Cambridge University Press, 1991); H. J. Leon, *The Jews of Ancient Rome* (Philadelphia: Jewish Publication Society of America, 1960). For Egypt we have Philo; much of the so-called Pseudepigrapha; and an even larger collection of papyri. Knowledge of specifically Corinthian Judaism is more limited; on it, see I. Levinskaya, *The Book of Acts in Its Diaspora Setting*, vol. 5 in The Book of Acts in its First Century Setting (Grand Rapids, MI: Eerdmans; Carlisle: Paternoster, 1996), 162–66.

[3] Earlier social approaches sometimes followed a Romanticist notion of the early Christian poor (e.g., S. J. Case, *The Social Origins of Christianity* [New York: Cooper Square, 1975; reprint of 1923 ed.]); this is corrected in more recent models (see Judge, Malherbe, Meeks and Theissen in the bibliography).

[4] See warnings in R. D. Anderson Jr., *Ancient Rhetorical Theory and Paul*, rev. ed. (Contributions to Biblical Exegesis and Theology, 18; Leuven: Peeters, 1999), esp. 114–17, 280

consist largely of argumentation, ancient rhetoric provides one of the most useful tools for analysis, because it structured formal patterns for argumentation. (The difference between Paul's and most ancient letters may be illustrated by their length; the average letters range from 18 to 209 words, although some writers such as Seneca tended to write longer moral epistles.[5] Shorter letters, like most papyri and most of Pliny's, were preferred.)[6]

Obvious rhetorical figures (such as anaphora) in Paul's letters prove that at the least he was familiar with pervasive speech conventions. It would be impossible to escape some exposure to rhetoric; it was one of two ancient forms of advanced education, and urban people heard its influence regularly at public events and in public places. One need not assume that Paul did tertiary study with a teacher of rhetoric to notice that his letters point to a Greco-Roman education in addition to studies in the Jewish Scriptures. He therefore must have been exposed to rhetoric, and his letters suggest that he developed rather than neglected what he learned. Corinthians of all classes encountered rhetoric in much entertainment and all legal and political discourse. Because most Corinthians would only hear Paul's letters read (and many would have been unable to read them), some consideration for rhetorical principles remains important.[7] The Corinthian Christians found his letters more compelling than his speech (2 Cor 10:10).

Many critics, however, felt that even spoken rhetoric should avoid excessive ornamentation,[8] and most expected letters to be even less weighted down with such ornament.[9] The excess of rhetorical devices in the Corinthian correspondence (esp. 1 Cor 1:12–13, 20, 26–28; also, e.g., 2 Cor 6:4–16) is therefore noteworthy. Local factors, in which rhetorical evaluation figured prominently (see 1 Cor 1:5, 17; 2:1–5; 2 Cor 10:10; 11:6), may help explain this emphasis, although other congregations also would have appreciated displays of learning (cf. Rom 5:3–5; 8:29–30, 35–39). Observing rhetorical devices helps us understand how Paul communicated in the idiom of his day, an essential prerequisite for anyone wishing to translate his ideas into other sociolinguistic settings.

(for 1 Corinthians in particular, 245–65); J. T. Reed, "The Epistle," 171–93 in *Handbook of Classical Rhetoric in the Hellenistic Period 330 b.c.–a.d. 400*, ed. S. E. Porter (Leiden: Brill, 1997); S. Porter, "Paul of Tarsus and his Letters," in ibid., 541–61, 562–67, 584–85; J. A. D. Weima, "Epistolary Theory," 327–30 in *DNTB*, 329; idem, "Letters, Greco-Roman," 640–44 in ibid.; D. L. Stamps, "Rhetoric," 953–59 in ibid., 958. Cf. Quintilian *Inst.* 10.1.36.
[5] See, for example, R. Anderson, *Rhetorical Theory* (1999), 113.
[6] Demetrius *Eloc.* 4.228. Given letters of such length, Paul may have even authored a draft first (cf., for example, Arrian *Alex.* 6.1.5).
[7] The common estimate of 10 percent literacy in the Empire is probably too low for urban centers like Corinth, but letters of this length and language would require better than average literary skill.
[8] For example, Dionysius of Halicarnassus *Dem.* 5, 6, 18 (admittedly an Atticist).
[9] See Cicero *Fam.* 9.21.1; Seneca *Lucil.* 75.1–3; Marcus Aurelius 1.7; Weima, "Theory," 328 (although cf. differently A. J. Malherbe, "Ancient Epistolary Theorists," *OJRS* 5 [2, October 1977]: 17).

The other form of advanced education was philosophy. Basic education included learning the sayings of famous thinkers and leaders from the past, including not only philosophers but moralists influenced by them. Despite the conventional enmity between rhetoric and philosophy, educated people usually drew from both realms. Orators used themes from moral and political philosophy in their discourses, and sages needing more students may have practiced their art by declaiming in public places to whoever would listen. Although most educated people were not trained in a particular philosophic school, they considered an eclectic knowledge and use of philosophy integral to a good education. Stoic philosophy was among the more pervasive forms in this era, so we should not be surprised to find recurrent (though not pervasive) contacts with philosophy, particularly (albeit not exclusively) Stoicism, in the Corinthian correspondence. (Platonic influences, growing and later dominant among intellectuals, also appear.) Because early Christian meetings involved moral teaching, one way many outsiders would have viewed Christians was as a philosophic school.[10]

Luke's claim that Paul was from Tarsus and spent several years there as an adult might have helped explain to ancient readers his grasp of basic philosophic language, because Tarsus was long a center of philosophy (Strabo 14.5.13), although Paul apparently lived longer in Jerusalem (Acts 22:3). Christians in centuries following Paul's letters to the Corinthians believed that the influence of pagan philosophy explained many of the attitudes of the Corinthians.[11]

Because Christian meetings lacked sacrifices and emphasized moral instruction, outsiders might view them more as a combination of a philosophic school, patronal banquets and (less acceptably) a religious association than a religious cult. (Gentile religion emphasized ritual and sacrifice, not moral instruction.) But, given their aniconic monotheism, basis in Scripture, and teachings on sexual matters, they would view them most closely in relation to Jewish associations, that is, synagogues (cf. Acts 18:4–8; sometimes to the embarrassment of local synagogue communities, Acts 18:12–13). God-fearers would be familiar with and new Gentile converts would become familiar with Jewish Scripture, which Paul quotes often.

ANCIENT LETTERS

A few comments on ancient letters (which in practice usually diverged from later handbooks' recommendations) are in order. Although the old distinction between letters and epistles is less emphasized today, it is important to note

---

[10] For example, S. K. Stowers, "Does Pauline Christianity Resemble a Hellenistic Philosophy?" 81–102 in *Paul Beyond the Judaism/Hellenism Divide*, ed. T. Engberg-Pedersen (Louisville, KY: Westminster, 2001); cf. Acts 19:9.

[11] See Chrysostom *Hom. Cor.*, *Proem*; Ambroasiaster *Commentary on Paul's Epistles*, *Proem*; Theodoret of Cyr *Comm. 1 Cor.* 163–64.

that Paul's extant letters are not pure letter-essays; although only Philemon is a purely personal letter, all the letters address concrete historical audiences. This is especially obvious in the Corinthian correspondence, in which Paul addresses at length a community of Christians he knew intimately.

Normally only literary letters were collected and published, and this practice was far more common in Rome than in the east. But later Christian communities that looked to the "apostle to the Gentiles" as their founder undoubtedly consulted with one another in collecting his letters as sample foundation documents that applied the apostolic message and ministry to particular situations.[12] Apart from "universal" paranesis and vice-lists, many philosophers (e.g., Seneca or even pseudepigraphic Cynic epistles) mixed apparently universal pronouncements with local applications. Similarly, we must read much in Paul's letters as a case study, a model for how he applied (and his successors can apply) the gospel to local situations. This seems particularly evident in much of the Corinthian correspondence.

The "occasional" nature of Paul's letters invites some interpretive observations. Ancient writers, like modern ones, typically assumed a measure of cultural and situational knowledge on the part of their audience.[13] Modern audiences can better understand the original letter if we can learn the implicit information the author shared with their audience without needing to articulate it explicitly. In contrast to those who think such concerns purely modern, sensitivity to writers' entire work (Quintilian *Inst.* 10.1.20–21), style (Seneca *Lucil.* 108.24–25; Philost. *Hrk.* 11.5), genre (Menander Rhetor 1.1.333.31–334.5), and historical context (Dionysius of Halicarnassus *Thuc.* 29) also were ancient concerns.

CORINTH

Corinth had been a leading center of Greek power before the Romans subdued it in 146 B.C.E. (although, contrary to Roman propaganda, archaeology reveals that some Greeks continued to live there). In 44 B.C.E., Caesar refounded Corinth as a Roman colony.[14] Although excavations suggest that the indigenous population never completely abandoned the site, it was the new Roman presence that later writers recognized (e.g., Pausanias *Descr.* 2.1.2). Corinth's official, public life in Paul's day was Roman, as architecture and most inscriptions indicate.[15]

---

[12] Collecting the letters was probably less difficult than we suppose; a second copy was probably retained in addition to the one sent, and subsequent copies could be made (Cicero *Fam.* 7.25.1; *Att.* 13.29; *Ep. Brut.* 3.1 [2.2.1]; cf. Seneca *Lucil.* 99). In rare emergencies, one might even send two copies by different means (Cicero *Fam.* 11.11.1).

[13] For example, Dionysius *Dem.* 46; Quintilian *Inst.* 10.1.22; Aulus Gellius *Noct. att.* 20.1.6.

[14] On its capture, see, for example, Polybius 39.2.–3.3; Virg. *Aen.* 6.836–837; perhaps even *Sib. Or.* 3.487–88; on its refounding, Strabo *Geogr.* 8.4.8; 8.6.23.

[15] See, for example, D. W. J. Gill, "Corinth: a Roman Colony in Achaea," *BZ* 37 (2, 1993): 259–64; D. Engels, *Roman Corinth: An Alternative Model for the Classical City* (Chicago: University of Chicago, 1990), 59.

Although many of the elite in Rome sought to imitate Greek ways, most of the elite in Corinth would seek to solidify their city's identification with Rome. In view of this evidence, it is not surprising that a higher than usual percentage of the names in Paul's circle in Corinth are Latin.

That being said, it is also not surprising that Paul wrote the letters in Greek. (Although Paul was likely a hereditary Roman citizen as Acts claims, this datum does not require his fluency in Latin; he grew up in the Greek-speaking East.) Even in Rome, educated Romans studied Greek language and culture;[16] still less could mercantile Corinth ignore its environment. Furthermore, despite its traditional base of Roman colonists, the city drew many immigrants from Greece and elsewhere in the eastern Mediterranean; most other Roman colonies had large populations that were not even Roman citizens. When Clement of Rome later wrote to the church in Corinth, he, like Paul before him, wrote in Greek. By the early second century C.E., Greek again became the city's official language, suggesting that the undercurrent of Greek language and culture had persisted.[17] Most relevantly, the congregation's likely Jewish and God-fearing Gentile founding center (cf. Acts 18:4) probably spoke Greek, as most Jews in Rome did. Understanding Paul's correspondence with Corinth requires knowledge of both Greek and Roman elements.

Corinth was widely known for its wealth in antiquity.[18] Its location on the Isthmus had long involved Corinth in trade (Thucydides 1.13.2, 5; Strabo 8.6.20), and some of our earliest references to the city portray wealth (Homer *Il.* 13.663–64). Local banking, artisans, and finally the current provincial seat would have further augmented the city's wealth. Despite the wide disparity between rich and poor that existed throughout the Empire, Corinth was particularly noteworthy for this problem (Alciphron *Parasites* 24.3.60, ¶1).[19] One particularly wealthy neighborhood was the Craneion.[20] Both excavations and inscriptions reveal that Corinth's prosperity had multiplied in the period between Augustus and Nero, that is, in the generations immediately preceding Paul's arrival.

Most Christians in Corinth were not well-to-do (1 Cor 1:26). But because nine of seventeen individuals Paul names there were on travels, it is a reasonable surmise that those named, who were probably particularly influential, were

---

[16] Cf., for example, Suet. *Claud.* 42; *Nero* 7.2. Both Musonius and Marcus Aurelius chose Greek as the language for their philosophic discourse, although Seneca preferred Latin.

[17] See R. M. Grant, *Paul in the Roman World: the Conflict at Corinth* (Louisville, KY: Westminster John Knox, 2001), 19; R. A. Horsley, *1 Corinthians* (Nashville: Abingdon, 1998), 25; cf. J. H. Kent, *The Inscriptions 1926–1950*, 8.3 in *Corinth* (Princeton, NJ: American School of Classical Studies at Athens, 1966), 18.

[18] Cf. Strabo *Geogr.* 8.6.19–20; *Greek Anthology* 6.40; for old Corinth, for example, Pindar *Ol.* 13.4.

[19] Archaeology, however, reveals a range between rich and poor in Corinth (D. Jongkind, "Corinth in the First Century AD: The Search for Another Class," *TynB* 52 [2001]: 139–48).

[20] It was also known in old Corinth (Xenophon *Hell.* 4.4.4; Plutarch *Alex.* 14.2). A Corinthian suburb provided an obvious example of wealth (Martial *Epig.* 5.35.3).

persons of means. This is especially clear in view of Erastus's office (Rom 16:23) and if Rom 16:23 means that Gaius hosted the entire church in his home. We cannot be sure whether Erastus was free or freed (or possibly even a public slave), hence what his status would have indicated in traditional Roman class distinctions; but in Corinth money defined status to some degree even for freedmen, and most likely he was free and purchased the office.

Condescending below appropriate status boundaries might be praiseworthy in terms of showing mercy but was considered shameful in terms of social intercourse.[21] Some other thinkers had challenged traditional class distinctions, though such challenges were apparently declining.[22] For Corinth's sexual reputation, see "A Closer Look" on 6:12–21.

Our only narrative (and only extra-Pauline) source for the church in Corinth is a limited passage in Acts (18:1–18). Although some dispute Luke's accuracy, the points of agreement are considerable; they are also often on secondary rather than primary points, suggesting that Luke wrote independently of any knowledge of the Corinthian correspondence.[23] According to Acts, the Corinthian church began in a synagogue (Acts 18:5–8); although this fits a pattern in Acts, it also helps explain (along with Paul's extended stay there, 18:11) Paul's ability to assume basic knowledge of biblical stories in his correspondence.

THE PARTICULAR SITUATION AND PAUL'S RESPONSE IN 1 CORINTHIANS

Although the majority of scholars still find at least two letters in 2 Corinthians, most commentators accept the unity of 1 Corinthians.[24] Whereas other ancient sources provide a fairly clear picture of life in ancient Corinth, it is especially from the letters themselves that we must reconstruct the particular situations that elicited them. Recent scholarship has challenged older reconstructions based on "mirror-reading," but some of the situation, at least, seems fairly clear. In the past, many suggested different "parties" in the Corinthian church (1 Cor 1:12) with diverging theologies (those who argued for Gnosticism in Corinth particularly favored this view). Today, scholars are more apt to emphasize divisions over favorite teachers and their styles (although for Paul any division warrants a theological critique).

---

[21] For example, Polybius 26.1.1–3, 12; Livy 41.20.1–3; Apuleius *Metam.* 10.23; Sir 13:2. But cf. Suetonius *Tit.* 8.2.

[22] T. Engberg-Pedersen, *Paul and the Stoics* (Louisville, KY: Westminster John Knox; Edinburgh: T. & T. Clark, 2000), 76.

[23] See further L. T. Johnson, *The Acts of the Apostles* (Sacra Pagina 5; Collegeville, MN: Liturgical Press, Michael Glazier, 1992), 325; B. Witherington III, *The Acts of the Apostles: A Socio-Rhetorical Commentary* (Grand Rapids, MI: Eerdmans, 1998), 537.

[24] For a thorough answer to remaining detractors, see M. M. Mitchell, *Paul and the Rhetoric of Reconciliation: An Exegetical Investigation of the Language and Composition of 1 Corinthians* (Louisville, KY: Westminster, 1991).

New issues arose after Paul left Corinth. Although Paul may lack "opponents" in 1 Corinthians, some Corinthians do wish to "evaluate" or "examine" him (1 Cor 9:3), a matter to which he is sensitive (2:14–15; 4:3).[25] Although neither Paul nor Apollos encouraged division (cf. 1 Cor 16:12), informal "schools" apparently formed around them in Paul's, and probably Apollos's, absence.

Audiences regularly evaluated speakers' rhetoric, and students chose teachers and defended them vigorously; this set the stage for the sorts of divisions in 1 Corinthians 1–4. Apollos's spoken rhetoric was superior to Paul's (although Paul's argumentation in his letters was skillful; 2 Cor 10:10). Like philosophers, however, Paul contended that his content (his "wisdom") mattered more than its form (1 Cor 1:17–2:10). The church ought to stop evaluating them by worldly (i.e., rhetorical) standards; only God's day of judgment would properly evaluate God's servants (1 Cor 3:13–4:5). Like a philosopher, Paul proved his character and provided a model by a hardship list (1 Cor 4:11–13).

As noted earlier, even if some have exaggerated Corinth's reputation for lewdness, male Gentile sexual behavior diverged significantly from biblical standards. That Paul must address Corinthian questions about sexuality and marriage, raised by their letter (1 Cor 7:1; perhaps 6:12–13) and reports about them (1 Cor 5:1), is not surprising. This topic also occasions a digression about church discipline, modeled after the intracommunity discipline allowed synagogues as communities of resident aliens (1 Cor 5:4–6:8).

Jews had long recognized both sexual immorality and food offered to idols as characteristic of pagan religion (cf. 1 Cor 10:7–8). The poor consumed the latter especially at religious festivals, and the well-to-do encountered both more regularly at banquets. Paul warns against knowingly eating food offered to idols in part because it could damage other believers' faith (1 Cor 8), and offers himself as an example of foregoing rights for others' sake (1 Cor 9). He opposes it, second, because the spirits the pagans worshiped in the idols are demons (1 Cor 10:20). After a digression about one matter of propriety (specifically, about women's head coverings) at Christian gatherings (which included meals), Paul turns to another, namely the meaning and consequent conduct of the Lord's supper (Ch. 11).

Continuing his discussion of propriety in the assembly, Paul turns to the proper use of spiritual gifts. The Corinthians apparently learned about most spiritual gifts, including tongues (14:18), from Paul's own practice. Because some were using tongues publicly in the assembly in a way that did not edify others, Paul emphasizes using gifts only to build up Christ's body (Chs. 12–14).

Strategically, Paul reserves his most important *theological* issue for his climax: the resurrection (Ch. 15; cf. 1:7). Many Greek philosophers emphasized the soul's

---

[25] The term appears nine times in 1 Corinthians and nowhere else in Pauline literature. Greek culture was intensely critical; for example, dramatists criticized heroes and even deities. Lamentation criticized deities more often than in OT analogies.

immortality, and none affirmed a future for the body; like other Jewish thinkers, Paul connected a future judgment in the body with moral living in the present (6:13–14; 15:32–33, 56–58; cf. 4:5). After addressing the life of the congregation itself, Paul concludes the letter with the collection, a letter of recommendation, and the epistolary closing (Ch. 16).

We cannot say for certain that all of the problems in the church were related, but it is possible that some socially "strong" elite members had initiated many of the problems. It was certainly they whom Paul accused of dishonoring the Lord's Supper (11:21–22). It was probably they who objected to wearing head coverings; preferred Apollos to Paul; most frequently ate meat hence found idol food least objectionable; and offered the philosophic rejection of the body's importance that required Paul's response (6:13–14; ch. 15). It also may have been they who faced sexual temptations at banquets or sponsored the philosophic defense of sex without marriage. That they also authored the division over tongues (perhaps adding it to their gifts in rhetorically skilled speech) also has been proposed, although the evidence appears more ambivalent.

II. Suggested Reading for Corinth and 1 Corinthians

S pace constraints prevent me from surveying and interacting with the full range of scholarship in this commentary (I have included perhaps 5 percent of my sources). The following list is a relatively concise sample introduction to some sources, omitting many good books and most good articles. More works were consulted than can be mentioned here; I will interact with them in my academic commentary on 1 Corinthians.

PAUL AND PHILOSOPHY

See A. J. Malherbe, *Paul and the Popular Philosophers* (Minneapolis: Fortress, 1989); several articles in *Paul in the Greco-Roman World: A Handbook*, ed. J. P. Sampley (Harrisburg, PA: Trinity, 2003). For Stoicism in particular, see T. Engberg-Pedersen, *Paul and the Stoics* (Louisville, KY: Westminster John Knox; Edinburgh: T. & T. Clark, 2000); D. A. deSilva, "Paul and the Stoa: A Comparison," *JETS* 38 (1995): 549–64. This must supplant the older view of Gnosticism in Corinth, argued most pervasively by W. Schmithals, *Gnosticism in Corinth: An Investigation of the Letters to the Corinthians*, trans. J. E. Steely (Nashville: Abingdon, 1971). The Hellenistic Jewish opponents of D. Georgi, *The Opponents of Paul in Second Corinthians* (Philadelphia: Fortress, 1986) are less subjective than Schmithals's Gnostic thesis but still require significant speculation and "mirror-reading."

RHETORIC AND 1 CORINTHIANS

Many scholars address the prominence of rhetoric in 1 Corinthians, esp. in 1–4; see esp. S. M. Pogoloff, *Logos and Sophia: The Rhetorical Structure of 1 Corinthians*, SBLDS 134 (Atlanta: Scholars, 1992); D. Litfin, *St. Paul's Theology of Proclamation: 1 Corinthians 1–4 and Greco-Roman rhetoric*, SNTSMS 83 (Cambridge: Cambridge University, 1994); B. W. Winter, *Philo and Paul among the Sophists*, SNTSMS 96 (Cambridge: Cambridge University, 1997); see also a number of articles by J. F. M. Smit. A commentary providing consistent attention to social and rhetorical questions is B. Witherington III, *Conflict and Community in Corinth: A Socio-Rhetorical Commentary on 1 and 2 Corinthians* (Grand Rapids, MI: Eerdmans; Carlisle: Paternoster, 1995).

The most sustained rhetorical analysis in terms of structure is that of M. M. Mitchell, *Paul and the Rhetoric of Reconciliation: An Exegetical Investigation of the Language and Composition of 1 Corinthians* (Louisville, KY: Westminster John Knox, 1991). Organizing the letter as a speech goes too far, and she may even overstate the pervasiveness of the theme of unity (the issues in 1 Cor 15, for example, do not easily reduce to this theme). Nevertheless, she has successfully demonstrated unity as a (possibly the) dominant theme and agenda in the letter; more significantly, her work is unsurpassed in analyzing the cultural context of argumentation for this theme. In 2 Corinthians, see, for example, J. D. H. Amador, "Revisiting 2 Corinthians: Rhetoric and the Case for Unity," *NTS* 46 (2000): 92–111.

For a survey of seminal studies in rhetoric and NT study, see D. F. Watson, "The NT and Greco-Roman Rhetoric: A Bibliography," *JETS* 31 (4, 1988): 465–72. For the rhetorical devices mentioned in the commentary, see G. O. Rowe, "Style," 121–57 in *Handbook of Classical Rhetoric in the Hellenistic Period 330 B.C.–A.D. 400*, ed. S. E. Porter (Leiden: Brill, 1997); R. D. Anderson Jr., *Glossary of Greek Rhetorical Terms Connected to Methods of Argumentation, Figures and Tropes from Anaximenes to Quintilian* (Leuven: Peeters, 2000); D. E. Aune, *The Westminster Dictionary of New Testament & Early Christian Literature & Rhetoric* (Louisville, KY: Westminster John Knox, 2003). For Paul and rhetoric, see R. F. Hock, "Paul and Greco-Roman Education," 198–227 in *Paul in the Greco-Roman World*, ed. Sampley (noted earlier). For a different approach (emphasizing literary structures), see J. D. Harvey, *Listening to the Text: Oral Patterning in Paul's Letters* (Leicester: Apollos; Grand Rapids, MI: Baker, 1998).

POLITICS AND 1 CORINTHIANS

Mitchell (see on rhetoric) is insightful here, arguing that Paul employs political rhetoric calling for unity. Whereas R. M. Grant (*Paul in the Roman World: The Conflict at Corinth* [Louisville, KY: Westminster John Knox, 2001]) sees Paul as more hierarchical and the Corinthian church as democratic, D. B. Martin (*Slavery as Salvation: The Metaphor of Slavery in Pauline Christianity* [New Haven, CT: Yale, 1990]) is among those who emphasize (undoubtedly rightly) the stratification of the Corinthian church.

SOCIAL SETTING OF 1 CORINTHIANS

The seminal work specifically on 1 Corinthians is G. Theissen, *The Social Setting of Pauline Christianity: Essays on Corinth*, trans. J. H. Schütz (Philadelphia:

Fortress, 1982); on Paul in general, see esp. E. A. Judge, *The Social Pattern of the Christian Groups in the First Century: Some Prolegomena to the Study of New Testament Ideas of Social Obligation* (London: Tyndale, 1960); A. J. Malherbe, *Social Aspects of Early Christianity*, 2nd ed. (Philadelphia: Fortress, 1983); and W. A. Meeks, *The First Urban Christians: The Social World of the Apostle Paul* (New Haven, CT: Yale, 1983). In the Corinthian correspondence, see especially P. Marshall, *Enmity in Corinth: Social Conventions in Paul's Relations with the Corinthians*, WUNT 2, Reihe 23 (Tübingen: Mohr Siebeck, 1987); and J. T. Fitzgerald, *Cracks in an Earthen Vessel: An Examination of the Catalogues of Hardships in the Corinthian Correspondence* (SBLDS 99; Atlanta: Scholars, 1988); more accessibly, idem, "Affliction Lists," 16–18 in *DNTB*.

For honor and patronage, see, for example, D. A. DeSilva, *Honor, Patronage, Kinship & Purity: Unlocking New Testament Culture* (Downers Grove, IL: InterVarsity, 2000); for patronage and the divisions in the church (esp. relevant to 1 Cor 5), see J. K. Chow, *Patronage and Power: A Study of Social Networks in Corinth* (JSNTSup 75; Sheffield: JSOT, 1992). Older works and some newer ones emphasize the relatively low social station of most Christians. More recent scholarship (Judge; Malherbe; Theissen, esp. 69–96) tends to focus on the influential minority with higher status.

PRIMARY SOURCES FOR CORINTH

The single most thorough primary text on Corinth (albeit from the second century) is Pausanias, *Description of Greece* Bk. 2. The most complete, accessible collection of primary texts is J. Murphy-O'Connor, *St. Paul's Corinth: Texts and Archaeology* (Wilmington, DE: Glazier, 1983). Scholars may pursue *Corinth: Results of Excavations Conducted by the American School of Classical Studies at Athens*, esp. vols. 8 (Cambridge: Harvard, 1931; Princeton, NJ: American School, 1966); 14 (American School, 1951); and 17–20 (American School, 1985–2003).

STUDIES OF THE LOCAL SITUATION IN CORINTH OR ITS CHURCH

See D. Engels, *Roman Corinth: An Alternative Model for the Classical City* (Chicago: University of Chicago, 1990), especially important for economic analysis. Besides sources mentioned under social setting above, see particularly for 1 Corinthians, B. W. Winter, *After Paul Left Corinth: The Influence of Secular Ethics and Social Change* (Grand Rapids, MI, Cambridge: Eerdmans, 2001); for 2 Corinthians, P. Marshall, noted earlier. Both reconstructions may be too detailed at points but offer significant insights.

ANCIENT LETTERS

See S. K. Stowers, *Letter Writing in Greco-Roman Antiquity* (LEC 5; Philadelphia: Westminster, 1986); D. E. Aune, *The New Testament in its Literary Environment*

(LEC 8; Philadelphia: Westminster, 1987), 158–225; A. J. Malherbe, "Ancient Epistolary Theorists," *OJRS* 5 (2, October 1977): 3–77; J. A. D. Weima, *Neglected Endings: The Significance of the Pauline Letter Closings*, JSNTSS 101 (Sheffield: Sheffield Academic Press, 1994). See here also L. L. Belleville, "Continuity or Discontinuity: A Fresh Look at 1 Corinthians in the Light of First-Century Epistolary Forms and Conventions," *EQ* 59 (1987): 15–37.

PAUL AND JEWISH TRADITION

See, for example, E. P. Sanders, *Paul and Palestinian Judaism* (Philadelphia: Fortress, 1977); on Paul's understanding of his Gentile converts, see especially T. L. Donaldson, *Paul and the Gentiles: Remapping the Apostle's Convictional World* (Minneapolis: Fortress, 1997). For Paul's use of Scripture, see C. D. Stanley, *Paul and the Language of Scripture: Citation Techniques in the Pauline Epistles and Contemporary Literature*, SNTSMS 69 (Cambridge: Cambridge University, 1992); esp. R. B. Hays, *Echoes of Scripture in the Letters of Paul* (New Haven, CT: Yale, 1989). For a patristic interpretation of 1 Corinthians, see especially Gerald Bray, ed., *1–2 Corinthians*, Ancient Christian Commentary on Scripture, NT 7 (Downers Grove, IL: InterVarsity, 1999), from which I have drawn several patristic citations.

THEOLOGY

J. D. G. Dunn, *The Theology of Paul the Apostle* (Grand Rapids, MI: Eerdmans, 1998); and V. P. Furnish, *The Theology of the First Letter to the Corinthians* (Cambridge: Cambridge University, 1999).

COMMENTARIES

The following list is by no means exhaustive but includes some of the commentaries that have made significant contributions. The boundaries for my categories (major scholarly commentaries; academic commentaries; and popular commentaries) are tentative and could be shifted at points. Commentaries from the 1990s and twenty-first century tend to employ more recent methodology (esp. social and rhetorical approaches), but some earlier commentators (e.g., Talbert) belong with more recent works methodologically. Furthermore some older commentaries (such as Conzelmann, Fee, Furnish, or Martin) remain among the most valuable because of their thoroughness and erudition, although offering less rhetorical criticism and sometimes overemphasizing realized eschatology. Even Moffatt's commentary, written in an earlier era of excessive focus on mystery cults, remains valuable because of his careful research on which others have been able to build.

Major Scholarly Commentaries

D. Garland, *1 Corinthians* (Grand Rapids, MI: Baker, 2003), thoroughly and critically engages a range of ancient and modern sources.

G. D. Fee, *The First Epistle to the Corinthians* (NICNT; Grand Rapids, MI: Eerdmans, 1987), interacts widely with earlier scholars, Paul's style and theology elsewhere, and in general exegetical and lexical matters. This is the most thorough commentary in text-critical matters.

A. C. Thiselton, *The First Epistle to the Corinthians: A Commentary on the Greek Text* (NIGTC; Cambridge, Grand Rapids, MI: Eerdmans, 2000), provides detailed attention to the details of the Greek text, a copious survey of contemporary and historical views, and is sensitive to cultural issues and the hermeneutical questions of moving from text to contemporary horizons.

Serious Academic Commentaries

C. K. Barrett, *A Commentary on the First Epistle to the Corinthians* (New York: Harper & Row, 1968), relatively concise and readable.

F. F. Bruce. *1 & 2 Corinthians* (NCB 38; London: Marshall, Morgan & Scott, 1971).

H. Conzelmann, *1 Corinthians: A Commentary on the First Epistle to the Corinthians*, trans. J. W. Leitch; ed. G. W. MacRae (Philadelphia: Fortress, 1975), thorough, balanced in most assessments.

J. Moffatt, *The First Epistle of Paul to the Corinthians*, Moffatt NT Commentary (London: Hodder & Stoughton, 1938).

C. H. Talbert, *Reading Corinthians: A Literary and Theological Commentary on 1 and 2 Corinthians* (New York: Crossroad, 1987), insightful with special attention to ancient sources.

B. Witherington III (noted earlier) provides the finest treatment from a social-rhetorical standpoint (the approach emphasized here); mid-level, useful to both students and scholars.

More Popular or Application-oriented Commentaries with Academic Interest

C. L. Blomberg, *1 Corinthians*, NIV Application Commentary (Grand Rapids, MI: Zondervan, 1994): not technical but academically informed.

R. F. Collins, *First Corinthians*, Sacra Pagina 7 (Collegeville, MN: Liturgical Press, Glazier, 1999): thorough (more than many mid-range commentaries), up-to-date, engaging ancient sources, although presented in a highly readable format.

J. D. G. Dunn, *1 Corinthians* (Sheffield: Sheffield Academic Press, 1995), concise and thematic.

R. B. Hays, *1 Corinthians* (Louisville, KY: Westminster John Knox, 1997), with careful literary and hermeneutical treatment.

R. A. Horsley, *1 Corinthians*, Abingdon NT Commentaries (Nashville: Abingdon, 1998): a fairly basic, brief, and reader-friendly format by a knowledgeable scholar; with attention to social method and background. Although usually balanced, he sometimes reconstructs the situation more speculatively than is preferred today.

J. Murphy-O'Connor, *1 Corinthians* (Wilmington, DE: Glazier, 1979; more recently, *1 Corinthians: The People's Bible Commentary*, rev. ed. (Oxford: Bible Reading Fellowship, 1999).

G. F. Snyder, *First Corinthians: A Faith Community Commentary* (Atlanta: Mercer University, 1992).

M. L. Soards, *1 Corinthians* (Peabody, MA: Hendrickson, 1999).

SAMPLE ARTICLES AND MONOGRAPHS

This is only a small percentage of those consulted.

1 Cor 1–4. For rhetoric in these chapters, see comments on rhetoric; also, for example, F. S. Malan, "Rhetorical Analysis of 1 Corinthians 4," *Theologia Viatorum* [Sovengo, South Africa] 20 (1993): 100–14; for politics (or politics alongside rhetoric), see (in addition to M. Mitchell, earlier), L. L. Welborn, "On the Discord in Corinth: 1 Corinthians 1–4 and Ancient Politics," *JBL* 106 (1987): 83–113; idem, *Politics and Rhetoric in the Corinthian Epistles* (Macon: Mercer University, 1997); A. D. Clarke, *Secular and Christian Leadership in Corinth: A Socio-Historical and Exegetical Study of 1 Corinthians 1–6*, AGAJU 18 (Leiden: Brill, 1993). On thanksgivings, see P. Schubert, *Form and Function of the Pauline Thanksgivings* (BZNW 20; Berlin: Töpelmann, 1939); P. T. O'Brien, *Introductory Thanksgivings in the Letters of Paul* (NovTSup 49; Leiden: Brill, 1977). For Hellenistic Jewish sources for some of Paul's language, including Philo, see B. Pearson, *The Pneumatikos-Psychikos Terminology in 1 Corinthians* (SBLDS 12; Missoula, MT: Scholars, 1973). On the nature of the division, see esp. Mitchell (under rhetoric); for the nature of congregations, see P. A. Harland, *Associations, Synagogues, and Congregations* (Minneapolis: Fortress, 2003).

1 Cor 5–7. On sexual morality, incest, and prostitution in antiquity and in these passages, see my "Adultery, Divorce and other irregular unions," 6–16 in *DNTB*. For the possibility of Scripture background to Paul's ethics in this section, see B. S. Rosner, *Paul, Scripture, & Ethics: A Study of 1 Corinthians 5–7* (Leiden: Brill, 1994); on courts, A. C. Mitchell, "Rich and Poor in the Courts of Corinth: Litigiousness and Status in 1 Corinthians 6.1–11," *NTS* 39 (1993): 562–86.

For the view that Paul was ascetic, see V. L. Wimbush, *Paul the Worldly Ascetic: Response to the World and Self-Understanding according to 1 Corinthians 7* (Macon: Mercer University, 1987); for the view that he was not, see W. Deming, *Paul on Marriage and Celibacy: The Hellenistic Background of 1 Corinthians 7*

(2nd ed.; Grand Rapids, MI: Eerdmans, 2003). On Paul's quotation of their letter and Paul becoming ascetic to ascetics and libertine to libertines, see especially the seminal article, H. Chadwick, "'All Things to All Men' (I Cor. ix.22)," *NTS* 1 (1955): 261–75 (developed by many other scholars). For the valuing or rejection of singleness and/or celibacy in antiquity, or other issues relevant to 1 Cor 7, see also D. L. Balch, "1 Cor 7:32–35 and Stoic Debates about Marriage, Anxiety, and Distraction," *JBL* 102 (1983): 429–39; my "Marriage," 680–93 in *DNTB*; . . . *And Marries Another* (Peabody: Hendrickson, 1991), 67–82; R. B. Ward, "Musonius and Paul on Marriage," *NTS* 36 (2, April 1990): 281–89; O. L. Yarbrough, *Not like the Gentiles: Marriage Rules in the Letters of Paul*, SBLDS 80 (Atlanta: Scholars, 1985). On divorce here, see D. Instone-Brewer, *Divorce and Remarriage in the Bible: The Social and Literary Context* (Grand Rapids, MI: Eerdmans, 2002); my *Marries Another*, 50–66.

1 Cor 8–11: Banquets, idol food, and head coverings. For ancient banquets, see D. E. Smith, *From Symposium to Eucharist: The Banquet in the Early Christian World* (Minneapolis: Fortress, 2003); for idol food, see W. L. Willis, *Idol Meat in Corinth* (SBLDS 68; Chico, CA: Scholars, 1985); see further P. D. Gooch, *Dangerous Food: 1 Corinthians 8–10 in Its Context*, SCJ 5 (Waterloo, ON: Wilfred Laurier University, 1993); cf. also D. W. J. Gill, "The Meat Market at Corinth (1 Corinthians 10:25)," *TynB* 43 (1992): 389–93; B. Witherington, "Not So Idle Thoughts about *eidoluthuton*," *TynB* 44 (2, 1993): 237–54.

For Paul's work in 1 Cor 9, see R. F. Hock, *The Social Context of Paul's Ministry: Tentmaking and Apostleship* (Philadelphia: Fortress, 1980); for issues in 9:19–23, see esp. D. B. Martin, *Slavery as Salvation: The Metaphor of Slavery in Pauline Christianity* (New Haven, CT: Yale, 1990); C. Glad, *Paul and Philodemus: Adaptability in Epicurean and Early Christian Psychagogy* (NovTSup 81; Leiden: Brill, 1995); also M. M. Mitchell, "Pauline Accommodation and 'Condescension' (συγκατάβασις): 1 Cor 9:19–23 and the History of Influence," 197–214 in *Paul Beyond the Judaism/Hellenism Divide*, ed. T. Engberg-Pedersen (Louisville, KY: Westminster John Knox, 2001). For 10:23–11:1, see D. F. Watson, "1 Corinthians 10:23–11:1 in the Light of Greco-Roman Rhetoric: The Role of Rhetorical Questions," *JBL* 108 (2, 1989): 301–18.

For 11:2–16, on headcoverings, see D. Gill, "The Importance of Roman Portraiture for Head-coverings in 1 Corinthians 11:2–16," *TynB* 41 (2, 1990): 245–60; C. Keener, "Head Coverings," 442–46 in *DNTB*; idem, *Paul, Women & Wives* (Peabody, MA: Hendrickson, 1992), 19–69; R. MacMullen, "Women in Public in the Roman Empire," *Historia* 29 (1980): 209–18; R. E. Oster, "When Men Wore Veils to Worship: The Historical Context of 1 Corinthians 11:4," *NTS* 34 (1988): 481–505; C. L. Thompson, "Hairstyles, Head Coverings and St. Paul: Portraits from Roman Corinth," *BA* 51 (1988): 101–15; B. W. Winter, *Roman Wives, Roman Widows: The Appearance of New Women and the Pauline Communities* (Grand Rapids, MI: Eerdmans, 2003), 77–96. For the Lord's Supper, see esp. Theissen, *Social Setting*, 145–74.

1 Cor 12–14: On rhetoric, for example, J. Smit, "The Genre of 1 Corinthians 13 in the Light of Classical Rhetoric," *NovT* 33 (3, 1991): 193–216. On the body of Christ, see, for example, J. A. T. Robinson, *The Body: A Study in Pauline Theology* (London: SCM, 1957); E. Schweizer, *The Church as the Body of Christ* (Atlanta: John Knox Press, 1976). For the Spirit in early Christian thought, see J. D. G. Dunn, *Baptism in the Holy Spirit* (Philadelphia: Westminster; London: SCM, 1970); C. Keener, "Spirit, Holy Spirit, Advocate, Breath, Wind," 484–96 in *WTWB*; esp. here G. D. Fee, *God's Empowering Presence: The Holy Spirit in the Letters of Paul* (Peabody: Hendrickson, 1991). For Paul's Jewish context, see M. Isaacs, *The Concept of Spirit: A Study of Pneuma in Hellenistic Judaism and its Bearing on the New Testament* (London: Heythrop College, 1976). On prophecy in antiquity and/or early Christianity, and spiritual gifts, see David E. Aune, *Prophecy in Early Christianity and the Ancient Mediterranean World* (Grand Rapids, MI: Eerdmans, 1983); J. Bowman, "Prophets and Prophecy in Talmud and Midrash," *EQ* 22 (1950): 107–14, 205–20, 255–75; T. Callan, "Prophecy and Ecstasy in Greco-Roman Religion and in 1 Corinthians," *NovT* 27 (2, 1985): 125–40; D. A. Carson, *Showing the Spirit: A Theological Exposition of 1 Corinthians 12–14* (Grand Rapids, MI: Baker, 1987); C. Forbes, *Prophecy and Inspired Speech in Early Christianity and its Hellenistic Environment* (Peabody, MA: Hendrickson, 1997; Tübingen: Mohr, 1995); D. Hill, *New Testament Prophecy* (Atlanta: John Knox, 1979); C. Keener, *The Spirit in the Gospels and Acts* (Peabody, MA: Hendrickson, 1997), 6–48; D. B. Martin, "Tongues of Angels and Other Status Indicators," *JAAR* 59 (1992): 547–589; S. Schatzmann, *A Pauline Theology of Charismata* (Peabody, MA: Hendrickson, 1987); M. Turner, *The Holy Spirit and Spiritual Gifts in the New Testament Church and Today*, rev. ed. (Peabody, MA: Hendrickson, 1998).

Of relevance to the particularly disputed passage 14:34–35, see, for example, L. A. Jervis, "1 Corinthians 14.34–35: A Reconsideration of Paul's Limitation of the Free Speech of Some Corinthian Women," *JSNT* 58 (1995): 51–74; C. Keener, *Wives*, 70–100 (with fuller documentation of earlier views); T. Paige, "The Social Matrix of Women's Speech at Corinth: The Context and meaning of the Command to Silence in 1 Corinthians 14:33b-36," *BBR* 12 (2002): 217–42; A. C. Wire, *The Corinthian Women Prophets: A Reconstruction through Paul's Rhetoric* (Minneapolis: Fortress, 1990).

1 Cor 15–16. J. R. Asher, *Polarity and Change in 1 Corinthians 15: A Study of Metaphysics, Rhetoric, and Resurrection*, Hermeneutische Untersuchungen zur Theologie 42 (Tübingen: Mohr, 2000); D. B. Martin, *The Corinthian Body* (New Haven, CT: Yale, 1995), esp. 104–36.

Because commentaries often cite many of the same primary sources except when a commentary introduces a new influx of ancient sources, I have tried to focus in the notes on "new" primary sources (while including some old ones). In this way, I trust that this commentary, although written for a much wider audience, also will prove valuable to scholars. Given this commentary's limited size, however, I can provide only a small percentage of my documentation even from ancient sources. Thus, in numerous cases, when much more documentation is available than can be cited and when I have provided more substantial documentation elsewhere, I refer students wishing further sources to treatments in my other works. (For example, the question of "nakedness" in antiquity, relevant to 2 Cor 5:3, and "sleeplessness," relevant to 2 Cor 11:27, are both treated extensively in passages in my John commentary.) My primary sources are often merely examples, drawn from various genres and periods but often typical of the wider range of evidence they represent. I hope to provide a fuller commentary on 1 Corinthians within the next decade.

III. Commentary on 1 Corinthians

1:1–3: PAUL'S GREETING

1:1: Paul, called to be an apostle of Christ Jesus by the will of God, and our brother Sosthenes,
1:2: To the church of God that is in Corinth, to those who are sanctified in Christ Jesus, called to be saints, together with all those who in every place call on the name of our Lord Jesus Christ, both their Lord and ours:
1:3: Grace to you and peace from God our Father and the Lord Jesus Christ.

Paul's letter introduction follows conventional forms for letter openings (especially for Jews writing in Greek). Conventional elements of letter openings could be expanded as needed, and Paul's specific departures from such convention reveal distinctive points about his apostolic understanding of God, Christ, and what the church is meant to be.

Letters always began by naming the sender. Paul introduces himself as an "apostle," a legate of Christ authorized to act as his representative (1:1).[1] Although his ministry is not yet in much dispute (contrast 2 Cor 2:14–7:3; esp. 11:5; 12:11–12), he has reason to emphasize his apostolic authority (1 Cor 9:1–2, 5; 12:28–29); for him, however, this calling is a mark of suffering (4:9) and undeserved favor (15:7, 9).

Composite authorship claims in Paul may function differently in different texts;[2] although the letter often uses "we" to include Paul's fellow-workers (e.g., 4:9–13), Paul does not limit it to Sosthenes (cf. 4:6; 9:4–5). Sosthenes may have been Paul's rhetorically proficient scribe (cf. Rom 16:22), helping with multiple rhetorical devices that counter criticism of his speech (see discussion later). But

---

[1] Backgrounds include ancient messenger conceptions, including as applied to prophets (see C. S. Keener, *The Gospel of John: A Commentary*, 2 vols. [Peabody, MA: Hendrickson, 2003], 310–15).

[2] See J. Murphy-O'Connor, "Co-Authorship in the Corinthian Correspondence," *RB* 100 (1993): 562–79 (who plausibly favors a significant role for Sosthenes).

Paul continues his rhetorical displays in 2 Corinthians, and sometimes claims of composite authorship simply served as special greetings in ancient letters.[3] If "Sosthenes" is the Corinthian synagogue official in Acts 18:17, he may have followed Crispus, another official of that synagogue, in joining the Christian movement (Acts 18:8; 1 Cor 1:14).

Although Corinth undoubtedly hosted multiple house churches, Paul emphasizes unity by addressing God's "church" in Corinth (1:2).[4] The phrase "church of God" (in the singular) appears four times in this letter, once in 2 Corinthians 1:1, and only one other time in Paul's undisputed letters. Despite their behavior (elaborated from 1:10 forward), Paul acknowledges them as "saints" "sanctified in Christ" (cf. also 6:11). These are biblical designations for the people God set apart by his own redemptive act. Like Israel, they were summoned to live holy (set apart, "sanctified") to God because God had chosen them; they were not chosen because of how they were living (1 Cor 6:9–11; cf. Lev 20:24; Deut 9:5–6). (In contrast to popular modern usage, this "sanctification," or being set apart, occurred when they joined God's people, that is, at conversion, and was first of all a ritual category. Being set apart for and dedicated to God meant being set apart from the profane things of the world. The Corinthians obviously needed to display in practice what they had been called to be [cf. 2 Cor 7:1]!) Paul further reminds them here that they belong to a larger community of believers worldwide, to whom they should be accountable in some ways (cf. 1 Cor 11:16; 14:33; 16:1, 19).

Greek letters frequently included the greeting *chairein*, which sounds similar to *charis*, "grace." *Shalom*, or "peace," was the traditional Jewish greeting, and Jewish letters written in Greek could combine these ("Greetings and true peace," 2 Macc 1:1). Most letters, Jewish or Greek, included toward their beginning a prayer for the recipients' welfare (one common form appears in 3 Jn 2). This prayer often took the form of a "wish-prayer," or blessing, in which one invoked God (or a deity) indirectly, such as *shalom*, "[May God bless you with] peace."[5] It was something like our modern, "God bless you." "Grace" means something like, "divine generosity"; "peace" something like, "prosperity." Thus, many early Christians (e.g., 1 Pet 1:2; 2 Pet 1:2; 2 Jn 3; Rev 1:4; 1 Clem title) opened letters with, "May God bless you generously and guard your welfare."

What is most striking, however, is Paul's divergence from the usual pattern. These opening wish-prayers invoked a deity; but Paul (and some other early

---

[3] See Cicero *Fam.* 16.1.title; 16.3.title; 16.4.title; 16.5.title; 16.6.title; 16.9.title; 16.11.1.

[4] Like "synagogue," Paul's term for "church" here in the LXX translates the Hebrew *qahal*, used for Israel's "assembly"; but it also applied to other assemblies, including citizen assemblies in free cities.

[5] On wish-prayers, see esp. Gordon P. Wiles, *Paul's Intercessory Prayers: The Significance of the Intercessory Prayer Passages in the Letters of St. Paul*, SNTSMS 24 (Cambridge: Cambridge University, 1974), 25–29. For such blessings of "mercy and peace," see 2 *Bar.* 78:2–3.

Christians) invoked not only "God our Father" for a blessing (as in Judaism) but also "our Lord Jesus Christ" (1:3). These letters thus open with a recognition of Jesus' deity in some sense (spelled out in 8:5–6; cf. also Theodoret *Comm. 1 Cor.* 166).

1:4–9: PAUL THANKS GOD FOR THE CORINTHIAN CHRISTIANS

1:4: I give thanks to my God always for you because of the grace of God that has been given you in Christ Jesus,
1:5: for in every way you have been enriched in him, in speech and knowledge of every kind –
1:6: just as the testimony of Christ has been strengthened among you –
1:7: so that you are not lacking in any spiritual gift as you wait for the revealing of our Lord Jesus Christ.
1:8: He will also strengthen you to the end, so that you may be blameless on the day of our Lord Jesus Christ.
1:9: God is faithful; by him you were called into the fellowship of his Son, Jesus Christ our Lord.

*A*ncient letter openings sometimes included a thanksgiving to a deity, as here (1:4);[6] of Paul's undisputed letters, only Galatians conspicuously omits one. Speeches and official letters (or other works with the same objectives as speeches) also typically opened with a complimentary *exordium*, praising the addressees.[7] Such introductory compliments, in thanksgivings or otherwise, established common ground with the audience and invited their favor.[8] This approach was crucial especially if (as in 1:10–17) one planned to challenge the audience's behavior afterward. Ancient orators praised people for native gifts (like beauty or high birth) as well as for deliberate virtues; that Paul praises only the Corinthians' gifts and not their behavior, however, may be noteworthy.

Introductory sections often outlined or summarized what would follow in a well-organized work.[9] Paul does not provide an outline, but does introduce themes he will treat in greater detail, such as spiritual gifts (notably speech and knowledge, Chs. 1–2; 12–14); evaluation at Christ's return (1 Cor 3:12–17; 4:5;

---

[6] E.g., 2 Macc 1:11; Fronto *Ad M. Caes.* 5.41 (56).
[7] In written works, e.g., Cicero *Fam.* 13.66.1; Statius *Silvae* 2.preface.
[8] E.g., Cicero *Inv.* 1.15.20; *De or.* 1.31.143; Quintilian *Inst.* 4.1.5. See here Theodoret *Comm. 1 Cor.* 166; Chrysostom *Hom. Cor.* 2.5.
[9] E.g., *Rhet. Alex.* 29, 1436a, lines 33–39; Dionysius of Halicarnassus *Lys.* 24; Seneca *Controv.* 1.pref.21; Quintilian *Inst.* 4.1.35. Outside speeches, see e.g., Polybius 3.1.3–3.5.9; 11.1.4–5; Dionysius of Halicarnassus *Thuc.* 19; Virgil *Aen.* 1.1–6.

Ch. 15); and possibly "fellowship" (1:10–17). "The day of our Lord Jesus Christ" (1:8) fulfills biblical prophecies about "the day of the Lord" (cf. comment on 1:3; 8:6). The term used for "fellowship" can imply intimate acquaintance or business partnership, but scholars especially dispute whether "fellowship of his Son" (1:9) means fellowship *with* his Son, or a community of fellowship based on his Son. If it means the latter, it addresses the very issue Paul must challenge in 1:10–12.

1:10–12: DEMAND FOR UNITY

1:10: Now I appeal to you, brothers and sisters, by the name of our Lord Jesus Christ, that all of you be in agreement and that there be no divisions among you, but that you be united in the same mind and the same purpose.

1:11: For it has been reported to me by Chloe's people that there are quarrels among you, my brothers and sisters.

1:12: What I mean is that each of you says, "I belong to Paul," or "I belong to Apollos," or "I belong to Cephas," or "I belong to Christ."

*A*lthough letters were not speeches, Paul's persuasive argument here follows the conventions of deliberative rhetoric: after praising the audience, he states his thesis (at least for the immediate matter) in 1:10, then turns to a narration of events leading to the current problem (1:11–12 or, as others argue, 1:11–17).[10] After his complimentary exordium, his letter invites attention with what appears to be an unexpectedly critical turn,[11] though mixing praise and blame was conventional. (For what it is worth, ancient handbooks would have viewed at least 1:10–4:21 as a letter of admonition.)

Paul's appeal for unity in 1:10 reflects a conventional (but widely needed) topic of exhortation in antiquity. (Urging one by a deity, here by Christ, was a familiar idiom; for example, Isaeus *Menecles* 47; Rom 15:30; 2 Cor 10:1.) Speeches or essays urging "harmony" or "concord" characterize orators, philosophers, moralists, and politicians.[12] Rivalry and enmity characterized Greco-Roman society, not only in politics and oratory but also in drama, sports, and so

---

[10] See G. A. Kennedy, *New Testament Interpretation through Rhetorical Criticism* (Chapel Hill: University of North Carolina, 1984), 24–25 (favoring 1:11–12); M. Mitchell, *Rhetoric* (1991), 184, 198, 200–01 (favoring 1:11–17).

[11] On the value of surprise (i.e., the device *paradoxon*) in ancient rhetoric, see R. Dean Anderson Jr., *Glossary of Greek Rhetorical Terms Connected to Methods of Argumentation, Figures and Tropes from Anaximenes to Quintilian* (Leuven: Peeters, 2000), 88.

[12] E.g., Xenophon *Mem.* 4.4.16; Dionysius of Halicarnassus *Ant. rom.* 7.53.1; Musonius Rufus 8, p. 64, line 13; Menander Rhetor 2.3, 384, lines 23–24; see further M. Mitchell, *Rhetoric* (1991), 60–64. For common speech and mind, see ibid., 68–69, 76–79.

forth.[13] Such rivalry made mixed loyalties dangerous; being friends with another's enemy made one a sharer in that enmity.[14] Sometimes people even found grounds to take their enemies to court (cf. 1 Cor 6:6; e.g., Cornelius Nepos 7.4.1). Yet everyone recognized that divisions weakened the state, making it susceptible to outside hostility;[15] the principle would be true of the church as well. Some scholars suggest that competing house churches abetted division; others favor a conflict between members of higher and lower status (a conflict that appears later in the letter).

Paul claims that he learned about the divisions from "Chloe's people" (1:11). Paul's charge in 1:11–12 invites naming a source; those who received news commonly named sources, except when doing so would injure the source.[16] If Paul had heard the same information from the church's delegation (16:17), naming a less controversial source might also protect those Paul recommends in 16:15–16, 18. Although we cannot be sure, the best guess is that Chloe was a well-to-do businesswoman, whose servants or freedpersons had traveled on business. Travelers were the usual means of sending letters, and also usually carried news by word of mouth.[17] Because the church knows her, she was probably a member or friend of the church and based in Corinth; but she could have been based in Ephesus and traveled to Corinth occasionally; or perhaps only her household members were part of the church.

The claims to be "of Paul," "Apollos," "Cephas" (translated into Greek as "Peter"), or "Christ" (1:12) need not, as some have argued, represent four distinct parties in the church. Nor need they represent theological divisions, as others have argued. Yet it is equally unlikely (against some commentators) that the only division is the entire church against Paul. Probably the two functioning divisions are followers of Paul versus followers of Apollos, as it is only Apollos who appears again in this section (3:5–7; 4:6).

Political parties were named for the founders to which adherents professed loyalty, and slogans analogous to, "I am of so-and-so" characterized rivalries of political, academic, and athletic factions.[18] Nevertheless, the "I am of so-and-so" is Paul's own hyperbolic caricature of the church's division. This caricature also allows Paul to demonstrate his (previously maligned) rhetorical skill, including

---

[13] For ancient examples of rivalries, see C. Keener, *John* (2003), 1061–62; on enmity, see P. Marshall, *Enmity in Corinth: Social Conventions in Paul's Relations with the Corinthians* (WUNT 2, Reihe 23; Tübingen: Mohr, 1987), 35–69.

[14] See, e.g., Lysias *Or.* 9.13, §115; Aeschines *Tim.* 193–95; Cicero *Scaur.* 17.38; P. Marshall, *Enmity* (1987), 67–69.

[15] E.g., Polybius 3.104.1; Livy 3.66.4; Sallust *Bell. Jug.* 73.5; Matt 12:25.

[16] For naming sources, see e.g., Xenophon *Mem.* 4.8.4; *Apol.* 2, 10, 14, 27; Alciphron *Fishermen* 21.1.18; for avoiding naming for the source's sake, see 5:1; Lysias *Or.* 8.8, §113.

[17] For oral news, see e.g., Euripides *El.* 361–62; Cicero *Fam.* 1.6.1; 3.1.1; 9.2.1; 9.6.1; *Apoll. K. Tyre* 8.

[18] See L. L. Welborn, *Politics and Rhetoric in the Corinthian Epistles* (Macon, GA: Mercer University, 1997), 1–42, esp. 11–16.

his use of *anaphora* (the parallel clause structure x . . . /x . . .) and *sermocinatio* (creating and attributing statements).[19]

Paul's formula here allows him to argue the opposite in 3:21–22: It is not the Corinthians who belong to their leaders, but their leaders who belong to them as the one church. That the Corinthians knew of Cephas in 3:22; 9:5; 15:5 need not mean that he had visited, any more than Galatians 2:9–12 shows that James had visited Galatia.[20] The parallel form in all four claims suggests that "I am of Christ" is one of the hypothetical slogans; creating a distinct Christ party, as if Christ were divided (1:13), would be *reductio ad absurdum*. Despite the grammatical parallel, however, those who suggest that "I am of Christ" is Paul's response to the other three claims have a point, at least in terms of Paul's overarching view in the letter as a whole, as suggested by the parallel in 3:21–23.

The Christian assemblies included a fellowship meal (the Lord's supper) that resembled other banquets (see comment on 11:17–34), and banquets often included lecturers among their entertainment. In such a setting it was natural for hearers of status to evaluate the speakers according to the norms their society used in such settings. (Audiences critically evaluated and compared speakers' rhetorical abilities, for example, in Cicero *De or.* 3.14.52.)[21] Like politicians, philosophers and orators competed for attention; more practically, they vied for pupils and their fees. Students evaluated speakers; chose those they favored; and vigorously advocated their schools' interests against those of other schools (Suetonius *Tib.* 11.3; Philostratus *Vit. soph.* 1.8.490), including in Corinth (cf. Dio Chrysostom *Or.* 8.9).[22] Sometimes this competition even came to blows. Not long after Paul's letter other visitors would appeal to this tendency of the Corinthians (2 Cor 10:12).

Whether or not Paul and Apollos liked it (they seem to be on favorable terms, 16:12), their supporters had made them into rival teachers (1:13–14). Thus, something like rudimentary schools, possibly rooted in separate house churches, now competed! Factions boasted in either Paul or Apollos versus the other (4:6). Because Paul goes on at great length about the divine wisdom he preached to them as opposed to the human wisdom by which they are divided, the Corinthians probably favored the rival teachers based on intellectual (perhaps philosophical and rhetorical) standards in their milieu.

---

[19] See also Stephen M. Pogoloff, *Logos and Sophia: The Rhetorical Situation of 1 Corinthians* (SBLDS 134; Atlanta: Scholars Press, 1992), 106.

[20] The sound of *Cephas* provided a rhetorical connection with *Christos* as *Paulos* matched "Apollos" (for *paronomasia*, see *Rhet. Her.* 4.21.29–22.31).

[21] Cf. even rhetorical evaluation of earlier orators, e.g., Dionysius of Halicarnassus *Isoc.* 13; *Thuc.* 29.

[22] See further S. Pogoloff, *Logos* (1992), 175–76; B. W. Winter, *Philo and Paul among the Sophists* (SNTSMS 96; Cambridge: Cambridge University, 1997), 170–76; idem, *After Paul Left Corinth: The Influence of Secular Ethics and Social Change* (Grand Rapids, Cambridge: Eerdmans, 2001), 34–40.

1:13–17: NOT A GOSPEL ABOUT PREACHERS

1:13: Has Christ been divided? Was Paul crucified for you? Or were you baptized in the name of Paul?

1:14: I thank God that I baptized none of you except Crispus and Gaius,

1:15: so that no one can say that you were baptized in my name.

1:16: (I did baptize also the household of Stephanas; beyond that, I do not know whether I baptized anyone else.)

1:17: For Christ did not send me to baptize but to proclaim the gospel, and not with eloquent wisdom, so that the cross of Christ might not be emptied of its power.

*B*efore reminding them of what the gospel is (1:17–2:5), Paul insists on what it is not (1:13–17); its messengers preach Christ, not themselves (2 Cor 4:5). Responding to divisions over "Paul" and "Christ" in 1:12, Paul demands whether Christ can be divided (as if belonging only to one faction) or if the Corinthians as a whole were baptized in Paul's name (hence into only one faction; 1:13). This is rhetorically effective *reductio ad absurdum* (making an opposing perspective appear ridiculous by extending it to an absurd conclusion).[23] The use of three parallel rhetorical questions further reinforces the point rhetorically (cf. 9:1; 2 Cor 6:14–16).[24]

Some propose that Paul responds in 1:13–15 to the Corinthians' abuse of baptism. It is possible that they misunderstood or overemphasized baptism (cf. 10:2; esp. 15:29), but it is much less likely that they actually think they were baptized in someone's name. The superviser of initiation into the mysteries could be the initiate's "father" in the rites, but the washing of initiatory purification did not hold the same significance of conversion that baptism held in early Judaism and Christianity.[25] This is simply another reduction to the absurd. Neither baptism nor rhetoric (which in antiquity often overshadowed the message) could be permitted to distract from the gospel message (1:17).

Crispus is probably a former synagogue official (Acts 18:8). Gaius, although a common name, may refer to a well-to-do patron who hosted all or much of the church in Corinth (Rom 16:23); some suggest that Gaius is the praenomen of Titius Justus (Acts 18:7). Both names reflect the Latin element of the city, possibly Roman citizens.[26] Much religion in pagan society focused around the

---

[23] For examples of *reductio*, see, e.g., Seneca *Lucil.* 83.9; 113.20; Aelius Aristides *Defense of Oratory* 336–38, §§111D–112D.

[24] Both orators (e.g., Lysias *Or.* 10.22–23, §118; Cicero *Rosc. Amer.* 1.2) and sages (Musonius Rufus 11, p. 80.22–25; 13B, p. 90.13–16; 15, p. 98.25–27; Epictetus *Diatr.* 1.19.2–6) accumulated rhetorical questions.

[25] On initiations in the mysteries versus Jewish baptism, see C. Keener, *John* (2003), 442–48.

[26] Other Jews could bear the Roman name "Crispus"; e.g., Josephus *Life* 382, 388; cf. *CIJ* 1:89, §126; 1:92, §132; 2:26, §762.

household, and the conversion of a household head usually invited that of the entire household (although cf. 7:12–16). Paul's apparent lapse in memory, adding Stephanas as an apparent afterthought, would be acceptable rhetorically in a letter or other casual discourse,[27] especially if he employed it to underscore how secondary his baptismal role was.[28] Corinth had copious baths and famous fountains (including the Fountain of Peirene, expanded in the next century); Paul could have used any of these for baptisms.

1:18–25: GOD'S FOOLISHNESS AND HUMAN WISDOM

1:18: For the message about the cross is foolishness to those who are perishing, but to us who are being saved it is the power of God.
1:19: For it is written,

"I will destroy the wisdom of the wise,
and the discernment of the discerning I will thwart."

1:20: Where is the one who is wise? Where is the scribe? Where is the debater of this age? Has not God made foolish the wisdom of the world?
1:21: For since, in the wisdom of God, the world did not know God through wisdom, God decided, through the foolishness of our proclamation, to save those who believe.
1:22: For Jews demand signs and Greeks desire wisdom,
1:23: but we proclaim Christ crucified, a stumbling block to Jews and foolishness to Gentiles,
1:24: but to those who are the called, both Jews and Greeks, Christ the power of God and the wisdom of God.
1:25: For God's foolishness is wiser than human wisdom, and God's weakness is stronger than human strength.

Although 1:17 concludes the example about baptism, it is transitional; it introduces the theme of this paragraph, contending that the cross of Christ is more powerful than human wisdom or eloquence. This paragraph argues that what appears foolish to the wisest humans may be the deeper, inscrutable wisdom of God. Like philosophers, Paul can use rhetoric to denounce abuse of rhetoric. Thus, for example, he holds attention with antithesis (1:18); citation of authority (1:19); a series of four rhetorical questions and the threefold repetition

---

[27] Cicero *Att.* 8.14.4; 14.5; (Ps) Dionysius *Epideictic* 4.269; Valerius Maximus 3.2.2. It is probably deliberate in Cicero *Verr.* 2.4.26.57.
[28] Epanorthosis (correction of a previous remark) was even an acceptable rhetorical device, if done deliberately (*Rhet. Her.* 4.26.36).

of "where is . . . " (1:20);[29] and finally in 1:25, antithesis and paradoxical, ironic oxymorons (God's "foolishness" and "weakness").[30]

Some apply the world's "wisdom" here only to rhetoric; others to philosophy or to skill in general. Paul's critique must at least include the abuse of persuasion techniques, since he mentions "eloquent wisdom" (1:17), "debaters" (i.e., sophists, 1:20), and "human wisdom" based on "lofty words" (2:1, 4–5). Like most philosophers, he disapproves of the way many orators valued persuasive form over truth content.

But the "wisdom" that blinded the world to God (1:21; 2:8) cannot be *limited* to rhetoric alone; it also implies philosophy (the other form of advanced education available to the elite) and other worldly assumptions. (Patristic interpreters also noted the influence of pagan philosophy and rhetoric among the Corinthians.) This warning applied also to Jewish "scribes" (1:20) and Jewish desire for "signs" (1:22; cf. Mk 8:11–12); although "scribes" in most villages were simply executors of legal documents, Paul's high-status sense here follows the Jewish usage for law teachers, also evident in the Synoptics.[31] His quotation in 1:19 also implies that Jewish tradition was inadequate (Is 29:13–14), as do many biblical prototypes for 1:20 (Is 19:12; 33:18; 44:25; 47:10; Job 12:17; Jer 8:8–9; 9:12, 23; Prov 21:30).

Crucifixion (1:23; 2:2) would prove the opposite of a messiah's success (cf. also Deut 21:23; Gal 3:13). The specific quest for wisdom, however, is attributed especially to Greeks, known for their philosophy (1:22). Paul must have concurred with the Jewish recognition that pagan wisdom led away from God.[32] Paul himself uses, as in 2:6, and agreed with, too much of the Jewish wisdom tradition to make that the focal point of his attack. But whereas he probably sympathized with the Jewish identification of wisdom and Torah (Bar 3:29–4:1; Sir 15:1; 24:23), he transfers the connection especially to Christ (1:24, 30; 8:6; 10:4), probably following earlier Wisdom Christology.[33]

More than the "signs" (probably miracles, literally "powers") and "wisdom" mortals seek (1:22), God offers his true "power" and "wisdom" in Christ (1:24). Although scholars offer various backgrounds for Christ as "power" here, Paul especially challenges elite status and worldly "power," that is, power in the *social* sense (see 1:26; cf. 8:7–12).[34] Just as some associated salvation or destruction

---

29 On the questions, see comment on 1:13; for repetition of elements, see, e.g., Cicero *Or. Brut.* 39.135 and *anaphora* in 1:12.

30 Everyone would recognize human reason as folly compared with divine wisdom (e.g., Xenophon *Mem.* 1.4.8; Pindar *Paean* 21, frg. 61.4).

31 See S. Pogoloff, *Logos* (1992), 160–63; Craig S. Keener, *A Commentary on the Gospel of Matthew* (Grand Rapids, MI: Eerdmans, 1999), 537–38.

32 *Jub.* 36:5; *Sib. Or.* 3.229, 584–90; *Let. Aris.* 137; see Rom 1:22; Col 2:8.

33 On early Wisdom Christology and its Jewish sources, see C. Keener, *John* (2003), 300–03, 350–63; B. Witherington, *Jesus the Sage: The Pilgrimage of Wisdom* (Minneapolis: Fortress, 1994). Cf. "power" in Acts 8:10.

34 As in, e.g., Xenophon *Mem.* 2.1.12; Musonius Rufus 15, p. 98, lines 5–6; Philostratus *Hrk.* 4.1–2; 33.25; Eunapius 462.

with people's response to God's wisdom (*1 En.* 5:8; 98:3; 99:10; *2 Bar.* 51:7), Paul links them with response to the cross (1:18). Most people would view this connection as "foolish" (1:23); crucifixion was the most degrading common form of execution.[35] Jesus' preaching of the kingdom, once offered in Jerusalem, would appear as a challenge to the Sadducees and potentially to Rome itself; to suspicious ears, the message of the cross was not only the folly of a dead and defeated leader but treasonous advocacy of a would-be usurper of the emperor's majesty. It was the height of folly! Paul uses his educated argumentation in the service of God's wisdom, not for the applause of the elite (cf. 3:18; 4:10); none of the marks of education or elite status among the world's powerful impressed the God who exercised all power and wisdom.

A CLOSER LOOK: PAUL'S USE OF RHETORIC

Corinthian Christians evidently criticized Paul for his rhetoric; Paul's letters reveal sophistication in argument, but his delivery may have been deficient (1 Cor 2:3; 2 Cor 10:10; 11:6). Certainly Paul was not an Atticist and lacked classical allusions, elements likely to be especially appealing to elite hearers. Educated church fathers (writing after the full-blown revival of Atticism) admitted that Paul did not exhibit the level of rhetoric their social peers expected. Paul's command of rhetoric was, however, better than the vast majority of literate people, and may have improved during his travels in the Diaspora. Yet the Corinthian elite may have found Apollos more acceptable rhetorically (Acts 18:24), making rhetorical prowess a major ground for the church's division (see comment on 1:10–12).[36]

It is probably for this very reason that Paul fills his Corinthian correspondence, including this chapter, with rhetorical devices (possibly, but not necessarily, with the help of his scribe or Sosthenes, and without necessarily knowing technical names for such devices). Rhetoricians warned against excessive use of the devices they taught, although students in declamation schools may have ignored such advice.[37] Letters were to use even more natural language. (Thus, for example, the renowned orator Cicero avoids excessive ornamentation in his letters.) Yet Paul includes in this letter more rhetorical devices than was rhetorically acceptable in letters (though not in speeches) – as if to say, "If it is rhetoric you want, I am able to offer it – for what, if anything, it is truly worth."

[35] See esp. Martin Hengel, *Crucifixion: in the ancient world and the folly of the message of the cross* (Philadelphia: Fortress, 1977).

[36] For rhetoric in Apollos's Alexandria, see B. Winter, *Philo and Paul* (1997), 19–112.

[37] See further R. Anderson, *Glossary* (2000), 90–91, 127. Many Greeks before Paul (and most after the second sophistic) deplored "Asianist" bombast; nevertheless, Romans still appreciated Cicero's abundant figures of speech, even in purely written form, long after Paul's day (Pliny *Ep.* 1.20.10).

The Greco-Roman world prized both "speech" and "knowledge" (1:5), and Corinth (whose Isthmian Games included speech competitions) was no exception.[38] Philosophy and rhetoric were the two forms of advanced education in antiquity, so the connection between wisdom and speech in this chapter may involve philosophic discourses or the widely prized rhetorical skill of ability to speak extemporaneously on topics proposed by the audience.[39] As in 1:5–7, skill in speech could be viewed as a divine gift as well as a discipline and achievement.[40]

Eloquence was a mark of education and respectability (e.g., Cicero *De or.* 3.14.55; Seneca *Controv.* 2.pref. 3); rhetoric was the language of law courts, politics, city assemblies, festival celebrations, and often even street side entertainment. Boys could be exposed to some rhetoric even at the grammar stage, although this may have been less common by Paul's day.[41] It was central, however, at the secondary level, with students in their teens.[42] Rhetorical theory and practice also influenced educated Jews like Josephus and (especially) Philo. Rhetorical principles affected even writing in genres other than speeches, because most of those writers had studied rhetoric.[43]

None of this suggests that Paul, despite his education, need have had tertiary rhetorical training; but it does suggest that he would have developed a sensitivity to the manner in which educated people in the Aegean communicated. (At least some basic rhetoric was probably available in Jerusalem for children of well-to-do Diaspora Jews receiving an elite education; cf. Acts 6:9; 9:1; 22:3.) Letters were not speeches, and even the later rhetorical handbooks that include them treat them differently from speeches; outlines of Paul's letters based on rhetoric may be excessive. Nevertheless, Paul's letters often include teaching and argumentation, and ancient rhetoric provides us a useful tool and objective control for analyzing his arguments.

But although rhetoric helps us understand and appreciate his arguments more closely, neither Paul's nor any other skilled writer's discourses reduce to rhetorical principles alone. Orators themselves adapted rhetorical principles with great flexibility; ancient orators were not confined by the basic exercises displayed in rhetorical handbooks. Great speakers thus varied widely in their own styles (Polybius 33.2.10; Cicero *Brut.* 56.204), and the best of ancient orators recognized diverse styles (Cicero *Or. Brut.* 5.20–6.21; 9.28; 23.77). Probably the

---

[38] For numerous concrete examples of oratory in Corinth, see B. Winter, *Philo and Paul* (1997), 126–44.

[39] Many valued extemporaneous speech; see, e.g., Seneca *Controv.* 4.pref.7; Tacitus *Dial.* 6; Suetonius *Gramm.* 23; Philostratus *Vit. soph.* 1.24.529.

[40] See, e.g., Menander Rhetor 2.17, 437.7–9; 446.11–13; *L.A.B.* 20.3.

[41] Dionysius *Dem.* 52; Quintilian *Inst.* 2.1; Suetonius *Gramm.* 4.

[42] See Quintilian *Inst.* 2.2.3; Tacitus *Dial.* 34–35; G. A. Kennedy, "Historical Survey of Rhetoric," 3–41 in *Handbook of Rhetoric,* ed. S. Porter (1997), 18–19.

[43] See, e.g., G. A. Kennedy, *The Art of Rhetoric in the Roman World: 300 B.C.–A.D. 300* (Princeton, NJ: Princeton University, 1972), 378–427.

greatest area of flexibility required was adaptability to one's audience.[44] (See further our "Closer Look" on Paul's critique of rhetoric, after 2:1–5.)

1:26–31: BOAST IN CHRIST, NOT IN STATUS

1:26: Consider your own call, brothers and sisters: not many of you were wise by human standards, not many were powerful, not many were of noble birth.
1:27: But God chose what is foolish in the world to shame the wise; God chose what is weak in the world to shame the strong;
1:28: God chose what is low and despised in the world, things that are not, to reduce to nothing things that are,
1:29: so that no one might boast in the presence of God.
1:30: He is the source of your life in Christ Jesus, who became for us wisdom from God, and righteousness and sanctification and redemption,
1:31: in order that, as it is written, "Let the one who boasts, boast in the Lord."

*P*aul introduces the principle of God choosing the weak by appealing to the church itself. Elite Christians apparently played a significant role in the congregation but were numerically a minority. (Early interpreters of rank recognized that Paul said "few" rather than "none"; Theodoret *Comm. 1 Cor.* 173.) Furthermore, they probably exhibited the status inconsistency of many of Corinth's emerging well-to-do: prosperous, but not part of a long-term hereditary nobility, and (possibly excepting Erastus, Rom 16:23) far from the highest ranks of the city. These elite Christians would be the church members most emphatic about education and rhetorical skill (see comment on 1:18–25).

Paul presupposes a passage from Jeremiah in this paragraph. In 1:26, Paul echoes Jeremiah 9:23, where the wise, powerful and rich should not boast (adjusted in Corinth to the wise, powerful, and well-born). In 1:31, he echoes the following verse in Jeremiah: boast in knowing and understanding the Lord (Jer 9:24). This perspective complements some Jewish expectations that God would invert human status (cf. Is 2:11, 17; Lk 14:11; 18:14).[45] Some other thinkers also relativized conventional status markers; more radical thinkers even rejected them (cf. 1 Cor 4:10).[46] In philosophic literature, true sages might be "nothings" to the world, as here and in 4:13.[47] Paul does not, however, simply echo philosophers:

---

[44] E.g., *Rhet. Alex.* 22, 1434b.27–30; Dionysius *Dem.* 15; Quintilian *Inst.* 11.1.1.
[45] See also Wis 5:3–4; *1 En.* 46:5–6; 104:2; *2 Bar.* 83:5.
[46] Cf. *'Abot* 4:1; Plato *Pol.* 257B; Cicero *Sest.* 9.21; *Verr.* 2.3.4.7–8; Seneca *Lucil.* 32.11; 44.1–2; Diogenes the Cynic in Diogenes Laertius 6.2.72.
[47] See G. Theissen, *The Social Setting of Pauline Christianity*, ed. J. Schütz (Philadelphia: Fortress, 1982), 71; cf. Gal 6:3.

the expected eschatological inversion has come in the Messiah. For Paul, Christ is divine wisdom (1:30; 8:5–6), the focus of God's plan to make people righteous, set apart and redeemed (cf. 1:2, 18; 6:11).

Despite his audience's dissatisfaction with his rhetorical skill in person (2:1–5; 2 Cor 10:10), Paul displays it lavishly in this paragraph. The threefold repetition of "not many . . ." in 1:26 is *anaphora* (x . . . /x . . .);[48] the threefold repetition of "God chose" in 1:27–28 is *antistrophe* (. . . x/ . . . x, because the phrase appears later in Greek than in the NRSV). Paul deliberately develops the same three elements in 1:27–28 that he introduced in 1:26.[49]

BRIDGING THE HORIZONS

On November 23, 1654, the inventor of a precursor of modern computers, the mathematician Blaise Pascal, had a profound spiritual experience that transformed his life. He described his encounter in part with these words: "God of Abraham, God of Isaac, God of Jacob, not of the philosophers and savants . . . God of Jesus Christ!"

Like philosophers who critiqued orators, Paul criticizes shallow forms of delivery at the expense of the message. Yet his critique offers a deeper challenge. Paul was neither impressed with nor coerced by the dominant intellectual trends of his day; for him, the deeper wisdom of God became the criterion for evaluating the shifting opinions of intellectual fashion. Biblical history was full of surprises, of a powerful God using weak agents like Moses or Gideon's three hundred (Ex 3:11–4:13; Judg 6:15; 7:2–7). The cross climaxes this divine irony, and apostolic ministry continues it (4:9–13; 2 Cor 4:7–12; 12:9–10).

Paul offers an uncomfortable example for scholars and preachers alike, not by offering a cheap anti-intellectualism but by demanding that we evaluate our own intellectual milieu critically in light of the cross. Sometimes graduate students are too beholden to "scholarly consensus," but reading the major scholarly works (e.g., on Jesus scholarship) chronologically from the nineteenth to the present generally cures that tendency. Recognizing that scholarly consensus reversed itself on some major points every decade or two (although British scholarship, for example, seems less given to extremes than my North American setting) invites us to evaluate arguments for positions rather than simply parroting them.

I was an atheist before my conversion to Christianity, partly out of intellectual fashion and partly out of revulsion for the allegedly Christian culture I observed. I rejected the shallow, unexamined faith of much of Western Christendom

---

[48] Some might prefer *epibole*, the repetition of more than one initial word. Paul was probably unfamiliar with most terminology in the rhetorical handbooks. "Not many" (i.e., "few") is *litotes*.

[49] Cf. a similar development of the categories in Jeremiah 9:23 in *b. Tamid* 32a.

because it seemed to me that even the Christians did not believe it. How could anyone genuinely believe they served their creator, yet fail to devote their entire life and property to their "lord"? But I also recognized that my finite intellect could not grasp a perfect deity, and in the end it was not Christendom but Christ that won me. After my conversion I discovered the difference between nominal and genuine commitment to Christ, and my conversion involved embracing the very shame against which I had once revolted: I was no longer intellectually fashionable. Once the cross had crucified my respectability, however, I was free to pursue unfettered what I believed to be truth.

If Paul were addressing us today, he would undoubtedly invite us to recover the costliness of the cross, to embrace it and articulate its claims even when they do not prove popular. At the most basic level, his critique addresses human pride that obscures God's infinite superiority; as Augustine declared, Jesus chose disciples of low status "to crush the necks of the proud" (*Tractates on Jn* 7.17.3).

Most wisdom traditions were universalistic, but by identifying Christ and wisdom Paul asserts the truth of Christ as a meta-narrative. Greco-Roman polytheism, like relativism today, allowed many truth-claims, provided that none was exclusivist; Paul, by contrast, relativizes other claims by asserting Christ as a meta-narrative through which all other reality must be construed. This claim would clash with worldviews in his day as well as in ours (cf. 1 Cor 8:5–6). The Roman world recoiled at the exclusivism of Jewish monotheism; early Christians further tightened that exclusivism in Christ (e.g., Acts 4:12; Jn 14:6; 1 Jn 2:22–23; Gal 2:21).[50] Like the Wisdom tradition, however, Paul is emphatically multicultural (e.g., Rom 1:16; 2:9–10; 3:9; 10:12; 1 Cor 10:32; 12:13; Gal 3:28); it is only his theological (and some moral) claims that he asserts as universals.

Paul's argument against division also challenges today's church. Whereas in some letters (most notably Romans) Paul reasons from the gospel to the common faith of Jewish and Gentile Christians, hence challenges ethnic and cultural division, in this letter he challenges especially division by class, status, and education. In this case, he challenges also our division over representative Christian celebrities. Today he would hardly be impressed by those who value denominational loyalties, rival theological traditions, political allegiances, or predilections for various worship styles over a common unity in Christ. Some are of Aquinas; others of Cranmer; others of Luther; still others of Wesley, Calvin, and so forth; but Christ must matter to Christians more than the teachers from whom we learned him, no matter how esteemed.

---

[50] Exclusive truth claims characterize traditional orthodoxies of most monotheistic religions and, in the sense of claiming their own truth, many other religions as well. Eastern religions, however, often do not fit this pattern, often embracing a different understanding of truth and reality.

2:1–5: CONVERTED BY "WEAK" SPEECH

2:1: When I came to you, brothers and sisters, I did not come proclaiming the mystery of God to you in lofty words or wisdom.

2:2: For I decided to know nothing among you except Jesus Christ, and him crucified.

2:3: And I came to you in weakness and in fear and in much trembling.

2:4: My speech and my proclamation were not with plausible words of wisdom, but with a demonstration of the Spirit and of power,

2:5: so that your faith might rest not on human wisdom but on the power of God.

P aul's own preaching, by which they were converted, relied on the Spirit's inspiration rather than on rhetorical skill for its "demonstration" and "power" (terms also used in rhetoric). When a speaker would first come to a city (2:1), he would advertise a meeting where he would declaim (normally praising the city); if he proved successful and attracted enough students, he would stay on in the city. Paul points out that he did not come to them like such sophists, pandering to popularity (see further 2 Cor 2:17).[51] Quite the opposite: his message was the stumbling block of a crucified Messiah (2:2; cf. 1:23).

In some respects, Paul may have been an adept speaker; his argumentation is often sophisticated, and often it was precisely the skilled orator who could afford to lower expectations and disclaim rhetorical skill.[52] When Isocrates claims to have abandoned the use of rhetorical devices (*Panath.* 3, *Or.* 12), then proceeds to employ them lavishly, hearers understand his disclaimer as itself a rhetorical device. Self-deprecation also appeared in other genres besides speeches,[53] and countered perceptions of boasting (say, in "lofty words of wisdom," 2:1), which was normally thought to display poor taste.[54]

The Corinthians had, however, heard Paul before, and his specific rhetorical weakness appears to involve his delivery (2:3; cf. 2 Cor 10:10; Plutarch *Dem.* 6.3). If Paul spoke with an accent, this too would invite scorn (Philostratus *Vit. soph.* 1.8.490; 2.31.624). People of status appreciated theatrical effect, recognizing appearance, gestures, and voice intonation as important components of good oratory.[55]

Few excuses would have satisfied elite members of the congregation, whose peers would judge them by the teachers they hosted. Some biblical predecessors

---

[51] See B. Winter, *Philo and Paul* (1997), 149–51; idem, *Left Corinth* (2001), 42.

[52] E.g., Lysias *Or.* 2.1, §190; 19.1–2, §152; Cicero *Fam.* 9.21.1; Sallust *Speech of Gaius Cotta* 4. As a calculated rhetorical strategy, see Quintilian *Inst.* 4.l.8–11.

[53] E.g., Catullus 49.5–7; Seneca *Nat.* 3.pref.2; Aulus Gellius *Noct. att.* Preface 10; 11.8.3.

[54] E.g., Cicero *Ag. Caec.* 11.36; Quintilian *Inst.* 11.1.15; see further discussion at 2 Cor 10–13.

[55] See, e.g., *Rhet. Her.* 3.11.19; Cicero *Brut.* 37.141; 43.158; 55.203; 66.234; *Or. Brut.* 17.55; Philostratus *Vit. soph.* 1.25.537–42.

like Moses were weak in delivery (Ex 4:10; cf. Jer 1:6), but this might provide Paul little defense; some high-status Jews claimed that Moses excelled in rhetoric (Josephus *Ant.* 4.25)! Stoics favored rational thought and rejected oratorical appeals to emotion;[56] but few agreed with them (including Paul; cf. 2 Cor 6:11–13). (Most considered use of emotion ethical, provided the speaker felt it; Cicero *De or.* 2.46.191.) Although even the best of speakers sometimes were too embarrassed to speak (Aulus Gellius *Noct. att.* 8.9; cf. Pliny *Ep.* 7.17.9–13), Paul's fear in speaking would dissatisfy both orators and philosophers![57] Trembling could be good rhetoric only when dramatically effective (Cicero *Verr.* 2.4.50.110); but Paul expects the Corinthians to view it as a weakness when addressing people. It was appropriate when directed toward God (cf. Ps 2:11; 2 Cor 7:15; Phil 2:12);[58] Paul, who speaks before God (2 Cor 2:17; cf. 5:13), might think of his humility as opposed to the self-commending, assertive vulgar rhetoric preferred in Corinth.[59]

Rhetoricians spoke of rhetorical "power"[60] and of rhetorical "demonstration" (an argument from indisputable premises, 2:4).[61] For Paul, however, the Spirit provided a demonstration of true power in a way that obviated purely rhetorical means of persuasion (2:4–5), even in the midst of his own weakness (2:3; cf. 2 Cor 13:3–4). For Paul, power's association or identification with the Spirit was paramount (cf. Rom 15:13, 19; 1 Thess 1:5; Eph 3:16), as often in early Jewish and Christian sources.[62] For Paul, this "power" was found not in some rhetoricians' enthusiastic style or in human status but in the cross (1:18, 24; cf. 2 Cor 12:9; 13:4). Contrary to the suggestions of some, Paul's dependence on the Spirit's inspiration in preaching the gospel had nothing to do with recent alleged failures in Athens or anywhere else (cf. 1 Thess 1:5; 2:13). Not only here but elsewhere he reminded Christians of the pattern of faith exhibited by the Spirit's inaugural work among them (Gal 3:3–5).

A CLOSER LOOK: PAUL'S CRITIQUE OF RHETORIC

Paul's valuing of substance over rhetorical form entered a centuries-old discussion about rhetoric's value. Many thinkers contended that rhetoric was necessary. If one has wisdom, Cicero contended, it profits society little if one lacks

---

56   Seneca *Lucil.* 108.7; Musonius Rufus frg. 36, p. 134.14–16; frg. 49, p. 142.4–12.

57   Aeschines *Fals. leg.* 34; Cicero *Brut.* 82.283; Plutarch *Cic.* 35.3–4. Fear was among the emotions Stoics rejected.

58   "Fear and trembling" appear together 13 times in the LXX; cf. also *1 En.* 1:5; 13:3; 14:13; 60:3.

59   For Paul's preference for "humble" rhetoric, see 2 Cor 10:1, 10; T. B. Savage, *Power through weakness*, SNTSM 86 (Cambridge: Cambridge University, 1996), 46, 71–73.

60   Aeschines *Fals. leg* 48; Dionysius of Halicarnassus *Ant. rom.* 7.4.5; Seneca *Controv.* 1.pref.16; Menander Rhetor 2.17, 437.25–26; cf. Sir 21:7; Acts 18:24.

61   Cf., e.g., Musonius Rufus frg. 44, p. 138.28; Porphyry *Marc.* 8.142–43. See further B. Winter, *Philo and Paul* (1997), 153–55.

62   Lk 1:17, 35; 4:14; Acts 1:8; 10:38; Zech 4:6; Wis 1:6; 7:7; 9:17; *Pss. Sol.* 17:37; *L.A.B.* 27:10. Persuasion succeeded by God's power (also *Let. Aris.* 266).

the eloquence to communicate it.[63] Eloquence was a great virtue (Cicero *De or.* 3.14.55), and helped not only with politics but with all other arts (Seneca *Controv.* 2.pref.3). Some apologists for rhetoric went so far as to claim that it was the one activity that distinguished humans from animals, or the "bond" that held together the cosmos.[64]

Rhetoric as the art of persuasion was easily subject to abuse if divorced from the speaker's conviction that the subject of persuasion was true. Thus one who deceived his audiences could still be viewed as an effective rhetor (Dionysius *Lys.* 18; *Is.* 16). Rhetorical training taught one how to turn the same argument to one's advantage, whichever side of a case one was arguing.[65] Much sophistry was playing with words to impress people (e.g., Aulus Gellius *Noct. att.* 8.10). Many thus complained that a better speaker could win an argument even if truth were on the other side (e.g., Philostratus *Vit. soph.* 1.483); aristocrats commonly protested demagogues swaying the masses (see comment on 9:19–23). Not surprisingly, a false accuser might find a new career in oratory (Suetonius *Rhetoricians* 4)!

Many ancient writers from classical Greece to the late Empire thus mocked or distrusted the arguments of sophists;[66] even other orators attacked the excesses, happily branding their rivals with the title.[67] Noteworthy for Paul's opposition between true wisdom and "clever speech," philosophers took a special interest in attacking the abuse of and focus on rhetoric,[68] starting with Socrates' denunciations of sophists.[69] Among Paul's contemporaries, the Roman Stoic Seneca emphasizes this theme repeatedly (*Lucil.* 20.2; 40.4; 86.16; 100.1; 108.12, 23, 38; 115.1–2); another, the Jewish philosopher Philo, criticized those who preferred sophistry to wisdom (Philo *Creation* 45). By rejecting the world's "wisdom" (1:20), Paul rejected much philosophic as well as rhetorical thought, but so did most philosophers who rejected the views of rival schools.

That philosophers and rhetoricians opposed each other became a traditional commonplace (Tacitus *Dial.* 42). Nor did the opposition derive solely from the philosophers' side. Orators responded that abuse of rhetoric did not make rhetoric itself evil.[70] Some also criticized philosophers for playing with words – simply doing so without the sort of skill orators exercised (Isocrates *Hel. enc.* 1).

---

63 Cicero *Brut.* 24.110; 31.117; *Inv.* 1.1.1; *Or. Brut.* 3.12–13; Plutarch *Cic.* 13.1.
64 Aelius Aristides *Defense of Oratory* 379, §126D; 403, §137D; 424, §144D; *Panath. Or.* 2, 150D.
65 E.g., *Rhet. Alex.* 15, 1432a.1–5; Cicero *Or. Brut.* 14.46; Tacitus *Dial.* 31.
66 E.g., Xenophon *Hunting* 13.1–2; Aristophanes *Nub.* 244–45; Plutarch *Statecraft* 5, *Mor.* 802 D–E; *Them.* 2.4; Philostratus *Vit. soph.* 1.15.499.
67 Demosthenes *Or.* 35.40–41, 56; Isocrates *Antid.*; *Soph.*; Dio Chrysostom *Or.* 4.35–37.
68 E.g., Anacharsis *Ep.* 1; Mus. Ruf. 8, pp. 62.40–64.4; Marcus Aurelius 1.7; 1.16.4; 1.17.8; Porphyry *Marc.* 17.284–85.
69 Plato *Theaet.* 164CD; *Apol.* 38D–39B; (Ps) Plato, *Hipp. maj.*; Xenophon *Mem.* 4.3.1; Val. Max. 3.4. ext. 1.
70 Isocrates *Nic.* 26–27, *Ad Nic.* 1–9; Cicero *Inv.* 1.3.4–1.4.5.

By Paul's day, however, the mediating position that valued both was dominant, including among those who criticized rhetoric's abuse.[71] Still, some rhetorically trained thinkers who valued both saw philosophy as more important (Tacitus *Dial.* 32; Maximus of Tyre 26.2). No less an orator than Cicero (a century before Paul) asked his friends to call him a philosopher rather than an orator (Plutarch *Cic.* 32.5)! A century after Paul, the prestigious orator Maximus of Tyre emphasized philosophy over rhetoric (*Or.* 1.7; 25.3, 6). If Paul employed some conventional rhetorical patterns while critiquing the abuse of rhetoric, he was hardly the first to do so. (See further our "Closer Look" regarding Paul's use of rhetoric, after 1:18–25.)

2:6–13: HUMAN WISDOM VERSUS WISDOM FROM THE SPIRIT

2:6: Yet among the mature we do speak wisdom, though it is not a wisdom of this age or of the rulers of this age, who are doomed to perish.

2:7: But we speak God's wisdom, secret and hidden, which God decreed before the ages for our glory.

2:8: None of the rulers of this age understood this; for if they had, they would not have crucified the Lord of glory.

2:9: But, as it is written,

> "What no eye has seen, nor ear heard,
>> nor the human heart conceived,
>> what God has prepared for those who love him" –

2:10: these things God has revealed to us through the Spirit; for the Spirit searches everything, even the depths of God.

2:11: For what human being knows what is truly human except the human spirit that is within? So also no one comprehends what is truly God's except the Spirit of God.

2:12: Now we have received not the spirit of the world, but the Spirit that is from God, so that we may understand the gifts bestowed on us by God.

2:13: And we speak of these things in words not taught by human wisdom but taught by the Spirit, interpreting spiritual things to those who are spiritual.

Normally only a speaker or writer who could trust the strength of his relationship with his audience would reprove them as firmly as Paul does

---

[71] E.g., Cicero *Off.* 1.1.3–4; Suetonius *Gramm.* 6; Ael. Arist. *Defense of Orat.* 342–343, §114D.

here.[72] Paul contends that the Corinthian Christians who think themselves wise are actually the opposite (cf. 3:18–20; 6:5; 10:15). If they neglect the true wisdom of the Spirit for the human wisdom focused on human status and power (2:6–13), their wisdom is "merely human" (3:4). Human wisdom could not grasp the divine wisdom that had saved them in the gospel (2:1–9), and that divine wisdom was available only through God's Spirit (2:10–16).

The "mature" (2:6) among whom Paul speaks the true wisdom (the wisdom of the cross, 1:23–24; 2:2) are those who have advanced beyond the stage of "infants" (3:1).[73] Their access to wisdom comes only from God's Spirit, as Paul will soon make explicit (2:10–16). Already his wording alludes to Wisdom 9:6, the only verse in later Septuagint collections that uses both "wisdom" (*sophia*) and this Greek term for "mature" (*teleios*): "for even one who is perfect [*teleios*] among human beings will be regarded as nothing without the wisdom that comes from you."[74] The Wisdom of Solomon went on to deny that one could know God's mind apart from the gift of his Wisdom and Spirit (Wis 9:17). God offered them this revealed wisdom, Paul contends, by inspiring Paul's preaching (2:4–5). Jewish tradition also affirmed that this Wisdom existed before creation (2:7).

Yet the Corinthians remain "infants," language philosophers applied to those unable to understand deeper truth (3:1). By focusing on worldly status and power (1:26–28), the Corinthians risk identifying with the supposedly powerful people of the world who crucified the truly powerful Lord of glory (2:8),[75] rather than celebrating the cross! Humans could not understand the unfathomable plan of God's wisdom (2:9) except by revelation from the Spirit (2:10), that is, from God who alone knows his mind (2:11, 16).[76] Jewish wisdom tradition also recognized that wisdom must be "revealed" because only God is truly wise (Sir 1:6–9, the only LXX passage using both "wisdom" and "reveal"; cf. Bar 3:31–32). That Paul

---

[72] See S. K. Stowers, *Letter Writing in Greco-Roman Antiquity* (LEC 5; Philadelphia: Westminster, 1986), 86; for letters of blame, *memptikai* (although Paul may not be thinking in terms of later formal categories), see ibid., 85–90.

[73] The repetition of "wisdom" beginning successive clauses is rhetorically appropriate (e.g., Cicero *Or. Brut.* 39.135); others also recognized the distinction between true and false philosophy (e.g., Aulus Gellius *Noct. att.* 10.22).

[74] Probably also the source for Philo *QG* 4.191. Paul might omit a citation formula (1:19, 31; 2:9; 3:19) out of knowledge of the different Judean canon; perhaps Apollos had used such wisdom texts as part of his Alexandrian canon, or they were in use in Corinth's synagogue before Paul's arrival.

[75] Cf. the demise of the world's rulers who neglected God's wisdom in Bar 3:14–19; cf. Ps 104[ET 105]:22; Is 19:11; Ezek 27:8; Dan 1:20; 2:48; 4:18 LXX; *Pss. Sol.* 8:20. Although Paul can refer to cosmic rulers (Rom 8:38–39), as in Judaism (Dan 10:13, 20; *Jub.* 15:31–32; 35:17; *1 En.* 61:10; 75:1), he thinks of earthly ones here (1:26–28).

[76] "Depths" could refer to God's secrets (Rom 11:33; cf. Rom 8:27; *1 En.* 63:3; polemic in Rev 2:23–24) or the inscrutability of wisdom (Sir 1:3–6, without the term), but probably especially recalls the analogy between God's and a human spirit in the familiar Jdt 8:14. That no one outside a person knew the person (2:11) was a commonplace (Prov 14:10; cf. Prov 20:27).

has Sirach 1:6–9 in mind is suggested by his midrashic adaptation of Isaiah 64:4 (LXX 64:3), by adding "those who love him" from Sirach 1:10, where they receive the gift of wisdom.[77] Thus, Paul argues, only those with God's Spirit, as opposed to the world, have true wisdom to understand God (2:12, 16).

2:14–3:4: SPIRIT-PEOPLE VERSUS MORTALS

2:14: Those who are unspiritual do not receive the gifts of God's Spirit, for they are foolishness to them, and they are unable to understand them because they are spiritually discerned.
2:15: Those who are spiritual discern all things, and they are themselves subject to no one else's scrutiny.
2:16:

> "For who has known the mind of the Lord
> so as to instruct him?"

But we have the mind of Christ.
3:1: And so, brothers and sisters, I could not speak to you as spiritual people, but rather as people of the flesh, as infants in Christ.
3:2: I fed you with milk, not solid food, for you were not ready for solid food. Even now you are still not ready,
3:3: for you are still of the flesh. For as long as there is jealousy and quarreling among you, are you not of the flesh, and behaving according to human inclinations?
3:4: For when one says, "I belong to Paul," and another, "I belong to Apollos," are you not merely human?

*J*ust as the world could not understand Jesus' mission (2:8), neither could they evaluate others moved by the Spirit's deeper wisdom (2:14–15; cf. Jn 3:8). That being the case, the Corinthians ought not to use worldly criteria to evaluate Paul's message (1:18–2:5). Paul later uses the term the NRSV translates by "discerned" and "scrutiny" (2:14–15) to reject worldly evaluations of his ministry (4:3; 9:3). This is not to say that Paul rejects any principle of evaluation (14:24; cf. 6:2–3; 10:15; 11:31); he merely rejects criteria based on worldly status (such as rhetoric or philosophy) rather than on the message of the cross.

Paul quotes two biblical texts to emphasize humanity's ignorance of God (2:9, 16a); in each case, he adds that we can understand God, knowing his

---

[77] "Those who love" God is admittedly a familiar phrase both in biblical (cf. Ex 20:6; Deut 5:10; 7:9; Neh 1:5; Ps 119:16; 122:6; 145:20; Dan 9:4) and extrabiblical (e.g., 1 Macc 4:33; *Pss. Sol.* 4:25; 6:6; 14:1; 4Q176 frg. 16.4) literature. The Isaiah passage was a favorite eschatological text among later rabbis; cf. the phrasing also in *L.A.B.* 26:13.

mind and heart, by the gift of his Spirit (2:10, 16b).[78] (Although Paul quotes the LXX of Isaiah 40:13, which speaks of the "mind" of the Lord, he undoubtedly knows that the Hebrew reads, the "Spirit" of the Lord, so that believers who have God's Spirit have his mind, 1 Cor 2:10–16.) What makes the difference is whether individuals are Spirit-people or simply dependent on human reasoning, "merely human" (3:4).

Like many philosophers, Paul divides humanity into the wise and the unwise, and demands that those converted to truth walk in a manner consistent with that truth.[79] "Unspiritual" (2:14) is literally *psychikos*, "soulish": God's "breath" or "Spirit" once made humans a "living soul" (Gen 2:7, literally; see comment on 15:44–46), but such souls still need the Spirit that formed them. (The NRSV captures the point: the "unspiritual," who lack the Spirit.) These are "people of the flesh" (3:1, 3), a description Paul uses in contrast to those dependent on the Spirit (cf. Rom 8:3–13).[80] (The Greek is literally merely "as fleshly" and "fleshlike," so he does not literally call them unconverted, as in the even harsher rhetoric of 2 Cor 5:20–6:2.)

Philosophers often described those unable to comprehend true wisdom as "infants" (3:1), maintaining the contrast with the "mature" (2:6). Sages charged that such infants were unready for solid food (their deeper teachings), enduring only their mothers' or nurses' milk (e.g., Epictetus *Diatr.* 2.16.39; Philo *Husbandry* 9).[81] Warning against infantile ways was common (e.g., Homer *Od.* 1.296–297), and Paul continues the parent metaphor in 4:15–17, 21. Paul's "merely human" (3:4) probably plays on some philosophers' division of humanity into the mortal masses, on the one hand, and philosophers whose experience with the innate divine spark or with divine knowledge progressively divinizes them, on the other.[82]

After Paul's lengthy theological excursus on the Spirit-revealed, divine wisdom of his preaching of the cross (1:17–3:3a), he returns to the practical issue that provoked it (3:3b-4; cf. 1:10–12). The series of rhetorical questions in 3:3–5 drives home the point. If the Corinthian Christians divide over favorite teachers the way worldly intellectuals did, they exhibit infantile wisdom rather than that given by God's Spirit.

---

[78] Philosophers sought unity of mind with God (Epictetus *Diatr.* 2.16.42; 2.19.26–27), but Christ and the Spirit take the role Stoics assigned to wisdom (this is esp. clear in Rom 8:5–9).

[79] See most fully T. Engberg-Pedersen, *Paul and Stoics* (2000), e.g., 70–72; cf. Maximus of Tyre 39–40.

[80] Genesis 6:3 introduces the contrast between human flesh and God's Spirit; the creaturely weakness of "flesh" in the OT develops moral connotations in the Qumran scrolls (e.g., 1QS 9.9; 11.12).

[81] In more detail, see C. Keener, "Milk," 707–09 in *DNTB*.

[82] E.g., Seneca *Lucil.* 32.11; 48.11; 124.23; Marcus Aurelius 4.16; Porphyry *Marc.* 15.263–65; more fully C. Keener, *John* (2003), 298–99. Even the rabbis were aware of such ideas (*Sipre Deut.* 306.28.2), although neither they nor Paul would have embraced genuine divinization.

3:5–4:5: ESCHATOLOGICAL EVALUATION

3:5: What then is Apollos? What is Paul? Servants through whom you came to believe, as the Lord assigned to each.

3:6: I planted, Apollos watered, but God gave the growth.

3:7: So neither the one who plants nor the one who waters is anything, but only God who gives the growth.

3:8: The one who plants and the one who waters have a common purpose, and each will receive wages according to the labor of each.

3:9: For we are God's servants, working together; you are God's field, God's building.

3:10: According to the grace of God given to me, like a skilled master builder I laid a foundation, and someone else is building on it. Each builder must choose with care how to build on it.

3:11: For no one can lay any foundation other than the one that has been laid; that foundation is Jesus Christ.

3:12: Now if anyone builds on the foundation with gold, silver, precious stones, wood, hay, straw –

3:13: the work of each builder will become visible, for the Day will disclose it, because it will be revealed with fire, and the fire will test what sort of work each has done,

3:14: If what has been built on the foundation survives, the builder will receive a reward.

3:15: If the work is burned up, the builder will suffer loss; the builder will be saved, but only as through fire.

3:16: Do you not know that you are God's temple and that God's Spirit dwells in you?

3:17: If anyone destroys God's temple, God will destroy that person. For God's temple is holy, and you are that temple.

3:18: Do not deceive yourselves. If you think that you are wise in this age, you should become fools so that you may become wise.

3:19: For the wisdom of this world is foolishness with God. For it is written,

"He catches the wise in their craftiness,"

3:20: and again,

"The Lord knows the thoughts of the wise,
that they are futile."

3:21: So let no one boast about human leaders. For all things are yours,

3:22: whether Paul or Apollos or Cephas or the world or life or death or the present or the future – all belong to you,

3:23: and you belong to Christ, and Christ belongs to God.

4:1: Think of us in this way, as servants of Christ and stewards of God's mysteries.
4:2: Moreover, it is required of stewards that they be found trustworthy.
4:3: But with me it is a very small thing that I should be judged by you or by any human court. I do not even judge myself.
4:4: I am not aware of anything against myself, but I am not thereby acquitted. It is the Lord who judges me.
4:5: Therefore do not pronounce judgment before the time, before the Lord comes, who will bring to light the things now hidden in darkness and will disclose the purposes of the heart. Then each one will receive commendation from God.

*I*n 3:5–4:5, Paul emphasizes again the folly of the Corinthians' division over himself and Apollos.[83] He points out the inadequacy of present human evaluations and that only the final judgment will arbitrate decisively what was in the hearts of God's servants (4:3–5). As Judaism (and a few Greek thinkers) taught, future judgment provided incentive for obedience in the present (cf. 15:32–34; 2 Cor 5:10–11).

Thus, the Corinthians should not follow their teachers the way worldly disciples did, like celebrities' fans or "groupies" (1:12), or the way some Christians follow denominations or popular speakers today. Rather, the teachers belonged to the Corinthians, as their servants before God (3:5, 21–22). Household "stewards" or managers (4:1–2) were often servants (4:1); Paul is but a servant manager over God's house (i.e., his temple; see comment on 3:10–17).

The focus must not be individual ministers but God who gives growth (3:5–9). Paul illustrates this point with the sort of agricultural and architectural illustrations common among sages. God promised to "plant" and "build" his people (Jer 1:10; 24:6; 31:28; 42:10; cf. Sir 49:7; 1QS 8.5–6; 11.8); they were his planting and field (cf. Is 5:6; *Jub.* 1:16; CD 1.7). Paul notes that others sowed God's message but that only God creates the fruit (3:6–9; cf. Mk 4:14, 26–29; 12); God rather than Paul had converted the Corinthians (1 Cor 1:13; 2:4–5). Echoing biblical descriptions for "building" God's people and perhaps Greek exhortations to unity, Paul often speaks of "building" believers (1 Cor 8:1, 10; 10:23; 14:3–5, 12, 17, 26; 2 Cor 10:8; 12:19; 13:10).

Whether the "working together" of 3:9 refers to Apollos and Paul being fellow-workers with each other (so NRSV; see 3:8) or to both as God's fellow-workers (so NASB; Theodore of Mopsuestia; cf. 2 Cor 6:1) depends on whether one reads the term translated "God's" (*theou*) as "with God" or "for God." One could justify either reading from context (3:6–8), although theological considerations and the rest of 3:9 incline many toward the NRSV translation. At the least, Paul would not have envisioned "working together" with a deity in the common but

---

[83] The division into two alternatives, both of which are then refuted (3:5–7), resembles rhetorical *dilemmaton* (see R. Anderson, *Glossary* [2000], 36; cf. also "removal" on 121).

more crass Greek sense,[84] because whatever the servants' contributions, only God causes the growth (3:6–7).

God's building did not serve ministers, but God would evaluate ministers according to how they served God's building (3:10–17). Until the day of God's fiery judgment burned away weaker contributions to the building, no one would really know which of God's servants had offered the best contributions, so no human evaluations now were certain (3:12–15; cf. 2:15; Matt 7:21–27). (Everyone knew which substances could endure fire [e.g., Num 31:23]; and the metaphor of testing or purifying substances by fire appears commonly in ancient literature, not least in the OT [Prov 27:21; Is 47:14; Zech 13:9].)[85]

When Paul speaks of "building," the structure he envisions is God's temple (3:16). Some philosophers spoke of spiritual temples and sacrifices; more importantly, some Jews viewed God's people as his temple (1QS 8.5–9; 9.6; CD 3.19A; 2.10, 13B; 4Q511 frg. 35.2–3), an idea widespread in early Christianity (e.g., Jn 4:21–24; Eph 2:19–22; 1 Pet 2:5). All peoples believed that defiling a temple merited divine vengeance (1 Cor 3:17); whoever introduced division into the church thus risked punishment![86] He challenges their supposed prudence with more biblical condemnations of foolish "wisdom" in 3:19–20 (Ps 94:11; Eliphaz in Job 5:13).

Thus, God's servants are for the church, not the church for God's servants (3:21–23). (Stoic and Cynic philosophers valued "having nothing," while claiming that everything belonged to them [cf. 2 Cor 6:10], so they could take whatever they needed. Commentators usually cite here the ancient philosophic axiom, "Friends share all things in common," and philosophers are "friends of the gods.")[87]

In view of their quest for wisdom (1:17–3:2), the Corinthians should recognize themselves unwise (3:18–19) to follow Paul, Apollos, or Cephas (3:22); they dare follow only Christ (3:23, echoing 1:12). They were but slave managers on the church's behalf (4:1–2; "stewards" were often servants or freedmen; 2 Cor 4:5). ("Mysteries" appear often in this letter, 2:7; 4:1; 13:2; 14:2; and perhaps 2:1; this is consistent with their interest in Hellenistic wisdom [cf. Wis 2:22; 6:22; as opposed to pagan mysteries in Wis 14:15, 23].) By contrast, it was only the estate's lord, Christ, whose evaluation of their performance counted (4:3–5). All Jews and Christians agreed that the Lord knew the secrets of all hearts and would reveal them in the judgment (4:5; cf. e.g., 1 En. 38:3; 49:4; 2 Bar. 83:3).[88] ("Human court" in 4:3 is literally "human day," probably implicitly contrasted with the "day of the Lord," 1:8; 3:13; 5:5.)

---

[84] See Xenophon *Cyr.* 3.3.58; Dionysius of Halicarnassus *Ant. rom.* 6.6.3; Philostratus *Hrk.* 2.8; 11.4; Menander Rhetor 2.17, 437.9–10.

[85] Cf. also, e.g., Seneca *Dial.* 1.5.10; 1 *En.* 48:9; 4 *Ezra* 7:50–61; *Gen. Rab.* 83:5.

[86] The wordplay, "Whoever does x will receive x," appears elsewhere (Ex 8:21 [MT 8:17]; Jer 34:17; *m. 'Abot* 2:7); and the idea is even more common (Prov 26:27; Sir 27:25–27).

[87] For sources, see C. Keener, *John* (2003), 1010–13, 1042.

[88] Cf. also Seneca *Lucil.* 102.29; more sources in C. Keener, *John* (2003), 531–32.

4:6–21: PERSONAL APPEAL TO HUMBLE THEMSELVES

4:6: I have applied all this to Apollos and myself for your benefit, brothers and sisters, so that you may learn through us the meaning of the saying, "Nothing beyond what is written," so that none of you will be puffed up in favor of one against another.

4:7: For who sees anything different in you? What do you have that you did not receive? And if you received it, why do you boast as if it were not a gift?

4:8: Already you have all you want! Already you have become rich! Quite apart from us you have become kings! Indeed, I wish that you had become kings, so that we might be kings with you!

4:9: For I think that God has exhibited us apostles as last of all, as though sentenced to death, because we have become a spectacle to the world, to angels and to mortals.

4:10: We are fools for the sake of Christ, but you are wise in Christ. We are weak, but you are strong. You are held in honor, but we in disrepute.

4:11: To the present hour we are hungry and thirsty, we are poorly clothed and beaten and homeless,

4:12: and we grow weary from the work of our own hands. When reviled, we bless; when persecuted, we endure;

4:13: when slandered, we speak kindly. We have become like the rubbish of the world, the dregs of all things, to this very day.

4:14: I am not writing this to make you ashamed, but to admonish you as my beloved children.

4:15: For though you might have ten thousand guardians in Christ, you do not have many fathers. Indeed, in Christ Jesus I became your father through the gospel.

4:16: I appeal to you, then, be imitators of me.

4:17: For this reason I sent you Timothy, who is my beloved and faithful child in the Lord, to remind you of my ways in Christ Jesus, as I teach them everywhere in every church.

4:18: But some of you, thinking that I am not coming to you, have become arrogant.

4:19: But I will come to you soon, if the Lord wills, and I will find out not the talk of these arrogant people but their power.

4:20: For the kingdom of God depends not on talk but on power.

4:21: What would you prefer? Am I to come to you with a stick, or with love in a spirit of gentleness?

*I*n 4:6–21, Paul appeals to his relationship with his audience, his images recalling those of other ancient moralists and philosophers. Sages often appealed to their relationship with disciples, typically including the father-children relationship.[89] As their father (4:14–15), Paul invites their imitation (4:16), of which

---

[89] For fictive filial language, including for the role of teachers, see C. Keener, *John* (2003), 921–23.

he offers Timothy as an example (4:17); he also threatens discipline (the "stick" or rod in 4:21).

Scholars debate the meaning of, "Nothing beyond what is written" (4:6). Some suggest that it means not to exceed the bounds of (i.e., to transgress) Scripture (the most common view); or a child tracing the lines of letters established by teachers (cf. 3:1–2);[90] or a plea to maintain terms of an agreement (used in ancient arguments for unity).[91] Perhaps the basic sense is, "Do not boast beyond the appropriate station God has given each one" (cf. 2 Cor 10:13, 15; Rom 12:3–8). (By pointing out that he is using parabolic speech [a claim obscured by NRSV's "applied"] rather than merely implying it, as appropriate for rhetors' "covert allusions," Paul probably treats them like children, as in 3:1.) Certainly, as ancients sometimes noted, it was foolish to boast in another's gift to one as if it were one's own achievement (4:7; cf. 1:7; 12:4–11).[92]

Their city valued wealth and status, and the church had followed its culture (cf. 4:8; 2 Cor 8:14). In words dripping with sarcasm (a common mode of discourse in antiquity; cf. 2 Cor 11:7),[93] Paul suggests that his converts should share their wealth and power with him, for the apostles were "last of all" (4:8–9). Sages claimed to have true wealth and royalty by having wisdom,[94] but Paul ironically appeals to the Corinthians' values of worldly wealth and status (4:8)! By their values, they must be wiser and nobler than Christ's servant who brought God's wisdom and power (4:10), which appeared foolish and weak to their society. Paul was a "fool" preaching God's "folly" (1:18–25).

Philosophers regularly provided moral examples for imitation, sometimes themselves (cf. 4:16; 11:1).[95] (Praising oneself was considered justifiable if explained as offered to inspire positive imitation; see comment on 2 Cor 10:12.) Here Paul offers himself as an example of genuine sacrificial service (4:9–13; cf. his example of sacrificing rights in Ch. 9) by listing his sufferings, the repetition driving home the point forcefully. Sages often used such *peristasis* catalogues (lists of hardships; also in 2 Cor 4:8–10; 6:4–5, 8–10; 11:23–33) to demonstrate their sincere devotion to the values they espoused.[96] If one must boast (cf. 4:6), it is in weakness that one ought to boast (2 Cor 11:16–12:10). Although respecting philosophy, most elite people viewed extreme philosophers, especially homeless

---

[90] See J. T. Fitzgerald, *Cracks in an Earthen Vessel: An Examination of the Catalogues of Hardships in the Corinthian Correspondence* (SBLDS 99; Atlanta: Scholars, 1988), 124–27.

[91] See L. L. Welborn, "A Conciliatory Principle in 1 Cor. 4:6," *NovT* 29 (4, 1987): 320–46.

[92] For surrendering God's gifts, see, e.g., Seneca *Ben.* 4.5.1; Epictetus *Diatr.* 4.1.107; 4.4.29; 2 Macc 7:11.

[93] E.g., Cicero *Phil.* 13.2.4; *Verr.* 2.1.6.17; 2.2.31.76; *Pro Sulla* 24.67; *Fam.* 5.2.8.

[94] E.g., Plato *Rep.* 5.472; Cicero *Fin.* 3.22.75; Musonius Rufus 8, p. 66.13–25; Plutarch *Flatterer* 16, *Mor.* 58E; Iamblichus *Pyth. Life* 35.250).

[95] For documentation, see C. Keener, *John* (2003), 924–26; cf. ibid., 15. For exceptions, see A. J. Malherbe, *Paul and the Popular Philosophers* (Philadelphia: Fortress, 1989), 57.

[96] Most fully on *peristasis* catalogues, see J. Fitzgerald, *Cracks* (1988); earlier, R. Hodgson, "'Paul the Apostle and First Century Tribulation Lists,'" *ZNW* 74 (1–2, 1983): 59–80.

Cynics (cf. 4:11), as weak and foolish beggars; like radical philosophers (or biblical prophets), Paul challenges social convention here.

Although Paul is their founding apostle (a high office, 12:28), the greatest has become the servant (cf. Mk 10:42–44)! Paul and other servants of the church (cf. 3:5; 4:1–2) suffer hunger and persecution. Stoic philosophers, respected by the Corinthians, claimed that such hardships mattered only to the body, hence should not disturb their tranquility;[97] from a different perspective, Jesus instructed his followers to endure this price for ministry (Mk 6:8–11; Lk 10:3–11). The apostles blessed when reviled (4:12), which perhaps resembled Stoic apathy toward external criticism, but also reflected Jesus' teaching (cf. Lk 6:22; Rom 12:14; 1 Pet 2:23). It certainly contradicted Cynics' propensity to revile their hearers, even unprovoked.

Elite members would view his manual labor as a mark of lower status inappropriate for the sort of sage they wished to support (see "A Closer Look" on 9:1–27). Paul even faces hyperbolic martyrdom; being exhibited "last" could refer to condemned captives led in triumph (2 Cor 2:14) or, more likely, criminals killed as the final act in the arena (1 Cor 15:32). (Scholars point out that some ancients used the terms for "rubbish" and "dregs" in 4:13 for criminals or others killed as expiatory offerings. Although this proposal fits the context, the terms also had a broader usage. Philosophers sometimes viewed the masses as "garbage," and the masses may have viewed Cynic beggars similarly.) That they were "spectacles" before the cosmos as in a theater (4:9) may reflect a common image (Philo *Creation* 78), but in contrast to some of his contemporaries Paul emphasizes the shame rather than the honor involved in this public display.[98]

Many ancient sages who corrected their hearers emphasized that they did so out of concern (4:14); except under extreme circumstances, they preferred admonishing gently rather than humiliating their hearers. Despite what may be an ironic denial (4:14), Paul's example is meant to shame them at least enough to make them follow his example. Stoics, traditional Romans, and many moralists advocated a rugged life and disdained luxury; it is Paul, not the Corinthians, who therefore models wisdom and virtue (cf. 4:8–10). Nevertheless, Paul's emphasis on his relationship with the Corinthians reflected the sort of affection commonly expressed between teachers and disciples, or in letters other than the sternest rebukes. "Guardians" (4:15; *pedagōgoi*) were slave-tutors who guarded children to and from school; such tutors (perhaps including Apollos) ranked nowhere as significant as fathers.

If the Corinthians will not as his children receive and imitate Paul's example (4:14–17) offered in "the spirit of gentleness," he will discipline them (4:21) like a father ought (4:15). (Although fathers were often portrayed as gentle, traditional

---

[97] E.g., Epictetus *Diatr.* 1.1.22; 2.1.13; cf. 4 Macc 18:2–3.

[98] Paul, like other Jews, adapted the familiar Greek phrase "gods and people" (i.e., everyone; e.g., Musonius Rufus 9, p. 76.10) to "angels and people."

Roman political rhetoric valued the stern and unbending patriarch.)[99] The Spirit that provided "gentleness" also provided "power" (4:21; cf. 2:4; Gal 5:22–23; 6:1). Paul would offer an initial demonstration of this power immediately (5:4–5) but also would offer more if necessary once he reached them in person (2 Cor 12:20–13:4). (His "if the Lord wills" in 4:19 reflects a familiar ancient idiom; cf. 16:7.)[100] The choice of how he comes to them, he warns them, is theirs.[101]

BRIDGING THE HORIZONS

The personal model Paul offers the Corinthians should challenge modern readers no less. Throughout history, many individuals and renewal movements have identified with the apostolic poverty lived by Jesus and his first agents, from Saint Anthony to Saint Francis to, in different ways, John Wesley, William and Catherine Booth, Mother Teresa, and others. It functioned as a practical necessity for many who, like Paul, traveled to bring the gospel to previously unevangelized cultures, such as Jesuits, Moravians, and evangelical Protestant missionaries (like David Livingstone or Mary Slessor), or many indigenous West African missionaries today. The frequent rediscovery of a sacrificial lifestyle by many of the most committed followers of Christ through history should warn us not to ignore what we find in these texts.

Paul's churches show us that Luke's ideal for the Jerusalem church (Acts 2:44–45; 4:32–35; cf. Lk 12:33; 14:33) was not a requirement for church membership; but Paul's personal example shows that it remained an ideal of service to Christ, especially for those called to ministry (see 9:15–18). It was voluntary, not mandated; but it was certainly a gracious invitation to the church. We too readily explain away such passages as irrelevant for today. If we embrace doctrinal aspects of the apostolic faith, we might remember (as did Athanasius and many other church fathers) that this faith also calls for lives of sacrifice for God's agendas.

5:1–13: DISCIPLINING THE SEXUAL OFFENDER

5:1: It is actually reported that there is sexual immorality among you, and of a kind that is not found even among pagans; for a man is living with his father's wife.

5:2: And you are arrogant! Should you not rather have mourned, so that he who has done this would have been removed from among you?

---

[99] Nevertheless, "meekness" was not a negative quality for authority figures; see Polybius 39.7.3–4; Plutarch *Brut.* 29.2; Menander Rhetor 2.4, 389.8; esp. Deirdre J. Good, *Jesus the Meek King* (Harrisburg, PA: Trinity Press International, 1999).

[100] See, e.g., Xenophon *Hell.* 2.4.17; *Anab.* 7.3.43. Letters often postponed business till arrival (e.g., 2 Jn 12; Cicero *Fam.* 2.3.2; 13.47.1; *Att.* 13.19).

[101] Some labeled the device of offering rhetorical choices *anacoenosis* (if the speaker feigns confusion, as in Gal 4:20, it also would be *aporia*).

5:3: For though absent in body, I am present in spirit; and as if present I have already pronounced judgment

5:4: in the name of the Lord Jesus on the man who has done such a thing. When you are assembled, and my spirit is present with the power of our Lord Jesus,

5:5: you are to hand this man over to Satan for the destruction of the flesh, so that his spirit may be saved in the day of the Lord.

5:6: Your boasting is not a good thing. Do you not know that a little yeast leavens the whole batch of dough?

5:7: Clean out the old yeast so that you may be a new batch, as you really are unleavened. For our paschal lamb, Christ, has been sacrificed.

5:8: Therefore, let us celebrate the festival, not with the old yeast, the yeast of malice and evil, but with the unleavened bread of sincerity and truth.

5:9: I wrote to you in my letter not to associate with sexually immoral persons –

5:10: not at all meaning the immoral of this world, or the greedy and robbers, or idolaters, since you would then need to go out of the world.

5:11: But now I am writing to you not to associate with anyone who bears the name of brother or sister who is sexually immoral or greedy, or is an idolater, reviler, drunkard, or robber. Do not even eat with such a one.

5:12: For what have I to do with judging those outside? Is it not those who are inside that you are to judge?

5:13: God will judge those outside. "Drive out the wicked person from among you."

Chapters 5 and 6 are closely related. Paul begins with the most notorious case of sexual immorality, and exhorts the church to exercise its own judicial discipline (5:1–13). By contrast, Paul points out, members have been resorting to secular courts (6:1–11; some think this involves the same offender, though that is not a necessary inference); Paul then returns to the question of sexual immorality (6:12–21).

The current passage also continues the previous context. The church's refusal to act against the offender in 5:2 provides the most striking *example* of their arrogance and doubt that Paul would execute discipline (4:18). Here, therefore, he does execute discipline (5:5). They may doubt his "power" (4:19–21), but he acts by Jesus' power (5:4).

The "father's wife" is presumably a stepmother (otherwise the title "mother" seems more obvious). Relations between sons and stepmothers were often notoriously uncomfortable in antiquity.[102] They also could prove sexually tempting: given the typical practice of Romans (and especially Greeks) marrying younger wives, second marriages often yielded stepmothers in the age range of elder sons.[103]

---

[102] E.g., Euripides *Alc.* 305–09; Callimachus *Epig.* 8; Hermogenes *Issues* 56.16–18; 58.20–22; see further S. Dixon, *The Roman Mother* (Norman: Oklahoma University, 1988), 49, 155–59.

[103] For the temptation, see, e.g., Euripides *Hipp.*; Appian *Hist. rom.* 11.10.59; Heliodorus *Aeth.* 1.9–14; Philostratus *Vit. soph.* 1.21.516–17.

Whereas modern discussions of incest usually involve an adult's abuse of a younger victim, the public instance in Corinth, like the majority of cases explicitly reported in antiquity, surrounds consenting adults. Although nearly all human cultures prohibit incest, specific definitions of the offense varied from one culture to another. Greeks, who permitted marriage to paternal half-sisters, found offensive the Egyptian practice of marrying full sisters, and claimed that Persians were permitted to marry even their mothers.[104] Roman law punished incest with banishment to an island. Although some philosophers regarded incest as unobjectionable, most people viewed it quite harshly, and laws treated it accordingly.

Paul echoes the language of Scripture in his astonishment that a man should have his father's wife (5:1; Lev 18:8). Although some rabbis suspected pagans of incest, Paul knows, as most other Diaspora Jews would have, that even Greeks and Romans prohibited this behavior. The tale of Oedipus, who unknowingly married his mother, is the most obvious instance of Greek horror about sleeping with a mother; alleged sleeping with a stepmother also invited punishment (Euripides *Hipp.* 885–90; Gaius *Inst.* 1.63).[105]

If even their culture repudiated such behavior, why were the Corinthians "boasting" in it (5:2)? Ancient literature frequently portrays arrogance about a sin as compounding the guilt all the more (e.g., Is 3:9; Jer 6:15; 8:12).[106] Lack of remorse could be used against an offender in ancient courts as it is today (Isaeus *Estate of Menecles* 24; Aeschines *Ctes.* 250). Condoning another's offense could be viewed as sharing in its guilt (e.g., Hesiod *Op.* 191–92), especially if those condoning it were a court assigned to punish it (Cicero *Verr.* 2.1.4.9; Seneca *Lucil.* 97.3).

Yet it is possible that the Corinthians here merely overlook the man's sin rather than boasting in it, and that what they boast in is the man's continuing presence in their church. In that case, he is likely one of the elite, perhaps even a patron of some members or host to a house church. (Theodoret *Commentary on 1 Cor.* 163–64 viewed him as an eloquent house church leader.) For clients or peers to criticize his behavior would then be a terrible breach of custom that could lead to his political enmity toward them and perhaps the entire church in Corinth. His mother-in-law, who is not addressed in the discipline, apparently does not belong to the church.

Incest was illegal under both Roman law and God's law, but Paul expected the church to exercise discipline rather than relegating it to secular authorities (6:1–2). Rather than waiting to come to demonstrate his authority (4:18–21), Paul acts in the present because his "spirit," unlike his body, is present (5:3–4). Paul neither refers to God's Spirit here nor to some metaphysical conception but

---

[104] Cf. also the charge that Nabateans slept with their mothers (Strabo 16.4.25).

[105] For fuller treatment and documentation regarding ancient incest, see C. Keener, "Adultery, Divorce," 6–16 in *DNTB*, esp. "3.5. Incest," 12–14.

[106] E.g., Lysias *Or.* 14.42, §143; Cicero *Parad.* 32; Publilius Syrus 239; Valerius Maximus 6.9. ext. 1; Seneca *Nat. Q.* 1.16.4–6.

employs the popular language that one could be with friends in one's heart.[107]
This language was especially common in letters, in which one could be absent
in body but present in spirit or thoughts (Col 2:5).[108] Likewise, because the
"spirit" counts for more, Paul was prepared to let the offender's "flesh" suffer so
he might repent and his "spirit" be saved (5:5). Some Jewish teachers believed
that earthly courts following God's laws issued their decrees on the authority of
God's own court; Paul affirms that he acts on God's authority.

Rome often allowed communities of resident aliens, including synagogues,
to judge their own members for violations of their own laws (cf. Acts 18:15);
Paul expects the church, which apparently began in a synagogue (Acts 18:7–8),
to function as synagogue communities did. Later in the passage Paul quotes
biblical law for executing offenders (5:13). Rome reserved capital jurisdiction
for its own agents, but Jewish courts could practice excommunication for any
crime for which the biblical sentence was death (such as consensual incest). This
left the physical part of the sentence to be carried out by God, as here (5:5).

Like the Qumran community and later rabbinic courts, Paul presumably
believed in various levels of exclusion (2 Thess 3:14–15).[109] The crime in question,
however, merited full banishment from the Christian community, a "handing
over to Satan" (5:5). God "handed" Job over to Satan for his testing (Job 2:6 LXX;
T. Job 20:3), but the image here appears harsher than testing alone. When an
Athenian court sentenced one to death *in absentia*, they instructed their priests
and priestesses to curse the offender (Plutarch *Alc.* 22.3–4). Greeks sometimes
cursed people by handing them over to destructive deities; for early Christians,
something placed under a ban for destruction (to use OT language) could be
handed over to Satan as the agent of destruction (1 Tim 1:20). Outside the sphere
of protection by the paschal lamb's blood (5:7), one remained susceptible to
"the destroyer" (cf. Ex 12:23; 1 Cor 10:10).[110] The purpose here, however, is
restorative: so the offender would be brought to repentance and his spirit "saved"
in the end (as in 1 Tim 1:20; Matt 18:15–22).

Because the feast of unleavened bread followed Passover, the completion of
Christ's sacrifice as Passover lamb required the new bread (his body, 10:16–17)
to be purified from leaven (5:6–8).[111] Although leaven was originally a symbol
of haste, sometimes Jewish teachers used it to symbolize evil;[112] perhaps it
functions here simply as a symbol of what spreads unchecked if not stopped.
Everyone understood that it was better to amputate a member of the corporate

---

107 E.g., Isocrates *Nic.* 51–52; Seneca *Lucil.* 32.1.
108 E.g., Cicero *Fam.* 3.11.2; Seneca *Lucil.* 67.2; *P. Oxy.* 32; Achilles Tatius 5.20.5. It becomes
     more metaphysical for Neoplatonists (Porphyry *Marc.* 10.175–79).
109 On the earliest Jewish forms of the ban, see C. Keener, *John* (2003), 208.
110 On the paschal connection, see R. B. Hays, *First Corinthians* (Louisville, KY: John Knox,
     1997), 85.
111 The blending of paschal and sacrificial imagery was natural; see Ex 34:25.
112 Philo *Spec.* 1.293; *b. Ber.* 17a; *Gen. Rab.* 17:8; cf. even Plutarch *R.Q.* 109, *Mor.* 289EF.

body than to let his behavior infect others (Cicero *Phil.* 8.5.15, urging destruction of Antony). The Corinthians' familiarity with Passover (5:7) and other festivals (16:8) was probably not unusual for early Christians (e.g., Acts 20:6, 16), and is certainly not surprising for a church birthed from a synagogue (Acts 18:4–8). (Jewish people had expected a new exodus; cf. Is 11:16; 40:3; 43:19; Hos 2:14–16; 11:1, 11.) Paul reminds them that their true identity is unleavened (5:7); he calls them to live according to their new identity in Christ (cf. 1:2; 2:16; 6:11).

Paul's admonition in an earlier letter (now lost, though some compare 2 Cor 6:14–7:1) to avoid immoral people (5:9) was meant to practice discipline within, not outside, the community (5:12; "those outside" meant nonbelievers, as in 1 Thess 4:12). That sexual immorality appears in the vice-lists (5:9–11) fits the context (5:1), but also is characteristic of most Pauline vice-lists (6:9; 2 Cor 12:21; Gal 5:19; Eph 5:3; Col 3:5); Rom 1:29–31 omits it only because it appeared earlier in Paul's argument (Rom 1:24–27). (Vice-lists were a conventional literary and rhetorical form.)[113]

Paul returns to his demand of 5:4–5 in 5:13. To "purge the evil from your midst" refers to capital punishment in Deuteronomy (13:5; 17:7; 19:9; 21:21; 24:7; cf. Josh 7:12–13), including for some sexual offenses (22:21, 24). As noted earlier, Paul, like his Jewish contemporaries, applied this punishment to banishment by an earthly court, leaving severer judgment, if necessary, to God.

It is important to keep in mind that Paul's application was tempered by sensitivity to the needs of the church. All sin merited punishment (6:9–10), but while many appear to have been committing serious sins (6:15–18), Paul makes an example of only the most serious offender. Without diminishing divine standards, he tempered them with a measure of grace (as in Matt 18:12–35).

6:1–8: CHRISTIAN VERSUS SECULAR COURTS

6:1: When any of you has a grievance against another, do you dare to take it to court before the unrighteous, instead of taking it before the saints?

6:2: Do you not know that the saints will judge the world? And if the world is to be judged by you, are you incompetent to try trivial cases?

6:3: Do you not know that we are to judge angels – to say nothing of ordinary matters?

6:4: If you have ordinary cases, then, do you appoint as judges those who have no standing in the church?

6:5: I say this to your shame. Can it be that there is no one among you wise enough to decide between one believer and another,

---

[113] E.g., Cicero *Mur.* 6.14; *Cat.* 2.4.7; *Cael.* 22.55; *Phil.* 8.5.16; Iamblichus *Pyth. Life* 17.78; see further J. D. Charles, "Vice and Virtue Lists," 1252–57 in *DNTB*.

6:6: but a believer goes to court against a believer – and before unbelievers at that?
6:7: In fact, to have lawsuits at all with one another is already a defeat for you. Why not rather be wronged? Why not rather be defrauded?
6:8: But you yourselves wrong and defraud – and believers at that.

On the one hand, the Corinthian Christians are failing to judge sin in their midst as a Christian court (5:2–13); on the other, they bring their own spiritual "siblings" (6:6, stronger than NRSV's "believer") to secular courts for arbitration. Communities of resident aliens, such as synagogue communities, could execute their own laws on members provided they did not violate Roman law; Corinth's church likely viewed itself in such terms (cf. Acts 18:4–8). Possibly Paul has in view lawsuits over the sort of sexual immorality he has already mentioned (5:1, 9), as he returns to the thought of immorality in 6:9–20. The likelier alternative is that 6:1–8 constitutes a digression on the subject of their juridical failures, and 6:9–20 an extension of the subject of their sexual immorality (with Ch. 7 criticizing the other extreme).

Roman society was notoriously litigious, and Corinth, with its rising class of *nouveau riche*, was even more so. Many ancient lawsuits addressed property matters among the wealthy; some grievances were simply pretexts for avenging insults and pursuing enmity. Arbiters sometimes settled property disputes, but these arbiters, too, were normally of high status (contrast 6:4). People of status also could charge those of lower status, but it was considered inappropriate for those of lower status, who were viewed as less credible and having more to gain, to charge those of higher status (see Gaius *Inst.* 4.183; Suetonius *Claud.* 15.4). Once a magistrate heard the charge, he summoned the accused; assuming the latter appeared, the magistrate then assigned the case as appropriate to a judge, jury, or (if the parties agreed to settle matters privately) to an arbitrator.

In secular courts, worldly status constituted a major factor for evaluation, in contrast to all that Paul has been arguing in the letter so far (1:26). Roman law effective in Corinth, like most other ancient laws except Israel's, decreed harsher penalties for those of lower status.[114] Thus an aristocrat might be banished but a low-status person crucified for the same crime (Josephus *Ant.* 18.79–80). Many recognized that this system was subject to abuse by the wealthy, either lamenting or warning against such abuse.[115] Social critics observed that those who offended the rich sometimes brought about their own deaths (Phaedrus 3.5; Apuleius *Metam.* 9.42). Another observer pointed out that laws were like

---

[114] Later formalized, e.g., *Digest* 47.21.2; Paulus *Sententiae* 5.23.14.19; see more fully P. Garnsey, *Social Status and Legal Privilege in the Roman Empire* (Oxford: Clarendon Press, 1970); B. Rapske, *The Book of Acts and Paul in Roman Custody*, BAFCS 3 (Grand Rapids, MI: Eerdmans, 1994), 56–62.

[115] E.g., Cicero *Verr.* 1.1.1; 1.3.8; 1.5.13; Libanius *Declamation* 36.8–9.

spider webs, capturing the weak but letting the strong escape (Valerius Maximus 7.2. ext. 14).

Again appealing to their identity in Christ (1:2; 5:7; 6:11), Paul reminds the believers of their future status: If they will someday judge the world and angels, how could they not judge by themselves relatively inconsequential matters of this life (6:2–3)? (Although Paul may include all matters of this life in "trivial matters," the Corinthians might expect the phrase to apply to matters of civil rather than criminal law.) We cannot be sure whether Paul expected them to know of their future role from his earlier teaching or simply from knowledge of Scripture among former synagogue members (Dan 7:22; Wis 3:8), but he shared elements of this teaching with some Jewish contemporaries.[116] Scholars debate whether Paul commands them to appoint those of lowest social status as judges (challenging societal prejudice) or demands mockingly whether they will depend on those of lowest status (perhaps outsiders, from the kingdom's view) or other alternatives. What context makes clear is that Paul is unimpressed with worldly courts and (presumably) their system of evaluation through the lens of status.

Suing a "brother" (*adelphos*, 6:6, 8; NRSV: "believer") in the literal sense was scandalous behavior (though it was actually quite common in property disputes). Communities of resident aliens (as well as members of other associations) generally preferred to settle matters among themselves rather than airing their dirty laundry before the larger society. This would have to be especially true for followers of Jesus (Matt 5:39–40; Lk 6:29–30). The elite in Corinth would also know (although rarely observe) the Stoic rejection of judicial remedies based on the worthlessness of anything that could be taken away.[117] "The sensible man," opined Musonius Rufus, "would not go to law nor bring indictments, since he would not even consider that he had been insulted" (10, p. 78.7–9; trans. p. 79, Lutz). Other philosophers also rejected lawsuits and preferred settling cases by their own wisdom to subjecting them to the unwise world (e.g., Iamblichus *Pyth. Life* 27.124–26).

6:9–11: LEAVING THE FORMER LIFE

6:9: **Do you not know that wrongdoers will not inherit the kingdom of God? Do not be deceived! Fornicators, idolaters, adulterers, male prostitutes, sodomites,**
6:10: **thieves, the greedy, drunkards, revilers, robbers – none of these will inherit the kingdom of God.**

[116] For judging the world, see *1 En.* 95:3; 1QpHab 5.4; 4Q418 frg. 69, 2.7–8; *Sipre Deut.* 47.2.8. Jewish tradition portrayed God as loving Israel more than angels; "judging" them may be a rarer view in this period or may be Paul's extrapolation.

[117] Musonius Rufus 10, p. 76.16–17. Cf. other thinkers in Maximus of Tyre 12.9–10; Philostratus *Lives* 1.25.532; Diogenes the Cynic in Diogenes Laertius 6.2.54.

6:11: And this is what some of you used to be. But you were washed, you were sanctified, you were justified in the name of the Lord Jesus Christ and in the Spirit of our God.

Those who "wrong" (*adikeite*) their Christian siblings in 6:8 will not inherit God's kingdom in 6:9, that is, they are "wrongdoers" (*adikoi*). Furthermore, these are the sort of wrongdoers Paul expects in the world (with its corrupt, status-based judicial system) but not in the church, which was why the church should not let unbelievers judge cases (so 6:1, one of only two other uses of *adikos* in the NT). The list of offenses (6:9–10) allows Paul to compare those wronging their siblings with more blatantly obvious vices. His list is heavy on sexual offenses (not unusual in Paul or unexpected for Jews appalled by typical male Gentile behavior, but relevant to the context in 5:1–13; 6:12–21), as well as concerning economic exploitation. Both categories could converge in the matter of prostitution (6:15). Slave prostitutes (the most common form) might be in view (cf. 6:20), though some think that Paul thinks specifically of high-class courtesans at banquets.

A CLOSER LOOK: *ARSENOKOITĒS* AND *MALAKOS*

The terms *arsenokoitēs* and *malakos* (6:9) are no more prominent in the list than others, but the considerable debate about them today invites our brief attention.[118] Although the question remains debated, Paul or (more likely) the ethical tradition he follows probably coined *arsenokoitēs* directly from the standard Greek translation of Leviticus 20:13, in which the two component terms refer to male homosexual intercourse. (The terms appear together there in this sequence, and the Greek Bible was one source for early Christian ethics that can be safely assumed.)[119] This interpretation makes sense given Paul's clear opposition to homosexual intercourse in Romans 1:26–27, and the pervasiveness of homosexual behavior in the Greek and Roman world. (He never addresses the modern question of homosexual "orientation" but presumably would view

---

[118] For homosexual intercourse here, see, e.g., D. F. Wright, "Homosexuals or Prostitutes? The Meaning of Arsenokoitai (1 Cor. 6:9, 1 Tim. 1:10)," *VigC* 38 (2, 1984): 125–53; D. F. Greenberg, *The Construction of Homosexuality* (Chicago: University of Chicago Press, 1988), 212–14; B. Winter, *Left Corinth* (2001), 118–20; R. A. J. Gagnon, *The Bible and Homosexual Practice* (Nashville: Abingdon, 2001), 306–32. Doubting this interpretation (preferring, e.g., homosexual prostitution or pederasty), see esp. the carefully argued R. Scroggs, *The NT and Homosexuality: Contextual Background for Contemporary Debate* (Philadelphia: Fortress, 1983); differently, D. B. Martin, "*Arsenokoitēs* and *Malakos*: Meaning and Consequences," 117–36 in *Biblical Ethics and Homosexuality: Listening to Scripture*, ed. R. L. Brawley (Louisville: Westminster John Knox, 1996).

[119] Out of sequence, the terms appear also in Lev 18:22; the two passages referring to all nonvirgins are less relevant in view of 1 Cor 7:7, 9. See *Sib. Or.* 2.74 (*arsenokoitein*); cf. Ps.-Phoc. 3, 191.

it as merely a sphere of temptation like its heterosexual counterpart, reserving sin only for a mental or physical act; cf. 7:9.)

Bisexuality was extremely common among Greeks, especially because of the shortage of available wives, which apparently occasioned the late age of marriage for most Greek men.[120] By the first century even many Romans had imbibed these social influences (though honorable Romans penetrated only non-Romans), so we should not be surprised about such influences in Corinth. Jewish literature regularly condemns such practices, which are generally viewed as the exclusive domain of Gentiles (e.g., Josephus *Ag. Ap.* 2.215; Philo *Spec. Laws* 3.37–39; *Sib. Or.* 5.387). Paul's language here reflects biblical tradition, but elsewhere he also employs the argument of some Roman Stoics, Diaspora Jews, and others that homosexual intercourse is "against nature" (Rom 1:26, of course not thinking in terms of modern genetics but the normal procreative function of sex in biology and the way male genitals normally fit those of females).[121]

The term *malakos* is more problematic, because it most frequently means "soft," appearing in condemnations of cowardice or (most commonly) leisure (cf. perhaps 16:13). Because the term can refer more specifically to the passive partner in male homosexual intercourse (in antiquity these were usually boys), some view it in light of Paul's context here as the passive partner of the *arsenokoitēs*.

If Jesus tells who will inherit God's kingdom (Mk 10:14; Matt 5:3, 10), some Pauline vice-lists announce who will not (Gal 5:21; Eph 5:5); this one emphatically begins and ends with that warning (1 Cor 6:9, 10).[122] (It might be relevant that in Paul's eschatology, God would subdue all Christ's enemies, death being the final one [15:24–26]; this might suggest the conquest of the unrepentant [cf. Rom 2:5–9; 2 Thess 1:7–9].) E. P. Sanders compares this threat with the "homiletical damnation" in rabbinic literature;[123] Paul believes that the Corinthians remain set apart for God (6:11), but their lifestyle so contradicts their profession (cf. comment on 3:1–3) that he questions whether they can continue in this ambiguous state (cf. Rom 8:13).

Paul's vice-list must correspond at some points to temptations some Corinthian Christians face (6:15–18), but Paul seeks to bring their behavior in line with their new status. He reasons from the indicative to the imperative; the

---

120 On homosexual behavior in antiquity, see esp. K. J. Dover, *Greek Homosexuality* (Cambridge, MA: Harvard University Press, 1978); briefly, C. Keener, "Adultery" (2000), 14–15.

121 E.g., Musonius Rufus frg. 12, p. 86.1, 9–10; Artemidorus *Oneir.* 1.80; Ps.-Phoc. 189–92; Philo *Abr.* 135; *Spec. Laws* 2.50; 3.39; for balanced discussion see D. Greenberg, *Homosexuality* (1988), 207–10.

122 "Inheriting" eschatological promises was conventional Jewish language (see further C. Keener, *Matthew* [1999], 167; James D. Hester, *Paul's Concept of Inheritance*, SJTOP 14 [Edinburgh: Oliver & Boyd, 1968]).

123 E. P. Sanders, *Paul, the Law, and the Jewish People* (Philadelphia: Fortress, 1983), 109; G. F. Moore, *Judaism in the First Centuries of the Christian Era*, 2 vols. (New York: Schocken, 1971), 2:388 n. 4.

disjunction between their identity in Christ and their non-Christian behavior should be jarring (6:11; cf. Rom 6:4, 11). Some philosophers reasoned similarly: those who have adopted philosophy have become wise, hence cannot (in practice, *must* not) follow the world's foolish ways.[124] The thought was, however, more generally intelligible: "Become such as you are, having learned what that is" (Pindar *Pyth.* 2.72; LCL).

In 6:11 he summons them to live according to what God has already made them in Christ (cf. Gal 5:25; Rom 6:11; Col 3:3–5), the sort of tension found in various rabbinic portraits of God's people and in Stoic descriptions of those converted to wisdom. Paul's teaching had presumably already familiarized the Corinthians with the sense and biblical background of his terminology here (cf. e.g., background for "justification" in Rom 1:17; 4:3–22; Gal 3:6, 11).

6:12–21: THE SANCTITY OF THE BODY, OR, WHY CHRISTIANS SHOULD NOT SLEEP WITH PROSTITUTES

6:12: "All things are lawful for me," but not all things are beneficial. "All things are lawful for me," but I will not be dominated by anything.

6:13: "Food is meant for the stomach and the stomach for food," and God will destroy both one and the other. The body is meant not for fornication but for the Lord, and the Lord for the body.

6:14: And God raised the Lord and will also raise us by his power

6:15: Do you not know that your bodies are members of Christ? Should I therefore take the members of Christ and make them members of a prostitute? Never!

6:16: Do you not know that whoever is united to a prostitute becomes one body with her? For it is said, "The two shall be one flesh."

6:17: But anyone united to the Lord becomes one spirit with him.

6:18: Shun fornication! Every sin that a person commits is outside the body; but the fornicator sins against the body itself.

6:19: Or do you not know that your body is a temple of the Holy Spirit within you, which you have from God, and that you are not your own?

6:20: For you were bought with a price; therefore glorify God in your body.

*H*aving listed various vices, including sexual sins, Paul now counters objections and establishes his case against immoral behavior to which some members of the church appear to be succumbing. In contrast to philosophers who denigrated or ignored the body, Paul emphasizes the body's sanctity, with an argument that climaxes in the exhortation to "glorify God in your body"

---

[124] See esp. T. Engberg-Pedersen, *Paul and Stoics* (2000), passim.

(6:20). The body, including its sexuality, was a divine gift to be used responsibly. Their new identity in Christ must shape their behavior (6:11, 13–17, 19–20).

Paul deftly employs the language of ancient ethics to answer objections in 6:12–14. Philosophers and orators regularly employed criteria such as "lawful" and "profitable" for ethical decisions.[125] Moralists often employed an interactive style in which they posed objections from an imaginary interlocutor; sometimes (as in 15:12; Rom 9:19; 11:19) they explicitly noted the interlocutor, but at other times (as here or Rom 3:1–9) they simply offered and refuted the objection (e.g., Cicero *Scaur.* 9.18; 18.41). The NRSV rightly identifies the objections in quotation marks; whether or not some Corinthians had actually used these phrases (cf. 1:12; 7:1), the thoughts the phrases embodied represented the Corinthians' best (potential?) objections.

Simply because an action was "lawful" (literally, one's "right," perhaps meaning not illegal under Roman law) did not make it good for a person (6:12; also 10:23). Paul also warns of being "dominated" by something one supposes one has authority over (6:12d, playing on *exestin* as "lawful" and a cognate word for authority). Greek thinkers regularly warned against being "enslaved" by false ideologies, passions, or a lustful relationship.[126]

Moralists sometimes used the "belly" to symbolize enslavement to gluttony and all other kinds of pleasure (also Rom 16:18; Phil 3:19; often in Philo).[127] "Food for the stomach" fits the common association of gluttony with intercourse; both were sometimes available in the banquets of the wealthy. This also represented the sort of logic by which some Greeks had justified promiscuity: as "food was for the stomach," so the body was designed for intercourse. Paul reminds the Corinthians, however, that God did not design the body only for passion on the level of other animals; it should be a tool for God's service, and God had a higher, eternal purpose for the body. Enemies of those who denied an afterlife (such as Epicureans) or a resurrection (such as Sadducees) typically accused them of lacking moral deterrents to hedonism (see 15:32). Paul here merely hints at an issue that he must develop more fully in Chapter 15: most Greeks and Romans did believe in an afterlife, but not for the body; their position was untenable, however, for those who believed that God raised Jesus from the dead.

Paul employs more than traditional ethical categories. Although echoing Scripture in his language, Paul develops his ethical position here most directly from implications of his gospel: those transformed by Christ have abandoned earlier behavior (6:11); the body belongs to the Lord and will be raised for judgment (6:13–14; cf. 2 Cor 5:10); believers' bodies are members of Christ's body and temple, which must not be defiled by immoral intercourse (6:15–21). If they knew that Jesus would not participate in such behavior, they ought not expose

[125] E.g., *Rhet. Alex.* 1, 1421b.25–1422a.22; 6, 1427b.39–10, 1430a.28; 34, 1440a.1–2; Musonius Rufus 16, p. 102.33–35; Hermogenes *Issues* 76.5–77.19.

[126] I collect scores of samples in *John* (2003), 748–51.

[127] E.g., *Spec. Laws* 1.148, 192, 281; 4.91; further sources in C. Keener, *Matthew* (1999), 342.

his members (themselves) to it; and although sacred prostitution might fit rumors of Aphrodite's temple in Old Corinth (cf. also 10:7–8), prostitution defiled God's true temple (cf. Hos 4:14; 2 Macc 6:4). Paul's prominent "Do you not know?" in this section (6:2, 3, 9, 15, 16, 19; although it appears elsewhere in his and other moralists' writings) assumes that they *ought* to know that he is right.

Genesis applied becoming "one flesh" to the marriage union, which formed a new, blended kinship unit (Gen 2:23–24; cf. Gen 29:14). (Greeks also recognized the unifying power of marital intercourse; Menander Rhetor 2.7, 407.22–23.) Yet because biblical law limited the physical union of intercourse to marriage (which it initiated),[128] Paul applies it to any sexual union, including that with prostitutes (6:16). So powerful was the sexual union that it established a relationship even if the parties involved sought to avoid emotional intimacy or the commitment the union was meant to consummate. Those united with Christ as "one spirit" (6:17), as members of his body, must not be "one flesh" with a prostitute! Being "united to the Lord" reflects OT imagery for God's "marriage" to Israel (cf. Hos 2:16–20; Jer 3:1; 50:5), eventually including converted Gentiles (Zech 2:11); its opposite was being joined to idols (Num 25:3; Hos 4:17).

Paul's graphic command to "Flee" (NRSV: "shun") might recall for some Joseph's escape from immorality (Gen 39:12–13), but the language is extremely common in ancient moral exhortation, including in early Judaism (Sir 21:2; Wis 1:5). It even appears in warnings to avoid prostitution (Cato *Collection of Distichs* 25; Aelian *Farmers* 9) and other forms of sexual immorality (*T. Reub.* 5:5). "Every sin that a person commits is outside the body" (6:18) may be another quotation from the objector;[129] Paul, maintaining his high Jewish view of the body and its sanctity, responds that sexual immorality sins even against one's own body (not to mention that of the other person and the Lord). (The argument would be intelligible even to Greeks for sexual practices they considered shameful; cf. Aeschines *Tim.* 29, 185, 188, and esp. 21: "they sin against their own bodies.")

"Bought with a price" (6:20) may suggest a contrast with slave prostitutes (7:23) or the price of prostitution; it alludes to the price of Christ's redemption (1:30), hence reinforcing once more the value of the individual's body. In contrast to pagan ideology, Christ's sacrifice and the sanctity of the bodies for which he paid obligate Christians to "glorify God" with their bodies.

A CLOSER LOOK: SEX IN THE CITIES

Old Corinth had a reputation for sexual immorality; an Athenian comic used "Corinthian lady" as a sexually significant remark (Aristophanes *Lys.* 91). Some

---

128 For sexual intercourse as the chief consummating feature of the marriage covenant, see G. P. Hugenberger, *Marriage as a Covenant: Biblical Law and Ethics as Developed from Malachi* (VTSup 52; Leiden: Brill, 1994; reprint: Grand Rapids, MI: Baker, 1998), 216–79.
129 See J. Murphy-O'Connor, "Corinthian Slogans in 1 Cor 6:12–20," *CBQ* 40 (3, 1978): 391–96.

even believed that old Corinth's temple of Aphrodite boasted a thousand cult prostitutes.[130] Although some may have applied the saying, "Not every man dare go to Corinth," to cutthroat competition, others plainly applied it to prostitution there.[131] As a city with two major ports, New Corinth would have harbored the same sorts of problems as its predecessor. By Jewish standards, Greek males were nearly always immoral; that Paul must address sexual improprieties among his converts (cf. 1 Cor 5–7) is therefore not surprising.

Sexual behavior that Paul, his Scripture, and most Christians, Jews, and Muslims in the world today would consider immoral was rife in Greco-Roman cities. Aristocratic Roman men could not sleep with women of rank, but they could sleep with those of lower station. If, as is often argued, Greeks abandoned more girl than boy babies, the consequent shortage of marriageable women explains why Greek men typically married women a decade their junior. Until age thirty, Greek men had access to intercourse primarily with slaves, prostitutes, and each other. As in virtually all slave cultures, female household slaves were often subject to abuse. Many abandoned girl babies rescued from death were raised as slave prostitutes, many of whom worked in inns and taverns, which doubled as brothels. Dio Chrysostom denounced the activities in brothels as humiliating "intercourse without love and passion without affection for gain" (*Or.* 7.133). A more expensive option was higher-status free prostitutes, traditionally called, somewhat euphemistically, *herairai*, "friends." Prostitution was legal (and a useful source of tax revenue), but if a prostitute married she had to retire from her trade.[132] Perhaps even more than today, sexually explicit comedy was also publicly accepted.

BRIDGING HORIZONS

Although the focus here is on the use of prostitutes, the principles Paul articulates (and some examples in his vice-list) prohibit all kinds of *porneia*, sexual immorality. Like other Jews, Paul defined as immoral any sexual intercourse apart from marriage (a union that in his day Jews and nearly all Gentiles assumed was heterosexual). Although many scholars question whether Paul refers to homosexual intercourse in 6:9, many of both his supporters and detractors think that he does. What is striking is that in this context Paul, unlike some of his modern followers, spends more space criticizing sexual misbehavior in general (5:11; 6:9, 13–18), presumably more often heterosexual than homosexual.

---

[130] Strabo *Geogr.* 8.6.20; 12.3.36. For skepticism about this claim, see J. Murphy-O'Connor, *St. Paul's Corinth: Texts and Archaeology* (Wilmington, DE: Glazier, 1983), 55–56. But for the continuing influence of Aphrodite there, see, e.g., Pausanias *Descr.* 2.4.6; 2.5.1; Alciphron *Parasites* 24.3.60, ¶3; for prostitutes and promiscuity there, e.g., Pindar *Encomia* frg. 122; Martial *Epig.* 10.70; Dio Chrysostom *Or.* 8.5; Athenaeus *Deipn.* 13.573c.

[131] Strabo *Geogr.* 8.6.20; Aulus Gellius *Noct. att.* 1.8.4.

[132] On prostitution, see sources in C. Keener, "Adultery" (2000), 10–12.

(Even in Romans 1, the particularly Gentile vices of idolatry and homosexual behavior are examples to pave the way for the broader human vice-list of Rom 1:29–31, allowing Paul's critique of Jewish alongside Gentile sin in Ch. 2.)

Yet even regarding heterosexual intercourse, modern Western society is no more comfortable with biblical sexual ethics than Paul's contemporaries were (although perhaps more tolerant of Paul for the sake of many of his other insights more widely accepted, such as spiritual unity across ethnic and class lines). Before modern readers dismiss him too readily, however, we should hear him (and his biblical and early Jewish tradition) clearly. Some modern readers hear the biblical tradition's emphasis on sexual restraint as if it were designed to inhibit pleasure, rather than to establish wholeness in relationships. This was certainly the case among some ascetics of late antiquity, including among both some philosophers and Christian monks; but it is not the point of Paul or most other first-century Jews (at least on our reading of 1 Cor 7). Much of Western culture, overreacting against late antiquity's tradition repressing sexuality, has come to value casual sex as a form of recreation.

Yet by rejecting any restraints (and practical judgments formed by many societies throughout human history), our world underestimates how deeply sexuality inheres in our humanity. As with other animals, our sexual drives serve a procreative function for the species as a whole; but for humans sexuality is also distinctively relational. For example, most female mammals are "in heat" only rarely, and females in few other species experience orgasm. Unlike most other animals, humans are able to mate face-to-face, and perhaps most significantly, romantically in the context of a relationship. Sexual intimacy is difficult to separate from emotional intimacy, and such intimacy flourishes in the context of vulnerability and trust, hence commitment. Counselors today must address the lives broken by betrayal and exploitation, where intercourse is often a self-gratifying act isolated from a person or a relationship.[133]

Israelites, like most other societies, sought to protect their children's innocence against sexual predators. They also took sexual acts (and the possibility of consequent pregnancy) more seriously than modern Western society does. In a society in which men controlled most wealth, they demanded that a man who risked getting a woman pregnant be committed to and provide for her; in this perspective, a prostitute sold herself cheaply, but casual sex was cheaper still. By contrast, valuing one's neighbor as oneself demanded reserving one's deepest gift of intimacy for a partner who would ideally offer one nothing less than their own life. Paul himself would have been dissatisfied with how far Israelite law took this: polygamy; a gender-based double standard for sexuality (challenged in Gen 38–39 and in 1 Cor 6–7); and other factors severely limited the fulfillment

---

[133] On a popular level, see these observations in P. Yancey, *Rumors of Another World: What on Earth Are We Missing?* (Grand Rapids, MI: Zondervan, 2003, 74–77).

of this ideal. Nevertheless, permanent, mutual commitment remained the ideal to which God's plan pointed (Gen 1:27–28; 2:24). To use another person's sexuality for one's own pleasure without genuinely committing oneself to that person was exploitive.

Today, as in antiquity, many people (most often men) exploit others' sexuality. Deceived by promises of education or legitimate jobs, thousands of girls from Bangladesh and Thailand are lured annually into an involuntary sex trade, a modern form of slave prostitution. In the West, tens of thousands of runaway teenagers end up as prostitutes to find places to sleep at night. My wife recounts horrifying accounts of men, often relatives and neighbors, raping young girls in her native Central Africa, a tragedy exacerbated further by recent wars there she witnessed. One of humanity's most precious gifts is also most easily abused by others who value momentary gratification over another human being's personhood.

Is it possible that, while thinking we are merely pursuing pleasures, modern people allow them to "dominate" our behavior (6:12) at the expense of our common sense and the common good? Christians must grapple especially with Paul's demand for spiritual fidelity: Members of Christ dare not defile Jesus' body by behavior inappropriate for his participation, or the sanctity of his temple with behavior inappropriate there. Dominated instead by the Spirit whose temple they are, Christians must live in ways that benefit others.

7:1–9: SEX WITHIN MARRIAGE

7:1: Now concerning the matters about which you wrote: "It is well for a man not to touch a woman."

7:2: But because of cases of sexual immorality, each man should have his own wife and each woman her own husband.

7:3: The husband should give to his wife her conjugal rights, and likewise the wife to her husband.

7:4: For the wife does not have authority over her own body, but the husband does; likewise the husband does not have authority over his own body, but the wife does.

7:5: Do not deprive one another except perhaps by agreement for a set time, to devote yourselves to prayer, and then come together again, so that Satan may not tempt you because of your lack of self-control.

7:6: This I say by way of concession, not of command.

7:7: I wish that all were as I myself am. But each has a particular gift from God, one having one kind and another a different kind.

7:8: To the unmarried and the widows I say that it is well for them to remain unmarried as I am.

7:9: But if they are not practicing self-control, they should marry. For it is better to marry than to be aflame with passion.

If 6:12–21 addresses the problem of sex outside of marriage, 7:1–7 addresses the danger of lack of sex within it. When Paul uses "Now concerning" (*peri de*; 7:1, 25; 8:1; 12:1; 16:1, 12; 1 Thess 4:9; 5:1), he is transitioning to a new subject (a common use of the phrase in antiquity);[134] some think that Paul is addressing different questions raised by the Corinthians' letter (7:1) when he uses the phrase.

Most scholars believe that Paul quotes the Corinthians' letter of inquiry in 7:1. Paul may refute their point about a man not "touching" a woman (a regular ancient idiom for intercourse), but if he is conceding it, he applies it to unmarried intercourse only (6:12–21); he goes on to demonstrate that married people must have intercourse (7:2–7). Contrast "It is well," *kalon*, in 7:1 with "It is not good," *ou kalon*, in Gen 2:18, a context Paul has just quoted in 6:16.

In verse 2, to avoid temptations to the sort of immorality just described (6:12–21; also 7:5), Paul wants each man to "have" his wife, and each wife to "have" her husband. This was often a euphemism for having the other sexually; thus Paul is saying, let them sleep together. Most people recognized marital intercourse as a deterrent to extramarital intercourse[135] (although some Gentiles saw even prostitution as a deterrent from adultery, and some Stoics valued intercourse only for procreation).

Ancients expected various "conjugal rights" (7:3) and obligations for each gender (spelled out in marriage contracts), but the reciprocal right intended in this context is clearly intercourse. First-century Pharisees emphasized that husbands must grant this right to wives, and even debated whether one week or two was too long for abstinence (*m. Ketub.* 5:6–7; *Sipre Deut.* 213.2.1). Although virtually all ancients agreed that the husband had authority over the wife's sexuality (7:4), most Gentiles refused to hold the husband to the same standard of fidelity (exceptions included the Stoic Musonius Rufus). By contrast, concern for both genders characterizes Paul's advice (7:2–5; 11:11–12; cf. Eph 5:21–25). Reasonable sexual "rights" over the other's body seems a natural extrapolation of the two being "one flesh" (6:16) and contrasts with the illegitimate power in prostitution (6:12d).

Paul concedes that those who wish to abstain for spiritual reasons (analogous to fasting)[136] might do so, but only by mutual consent and temporarily (7:5–6). Although using himself as a model in other ways (4:16; 11:1), he recognizes that not all are endowed with the ability to endure indefinite abstinence (7:7) or singleness (7:8–9). Paul accepts the value of celibacy for singles, but argues that it

---

[134] E.g., Theon *Progymn.* 1.60; 5.442; *P. Lond.* 1912.52.

[135] E.g., Xenophon *Oec.* 10.12; Publilius Syrus 492.

[136] Cf. Ex 19:15; Philo *Moses* 2.68–69; *T. Naph.* 8:8. On the character of the concession here, see D. Daube, "Concessions to Sinfulness in Jewish Law," *JJS* 10 (1–2, 1959): 1–13, p. 12.

is better to marry than to be even more distracted by passion (7:8–9). Although some think of burning as God's judgment (see plausibly 3:13–15), the NRSV rightly interprets the Greek's "aflame" as "with passion" in 7:9 (cf. 2 Cor 11:29). "Burning" was one of the most common descriptions of unfulfilled passion throughout Greek and Roman literature.[137] Like some other Jewish thinkers, Paul accepted marriage as the best antidote for such passion (cf. 7:2a, 5, 9).

A CLOSER LOOK: MARRIAGE, CELIBACY, AND PAUL

Most of Paul's contemporaries valued marriage and childbearing, a value especially prominent in mainstream Judaism and exemplified by Augustus's legislation to replenish the Roman aristocracy two generations before Paul's time. Augustus's laws rewarded with tax incentives widows and divorcées of childbearing age who remarried as quickly as possible. Many Stoic philosophers emphasized the importance of these virtues for maintaining the state. Some thinkers, however, believed that marriage proved a distraction from higher pursuits (e.g., Cynics in Epictetus *Diatr.* 3.22.69–76). Some radical philosophers (especially Cynics) therefore eschewed marriage, nevertheless condoning the release of sexual passions on prostitutes (cf. 6:12–21). It is therefore possible that the same people who justified sexual license by philosophy in Chapter 6 also opposed marriage in Chapter 7. It is, however, equally possible that 7:1–7 is directed toward members who abstain for spiritual reasons (7:5) and whose abstinence may tempt spouses to the behavior in Chapter 6 (see 7:2a). Jewish thinkers who viewed marriage as a distraction (including Philo's Therapeutae, for both genders; and most male Essenes) practiced celibacy, the option Paul expects of the unmarried.[138]

Paul's articulation of the spiritual value of singleness provided support for later Christians impressed with the rise of sexual asceticism in broader philosophic circles, but he addressed a mostly different philosophic environment than did his successors.[139] His reasons are not ascetic in the strict and later sense of the term; there is no denigration of the body (quite the contrary, 6:19–20), but an appreciation for the long-standing concerns of those who felt a higher calling. Cynics who thought marriage a distraction from intellectual pursuits were not celibate like Jewish monastics were; but Paul's congregations are very much in the world, not monastic communities (a resistance against society that their setting did not require). But Paul would have been sympathetic with a later rabbi

---

[137] E.g., Catullus 45.16; 61.169–71; Ovid *Fasti* 3.545–46; further in C. Keener, "Marriage," 680–93 in *DNTB*, 686–87.

[138] For a fuller description of the ancient options, see C. Keener, "Marriage" (2000), 680–83; ... *And Marries Another: Divorce and Remarriage in the Teaching of the New Testament* (Peabody, MA: Hendrickson, 1991), 68–78.

[139] See W. Deming, *Paul on Marriage and Celibacy: The Hellenistic Background of 1 Corinthians 7*, 2nd ed. (Grand Rapids, MI: Eerdmans, 2003).

who, while affirming the importance of replenishing the world (more forcefully than Paul would have), was so enamored with study of Torah that he had no time for marriage (ben Azzai in *b. Yebam.* 63b; *Gen. Rab.* 34:14). (Most rabbis, by contrast, felt that marriage prevented distraction, e.g., *b. Yebam.* 63ab.)

7:10–16: STAYING MARRIED

7:10: To the married I give this command – not I but the Lord – that the wife should not separate from her husband

7:11: (but if she does separate, let her remain unmarried or else be reconciled to her husband), and that the husband should not divorce his wife.

7:12: To the rest I say – I and not the Lord – that if any believer has a wife who is an unbeliever, and she consents to live with him, he should not divorce her.

7:13: And if any woman has a husband who is an unbeliever, and he consents to live with her, she should not divorce him.

7:14: For the unbelieving husband is made holy through his wife, and the unbelieving wife is made holy through her husband. Otherwise, your children would be unclean, but as it is, they are holy.

7:15: But if the unbelieving partner separates, let it be so; in such a case the brother or sister is not bound. It is to peace that God has called you.

7:16: Wife, for all you know, you might save your husband. Husband, for all you know, you might save your wife.

Whereas some Corinthian spouses wanted to abstain from intercourse (7:1–7), some others wanted to extricate themselves from marriage altogether (7:10–16). Divorce was extremely common in Corinth, so that many members of the church had likely been remarried before conversion; Paul must address, however, only the current behavior of those who are Christians.

Paul clearly distinguishes Jesus's teachings (7:10–11) from his own interpretation (7:12–13), although he appears to believe that his interpretation is inspired (7:40). As one Matthean form of Jesus's divorce saying expands OT law without denigrating it (Matt 5:31–32), so does Paul with Jesus's teaching: he will address a new situation that Jesus's general principle did not address.

Jesus's general principle was: Do not divorce (Lk 16:18; Matt 5:32). Given his Palestinian Jewish context (cf. Deut 24:1–4; Sir 7:26; 25:26), Jesus warned men against divorce; Greek and Roman law, however, predicated marriage on mutual consent, so the principle in this setting addresses both genders (Mk 10:12; 1 Cor 7:13–15). But what happens if one does not break up one's own marriage, yet it is broken against one's will by the other partner? That Matthew felt free to clarify that Jesus's principle does not restrict a spouse betrayed by an unfaithful partner

(Matt 5:32; 19:9) and Paul that it does not refer to spouses abandoned against their will (1 Cor 7:15) reveals early Christians' flexibility in applying Jesus's teachings to new situations according to the spirit rather than the letter of the law.[140]

Many Corinthians, mostly converted after their marriages, apparently wanted more "spiritual" unions (cf. 7:5), hence wanted to end their marriages on grounds of spiritual incompatibility. Paul admonishes them not to break up with spouses simply because they are unbelievers. Whether or not they may convert the spouse (7:16 can be read either hopefully, as in the NRSV, or pessimistically), staying together "sets apart" the children for God's influence (7:14). (In this period, the children nearly always went to the father in the case of divorce, at least if both parents were Roman citizens.) Ancient laws grappled with the status of children in mixed marriages between such groups as Roman citizens and noncitizens, and various classes in Judaism;[141] Paul here commends the influence of a godly parent.

But if the unbeliever, not following Christ's law, chose to divorce, the believer could not stop it. When Paul says that "the brother or sister is not bound" in such cases (7:15), he does not simply mean that they are free to divorce. He had no reason to state something so obvious, since they had no control over the situation: Under laws effective in Corinth, either party could dissolve the marriage without the other's approval. "You are not bound" or "you are free" was the language of ancient divorce contracts, always stipulating freedom to remarry (e.g., *m. Git.* 9:3; *CPJ* 2:10–12, §144; *P. Grenf.* 2.76.10–11); Paul affirmed believers' freedom to remarry if they did not break up their marriage.

7:17–24: REMAINING CONTENT WITH ONE'S SITUATION

7:17: However that may be, let each of you lead the life that the Lord has assigned, to which God called you. This is my rule in all the churches.

7:18: Was anyone at the time of his call already circumcised? Let him not seek to remove the marks of circumcision. Was anyone at the time of his call uncircumcised? Let him not seek circumcision.

7:19: Circumcision is nothing, and uncircumcision is nothing; but obeying the commandments of God is everything.

7:20: Let each of you remain in the condition in which you were called.

7:21: Were you a slave when called? Do not be concerned about it. Even if you can gain your freedom, make use of your present condition now more than ever.

---

140 C. Keener, *Marries Another* (1991), 28–37, 50–66.

141 E.g., Gaius *Inst.* 1.66–92; Ulpian *Rules* 5.8–9; *t. Demai* 3:9; *y. Qid.* 1:1, §8; *Git.* 1:4, §2; see fully C. Keener, *Marries Another* (1991), 56–58. Betrothal "set apart" brides (e.g., *m. Qid.* passim).

7:22: For whoever was called in the Lord as a slave is a freed person belonging to the Lord, just as whoever was free when called is a slave of Christ.

7:23: You were bought with a price; do not become slaves of human masters.

7:24: In whatever condition you were called, brothers and sisters, there remain with God.

In encouraging married people to remain married and (less forcefully) single people to remain single, Paul appeals to a wider principle of contentment with one's conditions (7:17, 20, 24). Many people, and particularly Stoic philosophers (who affirmed fate), stressed the value of contentment in circumstances one could not control (cf. 2 Cor 9:8; Phil 4:11; 1 Tim 6:6).[142] Of course, contentment with one's circumstances does not require one to oppose (or be discontent with) a change of circumstances that may prove more useful for the gospel (7:21–24).

As Paul had to address in other churches (Gal 5:2–11; 6:12–15; Phil 3:2–3), some Gentiles felt the need to be circumcised. Likewise, some Hellenized Jews ashamed of their circumcision had undergone operations to pull their prepuce forward, in effect uncircumcising them (1 Macc 1:14–15, which equates it with apostasy). Paul commonly observed that God values neither circumcision nor the lack of it, but the new life that flows from love (Gal 5:6; 6:15; cf. Rom 2:25–26), hence the *real* point of God's commandments.

Paul urged them to be content about something beyond their control. In urging contentment, Paul offers a limited analogy with slavery, relevant because Greek terms for "marriage" and "divorce" involved being "bound" or "freed" (7:15, 27). When Paul calls on slaves to be content with a situation they cannot control,[143] we should keep in mind the form of slavery he addresses. In urban Corinth he addresses neither the most repressed slaves in mines, gladiatorial shows, or to a lesser extent, in the fields, but household slaves. Many household slaves enjoyed economic and social conditions superior to peasants (who constituted the majority of the Empire's free population, although "free" must be used loosely with regard to those working feudal estates). A small minority who worked for powerful people even wielded more wealth and power than most aristocrats; some noble women married into slavery to improve their social station! Such observations are not intended to condone slavery of any sort, nor to deny its frequent dramatic abuse (e.g., beatings), especially for women (see comment on 6:12–21). But it is important for modern readers to understand that, on average, Roman household slavery proved quite different from slavery, even household slavery, in the Americas.[144]

---

[142] See, e.g., Valerius Maximus 7.2. ext. 1a; Seneca *Lucil.* 96.1–2; Marcus Aurelius 4.25; 5.27.

[143] For philosophic parallels regarding slavery, see, e.g., Diogenes Laertius 6.2.74 (Diogenes the Cynic); Seneca *Lucil.* 47.17; Epictetus *Diatr.* 1.1.23; 1.19.8.

[144] Slavery in the Islamic world included a different range of options; see esp. B. Lewis, *Race and Slavery in the Middle East: A Historical Inquiry* (New York: Oxford, 1990).

Paul recognized a limitation in his analogy with slavery, however: in contrast to being "freed" from a marriage, being freed from slavery could be desirable. Many (some argue most) first-century household slaves at some time in their life had the opportunity for manumission. They could save money on the side to buy their freedom. For the most part their continuing in slavery or being freed rested with the master's choice; certainly they could not reject manumission (7:21 means to make use of manumission, not, as in the NRSV, to continue one's present condition). Freedpersons remained members of their former holder's extended household, and their former holders as patrons were obligated to help them advance. Many in Rome became wealthy, often to the disdain of hereditary elites (e.g., Petronius *Sat.* 37–38). In Corinth, a high percentage of the population was freed or descended from freedpersons, and most (cf. Gaius *Inst.* 1.9–17) would have been Roman citizens (a status rarely available even to municipal aristocrats in the Greek East, outside Roman colonies).[145] Sometimes people bought slaves' freedom to turn them over for service in a temple; Paul envisions a different kind of service (7:23). As the Lord's freedperson, a Christian takes the Lord's name, functions as his dependent, and seeks to honor him.

7:25–35: UNMARRIED LIFE SIMPLER

7:25: Now concerning virgins, I have no command of the Lord, but I give my opinion as one who by the Lord's mercy is trustworthy.

7:26: I think that, in view of the impending crisis, it is well for you to remain as you are.

7:27: Are you bound to a wife? Do not seek to be free. Are you free from a wife? Do not seek a wife.

7:28: But if you marry, you do not sin, and if a virgin marries, she does not sin. Yet those who marry will experience distress in this life, and I would spare you that.

7:29: I mean, brothers and sisters, the appointed time has grown short; from now on, let even those who have wives be as though they had none,

7:30: and those who mourn as though they were not mourning, and those who rejoice as though they were not rejoicing, and those who buy as though they had no possessions,

7:31: and those who deal with the world as though they had no dealings with it. For the present form of this world is passing away.

---

[145] On slaves and freedpersons, see sources in C. Keener, "Family and Household," 353–68 in *DNTB*, 361–66; for this passage, esp. S. S. Bartchy, *First Century Slavery & the Interpretation of 1 Corinthians 7:21* (Eugene, OR: Wipf & Stock, 2003; originally SBLDS 11; Missoula, MT: Society of Biblical Literature, 1973); J. A. Harrill, *The Manumission of Slaves in Early Christianity* (HUT 32; Tübingen: Mohr Siebeck, 1995).

7:32: I want you to be free from anxieties. The unmarried man is anxious about the affairs of the Lord, how to please the Lord;

7:33: but the married man is anxious about the affairs of the world, how to please his wife,

7:34: and his interests are divided. And the unmarried woman and the virgin are anxious about the affairs of the Lord, so that they may be holy in body and spirit; but the married woman is anxious about the affairs of the world, how to please her husband.

7:35: I say this for your own benefit, not to put any restraint upon you, but to promote good order and unhindered devotion to the Lord.

*P*aul has already warned against applying the dictum of 7:1 ("It is good not to touch a woman") to married people (7:2–7); now he revisits the question of the never yet married and (by way of digression in 7:27) those whose marriages have ended. Continuing celibate singleness has advantages for those able to follow it (cf. 7:8–9).

Paul makes clear that his advice is not moral but practical (7:27–28). In 7:27 (using rhetorical parallelism), he reviews his earlier counsel in 7:10–16: the married should not divorce, and the divorced often should stay single (cf. 7:11). "Free from a wife" in the NRSV is literally "freed from a wife," using the same term as the preceding line's "do not seek to be free," an obvious reference to divorce. (In antiquity, when freeborn and freed status differed, Paul's first readers, who will recall his analogy between freed status and divorce in 7:21–23, would not have missed the point.) But as he also indicated in 7:15, remarriage is morally acceptable; now he notes that precisely the same situation obtains for those never yet married (7:28). (Most applied the term "virgin" to women, but occasionally, perhaps figuratively, males could be so designated;[146] the question is disputed here.) Paul is careful to address both virgins and others who are "unmarried" (*agamos*, 7:34; cf. 7:8), which may include divorced persons (7:11; although one might read, "the virgin unmarried woman," the definite articles preceding both terms renders this less likely).

Paul's first reason is a coming "crisis" (7:26; although *anagkē* can be rendered differently as in 7:37), probably referring to eschatological tribulation preceding the end. The language of inversion of normal relationships he uses fits many traditional Jewish expectations for the end (e.g., 2 *Bar.* 10:13–15; *m. Sotah* 9:15; although cf. Lk 17:27–28; Matt 24:38). Although this suffering did not materialize as quickly in Corinth as Paul expected, he probably would have considered the Neronian persecution in Rome and analogous events as part of the eschatological tribulation he expected, which always remained no less potentially imminent than Christ's return (cf. 1 Thess 3:3–4; 2 Thess 1:5–7; 2:2–7). Somehow marriage

---

[146]   Jos. and Aseneth 4:7/9; 8:1; Rev 14:4; Achilles Tatius 5.20.5; 5.27.

increases one's susceptibility to *thlipsis*, tribulation (7:28; NRSV, "distress"); if he relates this to eschatological distress, he may think of dangers associated with bearing or caring for infants (Mk 13:17) or grief at losing loved ones (cf. Jer 16:2–4).

Paul's second reason would be exacerbated by eschatological tribulation but remains important even without it. Like Cynic sages Paul recognizes that the activities necessitated by marriage (employment, childrearing, and so forth) can distract one from higher pursuits. ("Pleasing" a spouse was not intrinsically evil, of course [cf. 10:33], provided one pleased God first [cf. Gal 1:10]. Like most Stoics, Paul valued both marriage and singleness.)[147] Most later rabbis felt that marriage actually reduced distractions (e.g., *b. Qidd.* 29b–30a), and Paul would have conceded this point for those tempted by lust (7:9); yet he would have also understood a rare second-century rabbi who did not want marriage to distract him from Torah (*t. Yebam.* 8:7). Ultimately, even a homeless Cynic sage could marry if he found a woman who could endure the Cynic lifestyle (as in the rare – or perhaps unique – case of Crates and Hipparchia, Diogenes Laertius 6.7.96).

BRIDGING THE HORIZONS

Paul pointed to advantages of undistracted singleness for those with the constitution for such a lifestyle. One need not endorse ministerial celibacy as a requirement to note that the Catholic tradition has made a place for this form of devotion much better than the Protestant tradition, which too often views this passage as a problem to be resolved. For many years, I found that singleness permitted me to pursue my scholarly work undistracted, but social support for (or even acceptance of) my status was minimal.

At the same time, it is important to observe where Paul is conceding some value to a position he does not hold, rather than enthusiastically endorsing a position. Paul recognized that not all have or easily obtain the "gift" he had (7:7); in view of the relational and sexual "norm" in his Bible (Gen 2:18), only a special constitution or the overriding demands of one's call might surmount the usual pattern. This should give us special respect for those who, as a result of their calling, convictions about their sexual orientation, lack of available marriage prospects, or other life circumstances maintain a celibate single life. Someone living that lifestyle, such as Paul, can better understand its sacrifice and can articulate the value of celibate self-control more credibly than a person who has spent most of their adult life in a happy marriage (valuable as that lifestyle also is).

Paul's reason based on "impending distress" (7:29–31) fits a worldview often shared by Christians when they are persecuted minorities, but forgotten by

---

[147] For parallels, see esp. D. L. Balch, "1 Cor 7:32–35 and Stoic Debates about Marriage, Anxiety, and Distraction," *JBL* 102 (3, 1983): 429–39.

Christians who, as in Corinth, grow comfortable with the society in which they live (contrast Jesus's encouragement to the suffering churches of Smyrna and Philadelphia with his reproofs to the others in Rev 2–3). Although we recognize today that the end did not come in the first century, if Paul were among us today he would likely still insist that we remain ready for it. History certainly vindicates the perspective that comfortable situations change and Christians must always be ready to face tribulation. Times of crisis demand special sacrifice (2 Kgs 5:26). In the context of Paul's partly realized eschatology, such tribulation characterizes the present era (Rom 8:22; Col 1:24).

Paul's counsel on divorce (7:10–16, 27–28) bears special mention. Churches today often miss either Paul's emphasis on fidelity to the marriage covenant or mercy toward those in genuinely impossible situations. Paul regards Jesus's teaching on the subject as authoritative, but not complete. He addresses a new situation not specifically treated by Jesus's principle: What happens if the spouse breaks up the marriage against the believer's will? Paul's exception here resembles Matthew's principle of *porneia*, the partner's infidelity (Matt 5:32; 19:9); one partner's abandonment or choice of divorce, like *porneia*, is a breaking of the marital union caused by the unfaithful partner for which the faithful believer is not held responsible. Under such circumstances, Paul says, the believer is free to remarry (7:15). It is possible that 7:27–28 provides even more freedom.

But what about situations that Paul himself did not address? Would he not expect Christians to follow his model in applying Jesus's principles, rather than merely the explicit canonical exceptions? If we follow Paul's dynamic pastoral model, we are confronted with situations such as physical abuse, which breaks a marriage covenant; in this kind of case, the "innocent" party might even be one who files for divorce. Physical abuse is one obvious case; a spouse's illegal activities might be another. In pastoral practice, however, some other grounds offered for divorces are less obvious. It is all too easy to treat cheaply our covenant in a way that hurts spouse, children, society, and ourselves, when a marriage can be healed with work; most marriages face struggles, but many who persevere regain their joy. As a rule, it seems safest to work to heal marriages when possible; to make exceptions when they are necessary; to show grace when matters are unclear; and to work for both justice and healing for all involved in the tragic case of a marriage already irretrievably broken.

7:36–40: BETROTHED VIRGINS AND WIDOWS

7:36: **If anyone thinks that he is not behaving properly toward his fiancée, if his passions are strong, and so it has to be, let him marry as he wishes; it is no sin. Let them marry.**

7:37: But if someone stands firm in his resolve, being under no necessity but having his own desire under control, and has determined in his own mind to keep her as his fiancée, he will do well.

7:38: So then, he who marries his fiancée does well; and he who refrains from marriage will do better.

7:39: A wife is bound as long as her husband lives. But if the husband dies, she is free to marry anyone she wishes, only in the Lord.

7:40: But in my judgment she is more blessed if she remains as she is. And I think that I too have the Spirit of God.

*H*aving addressed primarily married people, virgins, and divorced people, Paul now wraps up his discussion with widows (7:39–40, whom he also mentions in 7:8) and a group whose identity was undoubtedly clearer to the Corinthians than to subsequent interpreters (7:36–38).

The two major interpretations of the debated group are the traditional interpretation, namely, fathers with their betrothed daughters (e.g., NASB) or the more common view today (and the view presupposed in the NRSV), namely prospective grooms and their betrothed fiancées. In favor of the first interpretation, fathers exercised the final say over their daughters' marriages (cf. Sir 7:24–25; *m. Qidd.* 2:1); thus he may "keep her virgin" (7:37, against the NRSV).[148] If one man refused to marry her, the father could betroth her to another. Further, *gamizō* (7:38), fitting normal *-izō* verbs, often means "give in marriage" as distinct from "marry" (Mk 12:25; Matt 24:38; again against the NRSV); but occasionally *gamizō* does mean simply "marry."

In favor of the latter interpretation, *gameō* (7:36, in the third-person plural) means "marry" (7:9, 10, 28, 33–34, 39); several terms also could be used for sexual desire. In this case, a betrothed couple may prolong the engagement while serving the Lord, but if passions become too strong they should marry quickly (cf. Achilles Tatius 4.1.4–5; 4.8.3). Also widespread is a third view, that Paul addresses celibate marriages; some later Christians had "spiritual marriages" or "spiritual betrothals," a situation that might explain this passage best but also may have arisen from one interpretation of it.[149] On the whole, the betrothal interpretation may be strongest.

Any of these interpretations presupposes a sizeable Corinthian church, if the couples' members are all Christians. They also reinforce Paul's general principle (hence he might have agreed with both): singleness is more useful if possible, but for those apt to be tempted sexually, marriage is better.

Although even Roman law advocated the remarriage of Roman widows, some still honored the romantic ideal of not remarrying after the death of a spouse;

---

148   This also would fit the rarer interpretation that the passage applies to slaveholders and slaves (7:21–23), although Paul offers no clue that he addresses slaveholders here.

149   There are a few isolated precedents for the idea, e.g., Pyrrho in Diogenes Laertius 9.11.66.

Paul does not require this (7:39–40). His claim that he may have the Spirit (7:40) might sound like a weak support for his opinion, but it is actually one of the strongest implied claims to inspiration in his writings, though not absolute (cf. 14:37); early Judaism associated the Spirit especially with various forms of prophetic empowerment.

8:1–13: KNOWLEDGE AND IDOL FOOD

8:1: Now concerning food sacrificed to idols: we know that "all of us possess knowledge." Knowledge puffs up, but love builds up.

8:2: Anyone who claims to know something does not yet have the necessary knowledge;

8:3: but anyone who loves God is known by him.

8:4: Hence, as to the eating of food offered to idols, we know that "no idol in the world really exists," and that "there is no God but one."

8:5: Indeed, even though there may be so-called gods in heaven or on earth – as in fact there are many gods and many lords –

8:6: yet for us there is one God, the Father, from whom are all things and for whom we exist, and one Lord, Jesus Christ, through whom are all things and through whom we exist.

8:7: It is not everyone, however, who has this knowledge. Since some have become so accustomed to idols until now, they still think of the food they eat as food offered to an idol; and their conscience, being weak, is defiled.

8:8: "Food will not bring us close to God." We are no worse off if we do not eat, and no better off if we do.

8:9: But take care that this liberty of yours does not somehow become a stumbling block to the weak.

8:10: For if others see you, who possess knowledge, eating in the temple of an idol, might they not, since their conscience is weak, be encouraged to the point of eating food sacrificed to idols?

8:11: So by your knowledge those weak believers for whom Christ died are destroyed.

8:12: But when you thus sin against members of your family, and wound their conscience when it is weak, you sin against Christ.

8:13: Therefore, if food is a cause of their falling, I will never eat meat, so that I may not cause one of them to fall.

s often elsewhere (7:1, 25; 12:1; 16:1, 12; cf. 1 Thess 4:9; 5:1; *Did.* 6.3; 7.1; 9.1, 3; 11.3), "now concerning" (8:1) signals a transition of topic. Paul addresses propriety in food and banqueting in most of 8:1–11:34 (apart from the digression in 11:2–16 that, like much of the rest of the letter, addresses decorum in Christian assemblies, which included banquets). Chapters 8–10 address the tables of other gods but provide hints of the coming contrast with the Lord's table in 11:17–34 (see 10:3–4, 21). After 8:13, Paul digresses to offer himself as an example of surrendering rights, providing a model for Corinthians to surrender their own (the term for "right" in 9:4–6, 12, 18, is the same term translated "liberty" in 8:9). Whereas Paul offers a theological critique of known idol food in 10:1–22, which harshly rejects it (at least when still on the sacred grounds of the temple, but probably anywhere that it will be explicitly associated with idolatry in observers' minds), he frames this argument with a social critique, based on his recurrent emphasis on love (8:1, 3; 13:1–14:1; 16:14), in 8:1–13 and 10:23–33. His concluding summary for Chapters 8–10 again appeals to his example (10:33–11:1).

For the sake of believers with "weaker" consciences, Paul in 8:1–13 summons elite Christians to surrender their "rights" to idol food. These "rights" may reflect their citizen rights at public festivals or their elite eating habits, and probably refers especially to their claims (following the example of philosophers) of superior knowledge and freedom. The elite members of the congregation vaunt their superior knowledge (8:1–2, 4, 7, 10–11); Paul reminds them that the only status that matters is how God views them (8:3, 12; cf. 1:30–31), and that this status rests not on their knowledge but their love (8:10–12; cf. 13:2, 8).[150] In at least 8:1 and 8:4 (and possibly a bit more, such as all of 8:8), Paul summarizes their own position (or a useful insight in it) as he sees it, then refutes or qualifies it (see comment on 6:12).

The particular knowledge to which the intellectually elite Christians here appeal is the claim that idols are really nothing (8:4). Whatever the status of their images,[151] Paul is less convinced that the "many gods" of Greeks and Romans (for statues in Corinth's marketplace, see Pausanias 2.2.6, 8; 2.3.1) are nothing (8:5); in fact, he follows common Jewish tradition in recognizing spiritual forces behind them (10:20). Paul does concede that these "so-called gods" are nothing in the sense that Christians recognized that only one God was true (8:6).

Apparently appealing to a conviction the Corinthian Christians share, Paul in passing describes Christian monotheism and creation in terms that Stoics and some other Greeks could understand, but which especially evoke the "one God" and "one Lord" of the regularly recited Shema' (Deut 6:4). Philo and some other Jewish thinkers distinguished "Lord" and "God" as representing separate divine attributes; the early Christian confession of Jesus as "Lord" (12:3; 16:22) naturally lent itself to such elucidation. Despite the doubts of some that Paul refers to Jesus's role in creation here, Jewish people viewed wisdom (cf. Philo's *logos*) as a divine attribute, through which God designed and created the world; less than three decades after Jesus's resurrection, Paul and his churches already see Jesus

---

[150] Indeed, for some philosophers like Socrates, wisdom began by claiming ignorance (cf. Philostratus *Vit. soph.* 1.480). But Paul would not advocate the thorough agnosticism of the Skeptics.

[151] The problem was not the artwork, but that idols were worshiped (cf. *m. 'Abod. Zar.* 3:4).

filling this role (cf. comment on 1:3).[152] Such a rapid identification of a movement's founder as divine seems unprecedented, certainly for a monotheistic
Jewish movement committed to the Shema'.

In any case, even if idols were nothing, Paul points out, those who fail to share
this conviction nevertheless participate in idolatry against their own faith when
they eat idol food (8:7). Because idol food holds a different social and theological
significance for the "weak" (the "uninformed," from the standpoint of the elite;
cf. Seneca *Lucil.* 94.50), they may follow the example of the "liberated" in a way
that compromises their own monotheism (8:10; cf. *t. Demai* 3:7). Causing one
to sin could "destroy" one eternally (8:11).[153]

Some scholars associate the strong Corinthians' "liberty" (8:9; literally, *exousia*, "authority"; the verb appears in 6:12) with special societal privileges that
belonged to Roman citizens or to members of the elite. This is likely part of
the picture, but it probably reflects even more fully the assumption of the elite
that they have superior knowledge. Popular philosophers often spoke of being
"free" in their decisions or having authority (cf. also 4:8; 6:12; Diogenes Laertius
7.1.125); some, such as Cynics and Skeptics, therefore disregarded social conventions. Paul insists that God is less interested in the status such rights confer
than in sacrificial love that surrenders such rights. Thus, in the example Paul
offers after this paragraph, although Paul himself is "free" (9:1), he surrenders
his "rights" (9:4–6, 12, 18), and even becomes a slave of everyone (9:19), to the
disdain of the elite (see comment on 9:19–23). Ancient statesmen recognized
that giving up "rights" and compromising were necessary for civic concord.[154]

Because philosophers valued their "freedom" from the vain ideas of the
masses, many (especially the Cynics) rejected the importance of others' opinions about them. Some did, however, recognize circumstances under which
considering others' opinions was important, for example, winning converts to
the true (philosophic) way of thinking. Paul is not concerned for his own honor
(4:3), but he is concerned for how his gospel will appear to others, even to the
point of sacrificing his personal freedom (9:19–23; 10:32–11:1).

Giving up meat (8:13) may sound like a radical solution, but such sacrifice
would demand more of the social elite (who had regular access to it at banquets)
than of others who ate it especially when it was distributed free (from large
amounts of meat roasted for sacrifices) at pagan festivals.[155] Paul offers himself
as an example of such sacrifice (9:1–27; even of "food and drink," 9:4) before

---

[152] See C. Keener, *John* (2003), 341–54, 374–81; L. Hurtado, *Lord Jesus Christ: Devotion to Jesus
       in Earliest Christianity* (Grand Rapids: Eerdmans, 2003).
[153] Cf. Num 31:16; *Sipre Deut.* 252.1.4. Judaism had already applied analogous language about
       "stumbling" to the "falling" of sin or apostasy; Sir 9:5; 23:8; 25:21; 32:15; 1QS 2.12; 3.24.
       The term "conscience," although important in Stoicism, was also common elsewhere,
       including Hellenistic Judaism.
[154] See documentation in M. Mitchell, *Rhetoric* (1991), 132.
[155] Scholars usually argue that the nonelite lacked access to nonsacrificial meat, although
       some (see J. J. Meggitt, "Meat Consumption and Social Conflict in Corinth," *JTS* 45
       [1, 1994], 137–41) dispute this claim.

turning to a theological argument against known idol food (10:1–22), or at least (on some views) idol food still connected with a temple (1 Cor 8:10). Paul would apply this principle even in other settings; when he addresses the tension between Jewish and Gentile food customs, Paul articulates a similar warning about causing "the weak" (Rom 14:1–2; 15:1; cf. 1 Cor 8:7, 9–12) to "stumble" (Rom 14:13, 20), and advocates willingness to give up meat (14:21) for the sake of those for whom Christ died (14:15).

A CLOSER LOOK: IDOL FOOD[156]

Just as Jews and Christians thanked God for food before they ate, others honored their deities at all meals, including ordinary banquets. When associations met for banquets, the food was often dedicated to their patron deity. Libations of wine were poured to a deity during banquets.

The association of dining with deities was even more obvious at public festivals honoring those deities, such as Poseidon or the emperor. Ancients generally did not waste much meat sacrificed to the gods, but ate most of it after it was cooked. Naturally festivals produced an excess of meat, so even the masses, which normally could afford little meat, could participate then. These were special occasions and privileges that few citizens would want to miss. (Meat was not the only sacrifice offered to idols, but it produced more "leftovers" from the sacrifice and constituted a special treat for those who shared it.)

Apart from festivals, people might eat meat from the idol's temple within the sacred precincts of the temple, but it also showed up in nearby restaurants and in the meat market. Apart from Jewish, kosher-butchered meat (which might, some think, have become unavailable under the anti-Jewish proconsul Gallio, in response to Claudius's anti-Jewish policy in Rome),[157] or meat specifically identified as from a temple, one might not know the source of all meat procured in the market. Most meat in urban markets may have come from temples (certainly much meat was sacrificial in some cities like Pompeii). But the possibility that some was not, and that much was not labeled, might allow one to not know for certain if one chose not to investigate (10:25). Some Judean teachers later criticized Diaspora Jews for attending pagan banquets with their children, even though these Diaspora Jews often brought their own food.

The patronage system, families, friendships, and business acquaintances all sometimes involved invitations to dinner. Paul seeks to minimize complications (10:27–29) but will not compromise with anything appearing to endorse idolatry (10:20–21).[158] Such conflicts would especially challenge Christians of status, such

---

[156] For greater detail, see esp. D. E. Smith, *From Symposium to Eucharist: The Banquet in the Early Christian World* (Minneapolis: Fortress, 2003), 1–172; W. L. Willis, *Idol Meat in Corinth* (SBLDS 68; Chico, CA: Scholars, 1985).

[157] See B. Winter, *Left Corinth* (2001), 296–99.

[158] Cf. *t. 'Abod. Zar.* 6:6; *b. 'Abod. Zar.* 6a.

as Erastus and Gaius (Rom 16:23); Jews were already accustomed to the struggles in avoiding such food.[159]

9:1–27: PAUL RELINQUISHES THE RIGHT OF SUPPORT

9:1: Am I not free? Am I not an apostle? Have I not seen Jesus our Lord? Are you not my work in the Lord?

9:2: If I am not an apostle to others, at least I am to you; for you are the seal of my apostleship in the Lord.

9:3: This is my defense to those who would examine me.

9:4: Do we not have the right to our food and drink?

9:5: Do we not have the right to be accompanied by a believing wife, as do the other apostles and the brothers of the Lord and Cephas?

9:6: Or is it only Barnabas and I who have no right to refrain from working for a living?

9:7: Who at any time pays the expenses for doing military service? Who plants a vineyard and does not eat any of its fruit? Or who tends a flock and does not get any of its milk?

9:8: Do I say this on human authority? Does not the law also say the same?

9:9: For it is written in the law of Moses, "You shall not muzzle an ox while it is treading out the grain." Is it for oxen that God is concerned?

9:10: Or does he not speak entirely for our sake? It was indeed written for our sake, for whoever plows should plow in hope and whoever threshes should thresh in hope of a share in the crop.

9:11: If we have sown spiritual good among you, is it too much if we reap your material benefits?

9:12: If others share this rightful claim on you, do not we still more? Nevertheless, we have not made use of this right, but we endure anything rather than put an obstacle in the way of the gospel of Christ.

9:13: Do you not know that those who are employed in the temple service get their food from the temple, and those who serve at the altar share in what is sacrificed on the altar?

9:14: In the same way, the Lord commanded that those who proclaim the gospel should get their living by the gospel.

9:15: But I have made no use of any of these rights, nor am I writing this so that they may be applied in my case. Indeed, I would rather die than that – no one will deprive me of my ground for boasting!

9:16: If I proclaim the gospel, this gives me no ground for boasting, for an obligation is laid on me, and woe to me if I do not proclaim the gospel!

---

[159] Cf. 4 Macc 5:2–3; *Jos. Asen.* 10:13–14; 11:9, 16; 12:5; *m. Abod. Zar.* 2:3; *Abot* 3:3.

9:17: For if I do this of my own will, I have a reward; but if not of my own will, I am entrusted with a commission.

9:18: What then is my reward? Just this: that in my proclamation I may make the gospel free of charge, so as not to make full use of my rights in the gospel.

9:19: For though I am free with respect to all, I have made myself a slave to all, so that I might win more of them.

9:20: To the Jews I became as a Jew, in order to win Jews. To those under the law I became as one under the law (though I myself am not under the law) so that I might win those under the law.

9:21: To those outside the law I became as one outside the law (though I am not free from God's law but am under Christ's law) so that I might win those outside the law.

9:22: To the weak I became weak, so that I might win the weak. I have become all things to all people, that I might by all means save some.

9:23: I do it all for the sake of the gospel, so that I may share in its blessings.

9:24: Do you not know that in a race the runners all compete, but only one receives the prize? Run in such a way that you may win it.

9:25: Athletes exercise self-control in all things; they do it to receive a perishable wreath, but we an imperishable one.

9:26: So I do not run aimlessly, nor do I box as though beating the air;

9:27: but I punish my body and enslave it, so that after proclaiming to others I myself should not be disqualified.

I n 9:1–27, Paul relinquishes his right of support. As part of his argument about food offered to idols (Chs. 8–10), Paul employs himself as an example of surrendering "rights" for the sake of others (the analogy even includes food, 9:4, 7, 9, 13). To this end, Paul's language of "freedom," "compulsion," and "slavery" all reflect standard philosophic discussions, including elite condemnations of "servile" flatterers and demagogues who appeal to the masses (cf. 9:19–23).

Paul also may be hinting at some dissatisfaction with his refusal to accept support, a dissatisfaction that becomes a major issue, probably exacerbated by traveling teachers competing with Paul, by the time he writes 2 Corinthians 10–13. (In a wealthy city such as Corinth, Paul's refusal to accept a particular standard of living could offend elite allies.) It is unlikely that the issue appears in both letters only by coincidence, and a lengthy chain of rhetorical questions (9:1–13) could function as a "defense" (9:3).[160] At this point, however, the "defense" remains primarily a mock one, assuming that his hearers will accept his argument; his primary purpose for writing about relinquishing rights is to set an example. He foregoes food and drink, so the Corinthians will forego food and drink to idols.

---

[160] Cf., e.g., Xenophon *Anab.* 5.8.4–5; Lysias *Or.* 24.24–25, §170; Cicero *Sest.* 21.47. But one could also use them to prosecute (Cicero *Phil.* 3.6.15) or to drive home any point (Musonius Rufus 11, p. 80.22–25; 13B, p. 90.13–16; 15, p. 98.25–27).

Paul begins by establishing his apostolic "right" to support (9:1–14); they themselves are the fruit of his "work" (9:1; cf. 2 Cor 3:2–3). (Many philosophers spoke of "freedom" [9:1] from false values or property concerns; see discussion at 8:9; 9:19.) Other apostles received hospitality for themselves and their wives traveling with them (9:4–5), but Paul and his earlier ministry companion Barnabas worked for their food (9:6; Paul did so in Corinth at least until gifts from Macedonia helped him, Acts 18:3–5; 2 Cor 11:8–9; Phil 4:16). Jewish disciples who went far from home to study with a teacher normally could not bring their wives;[161] but although this may have been true of Jesus's followers in the gospels (perhaps with children at home), it must have changed in time. ("Believing wife" in 9:5 is literally "a sister as a wife." Perhaps originally influenced by Egyptian marriages between literal siblings, Jewish people could employ "sister" affectionately, as in Song 4:9; Tob 8:4, 7. But the NRSV undoubtedly catches the point here; cf. 7:39.)

His comparisons in 9:7 reinforce the point: The army supported soldiers, and caretakers of vineyards and flocks expected to receive some of the fruit. Ancient teachers often employed such conventional images, and early Christians pictured the church as God's army (cf. Rom 13:12; 2 Cor 10:3–6), vineyard, and sheep (cf. 9:10–11; 3:9).[162] (The comparison's implications were self-evident; Greek-speakers sometimes applied *karpos*, translated "fruit," to nonagricultural "advantage" or "profit.")

Paul further advances his case from Scripture (9:9–11): If the law provides food from the field even for the laboring ox, it surely teaches that human laborers have that right (Deut 25:4; 11QTemple 52.12).[163] Ancients could understand "how much more" analogies from animals to humans (Heraclitus *Ep.* 9);[164] literal care for animals reflected a more general spirit of compassion (Josephus *Ag. Ap.* 2.213; Philo *Virtues* 140, 145). Although the OT seems to point to God's care for animals (Gen 6:20; 9:4; Ex 23:19; Lev 17:14; Jon 4:11) and many agreed,[165] others were more skeptical,[166] and interpreted the biblical text accordingly (*Let. Aris.* 144). Some who observed the texts literally explicitly argued that laws about animals were

---

[161] Cf. *Sipre Deut.* 48.2.4–6; but this was rarely for over a month, *m. Ketub.* 5:6.

[162] For varied images of the church, see P. S. Minear, *Images of the Church in the New Testament* (Philadelphia: Westminster, 1960); on background for some images here, C. Keener, *John* (2003), 799–802, 988–93.

[163] Some also point to Jewish applications of "ox" to all laborers (D. Instone-Brewer, "1 Corinthians 9.9–11: A Literal Interpretation of 'Do Not Muzzle the Ox,'" *NTS* 38 [4, 1992], 554–65).

[164] For this rabbinic analogy in Deut 25:4, see B. Cohen, *Jewish and Roman Law: A Comparative Study*, 2 vols. (New York: The Jewish Theological Seminary of America, 1966), 63; but contrast *Sipre Deut.* 287.1.1.

[165] See Matt 6:26; *p. Kil.* 9:3, §4; cf. Plutarch *Marcus Cato* 5.2–6; sources in C. Keener, *Matthew* (1999), 235.

[166] See Stoics in Cicero *Fin.* 3.20.67; Epictetus *Diatr.* 1.16.2. Cf. *m. Ber.* 5:3; *Meg.* 4:9, but the point may be different. Likewise, Solon's law cared not for slaves but to teach virtue to the free (so Aeschines *Tim.* 17).

for people's, not animals', sake (e.g., Philo *Special Laws* 1.260), and Paul's point is that God gave Scripture especially to benefit his people (10:11; Rom 15:4). Paul's final argument is "clerical" (cf. Rom 15:16). Perhaps particularly relevant to the context of sacred food (Chs. 8–10; esp. 10:18), priests ate a portion of the sacrifices (9:13). The Jesus tradition (the Q mission discourse) allows Paul to apply the principle to Christian ministers (9:14; Matt 10:10; Lk 10:7; cf. 1 Tim 5:18).

A CLOSER LOOK: TEACHERS' SUPPORT

To refuse a gift was to reject proffered friendship and declare enmity (e.g., Cicero *Fam.* 14.3.1); yet for Paul to depend on the Corinthians was to risk being seen as their client – or as the client of one faction over another.[167] No one could suspect that another's purse controlled his tongue. Similarly, by refusing to charge a fee (*misthos*), Socrates remained "free" (Xenophon *Mem.* 1.2.6); by lacking needs and dependence on anyone Cynics claimed to be "free" (e.g., Crates *Ep.* 7; 8; 29; Maximus of Tyre 36.5).

Teachers could be supported by several means: charging fees of pupils (tuition rates varied according to the teacher's notoriety; a few even charged on a sliding scale for poorer students); a wealthy patron (who might use their lectures as intellectual dinner entertainment); begging (most characteristic of Cynics);[168] and manual labor. (Among artisans, fine artists might be "free," but craftsmen were base; Menander Rhetor 1.3, 360.25–26.) The latter two were unacceptable to the elite, and elite members of the congregation may have been embarrassed to bring guests to hear a teacher who asserted his independence from their patronage by working with his hands (4:12). To some more "respectable" Corinthians, then, Paul's earning a "wage" (*misthos*, 9:17–18) was undoubtedly an embarrassment. Manual laborers, by contrast, seem to have respected their own trade, and nonelite members may have appreciated Paul identifying with them.

In contrast to elite ideology, some philosophers valued manual labor (especially for its compatibility with the old Roman virtue of hard work); most early Jewish sages also supported such labor (perhaps aristocrats excepted). Scholars debate whether Paul's trade in Acts 18:3 represents making tents from cloth (*cilicium*; a trade prominent in his native Tarsus) or (more commonly) leatherworking, perhaps making awnings for Corinth's Isthmian Games (although he also worked elsewhere; Acts 20:34; 1 Thess 2:9).[169]

---

[167] I use "patrons" and "clients" loosely for benefactors and beneficiaries, not implying the sort of clients who spent much of the day displaying political support for their patrons.

[168] Excepting Cynics and mendicant preachers, most people viewed begging as dishonorable, although sometimes necessary for the homeless.

[169] The classical study on Paul's work is R. F. Hock, *The Social Context of Paul's Ministry: Tentmaking and Apostleship* (Philadelphia: Fortress, 1980); see here more recently P. Marshall, *Enmity* (1987), 296–304.

Having established his "right" to support in 9:1–14, Paul now explains why he has voluntarily relinquished that right (9:15–18; anticipated in 9:12b); in so doing, he receives a better "wage" (*misthos*, 9:17–18; NRSV "reward"), perhaps evoking a teacher's "fee," than they could offer (cf. the same term in 3:8, 14). Paradoxically, this reward appears to be the sacrificial life itself (9:18), so that he might share the gospel's fruit, namely "gaining" many for Christ (9:19–23; NRSV uses "win"). He would sacrifice his profit so others could profit with salvation (10:33). One who offered service voluntarily was "free" (Xenophon *Cyr.* 8.1.4; Philostratus *Hrk.* 30.3).

If he did not accept the calling as a voluntary privilege, he would have to fulfill it nonetheless (cf. Ex 4:10–17), yet without reward (1 Cor 9:16–17). But he would "rather die" than relinquish this privilege and reward (9:15), a graphic expression to underline the point (cf. Rom 9:3). Ancients often claimed that death (or not being born, Matt 26:24) was preferable to some lamentable situation; this was common in Jewish, Greek, and Roman sources. One could use the expression rhetorically,[170] but more often it indicated severe emotional intensity.[171]

Paul was unwilling to compromise the opportunity to "gain" many (9:19–23) by accepting support; yet how would accepting support "put an obstacle in the way of the gospel of Christ" (9:12)? Because many wandering preachers exploited the masses (the equivalent of today's charge that affluent ministers are "in it for the money"), Paul must distinguish his ministry from theirs, no matter what the cost (cf. 2 Cor 2:17; 1 Thess 2:3–6).[172] A leader willing to sacrifice monetary gain due him would be viewed as honorable (e.g., Josephus *Life* 80).

Thus, the apostle has chosen to become as a slave to reach all (9:19–23), although he is technically "free" (9:1, 19) in the sense of having "authority" or a "right" to support (9:4–6, 12). He refused to be a client sage for any Corinthian patron, but serves all (cf. 2 Cor 4:5). A slave could earn wages (cf. *misthos*, 9:17–18, although this evokes rather teachers' fees; also *kerdaino*, "gain" [NRSV "win"] in 9:19–22)[173] and in a wealthy household might be better positioned than a free person outside it. Although wealth and power conferred some status, however, Romans born as aristocrats regarded even wealthy slaves as lower in dignity than themselves. Although adaptability for audiences was central to ancient rhetoric (and proselytism, for example, Hillel toward Gentiles), aristocrats despised those

---

170 Aeschines *Tim.* 55, 122; Demosthenes *Phil.* 4.25; Cicero *Fam.* 8.15.2.

171 Besides texts in C. Keener, *Matthew* (1999), 626, see, e.g., Jon 4:8; Aeschylus *Prometheus Bound* 747–51; *frg.* 229; Apollonius of Rhodes 3.774–75; Cicero *Att.* 11.9; *Fam.* 9.11.1; 9.18.2; Catullus 92.

172 In 1 Thess 2, see A. J. Malherbe, "'Gentle as a Nurse': The Cynic Background to I Thess ii," *NovT* 12 (1970): 203–17; for wandering preachers, see W. L. Liefeld, "The Wandering Preacher As a Social Figure in the Roman Empire" (Ph.D. dissertation, Columbia University, 1967), esp. 246–47.

173 Possibly this echoes Jewish language for proselytism also; commentators follow D. Daube, "κερδαίνω as a Missionary Term," *HTR* 40 (1947): 109–20.

who shifted too conveniently, as if without conviction (cf. the later charge of fickleness in 2 Cor 1:17). They viewed those who adapted themselves too flexibly as populist demagogues, who pandered to the less educated masses and hence reduced themselves to "slaves."[174] One orator emphasized that he had not made himself anyone's slave, but was a friend to all (Ps-Cicero *Invective Against Sallust* 4.11). Still, Paul's claim would make sense even to well-to-do members; even Cicero, who would not be "a slave to everyone" by letting himself be abused (*Fam.* 7.24.1), emphasized the importance of being a "slave" to those governed (*Quint. fratr.* 1.1.8.24). Pleasing others was considered good politics if it maintained peace (Fronto *Ad M. Caes.* 1.8.3).

Everyone understood that customs varied from one culture to another, but some Romans despised fellow-Romans who pandered to local tastes by becoming as a local (e.g., a German or Macedonian) to locals (cf. Herodian 4.7.3–4; 4.8.1–3; 5.5). Others, however, praised such adaptability (Nepos 7.11.2–6). Paul would be flexible with both Jews and Gentiles (9:20), reducing offenses (10:32) to reach both. The "law of Christ" (9:21) probably involves understanding God's law through Christ (Gal 6:2 with 5:18, 23; cf. Rom 3:31; 7:7, 25; 9:30–32; 10:4), perhaps written in the heart (Rom 8:2). Paul apparently applies it to the spirit of the law while allowing cultural accommodations for Gentiles otherwise alienated from it, although he does not spell out his means for distinguishing cultural and moral elements (cf. Acts 21:25). (Some other Diaspora Jews allowed such accommodations for God-fearers, for example, Josephus *Ant.* 20.41; but Paul differed in welcoming Gentiles into God's people on such terms.) Identifying with the "weak" (9:22) may reveal a deliberate policy of relinquishing a status (and perhaps potential academic and rhetorical level) to which he could have laid claim (and that higher-status members of the community expected from him). He models care for the weak (cf. 8:7, 9–10; 12:22; 1 Thess 5:14).

Paul explains his life of sacrifice by an athletic illustration about self-discipline to receive a prize (9:24–27). The biennial Isthmian Games were the second most popular events in Greece (after the Olympics), drawing large crowds of Greeks to Corinth (e.g., Livy 33.32.1; Alciphron *Courtesans* 2.1.29). These Games, recently restored to their original location, likely occurred at least once when Paul was in Corinth (Acts 18:11, 18).[175] Even outside Corinth, however, no one would miss Paul's point; athletic illustrations were among the most common employed by

---

174 See esp. D. B. Martin, *Slavery as Salvation: The Metaphor of Slavery in Pauline Christianity* (New Haven, CT: Yale, 1990), esp. 86–116; M. Mitchell, *Rhetoric* (1991), 134–35 speaks of a "political chameleon." The charge was often leveled against Cynics (W. Liefeld, "Preacher" [1967], 39, 59, 162). For antipathy toward demagogues, cf. also sources in C. Keener, *John* (2003), 732–33; against servile flatterers, e.g., Musonius Rufus 7, p. 58.3; Ambrosiaster loc. cit.

175 See further, e.g., O. Broneer, "The Apostle Paul and the Isthmian Games," *BA* 25 (1, Feb. 1962): 2–31.

philosophers and others for their labors.[176] The point is not competition but self-discipline (cf. Iamblichus *Pyth. Life* 9.49).

As Paul implies (9:25), training for major Greek games began long in advance and was a mandatory prerequisite for participation (Polybius 6.47.8), an image sometimes applied to virtue.[177] "Wreaths" were "perishable" (9:25). Whereas the victor's wreath in the Olympic games was wild olive, in the Pythian of laurel, and the Nemean of green wild celery, in various periods the Isthmian's wreath was of already withered celery or (before the end of the century) of pine. Like other athletic illustrations, the figurative use of crowns or wreaths was common in ancient literature, including in early Judaism (Wis 5:16; 2 *Bar.* 15:8; *T. Job* 4:10). Diaspora Jews also promised God's prize for those who sacrificed for virtue (4 Macc 9:8; 15:29); the prize for martyrdom was, as for self-discipline here, "immortality" (4 Macc 17:12). Jews obeyed the law with greater incentive than earthly treasures or victory wreaths (Josephus *Ag. Ap.* 2.217–18). In this context, what Paul "wins" or "gains" is human lives (9:19–22), striving not to lose any (8:11–13).

The pentathlon included both running (first) and wrestling, but boxing was a separate event. Orators could apply boxing figuratively as an illustration (Cicero *Brut.* 69.243). Because the sport was violent, boxers wore leather on most of the forearm and lacked the reprieve of rounds; the violent *pankration*, which combined boxing and wrestling (plus kicking and so forth), barred little but biting and gouging. One could practice by "beating the air" (9:26), or "shadow-boxing" (e.g., Philostratus *Hrk.* 13.2), but only genuine boxing was adequate preparation.[178]

But why does he bruise his own body (cf. Prov 20:30)? An illustration does not correspond to what it illustrates on every point, so mention of the "body" could simply evoke athletic discipline. Nevertheless, many ancient thinkers associated the body, if not carefully governed by reason, with seeking pleasure (including sexual pleasure, 6:13, 18; but Paul's treatment of the body is generally positive, e.g., 6:19; ch. 15). Stoics demanded discipline of the body, although not in the ascetic manner of later Gnostics (Seneca *Lucil.* 8.5; 14.1). In any case, failure to discipline himself would lead to failing the test or being "disqualified," a designation that for Paul probably includes eternal consequences (cf. 2 Cor 13:5–7; Rom 1:28). Likewise, the danger of undisciplined focus on their own desires will be judgment (10:5–6, 9–12).

---

[176] Examples are too many to enumerate (e.g., throughout Epictetus), but see V. C. Pfitzner, *Paul and the Agon Motif. Traditional Athletic Imagery in the Pauline Literature*, NovTSup 16 (Leiden: Brill, 1967).

[177] Cf., e.g., Isocrates *Ad Nic.* 11, *Or.* 2; Seneca *Lucil.* 80.3; Epictetus *Diatr.* 2.17.29; 3.22.52.

[178] Dio Chrysostom complained that philosophers who abdicated public affairs were like shadow-boxers (*Or.* 32.19–20; B. Winter, *Philo and Paul* [1997], 45).

10:1–22: EATING IDOL FOOD SUPPORTS IDOLATRY

10:1: I do not want you to be unaware, brothers and sisters, that our ancestors were all under the cloud, and all passed through the sea,

10:2: and all were baptized into Moses in the cloud and in the sea,

10:3: and all ate the same spiritual food,

10:4: and all drank the same spiritual drink. For they drank from the spiritual rock that followed them, and the rock was Christ.

10:5: Nevertheless, God was not pleased with most of them, and they were struck down in the wilderness.

10:6: Now these things occurred as examples for us, so that we might not desire evil as they did.

10:7: Do not become idolaters as some of them did; as it is written, "The people sat down to eat and drink, and they rose up to play."

10:8: We must not indulge in sexual immorality as some of them did, and twenty-three thousand fell in a single day.

10:9: We must not put Christ to the test, as some of them did, and were destroyed by serpents.

10:10: And do not complain as some of them did, and were destroyed by the destroyer.

10:11: These things happened to them to serve as an example, and they were written down to instruct us, on whom the ends of the ages have come.

10:12: So if you think you are standing, watch out that you do not fall.

10:13: No testing has overtaken you that is not common to everyone. God is faithful, and he will not let you be tested beyond your strength, but with the testing he will also provide the way out so that you may be able to endure it.

10:14: Therefore, my dear friends, flee from the worship of idols.

10:15: I speak as to sensible people; judge for yourselves what I say.

10:16: The cup of blessing that we bless, is it not a sharing in the blood of Christ? The bread that we break, is it not a sharing in the body of Christ?

10:17: Because there is one bread, we who are many are one body, for we all partake of the one bread.

10:18: Consider the people of Israel; are not those who eat the sacrifices partners in the altar?

10:19: What do I imply then? That food sacrificed to idols is anything, or that an idol is anything?

10:20: No, I imply that what pagans sacrifice, they sacrifice to demons and not to God. I do not want you to be partners with demons.

10:21: You cannot drink the cup of the Lord and the cup of demons. You cannot partake of the table of the Lord and the table of demons.

10:22: Or are we provoking the Lord to jealousy? Are we stronger than he?

$\mathcal{E}$ xamples were a standard form of proofs in antiquity, as were quotations from ancient authorities. Having established from his own example the importance of sacrificing rights for the greater good, Paul turns to biblical examples (10:1–13) to establish a more direct argument against idol food: participating in idolatry is wrong (10:14). He reasons also from the irreconcilability of the Lord's table and that of demons in 10:14–22. The remainder of his argument returns to the stumbling block principle: the problem is not the molded image per se but that people associated with it spiritual beings that genuinely were malevolent. He offers practical instructions in 10:23–30, and offers a concluding summary (which focuses on his opening argument about not causing others to stumble in Chs. 8–9) in 10:31–11:1.

Paul appeals to Israel's history because even the Gentile Christians have been grafted into that history as spiritual proselytes, no longer Gentiles (10:1, 32; 12:2; cf. Rom 2:28–29; 11:17–24; Gal 3:28–29; 1 Thess 4:5). The Israelites consumed food and drink provided by God (10:1–4), but God destroyed them because they practiced immorality (10:8) and idolatry (10:6), just as some Corinthian Christians were doing (6:9, 13–18; 8:1–10). In other words, as Paul soon declares explicitly, partaking of the Lord's table is meaningless if one also partakes of idols (10:14–21)!

Paul is not antisacramental in 10:1–4 (as some earlier writers, thinking that he polemicized against "sacramental cults," averred), but does challenge complacency by showing that baptism (cf. 1:13–17; 15:29) and the Lord's supper (the focus here; 10:14–22) no more protected them from divine judgment for idolatrous suppers than had their equivalent done among the Israelites. (Indeed, Paul has just relinquished any complacency of his own in 9:27.) Christians could void the trappings of Christian profession by behaving in a manner that negated the reality of that profession. Like the Wisdom of Solomon, Paul uses the wilderness narrative to challenge presumption among his audience. (This narrative would have already challenged former pagans in Corinth, where Poseidon, god of the sea, was heavily emphasized.)

Paul speaks of baptism "into Moses" on the analogy of baptism "into Christ" (12:13; Rom 6:3; Gal 3:27; cf. 1:13). Some later rabbis also drew a similar analogy between the immersion expected of converts to Judaism and Israel's past immersion (Moses sprinkling blood on them); Paul elsewhere compares descent into the Red Sea with Christ's death (Rom 10:7).

Spiritual food and drink (10:3–4) cannot protect those who also consume idol food (10:7, 20–21).[179] "Spiritual" could mean "allegorical" (cf. Rev 11:8); another Diaspora Jew regarded manna as God's "word" (Philo *Alleg. Interp.* 3.169–74) – although quite unlike Paul he also regarded the serpents (10:9) as

---

[179] "People of Israel" (10:18), literally "Israel according to the flesh," might contrast with "spiritual" food from God (10:3–4; but cf. Rom 9:3–8; 11:14).

pleasure (*Alleg. Interp.* 2.84–85).[180] In Paul's usage, however, it more likely means "from the Spirit" (cf. 2:13–3:11; 12:1; 14:1, 37; 15:44–46; probably even Rev 11:8), that is, "corresponding to the source you now depend on, the Spirit" (cf. 12:13; 2 Cor 3:17). (In this period, even the Greek term "allegory" sometimes applied to simple analogies; "type" could mean "pattern" or "example.") Some Jewish interpreters naturally inferred from references to the life-giving rock in different locations and years (Ex 17:6; Num 20:8) that the rock followed Israel (*L.A.B.* 11:15; some rabbis). Their rock, Paul says, corresponds to Christ as the source of life for his followers (10:4). In view of his wisdom Christology (1:30; 8:6), it is not surprising that Paul blends the water-giving rock (Ex 17:6; Num 20:8–11)[181] with the divine rock of the Hebrew text of Deut 32:13 (cf. 32:4, 15, 18, 30–31), whom he naturally identifies with Christ (cf. Rom 9:32–33); others had identified the source of water with Wisdom (cf. Wis 11:1, 4; esp. Philo *Alleg. Interp.* 2.86). This passage in Deuteronomy remains on Paul's mind later in this section (Deut 32:17, 21, in 1 Cor 10:20, 22).

Employing the rhetorical advantage of surprise (*paradoxon*; Demetrius *Eloc.* 152–53), Paul shifts suddenly to an emphasis on God destroying their spiritual predecessors (10:5, 8–10), as an "example" to God's people who would read about them in later eras (10:6, 11).[182] Just as the Israelites "fell" (10:8), the Corinthians must beware lest they "fall" (10:12; cf. Rom 11:11, 22; 14:4; 1 Cor 8:13; 2 Cor 11:29); as the Israelites were "destroyed" (10:9–10), so might the Corinthians be (8:11).[183] That some partakers of the Lord's table are therefore sick and dying (11:30) is not surprising.

Paul selects moral examples most relevant for his audience. "Desiring evil" (10:6) refers to the Israelites' greed (the related noun, a NT hapax, appears in Num 11:34; Paul may add "evil" from the language of Prov 21:26 LXX), an attribute probably relevant in Corinth (5:10–11; 6:10). That this "greed" was for food (namely, meat) other than the manna God had promised (Num 11:4–6, 20, 33; cf. 1 Cor 10:3) reinforces the point Paul is making in the context. Midianite women allured many to immorality to bring God's anger against the whole congregation (Num 25:1–18; 31:16); some Corinthians now committed immorality with Gentile prostitutes (6:15). The Israelites' "complaining" (10:10) was against the Lord (Ex 16:7–12; 17:3; Num 11:1; 14:27–29; 16:41); Stoics commonly warned

---

[180] For figurative interpretations of the manna and well in early Judaism (esp. as Wisdom imagery), see C. Keener, *John* (2003), 440–41, 681–83, 724, 727–28.

[181] Local mythology also attributed Corinth's chief spring to a struck rock (Strabo 8.6.21).

[182] Although "ends of ages" could refer to the overlapping of present and future ages (cf. Gal 1:4; *4 Ezra* 6:7; some rabbis), it probably simply refers to the climax of previous ages (1 Cor 2:7; Col 1:26). On the ancient pedagogic use of historical paradigms, see C. Keener, *John* (2003), 14–17.

[183] That God "overthrew" them in 10:5 [cf. Num 14:16] might just possibly involve a wordplay; because *katastrōnnumi* can occasionally mean "set a table" (e.g., Jdt 12:1).

against complaining about fate or the divine will[184] (although the Corinthians' complaining may be against each other; cf. 1:10–12; Phil 2:14). The Israelites tested "Christ" (their source of water in 10:4) as the Corinthians now did (10:9). When complaining, the Israelites tested God regarding water at Massah (Deut 6:16, also using *ekpeirazō*; Ex 17:2, 7, with *peirazō*; *ekpeirazō* appears also in Ps 78[LXX 77]:18 for their complaining while craving meat).

As in 10:7–8, Paul midrashically links two incidents in 10:9–10 (both leading to "destruction," using the verb *apollumi*). God did not destroy them for their complaints at Massah (where they tested Christ), but when they continued this behavior, he later kept the entire generation from entering the land, because of their cumulative testings (Num 14:22–23). When Israelites spoke against God still later, God sent serpents to destroy them (Num 21:5–6). The Pentateuch's connection with the serpent sign against Pharaoh (Ex 4:3; 7:15) may suggest that God punished rebellious Israel by the same means as the Egyptians. The "destroyer" (*olothreutēs*, 10:10) refers to the destroying angel that struck down (*olethreuonta*,) the Egyptian firstborn (Ex 12:23; cf. Wis 18:25; Heb 11:28). Paul may have in mind the Lord's angel, or perhaps Satan as "destroyer" (cf. 5:5), whom he associated with the primeval serpent of Gen 3:1–14 (2 Cor 11:3; cf. Rev 12:9). It is no coincidence that in both incidents they tested God regarding food or drink.

At the heart of Paul's argument here, however, is Ex 32:6, the text in 10:7: the idolatrous festival of the golden calf[185] involved eating and drinking, that is, idol food (contrast Ex 24:11). "Eating and drinking," though a common conjunction of terms, play an especially important role in this context (9:4; 10:3–4, 31; 11:22, 26–29). Paul's first example is "idolatry" (10:7), but only in this case does he neglect to mention the judgment (10:8–10).

This case might involve immorality (10:7; the same term for "play" appears in Gen 26:8 LXX) just as the next example (10:8) does (and these offenses often appeared together in ancient paganism; cf. Rev 2:14, 20).[186] In any case, Paul probably includes the judgment for both sins in 10:8. When Israelites slept with Midianite women, a plague from God struck 24,000 (Num 25:9), and the plague was stopped only by slaying one of the perpetrators (25:8). But it was midrashically logical to link that text with an analogous one: In the golden calf episode, God sent a plague because the people ate idol food and committed immorality (Ex 32:35), after the Levites struck down 3000 perpetrators (Ex 32:28). (Philo confuses the episodes in *Spec. Laws* 3.126.) This conflation might explain Paul's reduction of the round number 24,000 (attested in other ancient sources,

[184] E.g., Epictetus *Diatr.* 1.6.38–42; 1.14.16; Seneca *Lucil.* 96.1–2; Marcus Aurelius 2.16; 8.9; 10.1; 12.12; among others, Publilius Syrus 180.

[185] Later rabbis considered this the most shameful event in Israel's history; Josephus diplomatically omits it.

[186] Akiba by contrast read other texts' uses of the term in light of the idolatrous meaning in Ex 32:6 (*t. Sanh.* 6:6).

e.g., *L.A.B.* 47:1; Philo *Virtues* 41; *Moses* 1.304) to the more obscure 23,000, which might allow him to allude obliquely to both texts.[187]

God had provided an escape for or a limit to (*ekbasis* can mean either) the testing they needed to endure (10:13), so they must flee idolatry (10:14). Some Stoics claimed that nature equipped people to bear nature's vicissitudes (Marcus Aurelius 5.18), and the opinion that suffering was the lot of humanity was a frequently offered encouragement in antiquity.[188] Philosophers warned people to expect sufferings (e.g., Iamblichus *Pyth. Life* 32.224–25).

As he reasoned from the irreconcilability of God's temple and prostitution in 6:15, 19, he reasons also from the irreconcilability of the Lord's table and that of demons in 10:14–22 (cf. likewise 2 Cor 6:14–7:1). Drawing from the connection between idol food and idols in the exodus narrative (10:7), Paul warns the Corinthians to flee idolatry (10:14). Given Paul's longer emphasis on avoiding injuring others' faith (chs. 8–9; 10:23–11:1), his concern here is not so much an intrinsic problem with spiritually "contaminated" food or the material substance of idols (10:19) but with the symbolic compromise with idolatry that idol food communicated in a polytheistic social context. What others perceived as compromise with idolatry was important, because the spiritual entities involved in genuine idolatry were real, and few would dissociate the symbol from the reality.

Paul urges them to "flee" idolatry (for the admonition to "flee" in moral exhortation, see comment on 6:18). As in 10:15, orators sometimes invited audiences to "judge for themselves" (cf. 1 Cor 11:13) or rhetorically invoked their audience as "witnesses" (cf. 1 Thess 2:10; Acts 20:18, 34), appealing to their own moral sensibilities.[189] The "cup of blessing" (10:16) recalls the phrase for wine over which a Jewish patron offered a benediction to God at the end of meals (*b. Sot.* 38b; here often equated with the third cup at a Passover meal, but some suggest the fourth or even the second); early Christians often followed Jewish formulas (1 Tim 4:4–5; *Did.* 9.2–3). In this context it must refer specifically to the Lord's Supper, modeled on the Passover meal (see comment on 11:17–34). (Furthering the contrast in 10:21, Greeks poured libations to gods at banquets; they could treat this cup like other blessings to deities after the dinner.)

Priests burned some portions of the sacrifices, but ate other parts and shared still other parts with the people (10:18; e.g., Lev 6:29–30; 7:6: Deut 8:1). The "sharing" (*koinōnia*) "in Christ's body" plays on the two senses of his body: his physical body given on the cross as a sacrifice (11:23–24; cf. 5:7) and his body

---

[187] Covert allusions were good rhetoric but would be useless if (as might be the case here) few hearers could fathom them. A combination with the number of eligible Levites (Num 26:62) would not make sense here (cf. Ex 32:26). Cf. Josephus's 14,000 (*Ant.* 4.155).

[188] E.g., in dramatists (Sophocles *El.* 153–55; Euripides *Hipp.* 834–35), orators (Isocrates *Demon.* 21), moralists (Seneca *Lucil.* 96.1–2; 98.10; 99.6; 107.5; Ps.-Phoc. 27), and rabbis (*Pesiq. R.* 30:1); cf. 1 Pet 5:9.

[189] For judging, e.g., Aeschines *Tim.* 196; Alciphron *Courtesans* 7.1.34, paragraph 7; for witnesses, e.g., Aeschines *Fals. leg.* 56; Isocrates *Nic.* 46; 1 Thess 2:10.

the church (10:17; 12:12; cf. *Did.* 9.4). (In Mediterranean antiquity, sharing a meal established an enduring relationship, sometimes even multigenerational alliances.)[190] This reinforces the need to care for others' sensitivities, without digressing from the point of the incompatibility of two tables (10:21). Both priests (10:18) and Christians (10:16–17) partake of a sacrifice to God; by analogy, then, those eating idol food partake of a sacrifice to the demons the idols represent (10:20). (This was true even though the physical idols were nothing, 10:19; cf. Is 44:12–20; 45:20–25; 46:1–11). Most ancient Near Eastern temples were equipped with tables for offerings, and "the table of" such-and-such a deity (10:21), for example, "of the Lord Sarapis" (the god Sarapis as the dinner's host), appears in invitations to banquets explicitly using idol food; the dual repetition of the contrast is a rhetorical device (combining *anaphora* with *epiphora*). The Lord's "table" in the OT was where offerings were placed (Mal 1:7, 12), including bread shared by the priests (Ex 25:30).

Sacrificing "to demons and not God" (10:20) quotes Deuteronomy 32:17, perhaps with an allusion to Bar 4:7 (which follows Deut 32:17 and also speaks of "provoking" their creator). But surely they could not really provoke God to jealousy, Paul's imaginary interlocutor protests (10:22)? If this is a genuine question (its grammatically assumed negative answer suggests that Paul uses it ironically), Paul answers only indirectly in 10:23–11:1; his audience should know the context of his quotation well enough to answer affirmatively such a foolish question for themselves, especially Deut 32:21: they provoke him to jealousy with their nongods.[191] Scripture typically associated God's jealousy with idolatry.[192] Paul and most early Christians (Athenagoras *Leg.* 26; Tertullian *Apol.* 23.4; cf. *Did.* 6.3) shared the typical Jewish view that the beings worshiped by pagans were demons (in the LXX, see Deut 32:17; Ps 95[ET 96]:5; 105[106]:37; Is 65:3).[193]

10:23–11:1: CONCLUDING SUMMARY AND ARGUMENTS ON IDOL FOOD

10:23: "All things are lawful," but not all things are beneficial. "All things are lawful," but not all things build up.

10:24: Do not seek your own advantage, but that of the other.

10:25: Eat whatever is sold in the meat market without raising any question on the ground of conscience,

---

[190] See discussion in C. Keener, *John* (2003), 913.
[191] Paul quotes this text partly in Rom 10:19 and alludes to it in Rom 11:11, 14, his only other extant uses of the term. He prefers this to the more common LXX term in Bar 4:7. Cf. the idea in 1 Kgs 14:22; Ps 78 (LXX 77):58.
[192] Ex 20:5; 34:14; Deut 4:23–24; 5:9; 6:14–15; Josh 24:19–20; 1 Kgs 14:22; Ps 78:58.
[193] E.g., *Jub.* 1:11; 22:16–17; *1 En.* 19:1; *Sipre Deut.* 318.2.1–2.

10:26: for "the earth and its fullness are the Lord's."

10:27: If an unbeliever invites you to a meal and you are disposed to go, eat whatever is set before you without raising any question on the ground of conscience.

10:28: But if someone says to you, "This has been offered in sacrifice," then do not eat it, out of consideration for the one who informed you, and for the sake of conscience –

10:29: I mean the other's conscience, not your own. For why should my liberty be subject to the judgment of someone else's conscience?

10:30: If I partake with thankfulness, why should I be denounced because of that for which I give thanks?

10:31: So, whether you eat or drink, or whatever you do, do everything for the glory of God.

10:32: Give no offense to Jews or to Greeks or to the church of God,

10:33: just as I try to please everyone in everything I do, not seeking my own advantage, but that of many, so that they may be saved.

11:1: Be imitators of me, as I am of Christ.

*J*ust as not all things were profitable regarding sexual behavior (see comment on 6:12), so they were not with religious cuisine (10:23); Paul shifts the notion of "profit" in 10:23 to what profits the many (10:33). Seeking the advantage of one's neighbor (10:24) was conventional social ethics (e.g., Musonius Rufus 14, p. 92.17–18) as well as Christian virtue (Rom 13:8–10). Meat itself is pure as God's creation (10:25–26; citing Ps 24:1, which later Jewish teachers used to support thanks before meals); but the conscience that worships false gods is not (10:28; cf. Ps 24:3–4). What they did not know would not hurt them (10:25, 27); indeed, even scrupulous Jewish teachers considered inadvertent sins comparatively "light" (although they might not have adopted Paul's "Don't ask, don't tell" approach). (Apart from Jewish butchers, sellers might not always identify the source of their meat in the market; see the *Closer Look* section on Ch. 8.) In advising them to accept hospitality (10:27; cf. 10:25), Paul also may seek to conform to Jesus's teaching (Lk 10:7; cf. Mk 6:8–10).

The believer might protest that they gave thanks to the Lord, not to an idol (10:30); or that it was unfair to subject their "freedom" to the needs of another's conscience (10:29). (Cynics provide an extreme example of "freedom" in eating, for example, Diogenes in Diogenes Laertius 6.2.57–58.) Paul replies that freedom or authority is not the highest value (cf. 10:23); they should follow his example of avoiding offense so others could be saved (10:33–11:1), summarizing the substance of Chapter 9 (on imitating Paul, see also 4:16). As for giving thanks to the Lord (10:30), truly glorifying him meant causing others to praise him, not stumble against his way (10:31–33). (In 10:31, Paul agreed with Jewish teachers who emphasized doing everything for the sake of heaven and philosophers who emphasized pursuing only what is eternally significant.)

Recapitulating one's concerns in a section was common practice.[194] Reiterating his concern to avoid hindrances to the gospel in 9:19–23, Paul in 10:32 emphasizes that he is concerned with the opinions of Jews (who would not understand monotheists partaking of idol food; 4 Macc 5:2), Greeks (who would assume that meat-eating Christians, like everyone else, tolerated their gods), or the church (much of which would be confused by their eating). Ancients would recognize as virtuous concern for the "advantage" (*sumphoros*) of the whole (10:32; note the same expression in 2 Macc 4:5), a principle Paul will apply especially to the church in Chapters 12–14. Paul closes by appealing to his example (10:33–11:1), recalling 8:13–9:27, his wording especially recalling 9:19–23.

11:2–16: SEXUAL MODESTY IN CHURCH

11:2: I commend you because you remember me in everything and maintain the traditions just as I handed them on to you.

11:3: But I want you to understand that Christ is the head of every man, and the husband is the head of his wife, and God is the head of Christ.

11:4: Any man who prays or prophesies with something on his head disgraces his head,

11:5: but any woman who prays or prophesies with her head unveiled disgraces her head – it is one and the same thing as having her head shaved.

11:6: For if a woman will not veil herself, then she should cut off her hair; but if it is disgraceful for a woman to have her hair cut off or to be shaved, she should wear a veil.

11:7: For a man ought not to have his head veiled, since he is the image and reflection of God; but woman is the reflection of man.

11:8: Indeed, man was not made from woman, but woman from man.

11:9: Neither was man created for the sake of woman, but woman for the sake of man.

11:10: For this reason a woman ought to have a symbol of authority on her head, because of the angels.

11:11: Nevertheless, in the Lord woman is not independent of man or man independent of woman.

11:12: For just as woman came from man, so man comes through woman; but all things come from God.

11:13: Judge for yourselves: is it proper for a woman to pray to God with her head unveiled?

11:14: Does not nature itself teach you that if a man wears long hair, it is degrading to him,

---

[194]   E.g., Cicero *Fin.* 3.9.31; Demosthenes *Embassy* 177.

11:15: but if a woman has long hair, it is her glory? For her hair is given to her for a covering.

11:16: But if anyone is disposed to be contentious – we have no such custom, nor do the churches of God.

*B*efore addressing a major breach in decorum at the Lord's supper (11:17–34), Paul must address a minor one in 11:2–16; their breach of his "tradition" is more severe in 11:23 than in 11:2. It was good rhetorical practice to start with a subject in which one could "commend" or "praise" the audience (11:2) before moving to one in which one could not (11:17, 22). But even here, not all is well ("but I want," *thelō de*, as in 7:7; 10:20; 14:5); he must now add a tradition of sorts previously unnecessary (11:16). In contrast to earlier Greek culture, upwardly mobile Roman wives sometimes accompanied husbands to banquets, even though the homes where banquets were held intersected the boundaries between public and domestic spheres. Views on the appropriate decorum of respectable wives at such banquets, however, varied, introducing potential division (see comment on 14:34–35).

A CLOSER LOOK: THE NEED FOR HEAD COVERINGS

Some think that Paul refers only to hair as a covering; at least aristocratic women pinned their hair in specific styles, rather than wearing it loose. (The oft-mentioned "piled-up hair" style of aristocrats, however, grew popular especially a generation after Paul's time.) But artificial head coverings were common in the east and Paul employs hair only as an illustration from nature (11:14–15). Both men and women covered heads for shame, mourning, and, in Roman (but not Greek) culture, for worship, the setting envisioned here. The only gender-differentiated covering custom, however, was a sign of sexual modesty, intrinsic to a woman's honor (in her case, the avoidance of shame).[195] (Some viewed a wife's hair like a private part; cf. 12:23.) Far to the east and in Arabia, modest wives might wear even face veils, as in some Islamic countries today; in Jerusalem, Tarsus, and for some of the women of Corinth (including members of eastern immigrant communities, probably including many Jews), it sufficed to cover the hair, the most prized potentially public object of male desire (e.g., Apuleius *Metam.* 2.8; *Sipre Num.* 11.2.1–3). Traditionalists expected modest wives to shield their beauty from other men's gaze (e.g., Seneca *Controv.* 2.7.6).

Few expected single girls, who were supposed to need husbands, to cover their hair, but married women were to protect their hair from public view. Well-to-do Roman matrons, however, paid well for expensive hairstyles, following fashions

---

[195] E.g., Valerius Maximus 6.3.10; for Jewish use of head coverings, cf. Josephus *Ant.* 3.270; Philo *Special Laws* 3.56; *m. B.Qam.* 8:6; *Ketub.* 7:6.

generated by the empress; upper-class women were far less likely to cover their heads (cf. 1 Tim 2:9). In public, even well-to-do Roman women probably pulled a mantle over their heads;[196] but if the church met in homes, the need for such behavior may not have been evident. Because most Christians gathered in the wealthier homes, Christians of different social strata and backgrounds met together; "naked" hair held different social connotations for different women. To wealthier women, it signified at most ostentation; to most women from the east, it symbolized immodesty and, at worse, seduction.

As in the case of some other issues (e.g., 11:21), Paul must here address a clash of social values: just as to many idol food connoted idolatry hence should be avoided for others' sake, so uncovered hair to many connoted seduction and immodesty, hence should be avoided for others' sake. A modern Western equivalent might be someone walking into a religious service in a bathing suit; although this might not disturb some California beach churches during the Jesus movement, newcomers with such informal attire might disrupt traditional churches in, say, New England.[197]

In a series of interlocking arguments, Paul contends that by keeping her physical head uncovered, the wife also dishonors her figurative head, that is, her husband (11:3–5). (Both orators and rabbis often argued from plays on words.) Although some argue plausibly that "head" figuratively functions as "source" or "first part" (see 11:8–9, which may suggest the creation order in 11:3; also 8:6), ancient literature also applies it often to "authority" or to the "most honored [or prominent] part." Both "authority" and "honored part" fit Paul's Christology (11:3) as well as the normal structure of the household in Paul's environment (which he assumes, like most arguments in this passage, to argue for head coverings rather than to defend for its own sake).[198]

"Honored part" also would relate well to the contextual issue of a wife shaming her husband. Given the shame (often sexual) inherent in uncovered hair in the east (see *A Closer Look*, earlier), the wife speaking without this covering shames her husband (11:4–6). (Her behavior reflects on him because he is her "head," 11:3, and they are "one flesh," cf. 6:16.) Paul employs *reductio ad absurdum*: If a woman wants her head completely uncovered, she should shave it, an act that

---

[196] See A. T. Croom, *Roman Clothing and Fashion* (Charleston, SC: Tempus, 2002), 89, 106.

[197] For primary and secondary sources on head coverings and this passage, see C. Keener, "Head Coverings," 442–46 in *DNTB*; idem, *Paul, Women & Wives* (Peabody, MA: Hendrickson, 1992), 19–69.

[198] For this authority structure, see discussion in, e.g., D. L. Balch, *Let Wives be Submissive: The Domestic Code in 1 Peter* (SBLMS 26; Chico, CA: Scholars, 1981); D. C. Verner, *The Household of God: The Social World of the Pastoral Epistles* (SBLDS 71; Chico: Scholars, 1983); C. Keener, "Marriage," 680–93. Favoring especially preeminence (versus authority or source), see esp. A. C. Thiselton, *The First Epistle to the Corinthians* (NIGTC; Carlisle: Paternoster; Grand Rapids, MI: Eerdmans, 2000), 812–21.

most people in his culture would view as shameful (11:6; cf. 11:14–15). Rather than shame, the women should prefer what is honorable, especially through apparel that guards her husband's honor (11:7).

Paul now elaborates this argument with biblical examples. In the setting of worship, a man ought not to cover his head lest he obscure God's image and glory (11:7a), hence dishonoring his head, Christ (11:3–4). (Romans, unlike Greeks, covered their heads in worship; but some of the divine glory is recovered in worship [2 Cor 3:18], and it should be restricted only for the sake of those unable to endure it [2 Cor 3:13; 5:13].) The wife, however, reflects her husband's glory (11:7b). Perhaps Paul wants her to obscure her husband's glory (by covering her head) because human glory is not the goal of worship (cf. 10:31). But Paul also may be concerned that her uncovered head undermines her role of being his "glory," that is, of honoring him (because an uncovered woman disgraces or dishonors her husband; 11:5–6).

Paul's own Bible declared that both genders reflected God's image and glory (Gen 1:26–27; 5:1–2), and when not arguing for head coverings he recognized that all Christians were being conformed to God's image in Christ (1 Cor 15:49; Rom 8:29; 2 Cor 3:18). But in reading the second creation narrative as an elaboration of the first, he apparently argues that the woman, taken from the man (her "head" in 11:3), reflected God's image derivatively (Gen 2:23). He points out that God created the woman from the man (Gen 2:21–23; cf. the restoration of this flesh in Gen 2:24; 1 Cor 6:16) and for his strength, because he was incomplete (Gen 2:18).

Nevertheless, Paul does not wish to push the argument too far: subsequent men have come from women, and both are mutually dependent (1 Cor 11:11–12). (Paul here follows 1 Esd 4:15–17, a context which speaks of women bringing men glory in 4:17 and of women's authority in 4:14, 22.) It is possible that Paul thinks of this other side of the coin already in 11:10, in which he speaks of the wife's "authority over her head" (probably involving her literal head covering, but perhaps also over her husband in some sense; cf. mutual authority in 7:4). What is notable from the standpoint of Paul's eastern Mediterranean background is the level of mutuality assumed (as also in 7:2–5); such affirmations do appear in ancient writers, but only among the more gender-progressive ones.[199] Even most Greeks who insisted on women's public silence allowed prophecy; they attributed inspiration to a deity rather than to the woman herself. But Paul seems to envision women praying and prophesying fairly commonly in the gatherings (11:5).

---

[199] Cf. some mutuality in Xenophon *Oec.* 7.18–42; Musonius Rufus 12, p. 86.33–38; 14, p. 92.38–94.1; Plutarch *Bride* 11, *Mor.* 139CD. Roles often remained distinct, and none of these were modern egalitarians; but they stand out from the usual fare of antiquity.

Paul's most difficult argument for modern readers is in 11:10, in which Paul says that the wife ought to exercise authority over her own head responsibly (the NRSV's "symbol of authority on her head" is a weak interpretation) "because of the angels." Some think that Paul refers to the fallen angels, who lusted after women in Gen 6:1–4; although most later rabbis demurred, this was the most popular understanding of Gen 6 in Paul's day (cf. 1 Pet 3:19–20; Jude 6).[200] That Paul wished to safeguard the sanctity of angels present for the service is not impossible, but the empirical lack of many contemporary giants (Gen 6:4) probably suggested to most observers that angels were no longer falling. A more common proposal today relates to the expectation that angels were present for worship and could be offended by any breach of propriety (cf. 1QSa 2.3–9; 1QM 7.5–6), such as a wife dishonoring her husband. Paul did believe that angels watched God's servants (4:9).

But a third alternative might better explain the wives' "authority" (*exousia*). Paul alludes to angels he mentioned earlier: Just as the Corinthians' future judgment of angels should encourage them to judge rightly now (6:3), so the women's future authority over angels should motivate them to use properly their authority over their heads now. (The future authority may reflect a restoration of authority in Gen 1:27–28, fitting the context in 11:7.) She has a "right" to do with her head as she wills, but like Paul, she must give up her "rights" (the sense of *exousia* in 9:4–6, 12, 18; cf. 8:9) for the common good.

Paul further appeals to "nature" (11:14), a common argument (developed by many philosophers, most consistently the Stoics); nature supports the idea of women covering their heads by giving them longer hair (11:14–15). (Compare the Stoic argument that nature gave men beards to distinguish them from women; removing such gender markers violates nature.)[201] This returns to his natural analogy with hair (11:6). Nazirites, philosophers, "barbarians," and statues of ancient Greek heroes and deities all were exceptions Paul must have known, but his argument rested on the general practice of his day, when women's longer hair was honorable ("glory" in 11:15), as man's bare head honored God (NRSV's "reflection" in 11:7 is also "glory" or "honor").

His closing argument, appeal to authority, was the final default argument accepted even by Skeptics. (In contrast to Stoics, Skeptics rejected arguments from nature and saw no customs as transcultural; they argued only from custom.) He appeals to the practices of the churches in the eastern Mediterranean (11:16; also 7:17; 14:33; cf. 16:1; 1 Thess 2:14), all in a culture in which most respectable women covered their hair in public.

---

[200] E.g., *1 En.* 6:2; 16:2; 69:5; 106:13–14; *Jub.* 4:22; 7:21; CD 2.16–18; 4Q180 1.7–8; *2 Bar.* 56:10–15; cf. *T. Reub.* 5:5–6; in the Diaspora, Philo *Giants* 16.
[201] E.g., Musonius Rufus 21, p. 128.30–35; Epictetus *Diatr.* 1.16.10, 14; 3.1.27–31; cf. Ps.-Phoc. 210–12.

11:17–34: ABUSING A SACRED FELLOWSHIP MEAL

11:17: Now in the following instructions I do not commend you, because when you come together it is not for the better but for the worse.

11:18: For, to begin with, when you come together as a church, I hear that there are divisions among you; and to some extent I believe it.

11:19: Indeed, there have to be factions among you, for only so will it become clear who among you are genuine.

11:20: When you come together, it is not really to eat the Lord's supper.

11:21: For when the time comes to eat, each of you goes ahead with your own supper, and one goes hungry and another becomes drunk.

11:22: What! Do you not have homes to eat and drink in? Or do you show contempt for the church of God and humiliate those who have nothing? What should I say to you? Should I commend you? In this matter I do not commend you!

11:23: For I received from the Lord what I also handed on to you, that the Lord Jesus on the night when he was betrayed took a loaf of bread,

11:24: and when he had given thanks, he broke it and said, "This is my body that is for you. Do this in remembrance of me."

11:25: In the same way he took the cup also, after supper, saying, "This cup is the new covenant in my blood. Do this, as often as you drink it, in remembrance of me."

11:26: For as often as you eat this bread and drink the cup, you proclaim the Lord's death until he comes.

11:27: Whoever, therefore, eats the bread or drinks the cup of the Lord in an unworthy manner will be answerable for the body and blood of the Lord.

11:28: Examine yourselves, and only then eat of the bread and drink of the cup.

11:29: For all who eat and drink without discerning the body, eat and drink judgment against themselves.

11:30: For this reason many of you are weak and ill, and some have died.

11:31: But if we judged ourselves, we would not be judged.

11:32: But when we are judged by the Lord, we are disciplined so that we may not be condemned along with the world.

11:33: So then, my brothers and sisters, when you come together to eat, wait for one another.

11:34: If you are hungry, eat at home, so that when you come together, it will not be for your condemnation. About the other things I will give instructions when I come.

*I*n contrast with his earlier commendation for their attention to some other traditions (11:2), in this case he cannot commend them (11:17, 22), because they have ignored the tradition (11:23). ("What shall I say" in 11:22 may be rhetorical *aporia*, feigning such distress that one cannot decide what to do; cf. Gal 4:20.) They treat the Lord's meal like any association's banquet, which means that, despite the Greek and biblical ideals of equality,[202] their seating and treatment highlighted their social stratification. Whatever else was also wrong, some went hungry (11:21) and those with nothing were shamed in a status-conscious, honor-centered society (11:22). Paul earlier mentioned his knowledge of divisions (1:10–12), but expresses mock disbelief (rhetorical *dissimulatio*) that these could actually spill over into the Lord's Supper (11:18). Such mock unwillingness to believe a terrible report also appears in some other corrective literature, including calls to unity.[203]

Stratified treatment put the lie not only to the Greek ideal of friends' equality, but for Paul challenged the significance of the Lord's supper. Table fellowship was a binding covenant, and the one bread and body represented not only Jesus's sacrifice but those who partook together (10:16–17; cf. 12:12). This failure to discern the corporate body (11:29) led to sickness in their individual bodies (11:30; cf. the individual and corporate bodies as temples in 3:16–17; 6:19). Paul has returned to his emphasis on unity (1:10–4:21), which will continue through much of the letter (Chs. 12–14).

A CLOSER LOOK: SYMPOSIA AND THE LORD'S SUPPER

At Greco-Roman aristocratic banquets, people were seated (or more technically, usually reclined) by rank (cf. Plutarch *Table-Talk* 1.3, *Mor.* 619B–F); the necessary distinctions in such seating often rankled guests offended by being seated lower than they had hoped (cf. Lk 14:8–10; Prov 25:6–7).[204] Such guests complained about being served inferior food and inferior wine; the best was reserved for those in the highest position. But patrons normally invited only peers and clients of lower yet honorable rank; the church, like many religious associations, included a wider cross-section of society, including slaves.

Although the comfortable triclinium would host on couches the higher-status banqueters (nine or a maximum of 12, cf. Horace *Sat.* 1.4.86; but they could accommodate more if they sat rather than reclined; cf. 14:30), a wealthy host might use the atrium (an only partly covered, less comfortable court) for overflow crowds. Given the size of homes in Corinth's well-to-do Craneion district, some estimate room for 30–50 more worshipers, because they likely sat

---

202 Xenophon *Mem.* 3.14.1; Plutarch *Table-Talk* 1.2.3, *Mor.* 616E; *Sayings of Spartans* Agesilaus 1, *Mor.* 208BC; Athenaeus *Deipn.* 1.12c.

203 With M. Mitchell, *Rhetoric* (1991), 152–53, the likeliest of diverse proposals. Chrysostom *Hom. Cor.* 27.2 thinks Paul merely conciliatory here. The expectation of division (11:19) might echo unwritten Jesus tradition (Justin *Dial.* 35).

204 Cf., e.g., Seneca *Lucil.* 4; Juvenal *Sat.* 4.15–18, 24–25, 37–79, 146–58; Martial 3.49; 4.85; 12.28; Alciphron *Parasites* 37.1.20; G. Theissen, *Social Setting* (1982), 153–58.

(14:30).[205] The patron's peers would expect accommodations in the triclinium if anyone had them, leaving outside any "overflow" of lower status persons unable to be accommodated there.[206] Although in earlier times respectable Greek women did not attend male banquets (Cicero *Verr.* 2.1.26.66), developments in Roman custom certainly influenced banquets in Roman Corinth. Despite the traditional practice of gender-segregated banquets in some settings,[207] it seems unlikely that men and women sat far apart in the Corinthian house meetings; the atrium would allow little distance.

Older commentators' attempts to link the Lord's supper with "sacramental" mystery cults fail both because the mysteries in the first century were not sacramental and because any parallels found in mystery feasts characterized Greco-Roman banquets more generally. Jewish groups like Essenes (at least in Qumran texts, where seating was by rank, for example, 1Q28a 2.21) and (according to Philo) the Therapeutae practiced common meals. Possibly Pharisees banded together in meal associations; extended families also gathered for Passover banquets and some other meals.

Despite some detractors, it is clear that the model "Lord's supper" occurred in a Passover context (1 Cor 11:23–26; Mk 14:12, 22–25), as Paul was surely aware (cf. 1 Cor 5:7–8).[208] Although blessings over bread and wine belonged to every Jewish meal, the redemptive interpretation of the elements in a Passover setting provided the context for the sacrificial interpretation of Jesus's death Paul notes here (11:24–25; cf. 10:18–21; Mk 14:22–24). Jews had adopted Hellenistic banquet customs such as reclining for feasts such as the Passover. Accustomed to many other banquets, some Gentiles were apparently neglecting the Lord's supper's paschal or sacrificial origins – or perhaps just those origins' implications for relationships with one another. The custom of a common meal as Christians likely goes back to the earliest church (Acts 2:42, 46).

That the cup in question was "after supper" (*meta to deipnēsai*, 11:25) would not surprise even newcomers to Paul's audience. The main meal in aristocratic banquets (the *deipnon*, as in 11:20–21) was followed by the drinking party (the *symposion*), which included entertainment, sometimes prostitutes (cf. 6:13) and usually music. Intellectuals often preferred a sage's lecture, public readings, or intellectual conversation during this time. Christians probably sang and listened to exhortation (cf. 14:26, 35), as well as prayed and prophesied, after the Lord's supper.

---

[205] Less frequently, we may suppose that larger homes or villas might include even more, but again not with the sort of accommodations available in a triclinium.

[206] J. Murphy-O'Connor, *Paul's Corinth* (1983), 156–59. But of course the wealthiest could surpass even such limitations (e.g., Suetonius *Claud.* 32).

[207] Sources in C. Keener, *John* (2003), 503, 900; esp. (for changing customs), D. Smith, *Symposium* (2003), 40–44.

[208] See A. Thiselton, *Corinthians* (2000), 871–74; C. Keener, *Matthew* (1999), 622–23; idem, *John* (2003), 1100–03; the basic statement, although modified since then, was J. Jeremias, *The Eucharistic Words of Jesus* (Philadelphia: Fortress, 1966), 20–23, 62–84.

Social convention demanded providing the best couches in a triclinium to persons of status; to treat everyone equally would scandalize the host's peers. Moreover, to provide the same quality of food and wine for all guests as for one's peers would be expensive; but some suggest that Paul envisions guests bringing their own food (11:21, 34), an arrangement sometimes followed. If *prolambanō* means "goes ahead" (11:21, NRSV), as most contend, it is possible that slaves and many workers lacked the leisure to arrive for the dinner as early as people of higher status. Whether from food they had brought or from food provided for all, they defied the standard of the tradition of a genuinely common meal. Whatever the precise situation, members are not being treated equally (11:21).

At home wealthier members might have more freedom in how they should accommodate their culture's dictates (cf. 11:22), but not in God's church. By dishonoring fellow-believers, the elite are dishonoring Christ (11:29). That Paul "received" and "handed on" (11:23) is conventional ancient language for carefully transmitted tradition (e.g., Josephus *Ant.* 13.297, 408). Although Paul might mean he received the revelation directly from Christ (cf. Gal 1:12, 16), more likely he refers to the Jesus tradition (as in 7:10); when later sages claimed to have "received" words from "Sinai," everyone understood that the words had been mediated through tradition (often explicit, e.g., *m. Pe'ah* 2:6; *'Ed.* 8:7; *Yad.* 4:3).

Most elements in 11:23–26 are in fact paralleled in the Gospels, some even closely: Jesus was "betrayed" (or "handed over") at night (acting at night would appear as an unethical act of cowardice by his enemies);[209] he gave thanks for both bread and wine (Mk 14:22–23); he interpreted the broken bread as his body (Mk 14:22; the standard paschal interpretation was sharing in the unleavened bread of the ancestors' exodus); he identified the cup as a (new) covenant in his blood (Lk 22:20; cf. Mk 14:23; evoking the first covenant by blood, Ex 24:8). Just as many Jewish people at Passover looked forward to the final redemption it presaged (*t. Ber.* 1:10–11), the Lord's banquet would be fulfilled eschatologically at the messianic banquet (11:26; Mk 14:25).[210]

"In remembrance of Jesus" (also in most MSS of Lk 22:19) could evoke memorial meals for the dead (some were held annually in honor of dead teachers), yet modified in view of the resurrection (cf. 15:29). It is far more likely, however, that it evokes the original paschal context suggested by the sacrificial and covenant language (esp. "blood") and by 5:7.[211] As the Passover annually commemorated (and allowed new generations to share the experience of) the first redemption (Ex 12:14; 13:3; Deut 16:2–3; *Jub.* 49:15), so the Lord's supper regularly did the

---

[209] "Night" also fits the original paschal context (e.g., *t. Pesah.* 5:2; 10:9), although banquets in general began in the evening. But "handed over" might mean by God (Rom 4:25; 8:32; cf. LXX Is 53:6, 12).

[210] Cf. Is 25:6 (cf. Is 25:8 in 1 Cor 15:54); *2 Bar.* 29:4; perhaps 1QSa 2.11–12, 19–21.

[211] Although some argue that the OT Passover was not technically a sacrifice, it was so understood in Paul's day (Josephus *Ant.* 2.312; cf. the rabbis), and probably so by Paul (5:7; his other use of *thuō* is in 10:20, although the term is not exclusively cultic).

same for the climactic redemption. Traditions suggest that in annually reenacting the Passover, Jewish people felt that they shared their ancestors' experience (*m. Pesah.* 10:5). The regular reenactment of the Lord's supper was no doubt intended to have the same effect, conscious of the Lord's presence and act of redemption – which is not how the Corinthians were acting.

What then did it mean to eat and drink unworthily (11:27)? Most associations had regulations to prevent drunken abuse and quarrels at their banquets. Here, however, violators experience *divine* retribution (11:29); outside the sphere of grace (cf. "healings" in 12:9), they face sickness (11:30; cf. 5:5). Their transgression was failure to recognize the "body" (11:29) – not just the bread pointing to Jesus's physical body on the cross (11:24) but the spiritual body of those who died with him (10:16–17; 12:12). By treating members according to worldly status rather than God's perspective (cf. 1:26–28; 4:7–10; 6:4; Jas 2:2–4), they were dishonoring Christ's own body. Those not transformed by Christ's sacrifice would be liable for it (11:27). Some Jewish teachers believed that punishment in this life atoned for sin, delivering one from punishment to come. Although for Paul only Christ propitiates God's anger (Rom 3:25; 5:9; cf. sacrificial language in 1 Cor 5:7; 11:24–25; 15:3), he agrees that present suffering can lead to repentance, avoiding condemnation with the world (11:31–32).

12:1–11: GIFTS FROM THE SPIRIT

12:1: Now concerning spiritual gifts, brothers and sisters, I do not want you to be uninformed.

12:2: You know that when you were pagans, you were enticed and led astray to idols that could not speak.

12:3: Therefore I want you to understand that no one speaking by the Spirit of God ever says "Let Jesus be cursed!" and no one can say "Jesus is Lord" except by the Holy Spirit.

12:4: Now there are varieties of gifts, but the same Spirit;

12:5: and there are varieties of services, but the same Lord;

12:6: and there are varieties of activities, but it is the same God who activates all of them in everyone.

12:7: To each is given the manifestation of the Spirit for the common good.

12:8: To one is given through the Spirit the utterance of wisdom, and to another the utterance of knowledge according to the same Spirit,

12:9: to another faith by the same Spirit, to another gifts of healing by the one Spirit,

12:10: to another the working of miracles, to another prophecy, to another the discernment of spirits, to another various kinds of tongues, to another the interpretation of tongues.

12:11: All these are activated by one and the same Spirit, who allots to each one individually just as the Spirit chooses.

*W*ith his new "now concerning" (12:1), Paul turns to a new topic (7:1, 25; 8:1; 16:1, 12), namely, the proper function of spiritual gifts (or the spiritually gifted).[212] After demanding a unity of Christ's body (11:29; cf. 10:17; 11:24, 27) that transcends status (11:21–22), Paul turns to the demand for the body's unity by serving one another with and respecting the members' diverse gifts (12–14). As members of one body, Christians must use their public gifts to serve the church, not themselves (Ch. 12). The criterion for the best use of the gifts is love (Ch. 13); hence Christians should desire prophecy (which builds up the church) more than uninterpreted, public tongues (which does not). Given Paul's extended focus in Chapter 14 (and examples in 13:1, 8), at least one central conflict about gifts in Corinth must involve uninterpreted tongues-speaking. (Paul may reserve his strongest reproof for last, in Ch. 14, as in 2 Cor 10–13.) Happily for many later readers, however, Paul grounds his pastoral counsel concerning the purpose for particular gifts in the larger principles he introduces beforehand (Chs. 12–13).

Because some boast in their gifts, Paul points out that giftedness does not reveal which spirit inspires one, hence to which lord one belongs (12:1–3; cf. Matt 7:15–20). Some Gentile members of the church may have been spiritually inspired by "mute idols" before their conversion (12:2; cf. Lucan 5.97–193). The true test was thus not inspiration but content, especially the message of Christ (12:3; cf. 1 Jn 4:1–6). (Despite theories that some were "cursing" Christ [cf. 16:22; Gal 3:13; *anathema* is an Aramaic term from the church's Jewish background], Paul probably simply contrasts two extremes as hyperbolic illustrations of his content criterion.)

If exalting Jesus is the criterion of genuinely divine inspiration (12:3), believers should focus on God the giver rather than fixating on particular gifts (12:4–6). For the rhetorically astute Corinthians, Paul's rhetorical repetition in 12:4–6 (using rhetorical *anaphora*) graphically underlines his point. Paul's triple repetition here allows for a proto-Trinitarian perspective (to employ later terminology; cf. similar statements supporting unity in 2 Cor 13:14; Eph 4:4–6).[213] (Because two of the three nouns, "gifts," "services," and "activities," recur in 12:9–10, it is clear that Paul employs the different terms for rhetorical variation or clarification, not to distinguish categories of gifts.) The critical foundation for Paul's term

---

[212] "Spiritual" in 12:1 could refer to "things of the Spirit" or "spiritual things" in general, but many argue that it refers to people who think themselves particularly endowed by the Spirit (cf. 2:13; 3:1; Gal 6:1), as opposed to the NRSV's "spiritual gifts" (14:1 uses the neuter).

[213] For discussion, see G. D. Fee, *God's Empowering Presence* (Peabody, MA: Hendrickson, 1994), 827–45, esp. 839–42.

charisma (12:4, 9, 28, 30, 31)[214] is *charis*, grace (Rom 12:6; cf. Eph 4:7); gifts are expressions of God's generosity, not of human merit. To boast in a gift as if it were merit insults the patron or giver (cf. 4:7).

Paul emphasizes that the gifts come from God's Spirit, rather than "spiritual" individuals themselves, by framing his first list of gifts by this statement (12:7, 11). In 12:7, the Spirit gives gifts for "the common good" (a theme important in ancient speeches on unity and critical for the following context; 12:7).[215] In 12:11, the Spirit (cf. 12:4) rather than the individual determines one's gifts (though in a different context Paul can encourage an appropriate pursuit of gifts, 12:31; 14:1; like most early Jews and Christians, he embraced both God's sovereignty and human responsibility). (The verb *energeō* in 12:11 recalls the noun *energēma* in 12:6; although the terms are unrelated, the Spirit "giving" in 12:7 may also recall the *charismata* of 12:4.)

In 12:8–10, Paul offers examples of gifts (using different forms of "to another" for both rhetorical repetition and variation). Although Paul could have composed the list differently (12:28–30; 13:1–2, 8; 14:26; Rom 12:6–8; cf. Eph 4:11), he may focus here on gifts especially relevant in Corinth. Because his lists are ad hoc, the Corinthians may have had to determine the meaning of some of the gifts the same ways we do (by surveying his usage). The church prized wisdom and knowledge (12:8; see "A Closer Look" on 1:18–25; cf. 1:5; 8:1, 7–11; 13:2, 8). Paul probably defines the gift of wise speech in terms of the gospel (contrary to Corinthian emphasis on merely "clever" speech, 1:17–2:13) and knowledgeable speech as accurate spiritual teaching (cf. *1 En.* 14:3; 37:2; 99:10; *L.A.B.* 20:3). This would explain why "knowledge" does not appear in 12:28, but "teachers" does.[216] "Faith" as a distinct gift probably refers, as some church fathers opined, to extraordinary, mountain-moving faith (13:2). Early Christian narratives abundantly illustrate "gifts of healings" (e.g., Acts 8:7), which Paul seems to expect more commonly than his culture did; whereas ancients knew a few healer-prophets, they mostly sought healing at special shrines of Asclepius (like the famous one at nearby Epidauros) or sometimes Serapis (who had two shrines in Corinth). "Discernment [*diakriseis*] of spirits" might resemble prophetic ability to evaluate prophecies (cf. 14:32; 12:3; esp. *diakrinō* in 14:29); it might thus be connected to prophecy much like "interpretation" is related to tongues (12:10). He places tongues and their interpretation at the list's bottom (12:10; cf. 12:30) not to denigrate the gift (14:18, 39) but because the Corinthians were exalting it (cf. ch. 14).

---

214 Cf. also Rom 1:11; 1 Tim 4:14; 2 Tim 1:6; 1 Pet 4:10; and echoes of 1 Cor 1:7 in Ignatius *Smyrn.* 1; *Poly.* 2:2. The term supports unity in 1 Clem. 38.1–2. For differing "gifts" or endowments, cf. Xenophon *Hunting* 13.18; Eunapius *Lives* 500; esp. Homer *Il.* 13.730–34; Valerius Maximus 7.1.1; Aristides *Defense of Oratory* 397, §135D.

215 See the Stoic emphasis in Cicero *Fin.* 3.19.64; Seneca *Dial.* 8.1.4.

216 What some charismatics today call "word of knowledge" Paul probably would have classified as a form of prophecy (discussion in C. Keener, "Gifts, Spiritual," 155–61 in *WTWB*, 158).

12:12–30: ONE BODY, MANY MEMBERS

12:12: For just as the body is one and has many members, and all the members of the body, though many, are one body, so it is with Christ.

12:13: For in the one Spirit we were all baptized into one body – Jews or Greeks, slaves or free – and we were all made to drink of one Spirit.

12:14: Indeed, the body does not consist of one member but of many.

12:15: If the foot would say, "Because I am not a hand, I do not belong to the body," that would not make it any less a part of the body.

12:16: And if the ear would say, "Because I am not an eye, I do not belong to the body," that would not make it any less a part of the body.

12:17: If the whole body were an eye, where would the hearing be? If the whole body were hearing, where would the sense of smell be?

12:18: But as it is, God arranged the members in the body, each one of them, as he chose.

12:19: If all were a single member, where would the body be?

12:20: As it is, there are many members, yet one body.

12:21: The eye cannot say to the hand, "I have no need of you," nor again the head to the feet, "I have no need of you."

12:22: On the contrary, the members of the body that seem to be weaker are indispensable,

12:23: and those members of the body that we think less honorable we clothe with greater honor, and our less respectable members are treated with greater respect;

12:24: whereas our more respectable members do not need this. But God has so arranged the body, giving the greater honor to the inferior member,

12:25: that there may be no dissension within the body, but the members may have the same care for one another.

12:26: If one member suffers, all suffer together with it; if one member is honored, all rejoice together with it.

12:27: Now you are the body of Christ and individually members of it.

12:28: And God has appointed in the church first apostles, second prophets, third teachers; then deeds of power, then gifts of healing, forms of assistance, forms of leadership, various kinds of tongues.

12:29: Are all apostles? Are all prophets? Are all teachers? Do all work miracles?

12:30: Do all possess gifts of healing? Do all speak in tongues? Do all interpret?

In 12:12–27, Paul develops an extensive analogy with body parts to emphasize their organic unity. It is a short step from claiming that believers are one spirit with Christ (6:17), and that their bodies are a dwelling-place of God's Spirit (6:19), to claiming that they make up his body (12:12). (One may also consider that believers are betrothed to Christ [2 Cor 11:2] hence destined to be "one flesh" [1 Cor 6:16].) But Paul often uses the image in his exhortations for unity regarding diverse gifts (Rom 12:4–8; cf. Eph 4:4, 11), and it was a familiar image for urging a divided state to unity.

Many compared the state to a body. Ancient literature often repeats the "absurd fable" (as Karl Marx titled it) of Menenius Agrippa (a background for this text long acknowledged, e.g., by Calvin).[217] When the plebeians protested that they did all the work and patricians merely consumed their goods, Menenius explained that together they constituted a body, and even the less honored parts of the body were necessary for the whole. Whereas Menenius employs the rhetoric of unity to reinforce class hierarchy, however, Paul uses it to emphasize equality. After Menenius, many compared the state to a body.[218] Others, especially Stoics, compared the universe to a unified body.[219]

Philosophers could combine the images of a corporate body and its head, so Christ as "head" in 11:3 coheres with Paul's larger use of the body image. (Thus the senate could be a head and the people its body; Cicero *Mur.* 25.51; Plutarch *Cic.* 14.4–5.) The apparent identification of the body with Christ in 12:12 (cf. also Col 3:11) is organic rather than ontological; the figure is synecdoche or metonymy, commonly found in ancient literature.

In 12:13, Paul cites their baptism in the Spirit, which initiated them into one body (cf. Eph 4:4–5; for similar language but applied differently, see Acts 1:5). Baptism typically symbolized initiation (see comment on 1:13–16), and Paul probably connects this experience at least symbolically with their baptism in water (Rom 6:4). This forms them into a new community transcending the difference between Jew and Greek (cf. 10:1–4, 32) and class divisions (cf. 7:21–22; cf. Gal 3:28; Col 3:11). But in this case they also drink the water, which is the Spirit, presumably from the rock of Christ (10:4; cf. Jn 4:14; Wisdom in Sir 24:21); it also might evoke the image of the cup in which all believers shared (10:16).

A body consists not of a single member (examples in 12:15–17, 21) but of many, as Paul emphasizes by repetition (12:14, 18–20). Paul employs the rhetorical device *prosopopoiia* to generate speaking body parts (as if each has its own mouth!) in 12:15–16 (where they devalue themselves) and 12:21 (where they devalue others). (Others in his era also played on the shock value of parts of the body declaring their independence from the body, to its harm, e.g., Maximus of Tyre 15.3–5.)[220] As in 12:11, Paul emphasizes that God chooses each member's part according to his will and purpose (12:18; cf. 15:38). Each body part comes

217 E.g., Dionysius of Halicarnassus *Ant. rom.* 6.86.1–5; Livy 2.32.9–12; Plutarch *Coriolanus* 6.2–4; Dio Cassius 4.17.10–13.
218 E.g., Sallust *Rep.* 10.6; Cicero *Resp.* 3.25.37; *Phil.* 8.5.15; cf. Aristotle *Eth. nic.* 1.7; *T. Naph.* 2:9–10.
219 Seneca *Lucil.* 95.52; Epictetus *Diatr.* 1.12.26; Marcus Aurelius 7.13; cf. also Diodorus Siculus 1.11.6.
220 Treating intimate friends as members of one's body was also common (e.g., Hierocles *Fraternal Love* 4.27.20; Philostratus *Hrk.* 48.22).

with its own distinctive function; if it performs that function well, it contributes to the health of the whole. If we are to imagine specific purposes for specific parts (not necessary for Paul's analogy), the "eyes" probably perform a leading function, as in other analogies between people and body members.[221]

Even if we value some parts of our body more than others, we would not readily discard any part (Paul is not thinking of necessary amputations [cf. Mk 9:43, 45, 47; Col 3:5] or in modern terms of vestigial appendages).[222] Instead, we take special care to cover our less presentable members, such as private parts (or perhaps the stomach, as in Menenius's parable), not prominent parts like the head (12:22–24; he is apparently thinking of men; contrast 11:2–16). This fits a recurrent biblical and early Jewish perspective, namely, that God prefers those who humble themselves before his greatness, not those who exalt themselves.[223] Paul's point is that every member merits equal care and sympathy (12:25–26; cf. Rom 12:10, 15–16).[224] Ancients emphasized that true friends shared each other's joys and sorrows.[225] Rejoicing with any honored member of the body (12:26; not merely of one's own faction, 1:12) was the opposite of envy (3:3; 13:4; Phil 1:15), a tendency among those seeking honor only for their own gift.[226]

Paul concludes the discussion of body parts by reemphasizing that the church consists of one body and many members (12:27), as in 12:12, 14, 20, and proceeds to list gifts again (12:28). He enumerates the first three entries; in ancient texts this technique designated priority. This time he begins with apostles first, though in human honor they might be last (4:9). Ministries directly communicating God's message (apostles, prophets, teachers) take precedence (cf. Rom 12:6–8; Eph 4:11–12), then miracles, healings, and so forth; again he ranks tongues at the bottom, presumably because of the problem in Corinth. That he includes "leadership" distinct from apostles, prophets, and teachers suggests that Paul's emphasis on the value of all members does not rule out some supervisory roles, even if they are not hierarchically defined (cf. 16:16; 1 Thess 5:12–13; Phil 1:1). Perhaps patrons such as Stephanas (16:15), Phoebe (Rom 16:1–2), or Gaius (Rom 16:23) exercised "forms of assistance" and "of leadership" (cf. the "giver" and patron in Rom 12:8). Whereas normal patrons helped clients and bestowed benefactions on cities, however, Christian patrons would serve all God's people.

Paul lists most of these gifts again in an emphatic series of rhetorical questions meant to underline the point that none of these gifts is meant for all the members

---

221 E.g., Philo *Special Laws* 4.157; the Sanhedrin for Israel in *Song Rab.* 4:1, §2; 7:5, §2.
222 Many Corinthians may have been familiar with model body parts left at Asclepius's healing sanctuary near Corinth; but contrary to some scholars, this image probably contributes little to the chapter.
223 E.g., Prov 16:19; Is 2:11, 17; Zeph 3:11–12; Lk 1:52; 9:48; 14:11; 18:14; Jas 4:6; 1 Pet 5:5–6.
224 Contrast Aristotle's extrapolation from diversity of natural endowments (*Pol.* 3.7.2–3, 1282b); but Stoics emphasized that society should care for its weaker members (Cicero *Fin.* 3.20.66).
225 E.g., Cicero *Quint. fratr.* 1.3.3; *Let. Aris.* 241–42; *T. Jos.* 17:7.
226 Cf., e.g., Xenophon *Mem.* 3.9.8; *Cyr.* 1.4.15; Plutarch *Themistocles* 3.3–4.

(12:29–30). (It is possible, in view of 14:1, 5, 31, that the point is that none *have* all gifts, not that one *may* not have any gift;[227] cf. comment on 12:31. In any case, Paul's point remains that each one has different gifts and all are valuable.)

BRIDGING THE HORIZONS

Many gifts are obvious and impressive, but it is by their fruits, not by their gifts alone, that the gifted should be evaluated (12:1–3; cf. Matt 7:22; Deut 13:1–3). Some oratorically or exegetically gifted preachers have exploited followers sexually or materially; the gifts may be from God, but those who abuse them for their own ends must render account (cf. Judg 16:1–21; 1 Sam 19:20–24; Matt 7:23). Today many churches follow spiritual "celebrities" as in Corinth (cf. Chs. 1–4); meanwhile, other Christians feel inadequate to accomplish anything worthwhile compared with such leaders.

Yet in Paul's perspective, no one can genuinely know the hearts of God's servants before the judgment (3:12–15; 4:4–5). Humble village evangelists or people of deep prayer may well fare better than many great preachers, miracle workers, or scholars (some of the sorts of gifts valued in various church traditions; cf. 12:22–25). Christians, even famous Christians, dare not boast in their public gifts, because in Paul's theology the gifted are merely stewards of God's gifts for the entire body of Christ. (The gifts are "ministries" or "services," 12:5. And although inspired by God, they are partial, incomplete, and need to be conjoined with other gifts to fit together more of the full picture of God's will; see 13:9.)

The preacher-centered services common in some places today can end up marketing preachers as celebrities and treating the church as simply "services" to attend; this risks reducing "edification" to entertainment. Our success-driven culture measures churches by income, fame, or real estate; faithfulness to calling, which might look different in a persecuted underground church or a new Christian movement among impoverished urban immigrants, is harder to measure. Today's church has lost much of the character of the Pauline notion of church, just as it has lost much of the Pauline conception of the Lord's supper (a covenant meal together). Paul's ideal for house churches was that they would function as many members of one body serving each other; quality was defined by relationships, not by expensive buildings.

The problem is not numerical church growth, as if Paul would have disapproved of this (quite the contrary, he labored to expand the church wherever possible; Rom 1:13–17; 15:16–20; 1 Thess 1:8). The problem instead is neglect of the spiritual growth that lays the foundation for a numerical growth that only God's eyes can fully quantify: believers who can persevere when tested by adversity – and by judgment day (3:13). In free societies, it may be possible for

---

[227] G. D. Fee, *The First Epistle to the Corinthians*, NIGNT (Grand Rapids, MI: Eerdmans, 1987), 622.

even megachurches to recall the interpersonal dynamic by intimate cell groups (cf. Acts 2:46; 5:42), and for even small churches to neglect it by merely holding "services."

The key is emphasis on valuing and judiciously encouraging the contribution of every member to the work of ministry. Those who teach the rest of the church should view their task as mobilizing all believers for their ministry in the world, where their "parishes" are their physically and spiritually needy neighbors, coworkers, and other acquaintances (cf. Eph 4:11–13). If only 5 percent of Christ's body uses its gifts, only 5 percent of the church's work will be fulfilled. Whereas ancients expected particular supernatural activity especially at healing shrines or oracular centers, Paul democratizes God's activity among all of God's people.

Yet today gifts are often segregated even by church and denomination. Some churches emphasize social justice almost exclusively; others majestic or contemporary worship; others teaching (like this commentary); others tongues-speaking or healing; others evangelism; others the rich heritage of the church's past, or particular cultures' contributions. By cross-fertilizing and learning from other churches, Christians can make the entire church more effective.

12:31–13:13: THE CRITERION FOR EMPLOYING GIFTS

12:31: But strive for the greater gifts. And I will show you a still more excellent way.

13:1: If I speak in the tongues of mortals and of angels, but do not have love, I am a noisy gong or a clanging cymbal.

13:2: And if I have prophetic powers, and understand all mysteries and all knowledge, and if I have all faith, so as to remove mountains, but do not have love, I am nothing.

13:3: If I give away all my possessions, and if I hand over my body so that I may boast, but do not have love, I gain nothing.

13:4: Love is patient; love is kind; love is not envious or boastful or arrogant

13:5: or rude. It does not insist on its own way; it is not irritable or resentful;

13:6: it does not rejoice in wrongdoing, but rejoices in the truth.

13:7: It bears all things, believes all things, hopes all things, endures all things.

13:8: Love never ends. But as for prophecies, they will come to an end; as for tongues, they will cease; as for knowledge, it will come to an end.

13:9: For we know only in part, and we prophesy only in part;

13:10: but when the complete comes, the partial will come to an end.

13:11: When I was a child, I spoke like a child, I thought like a child, I reasoned like a child; when I became an adult, I put an end to childish ways.

13:12: For now we see in a mirror, dimly, but then we will see face to face. Now I know only in part; then I will know fully, even as I have been fully known.

13:13: And now faith, hope, and love abide, these three; and the greatest of these is love.

*A*s Paul digresses concerning church order when addressing sexual questions (6:1–8) or to offer himself as a model of surrendering rights while discussing foods (Ch. 9), so here he digresses to provide the ethical principle requiring use of gifts to edify the body. Love is more important than gifts (13:1–3) and is eternal in contrast to gifts (13:8b–13); its characteristics (13:4–8) contradict the behavior of the Corinthians specifically described earlier in the letter.

Love advises Christians which gifts to seek on the criterion of what will edify the church (12:31; 14:1). Paul frames his discussion on love (13:1–13) with exhortations to seek "the best" gifts, especially prophecy (12:31; 14:1). Love defines which gifts are the "best": those that build up the body. Some think that in 12:31 Paul claims that the Corinthians "*are* zealous for the best gifts," then shows them a better way (i.e., a better definition of "the best gifts," based on love); *zēloute* can be indicative (cf. Jas 4:2) or imperative (cf. Wis 1:12). The context, however, makes clear that Paul intends the imperative (14:1, 39, where Paul encourages pursuit of prophecy), hence that he exhorts them to seek the best gifts. (These gifts are defined by love, thus by what builds up others; probably this includes those ranked highest in 12:28, including apostolic ministry, prophecy, and teaching.) Although God is sovereign over the distribution of gifts (12:11, 18), believers can be zealous for (perhaps pray for) particular gifts rather than passively waiting for a random gift to materialize. Paul seems to imply that God often grants the requests (cf. 2 Kgs 2:9–15); in any case, zeal to build up Christ's body is always good. Elsewhere he encourages believers toward the right perspective on their service (Rom 12:1–3), by recognizing that they are gifted members of Christ's body (Rom 12:4–6).

Some earlier interpreters viewed 13:1–13 as poetry (though it lacks the meter of Greek poetry) or even a source that Paul reused. Repetition characterized Greco-Roman rhetoric, however, and Paul's exalted prose was appropriate for a lofty subject; such prose was sometimes even rhythmic.[228] Paul's central section uses anaphora (repetition of the first element) extensively. One of the three major types of rhetoric was epideictic (involving praise or blame), and one of the three types of epideictic rhetoric was the encomium, a praise of a person or subject. One common rhetorical exercise was an encomium on a particular virtue, as here (or Heb 11:3–31, also using anaphora). Sometimes the virtue was personified or deified (unlike here); wedding orations often included encomia on marriage or (erotic) love (Menander Rhetor 2.6, 399.11–405.13). Self-giving love was important in ancient ethics (esp. Greek thought on friendship)

---

[228] Cf. Aristotle *Rhet.* 3.8.1, 1408b; Dionysius of Halicarnassus *Comp.* 25; Cicero *Or. Brut.* 50.168–69.231; Fronto *Ad M. Caes.* 3.16.1–2. Exalted prose often appears with divine, "sublime" topics (e.g., Maximus of Tyre 11.1).

but not consistently central; Paul reflects its consistently central place in early Christian ethics, likely dependent on Jesus tradition (Mk 12:30–31; Jn 13:34–35; 17:21–23).

The most gifted individuals without love are worthless (13:1–3). He begins with the gift with which he left off, the one the Corinthians were overemphasizing (12:30, though mentioning the corollary "interpretation" afterward). Some have argued that Paul or the Corinthians believed their tongues-speech angelic (cf. *T. Job* 48–50), hence perhaps a sign of realized eschatology, or of participation in the heavenly liturgy (cf. 2 Cor 12:4; Col 2:18; Rev 4:2–3, 8; 7:11; 4Q403 frg. 1, 1.1–6). But would angelic tongues pass away at Jesus's return (13:8–12; indeed, some, at least, expected angels to speak Hebrew among themselves)? More likely, angelic speech merely reinforces the hyperbole of one able to speak "all" tongues (like one who knows everything or removes mountains, 13:2).

Such giftedness without love is mere noise, communicating nothing worthwhile. The "gongs" are more likely acoustic vases (used to amplify voices in the theater) or perhaps anything potentially noisy made from bronze, the most famous of which was produced in Corinth.[229] Cymbals were more deliberate musical instruments, some of which were also made of bronze (1 Chron 15:19; cf. Josephus *Ant.* 7.306). Eastern cults used such cymbals in music,[230] but they also could be used (alongside bronze vessels) in, say, a noncultic drinking party (Babrius 80.2).

A person's mountain-moving faith profits them nothing without love (13:2); here Paul alludes to Jesus's exhortation to exercise such faith (Mk 11:23; cf. Zech 4:7), employing a conventional Jewish hyperbole for doing what was virtually impossible.[231] For all Paul's interest in prophecy's value, prophets themselves are worthless without love. God may still use the gift he gave, but the instrument (and sometimes abuser; cf. 14:29–33) of that gift has no merit. Giving up possessions and offering one's body (presumably here in martyrdom; 13:3; cf. 4 Macc 18:3) fit the expectations of the Jesus tradition (Mk 8:34–38; 10:21–31; Lk 12:33; 14:33), but even these radical acts are void of merit if not motivated by love. Although strong arguments may favor "that I may boast" (with NRSV text; it is much easier to explain textually), there appears to be an echo of Dan

---

[229] Some ancients apparently viewed loud but worthless oratory as such clanging bronzes, although the alleged second-century source for this (Zenobius) is preserved in later documents and might possibly reflect Paul's influence on Christian rhetoric.

[230] E.g., those of the Mother (Lucretius 2.618–20; Martial 14.204; cf. Apuleius *Met.* 8.24, 30); Dionysus (Livy 39.8.8; Ovid *Metam.* 3.532–33; Arrian *Indica* 7.8); Israel (1 Chron 15:16; 25:1, 6); and others (*P. Hib.* 54.13). Contrary to some, this is irrelevant to Paul's point, unless he thinks here of "religious" sounds.

[231] Later rabbis used it for extraordinary halakic expertise (e.g., *'Abot R. Nat.* 6 A; 12, §29 B; *b. Sanh.* 24a).

3:95 LXX (referring to risking martyrdom; closer in Theodotion) if one reads "burned" with the NRSV footnote. If Paul wrote of burning, he would imply martyrdom (as in Dan 3:19–20; 2 Macc 7:5; 4 Macc 6:26–27; 7:12; 10:14; Josephus *War* 2.7).[232]

Paul frames his central virtue list about love (13:4–7) with contrasts between love and the gifts in 13:1–3 and 13:8–13. Between these sections Paul describes love's attributes or qualities in good epideictic fashion – yet as implicit reproof of his audience with the deliberative purpose of inviting them to change their behavior. Love was not envious (13:4), in contrast to the Corinthians (3:3); love was not conceited (13:4), in contrast to the Corinthians (4:6, 18–19; 5:2; 8:1; cf. 2 Cor 12:20; the term appears only one other time in the Pauline corpus). Love does not seek its own good (13:5), but its neighbor's, as Paul exhorted earlier (10:24; cf. Phil 2:21); love bears anything for others (13:7), as Paul's example illustrated (9:12). Paul often contrasts "wrongdoing" (*adikia*) with "truth" (Rom 1:18; 2:8; 2 Thess 2:10, 12), a quality they needed (1 Cor 5:8).

The final quality of love, its eternal durability (13:8a) frames (cf. 13:13) and transitions into the third segment of the praise (13:8–13): unlike mere gifts, love is eternal. (To intellectuals influenced by Greek philosophy, this claim would invite attention; cf. 2 Cor 4:18.) What is imperfect or incomplete is not eternal; this must include the gifts (13:8–10). That three of the four gifts in 13:1–2 (already narrowed from many more in 12:8–10, 28–30) recur in 13:8 (and two in 13:9) should not surprise us. Paul chooses examples especially relevant to the Corinthian situation – prophecy, tongues (Ch. 14), and knowledge (1:5; 8:1–11).

Because he contrasts the complete future with the incomplete present, Paul emphasizes in 13:9 that mortals do not have all knowledge (pace the hyperbole in 13:2), and, like teaching, prophecy remains fallible (14:29) and incomplete. The time of the gifts' passing to which Paul refers is when believers see God "face to face" (13:12; cf. LXX Gen 32:30; Judg 6:22) and "know fully" just as God knows them (13:12; cf. 8:2–3), that is, at Christ's return (1:7–8; 15:43–44, 50–54). However much pagan thought might resist corporate future eschatology, what the Spirit provides in the present is merely a foretaste of that future (2:9–10); the full picture remains to be known (4:5).

Paul's comparison of present dependence on gifts with the speech and knowledge of children (13:11)[233] does not imply that the gifted are more immature than the ungifted (though gifts hardly guarantee maturity, 14:20). Rather, he

---

232 Certainly not self-immolation as in the case of India's "gymnosophists" revered (e.g., Cicero *Tusc.* 2.17.40) or imitated (Lucian *Peregr.* 36; *Dial. Mort.* 416–17) by many pagan intellectuals, or the suicides of the shamed (Strabo 3.4.17) or of bereaved mothers (4 Macc 17:1) or lovers (Parthenius *L.R.* 10.4).

233 The rhetorically astute would notice Paul's *epiphora* or *antistrophe*, his threefold repetition of "like a child."

argues that even the fullest knowledge and experience of Christians now is incomplete, awaiting full completion when Christ returns (13:9–10; cf. Ambrosiaster). The present experience is immature *by comparison*, just as the present body is a mere seed of future glory (15:36–37). (In various ancient Mediterranean cultures, boys achieved manhood in their mid-teens. Boys from Corinth's Roman citizenry would exchange their boyhood toga for an adult one; cf. 15:53–54.)

Unlike other prophets, who saw only visions, Moses glimpsed God face to face (Num 12:6–8; cf. Ex 33:11; Deut 34:10), not merely enigmatically (Num 12:8, *di' ainigmatōn*; "dimly" in 1 Cor 13:12 is Paul's only use of *ainigma*). Paul believes that Christ was a fuller revelation of glory than what Moses saw (2 Cor 3:7–18; 4:4–6), and that Christians who learned of his glory are gradually transformed into the same image (2 Cor 3:18). Christians could see a reflection of God's glory now as in a mirror (13:12; by what they could see of Christ, his image, 2 Corinthians 4:4; Wisdom mirrors God as his image in Wisdom 7:26). Compared to the final revelation and transformation into his image, however (1 Cor 15:48–49), Christians presently see a mere reflection, only a little beyond what Moses and the prophets saw. (Some other thinkers also compared the difficulty of comprehending God with perception by mirrors.)[234] Paul mentions mirrors only here and in 2 Corinthians 3:18; some therefore find local color here, comparing Corinth's famous bronze industry (e.g., Pausanias 2.3.3), because its golden or silvery-colored bronze could be used in mirrors.[235] But archaeological evidence for bronze-work in Corinth is so far weak;[236] "Corinthian" bronze may not all have come from Corinth, any more than everything labeled "Swiss cheese" or "French fries" comes from those nations today.

When Christ would return, no need would remain for gifts spreading a degree of knowledge, for the knowledge of God would be perfect (cf. Jer 31:34; 1QS 4.20–23). Paul elsewhere emphasizes the value of gifts led by love until that time (12:31; 14:1, 5, 39); but they cannot begin to be compared with love, which comes from God's own character (cf. Gal 2:20; 5:6, 13–14, 22). Faith, hope, and love (cf. 13:7) constitute his triad of highest virtues for the present age ("now"; 1 Thess 1:3; 5:8; Col 1:4–5; cf. Rom 5:2, 5), one that other early Christians could also affirm (Heb 6:10–12; 10:22–24; 1 Pet 1:21–22). But even among these highest virtues, the greatest is love (13:13). Gifts are vital for accomplishing God's work; but only fruit (Gal 5:22–23) reveals one's character.

---

[234] See F. G. Downing, "Reflecting the First Century: 1 Corinthians 13:12," *ExpT* 95 (6, 1984): 176–77 (more relevant than self-knowledge suggested by some).

[235] Corinthian bronze characterized wealth (e.g., Petronius 31; Seneca *Dial.* 9.9.6; Josephus *War* 5.201; Pliny *Nat.* 34.1).

[236] C. Mattusch, "Corinthian Bronze: Famous, but Elusive," 219–32 in *Corinth, The Centenary 1896–1996*, ed. C. K. Williams II and N. Bookidis, vol. 20 in *Corinth* (Princeton, NJ: American School of Classical Studies at Athens, 2003).

14:1–25: PROPHECY MORE USEFUL THAN TONGUES

14:1: Pursue love and strive for the spiritual gifts, and especially that you may prophesy.

14:2: For those who speak in a tongue do not speak to other people but to God; for nobody understands them, since they are speaking mysteries in the Spirit.

14:3: On the other hand, those who prophesy speak to other people for their up-building and encouragement and consolation.

14:4: Those who speak in a tongue build up themselves, but those who prophesy build up the church.

14:5: Now I would like all of you to speak in tongues, but even more to prophesy. One who prophesies is greater than one who speaks in tongues, unless someone interprets, so that the church may be built up.

14:6: Now, brothers and sisters, if I come to you speaking in tongues, how will I benefit you unless I speak to you in some revelation or knowledge or prophecy or teaching?

14:7: It is the same way with lifeless instruments that produce sound, such as the flute or the harp. If they do not give distinct notes, how will anyone know what is being played?

14:8: And if the bugle gives an indistinct sound, who will get ready for battle?

14:9: So with yourselves; if in a tongue you utter speech that is not intelligible, how will anyone know what is being said? For you will be speaking into the air.

14:10: There are doubtless many different kinds of sounds in the world, and nothing is without sound.

14:11: If then I do not know the meaning of a sound, I will be a foreigner to the speaker and the speaker a foreigner to me.

14:12: So with yourselves; since you are eager for spiritual gifts, strive to excel in them for building up the church.

14:13: Therefore, one who speaks in a tongue should pray for the power to interpret.

14:14: For if I pray in a tongue, my spirit prays but my mind is unproductive.

14:15: What should I do then? I will pray with the spirit, but I will pray with the mind also; I will sing praise with the spirit, but I will sing praise with the mind also.

14:16: Otherwise, if you say a blessing with the spirit, how can anyone in the position of an outsider say the "Amen" to your thanksgiving, since the outsider does not know what you are saying?

14:17: For you may give thanks well enough, but the other person is not built up.

14:18: I thank God that I speak in tongues more than all of you;

14:19: nevertheless, in church I would rather speak five words with my mind, in order to instruct others also, than ten thousand words in a tongue.

14:20: Brothers and sisters, do not be children in your thinking; rather, be infants in evil, but in thinking be adults.

14:21: In the law it is written,

> "By people of strange tongues
>   and by the lips of foreigners
> I will speak to this people;
>   yet even then they will not listen to me,"

says the Lord.

14:22: Tongues, then, are a sign not for believers but for unbelievers, while prophecy is not for unbelievers but for believers.

14:23: If, therefore, the whole church comes together and all speak in tongues, and outsiders or unbelievers enter, will they not say that you are out of your mind?

14:24: But if all prophesy, an unbeliever or outsider who enters is reproved by all and called to account by all.

14:25: After the secrets of the unbeliever's heart are disclosed, that person will bow down before God and worship him, declaring, "God is really among you."

*D*irected by love, they should continue to be eager for spiritual gifts, but especially for those that edified the church (14:1). Apart from the Scripture exposition (i.e., the gift of knowledge and teaching, 12:8, 29; 14:6), the speech gifts that could dominate the Corinthians' gatherings were prophecy and tongues (inspired prayer in languages unknown to the speaker). Although careful not to denigrate the gift of inspired prayer in a tongue, Paul emphasizes articulate speech that directly builds up the church. (Paul can hardly denigrate prayer in unknown languages [cf. 14:5, 39], since he considers it a "gift" from God's own Spirit [12:7–10] and apparently does it often himself [14:18].) Some argue that those abusing tongues, like those Paul reproves most harshly elsewhere (cf. 1:26–28; 6:4; 8:1; 11:21), belonged to the social elite. This is possible, but they might also resort to tongues to compensate for lack of rhetorical eloquence, which the educated elite were abusing.

For Luke, "tongues" is Spirit-inspired worship in other languages, which symbolizes (on a narrative level) the power to cross cultural barriers (Acts 2:4; 10:45–46; 19:6; cf. 1:8). Paul describes it as prayer (again Spirit-inspired, 12:8–10) from the affective rather than cognitive aspect of the human personality (14:14). Many of Paul's contemporaries believed in a form of divine inspiration or possession that displaced the mind;[237] the Jewish philosopher Philo (who like many often divided the soul into rational and irrational components) sometimes articulated this view.[238] Paul apparently rejects that view for prophecy (at least normally); he does not view prayer in a tongue as cognitive but also does not require the mind to be inactive (14:15).

---

[237]   E.g., Euripides *Bacch.* 298–99; Virgil *Aen.* 6.77–102; Lucan *C.W.* 5.97–193.
[238]   E.g., *Drunkenness* passim; *Heir* 264–65; cf. *Creation* 71.

Against many interpreters today, Paul seems to believe that the gift employs genuine languages: he uses a term that normally means "languages"; speaks of "interpretation" (12:10, 30; 14:5, 13, 26–28); and compares human and angelic languages (13:1). (Contrary to some arguments, ancient Greek examples of inspired speech "interpreted" to arrange it in conventional oracular form, or uses of archaic "tongues" in liturgies, differ from the belief that one was inspired to speak in languages unknown to the speaker. Pagan parallels for early Christian glossolalia are thus more difficult to find than for prophecy.)[239] Although the speech is therefore articulate, however, the languages appear to be unknown to the speaker (14:13–14) and normally everyone else present (14:2, 16, 19); "tongue" here is early Christian shorthand for "unknown tongue." This probably makes it comparable to the experience of many modern charismatics.

Paul apparently defines prophecy as intelligible inspired utterance (normally distinct from the exposition of Scripture, although prophecy often echoed Scripture), the most common sense in the OT and early Christianity. Prophecy is more useful in the assembly than tongues because, being intelligible, it edifies all hearers and not merely the speaker (14:2–6). Rather than revealing "mysteries" (cf. 4:1; 13:2), the person praying in a tongue simply offers mysteries; the purpose of the utterance is prayer to God, not edifying others (14:2). By contrast, prophecy serves one's spiritual colleagues directly (14:3); the difference is between self-edification and edifying others (14:4). Although both purposes may be commendable, the former can be done privately (cf. 14:18–19) rather than at the rest of the assembly's expense. Paul regards the ability to pray in an (unlearned) language as desirable (14:5; cf. similarly 7:7); but prophecy was even more desirable because it served more people (14:5, 18–19).

To underline his point, Paul illustrates at length that what is unintelligible cannot communicate (14:7–11), whether with music (14:7–8) or languages (14:10–11). Everyone agreed that harps and flutes lacked language (Aristotle *Poetics* 1.5, 1447a; Sir 40:21); but, like the trumpet ("bugle"), they could communicate meaning (cf. 15:52). Ancients, including Israelites, used trumpets to summon armies, including giving instructions for battle (e.g., 2 Sam 2:28; 1 Macc 7:45); but "an indistinct sound" would leave hearers confused as to which instructions were intended. Although Greeks considered all non-Greeks "barbarians," the Greek term "barbarian" (NRSV: "foreigner," 14:11) originated as a depiction of foreign speech, and often continued to carry this connotation. Even non-Greek accents (Philostratus *Vit. soph.* 1.8.490) and slips in Greek (Appian *Hist. rom.* 3.7.2) could be reckoned "barbaric"; Romans borrowed the expression for slips in Latin as well (Quintilian *Inst.* 1.5.5–33). Speaking "into the air" (14:9) was as valueless as boxing the air (9:26). In 14:12, Paul reiterates his point from the

---

[239] See C. Forbes, *Prophecy and Inspired Speech in Early Christianity and its Hellenistic Environment* (Peabody, MA: Hendrickson, 1997; Tübingen: Mohr, 1995), 103–62; D. E. Aune, "Magic in Early Christianity," *ANRW* 2 (principat), 23.1.1507–57, pp. 1549–51.

beginning of the section (14:1) more directly: because they are commendably zealous for spiritual gifts, they should seek to use them to "edify" the church (as in 14:3–5; a term often used in exhortations to unity; five of Paul's eight uses of the verb, as well as a significant percentage of his uses of the noun, appear in this letter).

If a solution for the church as a whole is to pursue the gift of prophecy, a solution for those with the gift of praying in a tongue is to seek to "interpret" (14:13); public prayer, like prophecy, can be edifying so long as it is intelligible. In this context, "praying" and "singing with the mind" (14:15) refers to interpreting the prayer or song in a tongue (see further discussion on the nature of tongues-prayer at the beginning of this chapter). (Presumably, one could employ the gift of interpretation in private prayer also; but it is public prayer in which it is essential. The Corinthians are either less familiar with interpretation or less interested in it.) Inspired singing appears in the OT (1 Chron 25:1–3; cf. 1 Sam 10:5) and elsewhere.[240]

Public thanksgiving in tongues may be genuine praise, but how will outsiders say, "Amen" (an Aramaic affirmation of a prayer conventional in the church) to what they do not understand (14:16–17)? (*Idiōtēs,* "unlearned," the NRSV's "outsider," could mean "someone unfamiliar with the language"; but elsewhere in the context it seems to mean those unfamiliar even with the church's practice, 14:23–24.) Paul himself spoke in tongues more than all of them,[241] but preferred in the church to speak intelligibly (14:18–19; worth more than "10,000 words" was conventional hyperbole, e.g., Euripides *Med.* 965). This suggests that his abundant praying in tongues was largely in private devotion, as were some of his other intimate spiritual experiences (2 Cor 5:13; 12:1–4). (When he mentions these publicly it may often be to put less sound fellow charismatics in their place, 14:37–38; 2 Cor 12:1–10; cf. his mention of his own singleness to ascetics in 7:7.) It may also suggest that it was from Paul that they learned of this gift (although it was apparently more widespread, Acts 2:4; 10:46).

Paul encourages them to be mature in their thinking (14:20), as he had encouraged them before (3:1–2; for simplicity in evil, cf. Rom 16:19). He then quotes a prophet who, a few lines earlier, warned that Israel acted like infants just weaned from milk, who could handle only the most basic instruction (Is 28:9–10; cf. 28:13). (Although "the law" could refer to the books of Moses, it also applied more generally, as here, to the entire Jewish canon; e.g., *Sipre Deut.* 32.5.12.) He picks up the quote at the point where God then threatens to speak to the people by the judgment of foreign invaders (Is 28:11; cf. 33:19; Deut 28:49). They refused to hear the true prophets (29:10–12; 30:9–11); therefore, unintelligible speech is a sign of judgment that, ironically, they will understand.

---

[240] E.g., *L.A.B.* 32:14; Tg. Jon. on 1 Sam 19:23–24; Dionysius of Halicarnassus *Ant. rom.* 1.31.1.
[241] One could read this as a form of thanking God mentioned in 14:18a (cf. 14:16), but Paul's style supports the NRSV reading, "I thank God that" (cf. 1:4, 14).

Paul's apparently strange interpretation in 14:22 of the quotation in 14:21 makes more sense against the context in Isaiah, a context that 14:20 confirms that he knew. Tongues are a sign to unbelievers, like those in Isaiah's day who heeded only judgment; apparently they communicate in a way that confounds rather than converts unbelievers (14:23).[242] Given its associations with ecstatic frenzy in some (esp. pagan) circles, prophetic speech was often connected with madness (cf. 2 Kgs 9:11; Acts 26:24).[243] To point out that outsiders (in this case unbelieving or recently converted spouses or guests who might attend) would think a group mad was sometimes a way to provide an objective external control on their behavior.[244]

Prophecy (like Isaiah's own) was, however, a clear sign for those who already believe (14:22), though Paul ironically turns this so that it also leads to unbelievers' faith (14:24–25). The Lord knew (4:5; Prov 15:11) and could reveal by prophecy the secrets of hearts (2 Kgs 5:26; cf. Sir 1:30). Falling on one's face to worship God (14:25) is a common response of awe at his signs (2 Chron 7:3), or even before his vindicated people (Is 49:23; Dan 2:46). That "God is with you" (14:25) probably recalls the confession of Gentiles bowing to God's servants in Is 45:14 (cf. Zech 8:23). Although the ancient world knew of wandering prophets or stationary oracles, a community of prophets unattached to a sanctuary was unique, and prophetic accuracy in antiquity normally invited faith.

14:26–40: INSTRUCTIONS FOR ORDER IN WORSHIP

14:26: What should be done then, my friends? When you come together, each one has a hymn, a lesson, a revelation, a tongue, or an interpretation. Let all things be done for building up.

14:27: If anyone speaks in a tongue, let there be only two or at most three, and each in turn; and let one interpret.

14:28: But if there is no one to interpret, let them be silent in church and speak to themselves and to God.

14:29: Let two or three prophets speak, and let the others weigh what is said.

14:30: If a revelation is made to someone else sitting nearby, let the first person be silent.

---

[242] Alternatively, some interpret "tongues is a sign for unbelievers" as a rhetorical question or a statement that Paul refutes; or Paul may refute a Corinthian claim that tongues are a sign of their spiritual supremacy among believers; or Paul means that tongues produce unbelievers, and prophecy, believers.

[243] E.g., Ovid *Metam.* 2.640; see C. Keener, *The Spirit in the Gospels and Acts* (Peabody, MA: Hendrickson, 1997), 23–26. Hellenistic thought, however, follows Plato in distinguishing "divine madness" from lower forms ("Ecstasy," 505 in *OCD*).

[244] E.g., Dionysius of Halicarnassus *Isoc.* 17, quoting from Isocrates *Peace* 41–53.

14:31: For you can all prophesy one by one, so that all may learn and all be encouraged.

14:32: And the spirits of prophets are subject to the prophets,

14:33: for God is a God not of disorder but of peace. (As in all the churches of the saints,

14:34: women should be silent in the churches. For they are not permitted to speak, but should be subordinate, as the law also says.

14:35: If there is anything they desire to know, let them ask their husbands at home. For it is shameful for a woman to speak in church.

14:36: Or did the word of God originate with you? Or are you the only ones it has reached?)

14:37: Anyone who claims to be a prophet, or to have spiritual powers, must acknowledge that what I am writing to you is a command of the Lord.

14:38: Anyone who does not recognize this is not to be recognized.

14:39: So, my friends, be eager to prophesy, and do not forbid speaking in tongues;

14:40: but all things should be done decently and in order.

*I*n 14:26–40, Paul provides instructions for the ideal operation of gifts in the house-churches, then digresses (if 14:34–35 is not an interpolation) to address an apparently disruptive activity of some wives, concluding (as often in ancient rhetoric) with his general principle (14:39–40). That the Corinthians need such instructions (despite Acts 18:11) suggests new developments since his departure, and that the instructions are ad hoc rather than universal for all Paul's churches. The overriding principle, however, is edification (14:26; often reiterated, 14:3–5, 12, 17) and order (14:40), and this *was* common to all the churches (14:33). ("As in all the churches of the saints" belongs with the preceding context in 14:32–33, not what follows in 14:34–35, pace the NRSV. This is especially clear from Paul's style elsewhere in the letter [7:17; 11:16]; the repetition of churches in 14:34 also would be redundant if the thought continued.) "Disorder" (14:33) might also connote some hostility (cf. the same term in 2 Cor 6:5; 12:20); Christians were called to "peace" (cf. also 7:15).

In 14:26, each member brings distinctive contributions to the house gatherings, such as psalms (NRSV "hymn"; cf. Eph 5:18–19; Col 3:16), teachings (cf. 12:28–29; 14:6); revelations (cf. 14:6; this is prophecy, as in 14:30; cf. 2 Cor 12:1, 7), or a tongue or interpretation (14:26). (Although some psalms might be drawn from the OT, they could also be postbiblical, like some at Qumran. Some could be new songs in tongues if interpreted, 1 Corinthians 14:15; many OT psalms also originated in charismatic, although liturgical, worship – 1 Chronicles 25:1–6; cf. 16:4; 29:25, 30.) The gatherings were intensely interactive, more than what our few extant sources suggest for at least larger, formal synagogue gatherings in this period; the charismatic element might resemble Philo's Therapeutae, but for the most part is distinctly Christian.

Whether this is descriptive or, more likely, Paul's ideal, the regulating principle is edifying all those present (14:26). In the case of not only tongues but prophecy (the primary local issues), Paul issues instructions to ensure order. Speakers could not plead ecstatic frenzy (as in rites of Cybele or Dionysus) against following proper order; speaking in proper order was expected in formal assemblies,[245] and genuine prophets could control their spirits (14:32; cf. Prov 16:32). Thus, those offering prayer in a tongue should speak in turn, and after at most three utterances someone must interpret (14:27). They could pray for the gift of interpretation (14:13), but if no one yet had this gift, the person should employ the gift only quietly, to God and to oneself (14:28). ("To oneself" could mean either as a divine message to one's spirit, as in some OT prophecy [2 Sam 23:2–3; Jer 27:2; Hos 1:1], or, since the prayer is not interpreted, for one's personal edification.)

Just as two or three prayers in tongues must be followed by interpretation (14:27–28), two or three prophecies must be followed by evaluation (14:29), probably related to the gift of "distinguishing of spirits" (12:10, using the noun cognate of the verb in 14:29). Because prophecy was partial, incomplete revelation of God's will (13:9), it needed to be evaluated (1 Thess 5:20–22); ideally, senior prophets could mentor newer prophets in accuracy (cf. 1 Sam 19:20; 2 Kgs 2:3–7, 15; 6:1–7), but for first-generation Corinthian prophets, "peer review" was the only available approach. Just as those who prayed in tongues should remain publicly silent under certain conditions, for the sake of the entire group (14:28), so should one prophet fall silent if another signaled readiness to prophesy (14:30). Presumably most of the congregation was "sitting" (14:30) during this part of the meeting, and whoever was going to speak would stand, as was customary.[246] By prophesying in order (rather than all at once so no one could hear, appropriate only for self-edification; cf. perhaps 1 Samuel 10:5, 10; 19:20), they allowed all to learn and be encouraged (cf. 14:3). That "you can all prophesy one by one" emphasizes order, but also may point beyond the two or three prophecies before evaluation to the ideal possibility of an entire prophetic community (14:5), envisioned in the OT (Joel 2:28–29; cf. Num 11:29), even if not concretely fulfilled in a strict sense (1 Cor 12:29).

The digression in 14:34–35 is so disjunctive in its context that some argue plausibly that it is a post-Pauline interpolation. The only concrete textual evidence, however, is the passage's displacement in the Western text.[247] The passage is too brief for stylistic arguments against its Paulinicity to prove compelling; it stands in tension with much of Paul's teaching in this period (esp. Rom 16:1–7),

---

[245] Perhaps most strictly among Essenes (e.g., 1QS 6.10–13, 26–27; 7.9–10; Josephus *War* 2.132). Qumran assemblies even seated by rank in the community; most banquets did so by social rank (see C. Keener, *John* [2003], 905, 916).

[246] E.g., Homer *Il.* 1.68–69; Dionysius of Halicarnassus *Ant. rom.* 7.47.1; Plutarch *Coriol.* 16.2.

[247] See esp. G. Fee, *Presence* (1994), 272–81. Some others view it as a refuted quotation (cf. 6:12–13; 7:1–6).

but could be explained along the lines of 11:2–16. It is thus also plausible to read it as genuinely Pauline (as we suggest below), but as a parenthetical digression further expanding the topic of order in the churches.

Like tongues-speakers (14:28) and prophets (14:30), women were to remain "silent" under some circumstances.[248] Because the church met in homes, questions would arise as to whether women should comport themselves as if in the domestic or public sphere. Women had made serious gains in terms of public speaking in Roman culture, but some Romans and many Greeks still frowned on it,[249] potentially introducing cultural conflict in the church again. Some would consider women's speech in gender-mixed company "shameful" (14:35), just like public display of wives' uncovered hair (11:5–6). Paul appeals to "the law" to maintain the custom of wives' submission (presumably to their husbands), probably alluding either to the creation order (11:8–9) or the example of patriarchal wives (1 Pet 3:5).[250] Paul himself submitted to "the law" to avoid causing offense (1 Cor 9:20); perhaps even some local Jewish customs constitute a concern. Wifely submission remained an ideal in his day (although less practiced among aristocrats than in earlier times),[251] especially in terms of behavior to avoid shaming one's husband (14:35; cf. 11:5–6).

Yet Paul would not prohibit speech inspired by the Spirit (though the context shows his willingness to regulate it); in fact, he cannot be prohibiting women praying or prophesying without contradicting himself (see 11:5).[252] (Indeed, he had women coworkers even in Corinth; Rom 16:1–5; 1 Cor 16:19.) He refers specifically to "learning," a term that appears in the context only for those *hearing* prophecy (14:31; not judging it, as in 14:29).

Paul's solution to the problem may help us reconstruct the problem. To "ask their own husbands at home" (14:35) suggests that they were offering questions in the presence of other men in the assembly.[253] When Christians exercised their freedom in ways that caused others to stumble, Paul advised them to exercise their freedoms "at home" (11:34). We have touched briefly above on the problem

---

[248] Perhaps submitting themselves (to church order? 14:34) also echoes the requirement for the prophets (14:32).

[249] E.g., Plutarch *Bride* 32, *Mor.* 142D; Heliodorus *Aeth.* 1.21; Valerius Maximus 3.8.6; for mistrust of women's testimony, see comment on 15:5–8.

[250] Josephus likewise appeals to "the law" for wives' submission, despite lack of an explicit text (*Ag. Ap.* 2.200–01). Some early Jewish sources also appealed to Eve's fall.

[251] E.g., Philo *Creation* 167; Josephus *Ant.* 18.255; Marcus Aurelius 1.17.7.

[252] Though some argue that 11:5 was a concession and Paul's goal was to silence women (A. C. Wire, *The Corinthian Women Prophets: A Reconstruction through Paul's Rhetoric* [Minneapolis: Fortress, 1990], makes 14:34–35 central in reconstructing the letter's situation, at the other extreme from those who view it as an interpolation), he could have done so more effectively had he wished, and his attitudes elsewhere (Rom 16:1–7; Phil 4:2–3) probably argue against their universal silencing.

[253] Distant seating of men and women would be difficult in a house church, and we currently lack evidence for gender segregation in early synagogues.

of women speaking out publicly; but why were they asking questions? Learners asked questions in a variety of lecture settings.[254] Although some philosophic schools included women disciples[255] (and Jesus seems to have allowed them, Mk 15:40–41; Lk 8:1–3; 10:38–42), most schools, whether Jewish or Gentile, did not, and society expected men rather than women to absorb and question public lectures.

Furthermore, many hearers resented questions considered rude, inappropriate, or unlearned; these risked slowing other learners down.[256] It is possible, although not certain, that the women were more apt to ask unlearned questions. Although Judean boys learned to recite the law growing up (*m. 'Abot* 5:21), the privilege was rarer among girls even in regions where some are attested. Literate men may have outnumbered literate women five to one, and even among aristocratic Greeks and Romans, where education was most widely available, a woman's education usually ended by her mid-teens. Possibly Paul's ideals on gender (7:2–4; 11:11–12; Gal 3:28) had created conflict for the concrete milieu of the church.

To suggest that the women should learn by asking their husbands at home (14:35) would sound repressive to most of us today (at least where questions can be asked in public meetings), but probably seemed comparatively progressive in Paul's environment (and in some traditional cultures today). Most men considered their wives unable to grasp intellectual ideas; Plutarch notes that he is exceptional in advising a groom that his bride can learn (but then adds his own sexist twist, arguing that women if left to themselves produce only base passion; *Bride* 48, *Mor.* 145BE).[257] (Although the disparity in Roman and Jewish households was much less severe, on average Greek men married women twelve years their junior, probably because of a shortage of free women abetted by abandoning more female babies.) Most of the women would have "husbands at home"; because men outnumbered available wives, most women were married early in adulthood (and younger girls, like boys, would be restricted from speaking). Because conversions often followed households (cf. 1:16; 16:15), most of the wives Paul addresses would in fact have husbands who had heard the teaching and prophecies (although clearly this was not always the case; 7:12–16; cf. 1 Pet 3:1).

Reserving his harshest critique for the end (as rhetoric suggested for delicate matters), Paul finally challenges those who claim the Spirit's authority for their behavior (14:36–38). They need to recognize that the Spirit has also spoken to the churches (14:36; cf. 14:33, immediately before his digression), as well as to

---

[254] E.g., Aulus Gellius *Noct. att.* 1.26.2; 12.5.4; *t. Sanh.* 7:10.

[255] E.g., Diogenes Laertius 2.86; 4.1; 6.7.98; 8.1.42. But some ridiculed them (Juvenal *Sat.* 6.434–56).

[256] Plutarch *Lectures* 4, *Mor.* 39CD; 11, *Mor.* 43BC; 18, *Mor.* 48AB.

[257] Cf. Xenophon *Symp.* 2.9; *Oec.* 3.10–16; 7.11–22; 9.1. Stoic views of women's ability to learn were more positive, although focused on womanly roles (esp. Musonius Rufus 3–4).

their founding apostle (14:37).[258] Otherwise they themselves will be judged (cf. 14:29) as not speaking God's message accurately (14:38).

Paul closes the section, as speakers and writers often did, with a summary (14:39–40).[259] They should be zealous to prophesy, but should not mistake this preference as instructions to prohibit prayers in tongues (14:39). The overriding principle, however, was respectable ("decently"; cf. the concern in 14:23–25) order (14:40), indicating that tongues should be interpreted and prophecy evaluated (14:27–33).

BRIDGING THE HORIZONS

Many Christians read 1 Corinthians 12–14 as if it claimed that love makes gifts unnecessary. Instead, it was written by a charismatic and for charismatics to show that love must direct the gifts. Although the early Christian phenomena this chapter addresses are foreign to the experience of many readers today, Pentecostals and charismatics have exploded in some parts of the world and some denominations. Many observers estimate over three hundred million charismatics (including over one hundred million Pentecostals), making this group one of the largest blocs in Christendom next to the Roman Catholic church (with which it overlaps). Although others look for general principles, for these groups Paul's instructions are most directly relevant.[260]

Paul limited utterances for Corinthian house churches (14:27–30); he might have imposed fewer limits for smaller groups and more for larger ones. The basic principle, however, is what edifies those gathered; some things can be done at home (cf. 11:22, 34; 14:28, 35). A sermon devoid of content fails on the same criterion that unintelligible utterances would, squandering the worship time of those gathered. (On the contributions of all gifts in small groups, see our "Bridging the Horizons" section on 1 Cor 12.)

By contrast, Paul allows that inspired prayer in a tongue is a useful gift for private devotion. Defense mechanisms like rationalization and projection may obstruct cognitive prayer by deflecting admission of the genuine need; affective prayer with one's spirit, interpreted only afterward (14:15), might surmount such obstacles. (Paul seems unaware of the modern Pentecostal phenomenon of a

---

[258] Daring an audience to defy one's teaching (*epitrope*) or, more relevantly here, appealing to the justice of one's position (*dikaiologia*) were frequent rhetorical devices; some also compare OT and pagan curse formulas.

[259] See documentation in C. Keener, *John* (2003), 887, 1213.

[260] R. Hays, *First Corinthians* (1997), 219, even encourages those from noncharismatic churches to visit Pentecostal or charismatic churches to learn about the gifts more common there. This can be good advice, but visitors should keep in mind that not all charismatic churches are alike in practice or theology (see W. J. Hollenweger, *The Pentecostals* [London: SCM, 1972]; my *Gift & Giver* [Grand Rapids, MI: Baker, 2001], 190–203; A. Anderson, *An Introduction to Pentecostalism: Global Charismatic Christianity* [Cambridge: Cambridge University, 2004] cf. 14:29).

"message" – as opposed to a prayer – in tongues; but had he known of it, he may have allowed it; cf. 14:28.)

Particularly problematic for readers today are his words about wives in 14:34–35 (if judged original). Whereas Paul sometimes accommodated social conventions for the sake of peace, however (e.g., 9:19–23; 11:2–16), he did accept women's inspiration to pray and prophesy (11:5) and valued his women colleagues in ministry (Rom 16:1–7, 12; Phil 4:2–3; Col 4:15), probably including an apostle (Rom 16:7).[261] He employs for some of them the ministry terms he most commonly applied to his male colleagues (Rom 16:1, 3). On some points, as noted earlier, he was among the more progressive voices of his day on gender. Thus, had Paul faced today's social conventions rather than those of his day, he likely would have endorsed women's ministry more fully.[262]

15:1–11: JESUS ROSE

15:1: Now I would remind you, brothers and sisters, of the good news that I proclaimed to you, which you in turn received, in which also you stand,

15:2: through which also you are being saved, if you hold firmly to the message that I proclaimed to you – unless you have come to believe in vain.

15:3: For I handed on to you as of first importance what I in turn had received: that Christ died for our sins in accordance with the scriptures,

15:4: and that he was buried, and that he was raised on the third day in accordance with the scriptures,

15:5: and that he appeared to Cephas, then to the twelve.

15:6: Then he appeared to more than five hundred brothers and sisters at one time, most of whom are still alive, though some have died.

15:7: Then he appeared to James, then to all the apostles.

15:8: Last of all, as to one untimely born, he appeared also to me.

15:9: For I am the least of the apostles, unfit to be called an apostle, because I persecuted the church of God.

15:10: But by the grace of God I am what I am, and his grace toward me has not been in vain. On the contrary, I worked harder than any of them – though it was not I, but the grace of God that is with me.

15:11: Whether then it was I or they, so we proclaim and so you have come to believe.

---

[261] See here R. Bauckham, *Gospel Women: Studies of the Named Women in the Gospels* (Grand Rapids, MI: Eerdmans, 2002), 166–80.

[262] Many have argued this, including myself (*Paul, Women & Wives* [1992], passim; see also *Discovering Biblical Equality*, ed. R. W. Pierce, R. Merrill Groothuis, and G. Fee [Downers Grove, IL: InterVarsity, 2004]), although many others disagree (e.g., J. Piper and W. Grudem, eds., *Recovering Biblical Manhood and Womanhood* [Wheaton, IL: Crossway, 1991]).

*I*n 15:1–58, Paul contends for the common Judean doctrine of an end-time resurrection, despite its absurdity to Gentiles. For Paul, an eschatological resurrection has moral consequences (6:13–14; 15:32–34, 58), as in other early Jewish defenses of eschatological judgment on moral grounds (or pagan condemnations of "immoral" Epicureans' rejection of the afterlife). To argue for the eschatological resurrection, Paul begins in 15:1–11 with the component of that doctrine his hearers have already accepted, reinforcing the point with a list of eyewitnesses. Their acceptance of the kerygma invited acceptance of the Jewish salvation-historical framework of which it was a part.

A CLOSER LOOK: ANCIENT VIEWS ON RESURRECTION

Educated, elite Corinthians probably followed views held by many philosophers, such as immortality of the soul after the body's death.[263] Many viewed the body as earthly, the soul as heavenly (Heraclitus *Ep.* 9; Seneca *Dial.* 12.11.6), including some Jews (Wis 9:15–16; *Sipre Deut.* 306.28.2). Many philosophers viewed the immortal soul as the divine part of a person;[264] some Hellenistic Jewish thinkers concurred (Philo *Creation* 135). Contrary to the erroneous guesses of many NT scholars, most Jews in this period accepted this distinction between soul and body, and that the soul remained immortal after death.[265] But most Judeans, and at least some Diaspora Jews, also accepted the doctrine of a future bodily resurrection alongside the soul's immortality after death.

Some Greeks (like Epicureans and popular doubts on tombstones) denied even an afterlife. Yet even Greeks who expected an afterlife for the soul could not conceive of bodily resurrection (which they would view as the reanimation of corpses) or glorified bodies. The closest analogies were old myths about deceased souls brought back from Hades; annually returning underworld deities connected with spring vegetation;[266] witches magically resuscitating corpses; and (most common in novels) recovery from merely apparent death.

Most of Palestinian Judaism, however, emphasized bodily resurrection, as the canonical status of Dan 12:2 almost required.[267] Later rabbis felt that the Sadducees' denial of the resurrection deprived them of sharing the afterlife (*m. Sanh.* 10:1; *'Abot R. Nat.* 5A; 10, §26b). Some Diaspora Jews in this period also embraced the concept (e.g., *Sib. Or.* 4.179–82), although often accommodating it to Hellenistic understanding of immortality (Ps.-Phoc. 102–05), as Josephus

[263] E.g., Plato *Phaed.* 64CE, 67C; Cicero *De Re Publica* 6.24.26; Seneca *Dial.* 11.9.3; 12.11.7.
[264] Seneca *Nat.Q.* 1.pref. 14; *Lucil.* 78.10; Epictetus *Diatr.* 1.3.3.
[265] For summary see R. H. Gundry, *Sōma in Biblical Theology: with Emphasis on Pauline Anthropology* (Cambridge: Cambridge University, 1976); C. Keener, *John* (2003), 538, 553–54.
[266] In Corinth, cf. the cult of Persephone (R. S. Stroud, *Demeter and Persephone in Ancient Corinth* [Princeton, NJ: ASCSA, 1987]).
[267] E.g., 2 Macc 7:9, 14, 23, 29; 14:46; *Pss. Sol.* 3:12; *1 En.* 22:13.

does.[268] It is thus possible that Paul's Judean conceptions created friction not only with Gentile but even with Jewish elements in the congregation. Paul seems to move as far in their direction as possible here ("spiritual," heavenly bodies of glory; even further in 2 Cor 4:16–5:10) without compromising his insistence on the bodily character of future hope, rooted in the goodness of God's physical creation.[269]

Good rhetoric usually strove to appeal to common ground; Paul begins by appealing to the message by which they were converted, hence to which they gave assent (15:1–2; also 2:1–5; Gal 3:2–5; 1 Thess 2:1; 3:4). Paul warns them that if Christ was not raised, their faith is in vain (15:2, 14, 17; cf. 2 Cor 6:1; Gal 2:2; 3:4; 4:11; Phil 2:16; 1 Thess 2:1; 3:5), but assures them that this is not the case (15:10, 58). Their salvation depended on it (15:2). Early Christians saw the gospel events predicted or foreshadowed in Scripture (15:4), and Paul may think of texts like Psalm 16:10–11 and Isaiah 53:4–12, used by other Christians. If "third day" (counting inclusively, as ancients did, hence from Friday through Sunday) is included in "according to the Scriptures," Paul may think of Hosea 6:2; Jonah 1:17; but his point may simply be that Jesus was raised before he could experience decay (Ps 16:10; cf 3 *En.* 28:10).

Paul summarizes the gospel he preached to them (15:1–2); it did not originate with him, for he "passed it on" and they "received" it (i.e., as a deposit of earlier tradition; see comment on 11:23). Arguing from features such as non-Pauline words and Aramaisms, some find here a pre-Pauline creed. Paul may have reworded the summary substantially, but certainly it depends at least on pre-Pauline information. Despite correspondences, his most striking omission from the reports in the Gospels is the absence of the women witnesses. Given the prejudice against women's testimony,[270] it is unlikely the Gospels would have invented this claim and culturally intelligible that Paul would have omitted it.

Like the OT narrative framework for salvation history, Paul recites divine acts, in this case, a central act: this involves first of all Jesus's death "for our sins" (presumably with the same meaning as in 8:11; Rom 5:6, 8; 14:15; 2 Cor 5:14–15; Gal 1:4; 1 Thess 5:10; cf. 1 Pet 3:18), hence as a sacrifice or substitute (cf. Heb 7:27; 10:12; Rom 4:25; 5:9–10; Gal 2:20). Paul must have believed he had grounds for this belief in the Jesus tradition itself (11:23–25; cf. Mk 10:45; 14:22–24). Second, and Paul's focus here, is Jesus's resurrection. Although Paul affirms a different sort of body (a glorious, celestial, perhaps angelic sort of body), the embodied character of the resurrection (as opposed to a mere Greek

---

[268] *Ant.* 18.14; *War* 2.163; 3.374; *Ag. Ap.* 2.218. He accommodates Palestinian resurrection ideas to Neo-Pythagorean reincarnation language more acceptable to his Hellenistic audience.

[269] See fuller discussion of ancient resurrection and afterlife conceptions in C. Keener, *John* (2003), 1167–78.

[270] For mistrust of women's testimony, see Josephus *Ant.* 4.219; Justinian *Inst.* 2.10.6 (although contrast the earlier Gaius); *Sipra Vayyiqra Dibura Dehobah* pq. 7.45.1.1.

afterlife in the underworld, an Elysian paradise or heaven) is critical for him (15:35–44). Although he focuses on resurrection witnesses rather than the empty tomb, factors point to a transformation of rather than decomposition of Jesus's body: the burial (15:4); the very meaning of "resurrection" for most Jews; and his further discussion (15:35–37, 51).[271] Mere visions of some ghost or angel (cf. e.g., 2 Macc 3:24–26) do not fit the Jewish sense of "resurrection," the resurrection's centrality in apostolic proclamation, or public opposition. Ghost visions were not controversial, and confirmed no eschatological threat.

Ancients often listed witnesses for divine "epiphanies," but records close to the era they depict most often involved dreams or deliverances, differing from the scale here. Paul recites six individuals or groups that received appearances (15:5–8): first, Cephas (cf. Lk 24:34), about whom Paul must have spoken at times (1:12; 3:22; 9:5; Gal 1:18; 2:9–14). The "twelve" was a title for Jesus's closest followers, which Jesus as leader of a renewal movement undoubtedly chose to evoke the biblical tribes of Israel (cf. 1QS 8.1–2). Despite the number, one would hardly expect the Gospel writers to have invented apostasy by one of the twelve (betrayal from an inner circle constituted an embarrassment in ancient society); numerical group titles were common, and often remained even when numbers fluctuated.[272] This would be especially the case when the original number carried special (for the Jesus movement, eschatological) significance. (Cf. also Jn 20:24, although more detailed narrators usually preferred the more precise "eleven" for this period; Matt 28:16; Mk 16:14; Lk 24:9, 33; Acts 1:26; 2:14.)

The claim that many of the over five hundred on one occasion remained alive probably constituted an invitation to consult them if one wished (and had funds for travel).[273] Because Paul mentions but does not introduce James (15:7), they likely know of him from the Gospel tradition (cf. Gal 1:19; 2:9, 12), hence perhaps that he was a skeptic (Mk 3:21, 31; Jn 7:5). "All the apostles" (15:7) is a wider group than the twelve (15:5), reflecting Paul's wide usage of the term (Rom 16:7; Gal 2:19; 1 Thess 1:1; 2:7; contrast Luke-Acts).

He again uses himself as an example (4:16; Ch. 9; 10:33–11:1), although in 15:8–10 he credits God's grace (which suited rhetorical conventions for self-praise in addition to Paul's biblical theology). Following the rhetorical convention of comparison, Paul deprecates himself (probably more sincerely than some rhetoricians who used self-deprecation to fish for compliments). Paul was last, as a persecutor (cf. also Gal 1:13; Phil 3:6), still abasing himself in contrast to

---

[271] See further W. L. Craig, "The Historicity of the Empty Tomb of Jesus," *NTS* 31 (1, 1985): 39–67.

[272] Cf. e.g., classical Athens' "eleven" (Xenophon *Hell.* 1.7.10; 2.3.54); "thirty" (Xenophon *Mem.* 4.4.3); and "5000" really controlled by "400" (Plutarch *Alcib.* 26.2; 27.1; cf. Thucydides 8.86.3–6; 8.92.11; 8.93.2); or Rome's "ten" (Suetonius *Aug.* 36) and "fifteen" (*Julius* 79.3); esp. "one hundred," with fluctuating numbers (Cicero *Agr.* 2.17.44; Statius *Silvae* 1.4.24).

[273] For appeals to public knowledge, cf., e.g., Josephus *Ag. Ap.* 1.50–52; *Life* 359–62; Cicero *Verr.* 1.5.15; 2.1.40.103.

the Corinthians (cf. "the apostles" as "last of all," 4:9).[274] Paul compares his out-of-season experience with a stillborn child (always used as a comparison in the LXX: Num 12:12;[275] Eccl 6:3; Job 3:16), likewise presumably born out of season (but here *post*-maturely). Ironically, this stillborn embraces resurrection.

Paul graphically emphasizes the reality of his claims. A mass hallucination of over five hundred persons simultaneously is difficult to sustain; Paul cites as witnesses respected church leaders who had suffered for their claims, plus himself (and probably James) as former skeptics. Yet for all the evidence he marshals, Paul is establishing something his audience does not really doubt (15:1–2, 11), as a shared premise to demonstrate what he wishes to persuade them, namely that Jesus's resurrection is a piece of, hence guarantees, the resurrection of God's people (15:12).

15:12–34: ESCHATOLOGICAL RESURRECTION OF BELIEVERS

15:12: Now if Christ is proclaimed as raised from the dead, how can some of you say there is no resurrection of the dead?

15:13: If there is no resurrection of the dead, then Christ has not been raised;

15:14: and if Christ has not been raised, then our proclamation has been in vain and your faith has been in vain.

15:15: We are even found to be misrepresenting God, because we testified of God that he raised Christ – whom he did not raise if it is true that the dead are not raised.

15:16: For if the dead are not raised, then Christ has not been raised.

15:17: If Christ has not been raised, your faith is futile and you are still in your sins.

15:18: Then those also who have died in Christ have perished.

15:19: If for this life only we have hoped in Christ, we are of all people most to be pitied.

15:20: But in fact Christ has been raised from the dead, the first fruits of those who have died.

15:21: For since death came through a human being, the resurrection of the dead has also come through a human being;

15:22: for as all die in Adam, so all will be made alive in Christ.

15:23: But each in his own order: Christ the first fruits, then at his coming those who belong to Christ.

---

[274] He does not claim to be the last apostle (cf. 1 Thess 1:1; 2:7) or to have had the final vision (2 Cor 12:1), but to be the final resurrection witness in the chain of appearances he lists (cf. 9:1).

[275] Cf. the use of Num 12:6–8 in 1 Cor 13:12; but the specific connection here is tenuous.

15:24: Then comes the end, when he hands over the kingdom to God the Father, after he has destroyed every ruler and every authority and power.

15:25: For he must reign until he has put all his enemies under his feet.

15:26: The last enemy to be destroyed is death.

15:27: For "God has put all things in subjection under his feet." But when it says, "All things are put in subjection," it is plain that this does not include the one who put all things in subjection under him.

15:28: When all things are subjected to him, then the Son himself will also be subjected to the one who put all things in subjection under him, so that God may be all in all.

15:29: Otherwise, what will those people do who receive baptism on behalf of the dead? If the dead are not raised at all, why are people baptized on their behalf?

15:30: And why are we putting ourselves in danger every hour?

15:31: I die every day! That is as certain, brothers and sisters, as my boasting of you – a boast that I make in Christ Jesus our Lord.

15:32: If with merely human hopes I fought with wild animals at Ephesus, what would I have gained by it? If the dead are not raised,

> "Let us eat and drink,
>   for tomorrow we die."

15:33: Do not be deceived:

> "Bad company ruins good morals."

15:34: Come to a sober and right mind, and sin no more; for some people have no knowledge of God. I say this to your shame.

*P*aul uses reductio ad absurdum: if there is no resurrection (i.e., of believers in the future), then Jesus did not rise (15:12–13), a point on which he dwells at length (15:12–19, where Paul provides rhetorical emphasis through a series of seven if-then statements).

First he develops the practical implications of denying the resurrection (the first two points introduced in 15:14): the apostles have misrepresented God (15:15), hence would be equivalent to false prophets; their faith in a dead Lord is useless and they are not forgiven (15:16–17; contrast 15:3); those who died with resurrection hope died with a false hope (15:18–19, an implication he develops in 15:29–34). Some other Jews also noted that life's vicissitudes would be bitter were there no justice in the hereafter (*2 Bar.* 21:12–13).

Before developing the absurdity of suffering for a Christian faith without a genuine resurrection (15:29–34), Paul explains how denial of their own bodily resurrection logically entailed denial of Christ's (15:20–28). Because they must agree that Jesus rose (15:1–11), he explains the Jewish eschatology of the corporate resurrection, apart from which Jesus's individual resurrection was unintelligible.

Jesus's resurrection was the "first fruits" (15:20, 23), a phrase that meant the actual beginning of the harvest (cf. 16:8; Ex 23:19; Lev 23:10; Jer 2:3), something like a first installment (16:15; Rom 8:23; cf. 2 Cor 5:5).

On the principle that the end recalled the beginning (many Jews envisioned a future paradise analogous to Eden), Paul balances death in Adam with resurrection in Christ (15:22). (Most Jewish people affirmed both that Adam introduced sin and death and that people made their own choices;[276] see further 15:45–49.)

Although nothing else in Paul points in this direction, some have seen an intermediate messianic kingdom in 15:23–24 (cf. 15:27–28), similar to Revelation 20:4–6 and some Jewish apocalypses (*4 Ezra* 7:28–30; *2 Bar.* 29:3; 30:1–5; 40:3). The grammar allows this interpretation ("then . . . then"), but it accounts less well for Paul's exegetical basis for his argument (see 15:25–26, in which the reign is fulfilled at believers' resurrection); the resurrection also may directly precede God's kingdom in 15:50 (cf. 6:9). Paul's eschatological scheme here depends on his interpretation of Ps 110:1, which becomes clear in 15:25. Because "the Lord" will reign at God's right hand until all enemies are subdued beneath his feet (Ps 110:1), Christ must reign at God's right hand in the present until his enemies are subdued (15:25).

Death is an enemy (in contrast to the views of some philosophers, for example, Epictetus *Diatr.* 1.27.7), and therefore must also be subdued, something which could happen only at the resurrection; and there are no conceivable enemies to be subdued afterward (15:26).[277] The only exception to "all things" being subjected under him would be God, the subjecter (15:27), because the context of his quotation (Ps 8:6) specifically exempts God (Ps 8:5). In 15:27, Paul quotes from LXX Ps 8:7 (ET Ps 8:6), which he links by *gezerah sheva* (i.e., connecting texts by keywords, here, "feet"; and probably the idea of reigning in Ps 8:6 and Ps 110:2). Psalm 8's "son of man" (Ps 8:4; NRSV: "mortals") who is "a little lower than God" (8:5; although the LXX familiar to Paul's audience reads "lower than angels," as in Heb 2:7) probably alludes to the first human's commission to rule (Gen 1:26–28, a text Paul elsewhere mines: 1 Cor 11:7–9). Thus, Paul is already (as in 15:22) preparing for his exposition of the contrast between the first and eschatological Adam (15:45–49), and the humankind implied in each.

Once his enemies were subjected (15:25; Ps 110:1–2), Christ's reign at God's right hand would be fulfilled, and Christ himself would be subject to God's rule (15:28). (Despite Paul's affirmation of Christ's preexistence in 8:6, he also affirmed the Son's ultimate functional subordination to the Father; cf. 3:23; 11:3.) "All in all" (15:28) is rhetorically emphatic (e.g., Eph 1:23; 4:6; Philo *Embassy* 118) and presumably means, "everything that matters" (cf. Col 3:11); given the context

---

[276] E.g., emphasizing Adam's role, *2 Bar.* 17:2–3; 23:4; 48:42–45; 56:5–6; *4 Ezra* 3:7, 20–22; 4:30; emphasizing his descendants' responsibility, *2 Bar.* 54:15, 19; *4 Ezra* 7:118–19.

[277] Paul could not have conceived of the popular North American doctrine of a resurrection of saints before the final antichrist and tribulation, an idea plainly contradicting 2 Thess 2:1–4 and other texts.

of subjection, Paul can hardly be affirming the sort of pantheism accepted by earlier Stoics. (Most Jews did not use such language pantheistically.)[278]

The Corinthians would be reticent to claim that their own members died with a false hope, a corollary (Paul argues) of denying the resurrection (15:18, 29); Paul's own suffering would likewise be worthless without the resurrection (15:19, 30–32). Scholars have propounded numerous explanations of 15:29, one of the most obscure verses in the NT, often blaming the custom on the Corinthians themselves. (It could reflect influence from pagan cults of the dead; but would Paul cite it without correction? Jews washed corpses after death, but that does not fit the language of this verse.) Some suggest a reference to baptism for catechumens who died before baptism; although early Christian baptism was probably normally immediate (e.g., Acts 22:16), some take it as less urgent in Corinth (1 Cor 1:14). Although we lack evidence for vicarious baptisms, one ancient text analogously allows prayer for the dead, which is unreasonable "If" (in so many words) "the dead are not raised" (2 Macc 12:43–45).[279] Another possibility is that Paul refers to people baptized in hope of the future resurrection, in view of their own impending death (i.e., in view of their bodies under the sentence of death, Rom 8:10), or to share eternal life with Christians who have already died. Probably Paul's theological shorthand here made clearer sense to the Corinthians than it does to us.

More clearly, Paul offers the example of his own sufferings for the gospel, which would be foolish if there were no resurrection (15:30–32). Hourly danger (15:30; cf. *4 Ezra* 7:89) and especially daily dying (15:31; cf. 2 Cor 1:9; Rom 8:36) are hyperbolic, perhaps reflecting the tradition of sharing Christ's cross (Mk 8:34; Lk 9:23); but they underline the point that the resurrection provides courage to face death. This suffering is the basis of Paul's boasting in them (cf. 9:15; Gal 6:13), the proof of his ministry (9:1–2; 2 Cor 3:2–3). (The Greek affirmation reads something like an oath formula, "by your boasting," as in Gen 42:15–16; cf. Jerusalem Bible: "I can swear it by the pride that I take in you"; similarly NEB.) Paul's struggle with "wild beasts" at Ephesus (15:32) is figurative, alluding to public entertainment in which low-class criminals and captives were killed by wild beasts in the arena (cf. 4:9; Josephus *Ant.* 14.210; Apuleius *Metam.* 10.29).[280] But those who fought literal beasts rarely lived to tell of it; human enemies could be compared with beasts (e.g., Ps 22:16; 74:19), and the irrational so appear regularly in philosophic literature.[281] The phrase *kata anthrōpon* (NRSV's "with

---

[278] Sir 43:27; 4Q266; although cf. Philo *Alleg. Interp.* 1.44.

[279] We lack Jewish precedent for vicarious baptism, but some allowed an act prevented by one's death, such as punishment to atone for sin, to be carried out posthumously (*m. 'Ed.* 5:6). Later Christian "heretics" practiced vicarious baptisms, perhaps based on this text.

[280] Early Christians condemned such contests (Athenagoras *Leg.* 35; Tertullian *Spect.*). Stoics claimed to accept them only when necessary (cf. Epictetus *Ench.* 33.10; Dio Cassius 71.29.3).

[281] E.g., Musonius Rufus 10, p. 78.27–28; 14, p. 92.21; Marcus Aurelius 4.16; cf. 2 Pet 2:12, 16, 22.

human hopes") may even mean "figuratively" (cf. 9:8; Rom 6:19; Gal 3:15); Paul means that he faces potentially deadly conflicts in Ephesus (1 Cor 16:8–9), perhaps of the sort later epitomized by Luke in Acts 19:23–40.

Facing such suffering would be useless apart from the resurrection; one should rather eat and drink (although inappropriate eating and drinking take on a special meaning in the context of this letter; 10:7; 11:22, 27!) Paul here quotes from Isaiah 22:13, the words of the wicked who neglected to humble themselves (Is 22:12) and will face judgment (Is 22:14; cf. Sir 14:16).[282] Epicureans, who denied an afterlife,[283] were caricaturized as addicted to pleasures of "food and drink"; Jews similarly characterized those who denied an afterlife (e.g., Wis 2:1–20; *1 En.* 102:6–8). Without considering its philosophic underpinnings, however, countless dinner parties embodied the ethic.

Ancient sages often emphasized the importance of securing morally edifying companions (e.g., Prov 13:20; 14:7; 28:7; Sir 13:1); the metrical quotation in verse 33 was probably a popular proverb, earliest attested in Menander's comedy *Thais* (who may have borrowed it from earlier usage, as some argue). Paul's use of the proverb seems to suggest that the church is being influenced by some people who lack knowledge of God (15:34), possibly false teachers (cf. 2 Cor 6:14; 10:12; 11:4–5, 12–15), but probably simply outsiders or syncretistic members of their own church. Paul has to shame them (as in 6:5; contrast 4:14; 11:2).

15:35–58: NATURE OF THE RESURRECTION

15:35: But someone will ask, "How are the dead raised? With what kind of body do they come?"

15:36: Fool! What you sow does not come to life unless it dies.

15:37: And as for what you sow, you do not sow the body that is to be, but a bare seed, perhaps of wheat or of some other grain.

15:38: But God gives it a body as he has chosen, and to each kind of seed its own body.

15:39: Not all flesh is alike, but there is one flesh for human beings, another for animals, another for birds, and another for fish.

15:40: There are both heavenly bodies and earthly bodies, but the glory of the heavenly is one thing, and that of the earthly is another.

15:41: There is one glory of the sun, and another glory of the moon, and another glory of the stars; indeed, star differs from star in glory.

15:42: So it is with the resurrection of the dead. What is sown is perishable, what is raised is imperishable.

---

[282] Ecclesiastes accepts "eating and drinking" (2:24; 3:12; 5:18–19), but not as an end in itself (7:2, 14; 11:7–12:14).

[283] E.g., Lucretius 3.417–977; Plutarch *Pleasant Life* 23, *Mor.* 1103D.

15:43: It is sown in dishonor, it is raised in glory. It is sown in weakness, it is raised in power.

15:44: It is sown a physical body, it is raised a spiritual body. If there is a physical body, there is also a spiritual body.

15:45: Thus it is written, "The first man, Adam, became a living being"; the last Adam became a life-giving spirit.

15:46: But it is not the spiritual that is first, but the physical, and then the spiritual.

15:47: The first man was from the earth, a man of dust; the second man is from heaven.

15:48: As was the man of dust, so are those who are of the dust; and as is the man of heaven, so are those who are of heaven.

15:49: Just as we have borne the image of the man of dust, we will also bear the image of the man of heaven.

15:50: What I am saying, brothers and sisters, is this: flesh and blood cannot inherit the kingdom of God, nor does the perishable inherit the imperishable.

15:51: Listen, I will tell you a mystery! We will not all die, but we will all be changed,

15:52: in a moment, in the twinkling of an eye, at the last trumpet. For the trumpet will sound, and the dead will be raised imperishable, and we will be changed.

15:53: For this perishable body must put on imperishability, and this mortal body must put on immortality.

15:54: When this perishable body puts on imperishability, and this mortal body puts on immortality, then the saying that is written will be fulfilled: "Death has been swallowed up in victory."

15:55: "Where, O death, is your victory?
Where, O death, is your sting?"

15:56: The sting of death is sin, and the power of sin is the law.

15:57: But thanks be to God, who gives us the victory through our Lord Jesus Christ.

15:58: Therefore, my beloved, be steadfast, immovable, always excelling in the work of the Lord, because you know that in the Lord your labor is not in vain.

I n 15:35, Paul raises an objection by means of an imaginary interlocutor (a common rhetorical device; cf. Rom 3:1–9): What kind of body can the dead have (especially if their bodies have decomposed)? This was a commonsense objection to the doctrine, and both later Jewish teachers[284] and early Christians (Athenagoras *Leg.* 4) had to answer objections to the resurrection. Paul responds, "Fool!" – a common insult to rhetorical (including imaginary) opponents (Matt 23:17).[285] He explains that the fruit does not look like the seed from whose death

---

[284] Cf. *b. Sanh.* 90b (using the seed analogy as Paul does); *Pesiq. Rab Kah.* 9:4; *Gen. Rab.* 28:3; *Lev. Rab.* 18:1. For those lost at sea, see *1 En.* 61:5; *Sib. Or.* 2.233.

[285] E.g., Epictetus *Diatr.* 2.16.13; 3.13.17; 3.22.85; Libanius *Declamations* 36.22; many examples in C. Keener, *Matthew* (1999), 185, 526. In eschatological condemnations, see Lk 12:20; *b. 'Abod. Zar.* 3a; *Ruth Rab.* 3:3.

it grew (15:36–37; cf. Jn 12:24; *1 Clem.* 24:5); a seed provides an apt analogy for a seminal and fuller life. Employing various rhetorical devices (including lingering, anaphora, and antithesis), Paul points out that God is able to create very different kinds of bodies, including heavenly bodies of glory (15:38–41); an immortal body is not like our current flesh. The present body provides a pattern, not the substance – although Paul expects whatever remains of it to be transformed (cf. 15:51), because what is sown is raised (15:42–44).

Thus, although Paul contends for a bodily resurrection, it is a body of glory rather than of flesh (15:43, 50; Phil 3:20–21), a particular kind of heavenly rather than any earthly sort of body, aptly compared to heavenly bodies like the stars.[286] (Paul might exegetically infer "heavenly" from the earthly dominion "under [the new humanity's] feet" in the texts in 15:25–27.) Paul expects the body to be changed (15:37, 51–52); this might differ from a common ancient view that the resurrection body would initially retain the wounds before death, then be healed, to prove identity with the previous body.[287]

Most pagans considered the stars (15:41) divine,[288] whereas Jews saw them as angels;[289] many believed that the stars were composed of fire (Varro *Latin Lang.* 5.10.59), as Jews often believed angels were (e.g., Heb 1:7; *1 En.* 17:1). Many Greco-Roman thinkers believed the heavens to be lighter and purer, the native realm of the divine soul (cf. 2 Cor 4:17–5:1). Even in Judea, some compared resurrection bodies to angels (cf. Mk 12:25; Acts 23:8; *2 Bar.* 51:10).[290] As early as Daniel 12:2–3, resurrection bodies might be compared with stars (cf. also *1 En.* 43:3); because most Jews viewed stars as angels, Paul may think of bodies analogous to those of angels.[291] (In a secondary way, he might also midrashically draw on the prophetic theme of eschatological glory for God's elect; e.g., Is 60:1–2, 19; 61:3; 62:2.)

Paul stirs emotion with rousing rhetoric; the four parallel contrasts in 15:42–44 reflect the rhetorical devices *anaphora* (x . . . x . . .) and antithesis. ("It is sown" develops the seed analogy of 15:36–38.) Greeks yearned for "immortality" (15:42; cf. 15:50, 53–54), but not of bodies; in contrast to Paul's usage here, even philosophically inclined Jews could attach "imperishable" to the soul at death (4 Macc 9:22; 17:12; Philo *QG* 1.75). Raised "in glory" echoes the heavenly bodies' "glory" (15:40–41; cf. 2:7; Phil 3:21), a glory that reflects God's own (2 Cor 3:7–18; 4:4–6) and contrasts with mortals' present humiliation (2 Cor 6:8). The

---

286 For different sorts of bodies in antiquity, see esp. D. Martin, *The Corinthian Body* (New Haven, CT: Yale, 1995), 117–29 (quite useful, even if his reduction of the body to material *pneuma* goes too far; see comment on *pneumatikos* in 15:44).

287 E.g., *2 Bar.* 49:2–50:4; *Gen. Rab.* 95:1; 100:2; cf. Jn 20:27; Lk 24:40 (if original).

288 For astral immortality, e.g., Cicero *Resp.* 6.26.29; Ovid *Metam.* 15.749, 875–76; Lucan 9.1–9.

289 Ps.-Phoc. 71, 75; Philo *Plant.* 12, 14; *Sipre Deut.* 47.2.3–5.

290 Perhaps also *1 En.* 51:5; 104:2–4; *2 En.* 22:8–10; Ps.-Phocyl. 104; *Pr. Jac.* 19.

291 Note also the Jewish (although perhaps Jewish Christian) inscriptions in Corinth portraying the dead as angels (see J. A. Wiseman, "The Gymnasium Area at Corinth 1969–70," *Hesperia* 41 [1972]: 1–42).

antithesis in 15:43 between present human weakness and God's power revealed fully in the end reinforces Paul's teaching to status-conscious Corinthians (2 Cor 12:5, 9; 13:4), as do his contrasts between dishonor and glory (15:43; cf. 12:23–24; 2 Cor 6:8).

Paul's depiction of a *psychikos* ("soulish") body (15:44) sounds startling in Greek (lost in the NRSV's "physical"), as does his *pneumatikos* ("spiritual") body. But Paul cannot mean bodies "made of soul" or "made of spirit": elsewhere in the letter he uses "spiritual" for "of the Spirit";[292] *-ikos* adjectives (as opposed to – *inos* adjectives) normally denote mode of existence rather than substance.

The Corinthians have heard these terms in 2:14–3:4, and recognize the contrast between humanity in the images of Adam (moved by a "soul") and Christ (moved by the Spirit). Knowing the creation story in the LXX (11:7–9), they recognize that, as Paul says explicitly in 15:45, the first Adam became by God's breath "a living *psyche*," "soul" or "person" (but cf. also Gen 2:19).[293] They may have used this text, interpreted through the lens of Greek thought, to justify their emphasis on the soul apart from the body. (Paul may have preferred to prove the resurrection from a Pentateuchal text, like Pharisees often did against Sadducees, even if its connection to resurrection was less than obvious; but Jewish midrashic exegesis naturally linked Gen 2:7 with resurrection by God's Spirit/breath in Ezekiel 37.[294] Paul offers what appears to be a clearer proof-text from the prophets in 15:54–55.)

Paul argues in 15:45–46 that the natural (i.e., the first Adam, a *psyche*) precedes the "spiritual" (i.e., the second Adam energized by and energizing with the Spirit). Paul may reason that the Spirit characterizes the end-time (2:9–10; Rom 8:23) and raises bodies (Rom 8:10–13); no one who affirms resurrection would dispute that mortal bodies precede resurrection bodies. Yet this reverses the expectation in Philo (and perhaps some other Diaspora Jews), for whom the "heavenly" man of Gen 1:26–27 (connected with the Logos, *Conf.* 41, 146) was first, and the "living soul" of Gen 2 came afterward (*Alleg. Int.* 1.31–32; 2.4–5). Some think that Paul identifies Jesus with the Spirit on the level of Christian experience (one interpretation of 2 Cor 3:17); Paul may compare Jesus with God's life-giving breath in Genesis.

As Paul offered rhetorical contrasts in 15:42–43, so he contrasts Adam and those who bear his image with the second man and those who bear his in 15:47–49, which provides the theological rationale for the previous contrasts. Those in the image of the old Adam are earthly; those in the image of Christ are heavenly (the ancient principle of like begets like, Jn 3:6, 12–13; Col 3:1–5). Some Jews spoke

---

[292] For the resurrection body ruled by the Spirit, cf., e.g., Chrysostom *Hom. Cor.* 41.5; Augustine *Faith and Creed* 6.13; *Against Julian* 70 (although patristic views varied).

[293] God's breath in 2:7 could be rendered *pneuma*, but is not so rendered in the LXX.

[294] E.g., *Gen. Rab.* 14:8; J. A. Grassi, "Ezekiel xxxvii.1–14 and the New Testament," *NTS* 11 (1965): 162–64, esp. 164. For rabbinic resurrection exegesis, see, e.g., *Sipre Deut.* 306.28.3; 329.2.1.

of God stamping his image on people or all creation by his Wisdom or Logos, his perfect image (Philo *Creation* 16, 26, 36; cf. 2 Cor 4:4); some also emphasized the first man as God's image (11:7; Gen 1:26; Wis 2:23) to stamp on his successors (*m. Sanh.* 4:5). Although Paul responds to ideas current in Diaspora Judaism, Adam speculation was already part of Paul's Judean heritage as well;[295] Jewish sources comment on Adam's primeval glory, size, and abilities (although the most extreme of these are after Paul's era).[296] Adam introduced death (*2 Bar.* 23:4; 48:42–43); but for Paul, the new Adam inaugurates the life of a new creation (2 Cor 5:17). Members of Christ's body (12:12) belong to the new Adam, and will share his glory individually as well as corporately (cf. Rom 5:12–21).

Only those in the image of the heavenly Adam could inherit God's kingdom, thus mortals must be transformed (15:50–54). This clarifies the logic of Paul's transition from 15:41–49 to 15:50–54: if God's kingdom is heavenly, only heavenly bodies (15:40–41, 47–49) can inherit it (on "inheriting" the kingdom, cf. 6:10); and what was heavenly was considered imperishable and eternal (2 Cor 4:18). "Flesh and blood" was a familiar idiom for humans or human bodies,[297] which could not endure heavenly life. Thus he explains a "mystery" (a concept that must have interested the Corinthians, 2:7; 4:1; 13:2; 14:2; cf. "end-time" mysteries in Dan 2:28–30, 47): some would be transformed even while alive (15:51), instantly (the sense of blinking; cf. *T. Ab.* 4:5 A), at the "last trumpet" (15:52).[298] Given the collocation of trumpet and shout in 1 Thessalonians 4:16, the resurrection might be envisioned as at a final battle (cf. *4 Ezra* 6:23–25); trumpets also connoted gatherings (including in Jewish prayers and expectations for the end-time; cf. Is 27:13). Given the cluster of motifs echoing Jesus tradition in 1 Thessalonians 4:15–5:7 the trumpet may recall Jesus tradition about a final gathering after a period of tribulation (Matt 24:29–31).[299] Whether the trumpet connotes gathering or war or both, the description of "last" seems apt; the final enemy is subdued (15:26), and the "last" Adam has come (15:45; Paul's undisputed writings employ the term elsewhere only in 4:9; 15:8). This resurrection thus immediately precedes God's kingdom (15:50), as in 15:23–24.

In 15:53–54, Paul continues his use of rhetorical antithesis, specifically his contrast between "perishable" and "imperishable" (15:42, 50); others also used

---

[295] See W. D. Davies, *Paul and Rabbinic Judaism: Some Rabbinic Elements in Pauline Theology*, 4th ed. (Philadelphia: Fortress Press, 1980), 36–57; R. Scroggs, *The Last Adam: A Study in Pauline Anthropology* (Philadelphia: Fortress, 1966), 18–58; S. Hultgren, "The Origin of Paul's Doctrine of the Two Adams in 1 Corinthians 15.45–49," *JSNT* 25 (2003): 343–70.

[296] E.g., Philo *On Creation* 136; *Sib. Or.* 1.24; later, e.g., *b. Sanh.* 38b; *Hag.* 12a; esp. *Gen. Rab.* loc. cit.

[297] E.g., Wis 12:5; Sir 14:18; 17:31; *T. Ab.* 13:7 B; in Semitic texts, *1 En.* 15:4; *Mekilta Pisha* 1.120 and often in the rabbis.

[298] Cf. transformation into fiery bodies through the vision of God in *1 En.* 71:11; *3 En.* 15:1; on such vision, see comment on 2 Cor 3:18.

[299] See the arguments and supporting ancient sources for both suggestions in C. Keener, *Matthew* (1999), 565–66, 586–88.

the clothing metaphor ("put on") (see comment on 2 Cor 5:4). He also makes homiletic adaptations in his quotations to build to a rhetorical crescendo in 15:57; even in English translation, his recitation of triumph over death (15:25–26, 42–57) is stirring. As in 15:45, so in 15:54–55 he offers supporting texts for the resurrection, here blending Isaiah 25:7–8 with Hosea 13:14. In 15:54 Paul adapts the wording of Isaiah 25:8, "He will swallow death forever," to "death is swallowed *in victory*," a form preserved in some other Jewish translation traditions.[300] (Jewish interpreters commonly chose whatever textual tradition proved most suitable.) "Victory" recalls God subjugating Christ's enemies (15:25), especially the conquest of death as the "last enemy" (15:26); it also prepares for Paul's adaptation of Hosea 13:14 (15:55) and for his rousing application in 15:57. (Paul links the Isaiah and Hosea passages based on the keyword "death" and the resurrection concept, as well as by linkage of "victory" in his own paraphrase.)[301] This context naturally lent itself to a resurrection interpretation (Is 26:19) and remained fertile for early Christian interpreters; the same verse stands behind 2 Cor 5:4 (cf. the next line in Rev 7:17; 21:4; perhaps Is 25:6 in Rev 19:9).

In 15:55 Paul assumes the LXX indicative (promise) reading of the lines preceding his Hosea quote ("from the hand of Hades I will deliver them and from death I will redeem them"). Although the immediate context in Hebrew could be construed more negatively (as judgment on Israel), in light of God's promise of their restoration (Hos 14:4–7) a Jewish exegete might well infer this reversed interpretation. Paul naturally changes LXX *hades* to "death" (with which it is parallel). What appears most striking is Paul's transformation of the LXX's "punishment" ("Where, O death, is your punishment, *dikē*?") into "victory" (*nikē*) as another link with his Isaiah quotation; such wordplays were common in midrash (rabbis especially changed vocalization, since the Hebrew text lacked vowels).[302] The Corinthians may have known Paul's fuller connection among the law, sin, and death (15:56; see Rom 5:12–13; 6:13–15; 7:5–8:3);[303] the connection here between moral knowledge and death might recall Paul's comments about Adam (15:45–49; cf. Rom 5:12–14; Gen 2:17). Paul also may have connected death's punishment in Hosea 13:14 with Israel's "sin" in Hosea 13:12.

Paul concludes his argument by noting that God gives the victory to Christians, not to death (15:57; cf. 15:54–55); the last enemy will be subdued (15:26). "Thanks be to God" is familiar Pauline idiom (Rom 6:17; 2 Cor 8:16; 9:15), especially when commenting on his acts in Christ (Rom 7:25; 2 Cor 2:14).

---

[300] This reading appears in Theodotion (cf. closely also Aquila), who would not have borrowed it from Paul; the LXX ("strong") apparently construed the Hebrew "forever" based on an Aramaic cognate.

[301] Rabbis often linked texts based on a common key word (*gezerah sheva*); Greeks sometimes used the method as well.

[302] Once the LXX renders MT's "forever" as *nikē* (2 Sam 2:26), as Paul does here with the same Hebrew term in Is 25:8 MT; does this one LXX rendering provide Paul midrashic license here?

[303] Perhaps "power" (15:56) alludes back to "victory" (15:55).

Some contend that 15:58 concludes the entire argument of the body of Paul's letter; yet 1 Corinthians, for all its thematic unity, is not a unified argument and does not fit the usual outline of a speech. Still, Paul spoke publicly often enough to be sensitive to the importance of (sometimes summarizing) rhetorical conclusions, whether for sections of a work (as in 14:40; perhaps 6:20; 10:31–11:1; 11:33–34; and probably here) or for the body of a work itself (Rom 16:17, 25–26). His exhortation to remain steadfast and not to be moved (cf. Col 1:23) might recall the foundation metaphor (1 Cor 3:10–12; cf. Col 1:23) or the repeated "building" metaphor (3:9; 8:1, 10; 10:23; 14:3–5, 12, 17, 26). "The Lord's work" might allude to any labor for Christ (3:13–15; 9:1; 16:10; so also "labor" in 3:8). Like Paul (15:10), their labor is not in vain (15:58). Eschatology has moral implications (6:13–14; 15:30–32, 58).

BRIDGING THE HORIZONS

Some of Paul's arguments appear opaque to modern readers, such as his rationale for head coverings in 11:3–16 or his argument for the character of the resurrection body in 15:40–41. That Paul constructed these arguments to work for the Corinthians rather than in today's intellectual milieu should go without saying, although popular interpreters typically ignore this caution when approaching texts of less obvious difficulty.

Paul's analogy between resurrection bodies and bodies in the purer heavens fits ancient cosmology but is unintelligible in terms of modern astronomy. The basic point of his analogy, however, is that God is able to create various kinds of bodies; today we might appeal to quarks and dark matter, although we lack any notion of a pure spiritual location physically above us to confirm the analogy. With or without analogies, an imperishable body, not subject to decay or entropy, would have to be substantially different from our present bodies. Yet Paul insists on the Jewish notion of bodily life (as opposed to the common Greek philosophical goal of disembodiment). God's creation is good (Gen 1:31); it may be transformed, but it will not ultimately be abandoned. This emphasis on embodiment challenges the Neoplatonic spirituality that persisted in Gnosticism, some medieval theology, and some spirituality today. For Paul, what we do with our body matters because it bears some connection with a bodily future in a real (transformed) cosmos (2 Cor 5:10, 17).

16:1–12: PLANS AND INSTRUCTIONS

16:1: Now concerning the collection for the saints: you should follow the directions I gave to the churches of Galatia.
16:2: On the first day of every week, each of you is to put aside and save whatever extra you earn, so that collections need not be taken when I come.

16:3: And when I arrive, I will send any whom you approve with letters to take your gift to Jerusalem.

16:4: If it seems advisable that I should go also, they will accompany me.

16:5: I will visit you after passing through Macedonia – for I intend to pass through Macedonia –

16:6: and perhaps I will stay with you or even spend the winter, so that you may send me on my way, wherever I go.

16:7: I do not want to see you now just in passing, for I hope to spend some time with you, if the Lord permits.

16:8: But I will stay in Ephesus until Pentecost,

16:9: for a wide door for effective work has opened to me, and there are many adversaries.

16:10: If Timothy comes, see that he has nothing to fear among you, for he is doing the work of the Lord just as I am;

16:11: therefore let no one despise him. Send him on his way in peace, so that he may come to me; for I am expecting him with the brothers.

16:12: Now concerning our brother Apollos, I strongly urged him to visit you with the other brothers, but he was not at all willing to come now. He will come when he has the opportunity.

*M*ost ancient letters were brief, and a large number were business-related. Whereas most of Paul's correspondence more closely resembles philosophers' letters discoursing on moral topics, he is ready to address business as well. Here he addresses the collection, about which they already have some knowledge (as do we, from Paul's other letters), and his travel plans. "Now concerning the collection" provides a subject heading, such as many preferred when transitioning from one topic to another (Menander Rhetor 2.1–2, 372.14–18), especially if the subject is very important (372.19–20). Paul clearly wants the collection to cover all his churches (cf. Rom 15:26); Paul is working in Ephesus (1 Cor 16:8), but has recruited even the churches of Galatia (16:1; cf. Gal 2:10).

"Whatever extra you earn" (16:2) is literally, "if one should prosper," probably reflecting the principle of giving from abundance in Deuteronomy 15:14; 16:10, 17. The funds are voluntary, unlike most associations' membership dues (cf. Sir 14:13; Justin *1 Apol.* 67). That the believers set aside resources on the first day of each week (16:2) may suggest Sunday services (cf. Acts 20:7) or a connection with the resurrection (Mk 16:2), but need not do so. It might instead emphasize setting aside the Lord's offering first (cf. Ex 23:16; Lev 27:26), because most working believers worked and earned money daily, excepting Jewish believers on the Sabbath; believers had to meet in the evenings (cf. 11:23; *deipnon* in 11:20–21) or early morning, before work (Pliny *Ep.* 10.96). (Certainly the idea of Sunday as a "new Sabbath" is a later development; cf. Ignatius *Magn.* 9.1; *Barn.* 15.8.)

Paul wishes to take representatives from the local churches (16:3; cf. Acts 20:4) to guard the offering from false accusations (2 Cor 8:17–23); the letters (1 Cor 16:3) probably commend the bearers (cf. 2 Cor 3:1), hence further underline the operation's integrity (see "A Closer Look: Letters of Recommendation," at 2 Cor 3:1–3).

Paul planned to come to them through Macedonia (16:5; cf. Acts 19:21), though it appears that he later delayed his visit to Corinth because of their attitudes (2 Cor 1:15–23).[304] In most Western cultures, 16:6 sounds presumptuous, but in ancient Mediterranean culture the Corinthians would have counted it an honor to shower Paul with hospitality and send him off, that is, providing the expenses for his next journey (Rom 15:24). Travel was difficult and often dangerous during winter, especially by sea (cf. Acts 27:9; 2 Tim 4:21; Tit 3:12),[305] so Paul would need extended hospitality wherever he stayed during that season; and he preferred to spend that time with his friends in Corinth (16:7). The desire to spend time with someone was a familiar, if generally heartfelt, theme in ancient letters.[306] "If the Lord permits" (cf. 4:19) was a common turn of phrase among not only Stoics (Epictetus *Diatr.* 1.1.17) but many others.[307]

Because Paul writes before Pentecost (16:8), however, he is thinking of the following winter; if he writes in the weeks before Pentecost, it is not surprising that Passover (5:7) and first fruits (cf. 15:20; Ex 34:22; Num 28:26) are on his mind. Like Paul in 16:9, Luke emphasizes Paul's effective ministry in Ephesus (Acts 19:8–20) and summarizes opposition there (focusing in 19:23–41 on a subsequent dramatic scene that probably left Paul something of an embarrassment to his former patrons there; 19:31; 20:16). (Others used an "open door" as an expression for opportunity.)[308]

Paul sends Timothy as his own agent (16:10–11; cf. 4:17; Acts 19:22); one should receive an agent the way one would receive the sender (Mk 9:37; *m. Ber.* 5:5). Sending "him on his way in peace" also implies that they have received him well (Gen 26:29, 31; 2 Sam 3:21–23), as well as provided for his journey (cf. 16:6). It probably ultimately reflects the Hebrew idiom, "Go in peace" (Ex 4:18; Judg 18:6). Paul also demonstrates in 16:12 that he and Apollos work together, despite the conflicts among their followers (1:12; 3:4). (Sometimes leading figures were friends, despite popular perceptions that they were rivals; cf., for example, Cicero *Brut.* 1.2–3).

---

304 For plans to visit in Paul's letters, see, e.g., R. W. Funk, "The Apostolic Parousia: Form and Significance," 249–68 in *Christian History and Interpretation*, ed. W. R. Farmer et al. (Cambridge: Cambridge University, 1967).

305 See further documentation in C. Keener, *John* (2003), 823–24.

306 E.g., Cicero *Att.* 2.18; 12.3; *Fam.* 1.9.1; 7.15.1; 8.15.2; 15.20.2; 16.1.1; Rom 1:11; 1 Thess 3:6.

307 E.g., Homer *Il.* 8.142; Xenophon *Hell.* 2.4.17; 5.1.14; Josephus *Ant.* 2.333; 7.373; 20.267; Fronto *Ad M. Caes.* 3.11, 20.

308 E.g., Col 4:3; Rev 3:8; Epictetus's use for escape from life by suicide (*Diatr.* 1.9.20; 1.25.21; 2.1.19).

A CLOSER LOOK: PAUL'S COLLECTION

Paul promised that his Gentile mission would not lead him to neglect the poor in Jerusalem (Gal 2:10); some have argued that "the poor" was a pious title for the Jerusalem church (Rom 15:26; cf. later Ebionites), comparable to the use of some Jewish pietists.[309] Paul probably used the collection to establish unity between Jewish and Gentile Christians, a tangible offering of reconciliation that he hoped that even the more conservative elements in the Jerusalem church would recognize (Rom 15:25, 31). Some have compared the annual half-shekel tax Diaspora Jews paid for the upkeep of the temple, demonstrating their continued unity with Jerusalem; sending funds to Jerusalem was a recognized right before A.D. 70 (Josephus *Ant.* 16.171), but it generated Gentiles' scorn (Tacitus *Hist.* 5.5). Some also compare as background biblical passages about the nations bringing their offerings to Jerusalem (Is 60:5, 11–12; 61:6; 66:12).[310] Either or both of these patterns would have helped Paul's case for unity with the Jerusalem church, whose leaders accepted his mission with this condition (Gal 2:9–10). Perhaps Paul also hoped to make his people jealous, hence interested, partly through this collection (Rom 10:19; 11:11, 14; cf. Acts 24:17).

The Corinthian correspondence does not emphasize the Jewish-Gentile issue as much, because these concerns are less central in the Corinthian correspondence than in Romans and Galatians. For Corinth's famous wealth, see the introduction. Sacrificial sharing of one's goods with others in times of need was praiseworthy (e.g., Valerius Maximus 4.8).[311] Because Luke (Acts 24:17) and Paul's later letters make little of the collection, some think that it was not welcomed by the Jerusalem church. Others argue (perhaps more likely) that it simply did not achieve the grand goal Paul intended for it.

BRIDGING THE HORIZONS

Many conservative churches today raise funds by insisting that "tithes" must support the local church. But although ancient Israel's means of supporting clergy undoubtedly offers instructive principles for today's churches, translating from one cultural framework to another requires attentiveness. The "tithe" on

---

[309] 1QM 11.9–14; 1QpHab 12.3–10; 4QpPs 37, 1.2.10–11.

[310] For Jewish-Gentile unity, see K. F. Nickle, *The Collection: A Study in Biblical Theology*, SBT 48 (Naperville, IL: Allenson, 1966), 111–29; for the eschatological conversion or tribute of the nations, ibid., 129–42; for Jewish analogies, esp. the temple tax, see ibid., 74–99 (esp. 87–89). For eschatological pilgrims, see also T. L. Donaldson, *Paul and the Gentiles: Remapping the Apostle's Convictional World* (Minneapolis: Fortress, 1997), 69–74; on the temple tax, see S. Safrai, "Relations between the Diaspora and the Land of Israel," 184–215 in *JPFC*, 188–91.

[311] For ancient views on possessions and property, see the ancient sources in C. Keener, *Matthew* (1999), 229–30; M. Hengel, *Property and Riches in the Early Church: Aspects of Social History of Early Christianity* (Philadelphia: Fortress Press, 1974).

agrarian produce resembled royal taxes (also tithes) in surrounding cultures, and was only one of a large number of offerings required (such as the firstborn of livestock).

Early Christian references to tithing are rare and usually backward-looking (Matt 23:23; Lk 11:42; Heb 7:5–9). Apostolic teaching on possessions is in fact much more demanding than a tithe; the Gospels demand complete sacrifice, arguing that Jesus's followers should live like people matter more than possessions (esp. Luke-Acts, Lk 12:33; 14:33; Acts 2:44–45).[312] Paul's pastoral expectations apparently reinforce such ideals more pragmatically, but "if one prospers" (16:2) suggests an analogous approach. To the extent that God provides more than what one needs to live on (cf. Lk 3:11), it may be an opportunity to be God's conduit of supply to those who have less (2 Cor 8:13–15).

Wesley understood NT stewardship as care for the poor, and deliberately lived a simple life.[313] Many leaders of reform movements, whether Orthodox (like St. Anthony), Catholic (like St. Francis), or Protestant (like the Waldensians or Wycliffe's Lollards) embraced apostolic poverty, sowing their resources into care for the poor or for carrying out their mission. Many Christians today are more interested in competing with neighbors' status symbols than in caring for the poor. Contextualizing the gospel for one's culture is essential, but much of the Western church has capitulated to, rather than merely translated the gospel for, its materialistic culture.

16:13–24: CONCLUSION

16:13: Keep alert, stand firm in your faith, be courageous, be strong.

16:14: Let all that you do be done in love.

16:15: Now, brothers and sisters, you know that members of the household of Stephanas were the first converts in Achaia, and they have devoted themselves to the service of the saints;

16:16: I urge you to put yourselves at the service of such people, and of everyone who works and toils with them.

16:17: I rejoice at the coming of Stephanas and Fortunatus and Achaicus, because they have made up for your absence;

16:18: for they refreshed my spirit as well as yours. So give recognition to such persons.

16:19: The churches of Asia send greetings. Aquila and Prisca, together with the church in their house, greet you warmly in the Lord.

---

[312] For sources concerning ancient ideals, see, e.g., C. Keener, *Matthew* (1999), 229–30.

[313] See T. W. Jennings, Jr., *Good News to the Poor: John Wesley's Evangelical Economics* (Nashville: Abingdon, 1990).

16:20: All the brothers and sisters send greetings. Greet one another with a holy kiss.

16:21: I, Paul, write this greeting with my own hand.

16:22: Let anyone be accursed who has no love for the Lord. Our Lord, come!

16:23: The grace of the Lord Jesus be with you.

16:24: My love be with all of you in Christ Jesus.

S ome view 16:13–14 (or 16:13–18) as equivalent to a speech's rousing *peroratio*. Whether or not this is the case, it is noteworthy that skilled speakers liked to sum up their topic at its conclusion (Cicero *Or. Brut.* 40.137), a practice that would be relevant to many moralist letters whether or not they followed rhetorical structures (most do not). As a closing exhortation, 16:13–14 is strategic in understanding the letter. Although few of its words repeat earlier exhortations, they do summarize the response expected to them. "Keep alert" is common in paranetic contexts, sometimes with an eschatological coloring (1 Thess 5:6; cf. Rom 13:11; Mk 13:34–37); so also "stand firm" (Gal 5:1; Phil 4:1; 1 Thess 3:8). Although ancients could connect "be courageous" (*andrizesthe*) with maturity (13:11) or with avoiding effeminacy (6:9), the standard sense of the term (even when applied to women) is courage. In the LXX, this call to "take courage" is often paired with the call to be strong, including with the term used here (2 Sam 10:12; Ps 26:14 [ET 27:14]; 30:25 [ET 31:24]; more often with *ischuō*).[314] Paul provides a rousing call appropriate to a military audience: stand guard, do not retreat, be strong and courageous (16:13). The final component of this exhortation, however, relates directly to the Corinthian situation: he calls them to love (16:14; cf. ch. 13).

Paul's brief "letter of recommendation" (see "A Closer Look" at 2 Cor 3:1–3) for leaders he trusts (16:15–18) probably seeks to help unify the church. Because all but government mail in antiquity was carried by travelers (sometimes in the course of their other business),[315] presumably this letter is carried either by these visitors or by Timothy (16:10–11; cf. the probable epistolary aorist in 4:17). "First converts in Achaia" (16:15) is literally "first fruits," not only because Pentecost is on Paul's mind (16:8) but perhaps originally as a faith prospect for a greater harvest (Rom 16:5) and because "first fruits" are holy, devoted to the Lord (Rom 11:16; Sir 7:31; *Did.* 13.3–7). (It is possible that many first converts also achieved leadership in Pauline churches; *1 Clem.* 42.4.) Paul's particular wording in 16:17 might imply not only making up for the Corinthians' absence (so NRSV; cf. 5:3–4) but also for their obligation to his ministry (cf. *husterēma* in Phil 2:30; cf. 2 Cor 8:14; 9:12; 11:9); although Paul apparently stirs controversy by refusing to be the Corinthian church's "client" (9:3–4; 2 Cor 11:7–10; 12:13–15), he does not

---

314 In the MT, see esp. 1 Sam 4:9, a military exhortation to Philistines, whose original cultural sphere was more Greek than Semitic.

315 E.g., Cicero *Att.* 8.14; *Fam.* 1.7.1; 2.1.1; 5.5.1; Diogenes *Ep.* 6.

reject their gifts. "Refreshing" someone's "heart" or "spirit" (16:18) probably also suggests some provision (2 Cor 7:13; Phlm 7, 20). Paul's desire that they receive "recognition" (16:18) fits his concern for others who traveled long distances to supply his needs (Phil 2:29–30). Like ancient hospitality, the expectation that teachers be honored is foreign to modern Western culture but remains alive in many cultures today.

Letters often closed with secondary greetings from others who knew the author was writing (16:19–20; cf. Rom 16:21–23; 2 Cor 13:12; Phil 4:21–22; Col 4:10–14),[316] reflecting a custom of respectful acknowledgment preserved in many cultures today (more often than in the West).[317] The Corinthian church apparently knew Prisca and Aquila (16:19) from their ministry in Corinth (cf. Acts 18:1–3), before they left (like Paul) for Ephesus (cf. Acts 18:18–19, 26), and later preceded him to Rome (Rom 16:3–5), where they had lived before (cf. Acts 18:2). Like patronal banquets, cult associations, and some less endowed synagogues, the earliest churches met in homes (Acts 2:46; 5:42; 12:12; 18:17; 20:20; Rom 16:5; Col 4:15; Phlm 2).[318] This was convenient, economic, and, given restrictions on unregistered associations, eventually a matter of safety.

Paul sometimes sends greetings to particular recipients (Rom 16:1–16; Col 4:15–17; Phlm 2), and as in 16:20 often encourages greeting one another with a holy kiss (Rom 16:16; 2 Cor 13:12; 1 Thess 5:26; cf. 1 Pet 5:14). Light kisses, typically on the lips, were used as affectionate greetings among relatives and others who were close; they were distinguishable in kind from erotic kisses. (Still, cross-gender kissing could be abused [cf. Suetonius *Tib.* 34.2], and later Christians had to establish boundaries when this problem arose.)[319] This was a natural way to express affection for one's Christian "brothers and sisters" in first-century eastern Mediterranean culture, although Christians today in many cultures (especially those that reserve kissing for erotic settings, in contrast to say, Russian or French cultures) prefer to express sibling affection differently (e.g., often light embraces in many churches in the United States). In greetings, a reader might convey the writer's kiss to another on behalf of the writer.[320]

Paul often used an amanuensis (Rom 16:22; the poor often used scribes because they could not write; the wealthy dictated to scribes because they could afford to). Thus he often closed letters by adding his signature (Gal 6:11; Col 4:18; 2 Thess 3:17; cf. Phlm 19), as here (16:21). Writing a letter (or in this case a part of it) in one's own hand conveyed affection (e.g., Fronto *Ad M. Caes.* 3.3). Affirming

---

[316] See, e.g., Cicero *Att.* 5.9; Fronto *Ad M. Caes.* 3.8.3; 3.12; 4.10.
[317] On ancient letter-closing conventions, see J. A. D. Weima, *Neglected Endings: The Significance of the Pauline Letter Closings* (JSNTS 101; Sheffield: JSOT, 1994), 28–56.
[318] See at length B. Blue, "Acts and the House Church," 119–222 in *Greco-Roman Setting*, ed. D. W. J. Gill and C. Gempf, vol. 2 in BAFCS (Grand Rapids, MI: Eerdmans; Carlisle: Paternoster, 1994).
[319] See documentation for the ancient custom in C. Keener, "Kiss, Kissing," 628–29 in *DNTB*.
[320] Fronto *Ad M. Caes.* 1.8.7; 5.33 (48); 5.42 (57).

again love for the Lord (cf. 2:9; 8:3) in 16:22, he pronounces a curse (*anathema*) on those who do not love him (see 12:3; cf. Rom 9:3; Gal 1:8–9). *Anathema* is an Aramaic term reflecting the church's Jewish background (found eighteen times in the LXX). Paul adds another Aramaic expression in the verse, which reflects the prayer life of the early church (cf. similarly *Abba* in Rom 8:15; Gal 4:6). *Marana tha* (probably echoed *Did.* 10.6) is probably best translated "Our Lord, come" (with the NRSV; cf. Rev 22:10), reflecting eschatological anticipation (a fitting climax to this letter, 1:7–8; 2:9; 3:13–15; 4:5; 5:5; 6:2–3; 7:29–30; 11:26; 13:8–12; Ch. 15). It also very likely suggests that Jesus was already identified as "Lord" in the earliest Aramaic-speaking Jerusalem church (much less likely originating in Antioch), before the spread of the movement among Greek speakers there. He offers a closing "wish-prayer" about God's grace (16:23; cf. Rom 16:20; 2 Cor 13:13; Col 4:18; 1 Thess 5:28; 2 Thess 3:18; see comment on 1:3); and reminds them of his love (16:24; cf. 2 Cor 12:15).

IV. Introduction to 2 Corinthians

GENRE

No one disputes that 2 Corinthians is a letter. More specifically, many also view it (or some of its constituent parts) as an apologetic letter. Such letters often open by listing charges to be refuted, but (as in 2 Corinthians) they can allude to these charges later. Technically, our letter may not fit the precise contours laid out for such letters in later handbooks; but such handbooks did not dictate practice even in their own day, much less Paul's. Much of Paul's letter is indisputably apologetic in character.

Although Paul disclaims the need for letters of recommendation (3:1), some argue plausibly that this letter, or part of it, is an apologetic letter of self-commendation. Because Paul parodies and inverts the values of his opponents, some even view the letter (or part of it) as a parody of apologetic; but Paul may simply offer apologetic based on different values than the Corinthians hold.

We treat the major questions of situation, opponents, and partition below, reserving other comments for the texts in 2 Corinthians that raise them.

THE SITUATION IN 2 CORINTHIANS

For general background on Corinth and its churches, see the introduction to 1 Corinthians. The specific situation has advanced beyond that described in 1 Corinthians, but exact reconstructions of it vary, not least according to the number and sequence of component letters reconstructed in 2 Corinthians. Even viewing the letter as a unity written sequentially, as a growing minority of scholars do, leaves questions about the exact reconstruction of the situation.

Although there is obviously a non-Pauline faction in the church in 1 Corinthians (1:12; 3:4–5), no clear opponents had yet emerged. Apollos is an ally (16:12), and those leading the members astray (15:33) may not claim to be Christians. Some are evaluating Paul negatively because of his rhetoric (2:1, 14) and refusal to accept their patronage (9:3, 15); but it is only after Jewish Christian outsiders other than Apollos (2 Cor 10:12, 18; 11:5, 12–15, 18–23) provide a competing model for apostleship that rhetoric (2 Cor 10:9–11; 11:6) and refusal to accept patronage (2 Cor 11:7–11; 12:13–15) become part of a major power struggle. Even here, however, Paul quickly turns from addressing the outsiders to addressing the Corinthian believers themselves (12:19–13:10).

Paul addresses opposition more subtly earlier in the letter, as in 1 Corinthians (and accepted rhetorical practice for controversial matters) reserving the harshest confrontation for later. Still, Paul's defense of his ministry earlier in 2 Corinthians (2:17–3:1; 4:1–2; 5:11–12; 5:20–6:13; 7:2–3) is clearly more than mere apologetic convention (perhaps in contrast to 1 Thess 2:3–12).[1] He already criticizes those who speak God's word for funds (2:17). Those alienating the Corinthians from Paul (6:13; 7:2) are probably called or compared with unbelievers (6:14). Paul's competitors likely boast letters of recommendation (3:1), and engage in self-commendation (5:12), an issue he challenges more directly later. They also may claim the authority of Moses's law (as suggested, but not required, by the antitheses in 3:7–11), as only "Hebrews" (11:22; cf. Phil 3:5) could easily do. At least some of the Corinthians seem to accept these teachers (3:1), and certainly some are criticizing Paul.[2] This may jeopardize the collection (Chs. 8–9).

It seems likely that Paul was soon reconciled with the Corinthians, given the evidence that he chose to winter with them (Acts 20:3, 6) and sent his letter to the Romans from this Roman colony (cf. Rom 15:26; 16:1).

OPPONENTS

Clearly the situation has advanced beyond some friction between Paul and many Corinthians in 1 Corinthians. On the common view that Chapters 10–13 depict a situation after Chapters 1–7, the situation advances further still within our 2 Corinthians; if the letter is a unity, as we favor, the end of the letter nevertheless signals serious conflict.

Clearly by the time Paul writes Chapters 1–7, he is aware of some rival teachers presenting their credentials to the Corinthians and vying for their loyalty (2:17; 3:1; 5:12). This makes it paramount for Paul to put behind him other conflicts between himself and parts of the church (cf. 2:7–11) before firmly confronting them on nonnegotiable issues. If some Corinthians fail to recognize that they cannot be on good terms with both Paul and his rivals (a situation unlike that in 1 Cor 1:12), Paul makes this demand clear in no uncertain terms, demanding that they be reconciled with God, Christ, and with Paul the divine agent (2 Cor 5:20–6:2; 6:11–13), while breaking with "unbelievers" compromising with paganism (6:14–16). (If 6:14–7:1 is original to the letter, as I think, it might suggest

[1] See A. Malherbe, "Gentle" (1970).
[2] Paul's "majority" support in 2:6 may be diplomatic language as well (cf. 9:2; 1 Cor 10:5; 15:6; Phil 1:14), although many think it a Semitic idiom for "the community."

that Paul's rivals, who appeal to the rhetorically appreciative elite, reflect a more liberal brand of Jewish Christianity than he, at least regarding idol food; cf. 1 Cor 8–10. But Paul or his source might simply employ "idols" for rhetorical antithesis.)

Scholars have identified Paul's rivals variously as Gnostics, legalists, pneumatics, or some combination thereof. No consensus exists; the Gnostic designation has become particularly problematic given the later date most scholars now assign for Gnosticism. More clearly, the opponents are Jewish (11:22); some scholars also think that they appeal to Moses (cf. 3:7–13). We might compare Josephus's itinerant opponents, who sought to undermine his influence in each city and town, claiming to represent the leadership in Jerusalem. Josephus, who also had Jerusalem ties, had to keep traveling and winning back people's favor (e.g., *Life* 272–75).

Their Jewishness does not, however, invite us (with some early interpreters) to equate them with Paul's opponents in Galatia. *Most* early Christian leaders were Jewish, apart from several younger ministers mentored by Paul. Paul's conflict with them is probably not over circumcision; the Corinthian correspondence lacks Paul's typical polemic against advocates of circumcision (Gal passim; Phil 3:2). In contrast to the likely situation in Galatians, the oft-claimed connection of his rivals with Jerusalem is unclear here (certainly the rhetorically skilled "super-apostles" of 11:5–6 refer to the rival missionaries themselves, not to the Jerusalem leaders; cf. 11:12–15). Indeed, whereas Paul wanted funds for the Jerusalem church, these teachers apparently kept money for themselves (11:7)! If these "missionaries" resemble those in Galatia, they have changed their strategy for a more Hellenistic-Roman church.

Whether from Judea (as some understand "Hebrews" in 11:22) or elsewhere, their apparent Greek rhetorical proficiency suggests that they could appeal to Greeks and Romans. It is quite possible that they stem from a background like that of Apollos (Acts 18:24–28), and appeal especially to his prior constituency in Corinth. Many scholars have followed Dieter Georgi's brilliant reconstruction of Hellenistic Jewish missionaries in Corinth.[3] Although the rivals are likely Hellenistic Jews, however, and Diaspora Jewish apologetic sources are therefore useful in understanding them (as well as Paul), Georgi's detailed reconstruction of their character is too confident. Some of Paul's attacks and apologetic are conventional rhetoric, reducing what we can actually discern about the opponents from his words.

The clearest evidence for the opponents' character is simply that they urged different criteria for evaluating apostleship than Paul did, affirming their own while questioning his, probably based on their apparent rhetorical or possibly charismatic superiority.[4] The Corinthians would naturally give attention to

---

[3] D. Georgi, *The Opponents of Paul in Second Corinthians* (Philadelphia: Fortress, 1986).

[4] Cf. J. L. Sumney, *Identifying Paul's Opponents: The Question of Method in 2 Corinthians* (JSNTS 40; Sheffield: Sheffield Academic Press, 1990), passim.

rhetorical skill (see our discussion at 1 Cor 1–2), and at least some of Paul's rivals outstrip him in this (11:6). Paul's charismatic experiences in 12:1–4 could constitute a response to his opponents' charismatic claims (otherwise why raise them only now?; cf. also 12:7), but this is less clear than many have supposed (he might simply trump less supernatural claims). What is clear is that his opponents cannot match his record of sufferings for the gospel (11:23; 12:10), a criterion for Christ's agents in the Jesus tradition (e.g., Mk 8:34–38; 13:9–11; Matt 10:24–25; Lk 10:16). From Paul's perspective, Christ's suffering and a theology valuing God's power in brokenness do not sufficiently permeate their ministry; thus they preach another Christ (11:4).

UNITY?

The question of literary integrity is important for reconstructing the character of the opposition Paul confronts, hence for understanding various responses in the letter. In this introductory section I address only the proposed partition of Chapters 10–13 from the preceding chapters (a separation most scholars accept, although the dissenting minority is growing). Other, less frequently accepted divisions (such as separating 2:14–7:4 from its context; 6:14–7:1 from its context; and either or both of Chapters 8 and 9 from Chapters 1–7) will be addressed briefly at the appropriate points in the commentary.

The letter's style and interests are unquestionably Pauline, but this need not mean it was written and sent all at once. Partition theories of 2 Corinthians somewhat resemble those of 1 Corinthians, though the latter have fallen from favor; certainly digressions such as 1 Corinthians 9 or 13 are now widely accepted as integral to that letter (cf. similarly Chapters 9–11 in Romans). Yet if such approaches work anywhere in the Pauline corpus, it would be in 2 Corinthians.

Given literary-critical trends to read documents as wholes and rhetorical-critical analysis on the function of elements in letters, it is not surprising that an increasing minority of scholars support the letter's unity, including a number of the recent commentators on the letter.[5] Arguments for any work's composite

---

[5] E.g., B. Witherington III, *Conflict and Community in Corinth* (Grand Rapids, MI: Eerdmans, 1995); P. Barnett, *The Second Epistle to the Corinthians* (Grand Rapids, MI: Eerdmans, 1997), 16–23; D. Garland, *2 Corinthians* (Nashville: Broadman & Holman, 1999); J. Lambrecht, *Second Corinthians* (Collegeville, MN: Liturgical, 1999); J. W. McCant, *2 Corinthians* (Sheffield: Sheffield Academic Press, 1999), 20–23; F. J. Matera, *II Corinthians: A Commentary* (Louisville, KY: Westminster John Knox, 2003); earlier, e.g., E. B. Allo, *Seconde épître aux Corinthiens* (Paris: Gabalda, 1953), l–lvi. Studies include F. Young and D. F. Ford, *Meaning and Truth in Second Corinthians* (Grand Rapids, MI: Eerdmans, 1987), 27–59; F. W. Danker, "Paul's Debt to the *De Corona* of Demosthenes: A Study of Rhetorical Techniques in Second Corinthians," 262–80 in *Persuasive Artistry: Studies in NT Rhetoric in Honor of George A. Kennedy*, ed. D. F. Watson (JSNTS 50; Sheffield: Sheffield Academic, 1991); D. A. deSilva, "Measuring Penultimate Against Ultimate Reality: An Investigation of the Integrity and Argumentation of 2 Corinthians," *JSNT* 52 (1993): 41–70; idem,

character must bear the burden of proof. By itself, however, such a claim cannot resolve the question of unity. Whereas literary criticism accustoms us to reading texts as entire units in the forms in which they reach us, most biblical scholars also ask how our ancient texts were heard in the framework of the original authors' and audiences' situation. This focus compels scholars with historical interests to ask questions about the original shape of documents and traditions, in addition to how most readers approach them in their current canonical form. In general, a straightforward reading of a work as a unity is more historically probable than any particular competing hypothesis; this does not necessarily make it highly probable, but simply more probable than specific hypothetical reconstructions, any one of which individually is less probable than the straightforward reading. Despite this general premise, everyone agrees that some documents are composite, and would differ only in determining how much evidence is necessary to shift the burden of proof toward a particular reconstruction's probability.

Arguments Favoring Partition

The most commonly argued division in the letter, first proposed by J. S. Semler in 1776 and now accepted by the majority of scholars, divides Chapters 10–13 from the other chapters. Many have argued that 10–13 was Paul's "tearful letter" (2:3–4; 7:8–12), a view first popularized by Adolf Hausrath in 1870. Most scholars today question this view; the "tearful letter" focuses on a single perpetrator, and was offered in lieu of a visit, unlike 10–13, which prepare for a visit.[6] More argue plausibly that Paul wrote Chapters 10–13 after Chapters 1–9.

There is certainly good reason to notice disjunction between these two sections. For example, would Paul follow his appeal for generosity in Chapters 8–9 with such harshness as we find in Chapters 10–13? Further, Paul shifts from mostly using the first-person plural in Chapters 1–9 to the first-person singular in Chapters 10–13. (Proponents of unity could account for this by a lapse in time of writing, or better yet a shift in rhetorical strategy to more direct responses to charges; Paul uses both forms in both sections.) Perhaps most tellingly, many think that 12:16–18 look back on Paul's agents' visit for the collection, whereas 8–9 anticipate it. Proponents of unity can argue that 12:18 might refer to an earlier trip (7:13), when Titus had "made a beginning" (8:6). Likewise, we could read 12:18a as an epistolary aorist, precisely as it is regarding the same agents in

---

The Credentials of an Apostle (N. Richland Hills, TX: BIBAL, 1998), 36–43; D. A. Hester, "The Unity of 2 Corinthians: A Test Case for a Re-discovered and Re-invented Rhetoric," *Neotestamentica* 33 (2, 1999): 411–32; J. D. H. Amador, "Revisiting 2 Corinthians: Rhetoric and the Case for Unity," *NTS* 46 (2000): 92–111.

[6] See, e.g., M. E. Thrall, *A Critical and Exegetical Commentary on the Second Epistle to the Corinthians*, 2 vols. (Edinburgh: Clark, 1994–2000), 13–18; L. Kreitzer, *2 Corinthians* (Sheffield: Sheffield Academic Press, 1996), 23–25. Welborn, however, rightly notes that conciliatory letters did not explicitly address the former dispute (*Politics*, 86–93).

8:18, 22 (although this would require Paul's faith that it turned out this way!) But if one does not have reason to argue for unity, such phenomena would point more easily to disunity.

Some have pointed out rhetorical connections between 10:1–11 and 13:1–10, which could bracket 10–13 as a cohesive unit. But although all agree that 10–13 is a cohesive rhetorical unit, this does not necessarily make it a distinct *letter*. Letters were not speeches, and even speeches often failed to conform to standard rhetorical outlines. Paul's individual as well as overarching arguments sometimes follow conventional arrangements for persuasion (rhetorical outlines for 10–13 prove a distinct letter no more than similar outlines proposed for 1 Cor 8–11 or 15).

Arguments against Partition

Nevertheless, supporters of partition must provide explanations for why redactors united these distinct letters. An accident is implausible; the earliest copies would have been scrolls, not codices with pages, and even if they were codices one would need to presuppose not just carelessness but that one page in question fortuitously ended with a complete sentence and the other began a new paragraph. Deliberate literary explanations are better, but usually more difficult than assuming unity: If we can explain why a redactor would have united sections, the same explanation might show why Paul wrote them together.

Not only the Christians in Corinth, but probably Christians elsewhere (if we may judge by use of 1 Corinthians in Clement of Rome a generation later) knew something of Paul's correspondence with the Corinthians. Granted, 2 Corinthians was not widely circulated like 1 Corinthians, and (unlike its extant predecessor) is not quoted or echoed before the mid-second century. Yet if 2 Corinthians were composite, one would expect some recognition of this fact at least in Corinth, hence in some early manuscripts or church fathers; but such is not the case. Neither Marcion nor his early detractors seem aware of fragments.

More important, ancient letter collections (e.g., from Cicero, Seneca, or Pliny) normally distinguished letters. This is not a foolproof argument; such mingling of letters as is proposed for Paul apparently did occur on rare occasions.[7] Furthermore, although distinguishing letters, some collections, like Seneca's letters to Lucilius, also omitted opening addresses, where these were simply standard. Yet Paul often has significant letter closings, sometimes with hortatory summaries (cf., e.g., 13:11–12; Rom 16:17–27; 1 Cor 16:22). Would Christian editors simply suppress the closing of one of the earlier component letters in our 2 Corinthians? More problematic, would the editor remove Paul's usual thanksgiving periods?

---

[7] Cf., e.g., Cicero *Fam.* 10.21.7; 11.13a.4. Nor is our current sequence of letters always the sequence in which they were written (e.g., Seneca *Nat.Q.* 4.1.1, probably alluding to 6.8.3–5; Pliny *Ep.* 1.1).

Later chapters may echo earlier chapters: for example, "we speak before God in Christ" in 2:17 and 12:19; "crafty/craftiness" and "deceive/deceit" in 4:2 and 12:16; "exhort" and "beg" in 5:20 and 10:1–2. Paul tests the Corinthians (2:9; 8:8) and warns them to test themselves (13:6). The language of "boasting," "joy," and "commendation" appear in both sections.[8] Power in weakness characterizes apostolic ministry and hardship lists in both (though also in 1 Cor 4:8–13). It may even be relevant that Paul elsewhere offers appeals (using *parakalō*) after thanksgivings (Rom 11:33–12:1; 1 Thess 3:11–4:1), which could unite 9:15 with 10:1. If the work is a unity, Paul sandwiches between the epistolary introduction and conclusion two defenses of his apostolic ministry (1:12–7:16; 10:1–13:10), which in turn frame his discussion of the collection and its urgency (8:1–9:15).

Resolving Tensions between the Sections

Such factors leave the burden of proof heavily on supporters of partition, but only *if* the letter can be plausibly explained as a unity. Are the differences between the sections sufficient to carry the burden of proof against unity? Although 2 Corinthians 1–7 notes some issues that have been resolved (the discipline of the offender and the Corinthians repenting; 2:6–11; 7:7–13), it also presents the reconciliation as incomplete (5:20–6:2): the Corinthians must be reconciled to God (5:20) and not accept his grace in vain (6:1–2); they must open their hearts to Paul (6:12–13; 7:2), though Paul can be conciliatory in the same breath (7:3–4; cf. 11:11; 12:14–15, 19; 13:7–8). The opening chapters consolidate his position vis-à-vis the fairly sympathetic, but less than solidified, majority.[9]

The often-noted tensions between the two sections of the letter are no greater than apparent contradictions within one section; for example, Paul commends himself (4:2; 6:4) yet does not commend himself (3:1; 5:12). Paul offers sudden shifts in topic in this letter (esp. at 8:1; 10:1), but did the same in 1 Corinthians (1 Cor 1–4; 5–7; 8–11; 12–14), albeit there with optional "now concerning" markers.

In saving the most direct challenge for the later chapters, Paul probably follows what was a rhetorically prudent strategy. Rhetorically, it makes sense to establish common ground earlier in a speech or letter and reserve the most controversial elements for the final part of a speech (cf. e.g., *POxy.* 1837).[10] Thus many rhetorical critics argue that Paul saves his strongest complaint – the church's toleration of rival teachers – for the end. Speeches typically climaxed with special emotional appeal toward the conclusion. (Many compare the concluding harangue in Demosthenes's second epistle, although advocates of partition could equally

---

[8] For these and other possible connections, see P. Barnett, *2 Corinthians* (1997), 19–21; J. McCant, *2 Corinthians* (1999), 22–23.

[9] With, e.g., F. Matera, *II Corinthians* (2003), 29–32.

[10] Cf., e.g., the treatment of *insinuatio* (*Rhet. Her.* 1.9–11) in G. Kennedy, *Interpretation* (1984), 36 (although he treats the letter as composite, 92). Contrast, however, the structure of some OT prophetic books (cf. Amos 9:11–15; Ezek 40–48; *Sipre Deut.* 342.1.2).

compare its emotions with Paul's in 7:8–16.[11] Somewhat less relevant, a writer could also reserve a clinching surprise for the end, as in Cicero *Quinct.* 25.78–80; in Romans, Paul saves his most explicit texts for including Gentiles for near the end, 15:7–13.)

Good speakers and writers often varied style and especially tone within the same speech or work (e.g., Pliny *Ep.* 2.5.7–8), and Paul was no exception.[12] Nevertheless, Paul does prepare for this conclusion with significant apologetic digressions (esp. 2 Cor 3–6, which seems unnecessary unless significant opposition remains) and concerns about some alienating the Corinthians from Paul (2:17–3:1; 5:20–6:1, 6:11–7:2). The issue of offerings in 12:16–18 was treated at length in Chapters 8–9 (cf. also 7:2; 12:16–18), as was the issue of greed (2:17; cf. 4:2). If Paul's tone is more positive in earlier chapters, it is not without hints of serious problems (5:20; 6:2; 6:12–13; 7:2).

It is also possible (although not demonstrable) that Paul's tone shifted because of new reports. Letters were often dictated in stages (e.g., Fronto *De Fer Als.* 4), and a writer could add an addendum when receiving fresh news (e.g., Cicero *Fam.* 12.12.5), although it seems odd that Paul does not mention it. Another possibility is that if Titus carried on the same trip both letters, written and sealed separately, the Corinthians would have read them together as a unity. Once a letter was sealed, an author might simply enclose another for the same carrier (Cicero *Att.* 8.6; Fronto *Ad M. Caes.* 3.4). Although the writer usually mentions the addition, the collection's editor could have deleted it as theologically inconsequential.

Paul's opponents may question his refusal to accept pay both in 2:17 and 11:7–9, and may question the proof of his apostleship both in 3:1 and 12:12. Likewise, Paul rejects their criteria for self-commendation in 5:12 and 10:10–18.[13] An apologetic defense of Paul's ministry as genuinely apostolic characterizes both sections (if we admit the unity of 1–7); whereas 2:14–7:4 lay the theological groundwork for true apostleship (along with personal appeals and defenses in 1–7), 10–13 get down to business with a more direct personal attack and defense. Some of Paul's other letters offer transitions from theological groundwork to practical advice (e.g., Rom 1–11 and 12–15); here he transitions from theological groundwork to polemic. Although less polemical, Galatians 5–6 offers a similar abrupt transition developing more forcefully the ideas of Galatians 1–4.[14]

The "second letter" displays its own variations. Omitting Paul's direct challenges to the false apostles in 10–13 would decrease the harshness in those

[11] Rhetorical arguments allow but do not require unity, since they could be used to support partition as well (see B. K. Peterson, *Eloquence and the Proclamation of the Gospel in Corinth*, SBLDS 163 [Atlanta: Scholars, 1998], 53–57, 132–39), depending on the burden of proof.

[12] See esp. P. Marshall, *Enmity* (1987), 392; cf. Gal 4:20.

[13] J. L. Sumney sees two letters, but finds the same opponents in both (and only in these two letters; e.g., *Paul's Opponents* [1990], 128–29, 177, 183–84).

[14] W. H. Bates, "The Integrity of 2 Corinthians," *NTS* 12 (1965–1966): 50–69.

chapters; most of his reproof of the Corinthians themselves is gentler, resembling earlier appeals or reproofs. Within 10–13, Paul varies between challenging his opponents' claims to be equal to him as Christ's servants (10:7; 11:23) and denouncing them as Satan's servants (11:13–15). He is harshest with the Corinthians when threatening discipline (12:20–13:3), but in a conspicuously affectionate context (12:14–15; 13:9–13) – the same tension we find in 6:11–7:4. Even within 1 Corinthians (where he was not addressing false apostles), Paul sometimes pleaded with the Corinthians as if they were wayward (4:18–21; 6:5; 11:22; 15:34), and even here he pleads with them affectionately (2 Cor 11:11, 28–29; 12:14–15, 19; 13:7–10).

I currently favor reading the entire letter as a unity, but my conclusion and the situation it implies (identical, fully engaged opponents throughout the letter) remain a minority view. Because differences between the two major sections are not in dispute, one's conclusion depends on how heavily the burden of proof rests on specific hypothetical reconstructions (such as partition) or on those defying scholarly consensus (such as advocates of unity). I believe that the Ockham's Razor principle of the simplest solution warns against finding interpolations and additions without clear evidence. Nevertheless, many still regard the evidence for partition (more convincing here than in other letters) as sufficiently clear to meet this criterion. Most partition theories on this letter might eventually go the way of alleged partitions in 1 Corinthians, but the proposed partition between Chapters 9 and 10 is more defensible than the others and more likely to endure.

V. Suggested Reading for 2 Corinthians

See further relevant resources on Corinth, rhetoric, epistles, and so forth, in the suggested reading for 1 Corinthians.

SITUATION

See, e.g., S. Hafemann, "'Self-Commendation' and Apostolic Legitimacy in 2 Corinthians: A Pauline Dialectic?" *NTS* 36 (1, 1990): 66–88. For one detailed reconstruction of the situation, see P. Marshall, *Enmity in Corinth: Social Conventions in Paul's Relations with the Corinthians*, WUNT 2, Reihe 23 (Tübingen: Mohr Siebeck, 1987). Despite the overconfidence of his reconstruction in details (especially when addressing the problems in 1 Corinthians), the work's strong grounding in ancient social and rhetorical evidence makes its primary theses likely. By rejecting the patronage of the Corinthian elite, Paul has violated their expectation of "friendship," risking conventional forms of enmity relationships.[1] Against the frequent practice of mirror-reading Paul's opponents (but concluding that the opponents in 10–13 are "pneumatics"), see J. L. Sumney, *Identifying Paul's Opponents: The Question of Method in 2 Corinthians* (JSNTS 40; Sheffield: Sheffield Academic Press, 1990).

THEOLOGY

In addition to Dunn (see 1 Corinthians), J. Murphy-O'Connor, *The Theology of the Second Letter to the Corinthians* (Cambridge: Cambridge University, 1991).

---

[1] On "friendship" patterns, see further *Greco-Roman Perspectives on Friendship*, ed. J. T. Fitzgerald (SBLRBS 34; Atlanta: Scholars Press, 1997); C. Keener, "Friendship," 380–88 in *DNTB*.

OTHER QUESTIONS

D. A. deSilva, "Measuring Penultimate against Ultimate Reality: An Investigation of the Integrity and Argumentation of 2 Corinthians," *JSNT* 52 (1993): 41–70; J. T. Fitzgerald, "Paul, the Ancient Epistolary Theorists, and 2 Corinthians 10–13," 190–200 in *Greeks, Romans, and Christians: Essays in Honor of Abraham J. Malherbe*, ed. D. L. Balch et al. (Minneapolis: Fortress, 1990); A. Stewart-Sykes, "Ancient Editors and Copyists and Modern Partition Theories: The Case of the Corinthian Correspondence," *JSNT* 61 (1996): 53–64.

COMMENTARIES

I exclude here those that include also 1 Corinthians; the boundaries among commentaries below are approximate. For example, although Danker's commentary is packaged as fairly popular, he provides considerable fresh research in primary sources; even some scholarly commentaries largely recycle the information he and others have introduced.

Major scholarly commentaries (all of them excellent, though I have not cited them all in equal proportion):

V. P. Furnish, *II Corinthians* (AB 32A; Garden City, NY: Doubleday & Company, 1984).

M. J. Harris, *The Second Epistle to the Corinthians* (NIGTC; Grand Rapids, MI: Eerdmans; Carlisle: Paternoster, 2004).

R. P. Martin, *2 Corinthians* (Waco, TX: Word, 1986).

M. E. Thrall, *A Critical and Exegetical Commentary on the Second Epistle to the Corinthians*, 2 vols. (Edinburgh: Clark, 1994–2000), probably the most thorough, current commentary surveying various views and grammatical options; detailed on the Greek text; she always credits her sources.

Serious academic commentaries:

P. Barnett, *The Second Epistle to the Corinthians* (Grand Rapids, MI: Eerdmans, 1997).

C. K. Barrett, *A Commentary on the Second Epistle to the Corinthians* (New York: Harper & Row, 1973).

J. Héring, *The Second Epistle of Saint Paul to the Corinthians*, trans. A. H. Heathcote and P. J. Allcock (London: Epworth, 1967): one of the most insightful for his era, sometimes even offering rhetorical insights.

F. J. Matera, *II Corinthians: A Commentary*, NT Library (Louisville, KY: Westminster John Knox, 2003): a careful and up-to-date, readable, and mid-level analysis of 2 Corinthians fully informed by current scholarship.

B. Witherington III, *Conflict and Community in Corinth: A Socio-Rhetorical Commentary on 1 and 2 Corinthians* (Grand Rapids, MI: Eerdmans; Carlisle: Paternoster, 1995).

More popular or application-oriented commentaries with academic interest:

L. L. Belleville, *2 Corinthians* (Leicester, Downers Grove, IL: InterVarsity, 1996).

E. Best, *Second Corinthians* (Atlanta: John Knox, 1987): highly readable and application-oriented.

F. W. Danker, *II Corinthians* (Minneapolis: Augsburg, 1989). Despite the book's popular format and brevity, it provides more fresh insight on the letter's Greco-Roman setting and rhetoric (esp. from epigraphic sources) than do most "academic" commentaries (some of which reuse its information); highly recommended.

J. Lambrecht, *Second Corinthians* (Collegeville, MN: Liturgical, 1999).

J. W. McCant, *2 Corinthians* (Readings; Sheffield: Sheffield Academic Press 1999): fairly basic and readable level but rhetorically sensitive.

J. M. Scott, *2 Corinthians*, NIBC (Carlisle: Paternoster; Peabody, MA: Hendrickson, 1998): basic level (but well-informed on Jewish sources, and esp. illuminating on *merkabah* mysticism).

N. Watson, *The Second Epistle to the Corinthians* (Epworth Commentaries; London: Epworth, 1993): fairly popular level.

ARTICLES AND MONOGRAPHS

2 Cor 1–2. See, e.g., C. Breytenbach, "Paul's proclamation and God's 'thriambos' (Notes on 2 Corinthians 2:14–16b)," *Neotestamentica* 24 (2, 1990): 257–71; P. B. Duff, "Metaphor, Motif, and Meaning: The Rhetorical Strategy behind the Image 'Led in Triumph' in 2 Corinthians 2:14," *CBQ* 53 (1, 1991): 79–92; S. Hafemann, *Suffering and Ministry in the Spirit: Paul's Defense of His Apostolic Ministry in II Corinthians 2:14–3:3* (Grand Rapids, MI: Eerdmans, 1990); P. Marshall, "A Metaphor of Social Shame: *thriambeuein* in 2 Cor. 2:14," *NovT* 25 (4, 1983): 302–17.

2 Cor 3. W. R. Baker, "Did the Glory of Moses' Face Fade? A Reexamination of καταργέω in 2 Corinthians 3:7–18," *BullBibRes* 10 (1, 2000): 1–15; L. L. Belleville, *Reflections of Glory: Paul's Polemical Use of the Moses-Doxa Tradition in 2 Corinthians 3.1–18* (JSNTS 52; Sheffield: Sheffield Academic Press, 1991).

2 Cor 5. See W. L. Craig, "Paul's Dilemma in 2 Corinthians 5:1–10: A 'Catch-22'?" *NTS* 34 (1, 1988): 145–47; A. T. Lincoln, *Paradise Now and Not Yet: Studies in the Role of the Heavenly Dimension in Paul's Thought with Special Reference to his Eschatology* (SNTSMS 43; Cambridge: Cambridge University, 1981).

2 Cor 8–9. H. D. Betz, *2 Corinthians 8 and 9: A commentary on Two Administrative Letters of the Apostle Paul* (Hermeneia; Philadelphia: Fortress, 1985) (full

of useful insights despite the identification of two distinct letters here). On the collection, see, e.g., K. F. Nickle, *The Collection: A Study in Biblical Theology*, SBT 48 (Naperville, IL: Alec R. Allenson, 1966), esp. 100–43; D. Georgi, *Remembering the Poor: The History of Paul's Collection for Jerusalem* (Nashville: Abingdon, 1992). For background, see esp. F. W. Danker, *Benefactor: Epigraphic Study of a Graeco-Roman and NT Semantic Field* (St. Louis: Clayton, 1982); James R. Harrison, *Paul's Language of Grace in its Graeco-Roman Context*, WUNT 2.172 (Tübingen: Mohr Siebeck, 2003), esp. 289–332.

2 Cor 10–13. See esp. P. Marshall, *Enmity in Corinth*, as noted above; C. Forbes, "Comparison, Self-Praise and Irony: Paul's Boasting and the Conventions of Hellenistic Rhetoric," *NTS* 32 (1, 1986): 1–30; also T. B. Savage, *Power through weakness: Paul's understanding of the Christian ministry in 2 Corinthians* (SNTSM 86; Cambridge: Cambridge University, 1996) (relevant to the entire Corinthian correspondence, but esp. this section), stresses Paul's "meek" demeanor in contrast to more authoritarian Corinthian expectations. B. K. Peterson, *Eloquence and the Proclamation of the Gospel in Corinth* (SBLDS 163; Atlanta: Scholars Press, 1998) offers a significant rhetorical study (whether or not one accepts his structure of this section as a speech). H. D. Betz, *Der Apostel Paulus und die sokratische Tradition* (Tübingen: Mohr/Siebeck, 1985), provides analogies between Paul's argument against his opponents and philosophic critiques of sophists (and defenses of the outwardly lowly Socrates). L. L. Welborn, "The Runaway Paul," *HTR* 92 (2, 1999): 115–63, finds four stock characters of mime in Paul's fool's speech (not all equally compelling). For 12:1–4, see, e.g., Lincoln, *Paradise Now Not Yet*, noted earlier; C. R. A. Morray-Jones, "Paradise Revisited (2 Cor 12:1–12): The Jewish Mystical Background of Paul's Apostolate. Part 1: The Jewish Sources," and "Part 2: Paul's Heavenly Ascent and its Significance," *HTR* 86 (1993): 177–217, 265–92.

VI. Commentary on 2 Corinthians

1:1–11: EPISTOLARY INTRODUCTION

1:1: Paul, an apostle of Christ Jesus by the will of God, and Timothy our brother, to the church of God which is at Corinth with all the saints who are throughout Achaia:

1:2: Grace to you and peace from God our Father and the Lord Jesus Christ.

1:3: Blessed be the God and Father of our Lord Jesus Christ, the Father of mercies and God of all comfort;

1:4: who comforts us in all our affliction so that we may be able to comfort those who are in any affliction with the comfort with which we ourselves are comforted by God.

1:5: For just as the sufferings of Christ are ours in abundance, so also our comfort is abundant through Christ.

1:6: But if we are afflicted, it is for your comfort and salvation; or if we are comforted, it is for your comfort, which is effective in the patient enduring of the same sufferings which we also suffer;

1:7: and our hope for you is firmly grounded, knowing that as you are sharers of our sufferings, so also you are sharers of our comfort.

1:8: For we do not want you to be unaware, brethren, of our affliction which came to us in Asia, that we were burdened excessively, beyond our strength, so that we despaired even of life;

1:9: indeed, we had the sentence of death within ourselves in order that we should not trust in ourselves, but in God who raises the dead;

1:10: who delivered us from so great a peril of death, and will deliver us, He on whom we have set our hope. And He will yet deliver us,

1:11: you also joining in helping us through your prayers, that thanks may be given by many persons on our behalf for the favor bestowed upon us through the prayers of many.

*P*aul offers a brief, basic greeting (cf. comment on 1 Cor 1:1–2) to Christians in Achaia even beyond Corinth.[1] Afterward, he introduces a theme of comfort in suffering in his thanksgiving, which he then develops more fully in the following paragraph (1:8–11, closing with the prospect of future thanksgiving in 1:11; cf. 2:14; 4:15; 9:11–12; 1 Thess 1:2; 2:13; 3:9). Paul will return to this theme of suffering and comfort, weaving his introductory *narratio* about his recent experiences, especially concerning them and Titus's visit to them, into the defense of his reliability. "Comfort" or "consolation" for sorrow was a common topic of speakers and writers in Paul's day (although some conventions, like Stoic admonitions not to grieve, hardly sound comforting to us).

In place of Paul's usual thanksgiving for his audience (e.g., Rom 1:8–15; 1 Cor 1:4–9) we find a blessing (1:3–5), following the form of a traditional Jewish *berakah*;[2] the focus is thus on God's activity on Paul's behalf, not gratitude for the state of the Corinthians (cf. 1:11; 2:14). (In various texts, the first-person plural may include Timothy, may include all Paul's fellow-workers, or simply represent Paul himself.)[3] Although the use of such blessings is not intrinsically negative (Eph 1:3; 1 Pet 1:3), the rest of the letter suggests that not all is well in Paul's relationship with this church (5:20–6:1), despite moments of concord (7:9–16). In a sense, though, Paul is thanking God partly for the Corinthians: his greatest anxiety is for the churches (11:28–29), and his greatest comfort is the good news of their love for him (7:6–7, 13). "Father of mercies" (1:3), that is, "merciful Father," was, like the blessing form, common in Jewish prayer; the same is true of "God who raises the dead" (1:9; cf. the "Eighteen Benedictions").

Although Paul technically does not use a thanksgiving, he establishes goodwill as much as in any exordium (see comment on 1 Cor 1:4–9). He emphasizes his affection for the Corinthians, noting that his sufferings are for their sake, as their apostolic representative on the front line of God's mission (1:6; cf. 4:12, 15). And just as Paul shares both Christ's sufferings and his grace (1:4–5), so the Corinthians, who are connected with him, share not only his sufferings but also the comfort he has received from God (1:6–7). Paul later returns to this theme of comfort (1:3–7) in 7:4–7, 13: their love for him proves to be his greatest comfort in all of his affliction.

Whatever Paul's suffering in Asia (1:8), it appears life-threatening. (Suggestions of temporary detention are plausible but uncertain; the "sentence of death" in 1:9 may be figurative like the "beasts" in 1 Cor 15:32). Given Luke's narrative form, it is not too surprising that he focuses on a dramatic scene climaxing

---

[1] Roughly forty settlements (with perhaps twenty thousand inhabitants) surrounded Corinth itself (see D. Engels, *Roman Corinth* [1990], 82), including Cenchreae, which had a church (cf. Rom 16:1).

[2] Pervasive in Jewish texts, e.g., Ps 72:18; Tob 13:1; 3 Macc 7:23; *1 En.* 63:2; *m. Ber.* passim.

[3] For the authorial "we," see, e.g., Dionysius of Halicarnassus *Dem.* 58; probably Josephus *Life* 10.

Paul's opposition in Asia (Acts 19:23–41); but it is clear that Paul had faced opposition there, as well as successes, for some time (1 Cor 15:31–32; 16:9). Yet just as sharing Christ's sufferings guaranteed his comfort, so those who suffered with him would share his resurrection (Rom 8:11, 17–18; 1 Cor 15:30–34; Phil 3:10–11). Paul experiences a foretaste of the ultimate deliverance from death when God protects him from the dangers he regularly faces in Ephesus (including a particularly dramatic incident here of which his hearers seem already aware; 1:8–10). (Given common liturgical hyperbole involving deliverance from death [e.g., Ps 30:3; 40:2; 119:25], viewing deliverance as foreshadowing resurrection was not difficult; cf. Chrysostom *Hom. Cor.* 2.4.) An essential element of ancient ethics was that beneficiaries should lavish gratitude on their benefactors, human or divine; God is the benefactor in 1:11 (see further 4:15; 9:11–12).

1:12–22: PAUL'S RELIABILITY

1:12: For our proud confidence is this, the testimony of our conscience, that in holiness and godly sincerity, not in fleshly wisdom but in the grace of God, we have conducted ourselves in the world, and especially toward you.

1:13: For we write nothing else to you than what you read and understand, and I hope you will understand until the end;

1:14: just as you also partially did understand us, that we are your reason to be proud as you also are ours, in the day of our Lord Jesus.

1:15: And in this confidence I intended at first to come to you, that you might twice receive a blessing;

1:16: that is, to pass your way into Macedonia, and again from Macedonia to come to you, and by you to be helped on my journey to Judea.

1:17: Therefore, I was not vacillating when I intended to do this, was I? Or that which I purpose, do I purpose according to the flesh, that with me there should be yes, yes and no, no at the same time?

1:18: But as God is faithful, our word to you is not yes and no.

1:19: For the Son of God, Christ Jesus, who was preached among you by us – by me and Silvanus and Timothy – was not yes and no, but is yes in Him.

1:20: For as many as may be the promises of God, in Him they are yes; wherefore also by Him is our Amen to the glory of God through us.

1:21: Now He who establishes us with you in Christ and anointed us is God,

1:22: who also sealed us and gave us the Spirit in our hearts as a pledge.

The opening section of the letter's body is the narrative introduction to Paul's case (1:12–2:13). Not only speeches but other ancient works (even ancient Near Eastern treaties) often opened with narrative introductions, setting the stage for the current situation.

Ancient travel could be complicated, but Paul's unexpected change of travel plans (1:15–16) had disappointed the church and apparently exacerbated criticism (1:17). Paul had not only rejected their benefaction (11:7–9; 12:13); he had even more offensively robbed them of the privilege of showing an apostle hospitality. Although such protests were often friendly signs of affection (e.g., Cicero *Att.* 1.9; *Fam.* 2.10.1), even inviting an affectionate defense (Fronto *Ad Verum Imp.* 1.3–4), in Corinth they reflected genuine offense.

Paul thus emphasizes the integrity of his conduct toward them (1:12) against insinuations of dishonesty (12:16–18), and perhaps by contrast with his accusers and wandering charlatans in general (see comment on 2:17; cf. 1 Thess 2:3–11). In this period in his ministry, Paul often states a central proposition shortly after the thanksgiving (Rom 1:16–17; 1 Cor 1:10–12), and he seems to offer such a statement in 1:12. Paul continues to emphasize terms like "sincerity" (2:17) and "frankness" (3:12; 7:4); he demonstrates the latter in his claim to transparency in 1:13.[4] "Boasting" (1:12) was normally frowned on unless properly justified (see comment on 10:12); Paul justifies it here because he offers the Corinthians occasion to boast about him as he does about them (1:14; cf. 7:4, 14; 8:24; 9:2–3). They will be each other's cause for boasting in the day of Christ (1:14), but Paul also hopes that they will use the opportunity to counter his rivals (5:12; cf. 11:12, 18, 21).

A CLOSER LOOK: FICKLENESS

Ancient literature regularly condemns fickleness and unreliability while praising those who keep their word even under duress. Many thought fickleness inappropriate for a virtuous person (Maximus of Tyre 5.3); the Roman world despised it in leaders.[5] Those who changed stated plans had to explain their reasons and prove that they were not fickle (*CPJ* 2:219, §431; Phaedrus 4.prologue, lines 8–9); one might argue that it is impossible to foresee the future (Libanius *Declamation* 36.42; 44.50–52, 61) or that one was avoiding danger (Cicero *Att.* 3.4). Failure to carry through on one's word led to ridicule (e.g., Suetonius *Tib.* 38); keeping an agreement despite another's failure was honorable (Iamblichus *Pyth. Life* 30.185).[6]

Some Corinthians may have already been dissatisfied with Paul's "servile," apparently populist, flexibility, even before this change in plans (cf. 1 Cor 9:19–23). From Paul's perspective, however, the Corinthians are the fickle ones, flirting with his rivals (6:11–7:4). The elite typically portrayed the masses as fickle in their taste for leaders (see comment on 1 Cor 9:19–23); later citizens of Corinth itself proved fickle in their appreciation of others (cf. Dio Chrysostom 37.33).

---

[4] Ancients contrasted frankness with insincere flattery; see discussion in C. Keener, *John* (2003), 705–06.

[5] See Suetonius *Tib.* 67.4; *Claud.* 15.1; 16.1; 39–40; *Dom.* 3.2; Tacitus *Hist.* 2.57, 101.

[6] Dependability in matters of loyalty was particularly important (Cicero *Fam.* 5.2.10; Fronto *Ad Amicos* 1.19).

The Corinthian criticism must have gone deeper than their severe disappointment over his delay. Apparently for some, if Paul's word was not dependable when it involved his relationship with them, how could they trust his apostolic message (cf. 1:18–22; 11:4) and ministry (cf. 2:14–7:4)? Probably his "unreliability" with regard to his visit has also fed charges of unreliability regarding the collection (cf. 2:17; 4:2; 8:20–21; 12:16–18), at a critical time when Corinthian reluctance could stall that ministry's momentum (9:3–5). If Paul's word cannot be trusted, he cannot hold the Corinthians to their "promises" concerning the collection (9:5).

Thus, in 1:18–22, Paul digresses from explaining his changed travel plans to defend the integrity of his ministry, of which those changes have occasioned questioning. Paul grounds his ministry in the gospel that shapes it (1:18–19), as he will continue to do (5:18–6:2). He insists on defending not himself apart from his gospel but, rather, the gospel that shapes his ministry (repeatedly in 2:14–7:4), turning to a more specific and less theological defense of his conduct in the "fool's speech" of 11:17–12:13.

His ministry is reliable not because his plans never change but because the God who established his ministry (and theirs, 1:21–22) is reliable (1:18–19); God keeps his promises (1:20; 7:1; cf. Rom 3:3–4; 9:6). (Paul usually refers to biblical "promises" to Israel; he regards an initial fulfillment of the promise as available through the Spirit [Gal 3:14], as here [2 Cor 1:22].) Just as the Corinthians recognize Paul's Jewish "blessing" form (1:3), they understand the "Amen" (1:20) as a confirmation following prayer or thanksgiving (1 Cor 14:16; 16:24); confirmation meant that a matter was sure.[7] Like the Corinthians (1:24), Paul was "firm" or "established" (1:21), hence not unreliable. The reason they were firm was the Spirit, the first installment (1:22; cf. 5:5) on all God's promises (cf. 1:20). The "first installment," as a pledge or downpayment, functioned as a guarantee of the promise; in this context, "sealing" might imply the same connotation (Xenophon *Anab.* 2.2.9). If the Corinthians could not trust Paul's own "Yes, yes" (1:17), Paul as God's agent, forced by his audience to make this oath (Matt 5:37), could call to witness the true guarantor of his word, God himself (1:23).

1:23–2:11: DISCIPLINE AND FORGIVENESS

1:23: **But I call God as witness to my soul, that to spare you I came no more to Corinth.**
1:24: **Not that we lord it over your faith, but are workers with you for your joy; for in your faith you are standing firm.**

---

[7] Cf. perhaps a Christian adaptation of Jewish prayers for the fulfillment of God's kingdom promises (Matt 6:10//Lk 11:2), here offered "through him" (cf. prayer in Jesus's name, Jn 14:13–14; Acts 3:6).

2:1: But I determined this for my own sake, that I would not come to you in sorrow again.

2:2: For if I cause you sorrow, who then makes me glad but the one whom I made sorrowful?

2:3: And this is the very thing I wrote you, lest, when I came, I should have sorrow from those who ought to make me rejoice; having confidence in you all, that my joy would be the joy of you all.

2:4: For out of much affliction and anguish of heart I wrote to you with many tears; not that you should be made sorrowful, but that you might know the love which I have especially for you.

2:5: But if any has caused sorrow, he has caused sorrow not to me, but in some degree – in order not to say too much – to all of you.

2:6: Sufficient for such a one is this punishment which was inflicted by the majority,

2:7: so that on the contrary you should rather forgive and comfort him, lest somehow such a one be overwhelmed by excessive sorrow.

2:8: Wherefore I urge you to reaffirm your love for him.

2:9: For to this end also I wrote that I might put you to the test, whether you are obedient in all things.

2:10: But whom you forgive anything, I forgive also; for indeed what I have forgiven, if I have forgiven anything, I did it for your sakes in the presence of Christ,

2:11: in order that no advantage be taken of us by Satan; for we are not ignorant of his schemes.

*P*aul continues his affectionate, conciliatory appeal here, continuing to "soften" his relationship with the Corinthians before going on to challenge them on other issues later in the letter. Conciliatory letters and speeches generally did not draw unnecessary attention to the point that had actually caused the breach in their relationship (cf. e.g., Pliny *Ep.* 1.5.11). In ancient defense speeches one could deny a deed; or admit to doing it but deny that it was wrong; or admit to doing it but attribute it to accident or innocent motives. One who had failed to write or visit might explain that he did so out of consideration for the other's time or welfare (Fronto *Ad M. Caes.* 3.13.3).

Paul defends his failure to come as an act of consideration on his part, because he wished to avoid coming harshly (1:23; 12:20–21; 13:10; 1 Cor 4:18–21). (Nevertheless, at the letter's end he notifies them that he will finally do so if necessary; 2 Cor 13:2, 10.) He wishes to build up and not tear down (10:8; 13:10; cf. 12:19), to bring life and not kill (3:6–7; cf. 2:15–16; 7:10), and like Moses (3:7, 13), restrains some of his righteousness for their sake (5:13; cf. 12:4). He did not wish to inflict sorrow, because their sorrow would cause him sorrow (2:3; affectionate letters expressed sharing the recipient's sorrow, for example, Cicero *Fam.* 13.1.1). That he had not come in person to execute discipline undoubtedly contributes to accusations that he is too "soft," in contrast to harsher leadership models prevailing in Corinth (10:9–11; 12:21–13:3).

Paul delayed his visit in part to test their obedience (2:9); if fickleness was bad (1:17), they must prove loyal to him. (He returns to testing them further later in the letter; 8:8; 9:13; 13:5.) He tested them by a letter much firmer (and more successful) than 1 Corinthians (2:3–4; 7:8).[8] The letter caused him great anguish; tears were common signs of affection even in public orations (and other "tearful letters," e.g., Catullus 68.1–2), and letters frequently emphasized "abundant love," as here (e.g., Cicero *Fam.* 2.4.2).

They responded to his letter by disciplining the offender (2:5–6; 7:9). Now the disciplined person has repented and Paul urges them to forgive him. The disciplined man may have been, as most modern scholars think, a vocal critic of Paul (though see "the one wronged" in 7:12). Apparent literary connections may allow that he was the incestuous man mentioned in 1 Corinthians 5:1–5, as most church fathers thought. (If he was the latter, however, it took Paul's harsh letter [2:3–4] to achieve his discipline; the Corinthians had not disciplined him after receiving 1 Cor 5.)[9] A few have suggested that he was both the incestuous man and a vocal critic, influenced by Paul's opponents. Now that the man had repented, there was no need to continue the discipline (2:5–8, 10). Although Satan could be an agent of divine discipline (12:7; 1 Cor 5:5), he would gladly exploit a situation like excessive alienation for harm (2:11; cf. 11:14; 1 Cor 7:5).

2:12–13: PAUL'S CONCERN FOR TITUS

2:12: Now when I came to Troas for the gospel of Christ and when a door was opened for me in the Lord,
2:13: I had no rest for my spirit, not finding Titus my brother; but taking my leave of them, I went on to Macedonia.

*P*aul weaves the narrative about Titus's mission to them, which was to precede and test the advisability of his own, into his pleas to them to embrace his ministry again (see esp. 7:5–7, 13–15). (Contrary to what one might expect from most conventional outlines in rhetorical handbooks, ancient writers could mix narrative and proofs.)[10] Titus had delivered the instructions for the man's discipline (2:3–4; 7:8–13); Paul's concern for how Titus has been received is part

---

[8] For "testing" intentions, see Caesar *C.W.* 2.32–33; C. Keener, *John* (2003), 665.
[9] Most commentators from the Fathers through the Reformers thought that Paul addressed the incestuous man here; but they also unpersuasively identified his tearful letter with 1 Corinthians.
[10] See, e.g., F. W. Hughes, "The Rhetoric of Reconciliation: 2 Corinthians 1.1–2.13 and 7.5–8.24," 246–61 in *Persuasive Artistry*, ed. D. Watson, 252–53.

of his display of affectionate concern for how the church has responded to him, hence to his gospel (1:19–22; 2:14–7:4). The uncertainties of travel and correspondence sometimes led to crossed plans, with parties waiting in separate places (e.g., Cicero *Att.* 3.8).

2:14–17: GOD SENT PAUL

2:14: But thanks be to God, who always leads us in His triumph in Christ, and manifests through us the sweet aroma of the knowledge of Him in every place.
2:15: For we are a fragrance of Christ to God among those who are being saved and among those who are perishing;
2:16: to the one an aroma from death to death, to the other an aroma from life to life. And who is adequate for these things?
2:17: For we are not like many, peddling the word of God, but as from sincerity, but as from God, we speak in Christ in the sight of God.

The next major section of Paul's letter is 2:14–7:4. Here Paul is an ambassador of a revelation greater than that to Moses; those with eternal perspectives can recognize this revelation's glory. Thus Paul pleads with the Corinthians to be reconciled to him – hence to the Lord whose representative he is.

The invitation to be reconciled to God seems in tension with a context that suggests a resolution already accomplished (7:7–13). Although 2:14–7:4 (or the bulk of it) seems to intrude so abruptly into the narrative that many scholars regard it as a separate Pauline letter interpolated here, contemporary literary criticism invites us to at least explore the possibility of the letter's unity (easier here than with the break at 10:1). (Possibly 2:14–7:4 depends on a draft of a letter Paul was preparing before receiving Titus's good news, but he would hardly have included it in the new letter if reconciliation were already complete.) Because ancient letter collections usually preserved some indications (such as introductory or concluding remarks) of breaks between discrete letters; and an accidental interpolation of this nature, possible in pages of a later codex, is unlikely to have appeared this early in a scroll without leaving traces in our textual tradition, the burden of proof should rest with those arguing for disunity. In this case, the evidence is insufficient to carry the burden of proof.[11]

It might seem more likely that 2:14–7:4 is an argument section following a *narratio*, a frequent pattern in argumentation, if the "narrative" of 2:12–13 did not resume at 7:5. But orators did sometimes weave their *narratio* into their argument,[12] and Homer could digress for seventy-five lines and then expect

---

[11] For more detailed arguments supporting the unity of 2:14–7:4 with its context, see, e.g., D. deSilva, *Credentials* (1998), 4–14.
[12] See F. Hughes, "Rhetoric" (1991), 252–53.

his audience to return to the point simply by repeating the verb where he left off.[13] Digressions were frequent, and Paul's narrative here, establishing the common ground and fond feeling between Paul and the Corinthians, provides a useful framing device for Paul's apologetic appeal. This framing need no more betray an interpolation than the B element in the A–B–A' pattern often found in 1 Corinthians (6:1–8 in Chs. 5–6; Ch. 9 in Chs. 8–10; Ch. 13 in Chs. 12–14). Given Paul's frequent use of framing devices, an interpolation is unlikely in 2:14–7:4, and (despite some apparently non-Pauline expressions) in 6:14–7:1. Instead, Paul seems to use the narrative of Titus to frame his exhortation to them here. See further comments at 7:5–16.

In 2:14–16, Paul depicts the ministry of himself and his colleagues by employing the images of triumphal processions and the sacral use of incense, perhaps at such processions (cf. Josephus *War* 7.72), although the image is also biblical (e.g., Ps 141:2; Phil 4:18). Christ, not himself, is central in his ministry, in contrast with the activity of charlatans (2:17; cf. 4:2). In contrast to the Roman Republic, under the Empire, only the emperor celebrated triumphs.

Most captives led in triumphal procession were executed afterward, but Paul's participation here is *both* his death (his suffering for the gospel) and eternal life (sharers of Christ's death will also share his resurrection).[14] His ministry (cf. 2:17; 4:2) announces death to the spiritually dead, who find only death in the stench of his apostolic suffering. The cross speaks death for those for whom the cross reveals nothing beyond itself. But his ministry proclaims life to those with faith to trust the resurrection promise implicit in Christ's cross and the broken vessel of its bearer. The watching world (cf. 1 Cor 4:9) is thus destined to become captives led to death as well, as perishing followers of the god of this age (2 Cor 4:3–4; cf. 1 Cor 1:18).

This theme continues in following paragraphs. Those who depend only on the letter get death (3:6), but those who bring the new covenant message revealed by the Spirit offer life (3:6). The world perceives in the gospel's agents only their suffering and death, but these messengers have life inside (4:16–5:1, 5) and eternally (4:11, 14–15; 5:1–4), and by their dying bring life to others (4:12). Whether the audience is led to death or life depends on whether one looks to the heart or appearance (5:12, 16), to letter or spirit (3:6), by sight or by faith (4:13–14; 5:7).

Paul recognizes the inadequacy of all human agents to bring life (2:16: "Who is sufficient?" *hikanos*), but affirms that true apostolic competence (*hikanos* and cognates) to bring life comes from God's Spirit (3:5–6; cf. Ex 3:11, 14).

---

[13] See J. D. Harvey, *Listening to the Text: Oral Patterning in Paul's Letters* (Leicester: Apollos; Grand Rapids, MI: Baker, 1998), 58.

[14] Other honorees might join a procession (e.g., Livy 40.43.4–7; Valerius Maximus 5.2.6), but the term for "leads in triumphal procession" here normally specifies captives as its object. Triumphs included public thanksgiving (cf. 2:14; 8:16; 9:15).

The language of 2:17 reflects stock charges against charlatans and sophists (e.g., *Rhet. Alex.* pref. 1421a.32–34; Iamblichus *Pyth. Life* 34.245). (The charge against ancient speakers was often deserved; many handbooks on forensic rhetoric in effect explained how to deceive effectively.) Although anticipating and distancing oneself from such charges was good rhetoric in any case, the hucksters with whom Paul contrasts himself here probably represent the opponents who surface (whether or not the letter is a unity) in 11:4–5, 22. Unlike Paul, they are happy to accept the Corinthians' support (11:7–9), allowing Paul to denigrate them with the tradition of ministers with convictions for sale (Jer 6:13–14; 8:10–11; Micah 3:5, 11). (Those wishing to apply the text may note that some professional clergy and scholars still cater more to their paying clientele or institutions than to personal convictions.)

Paul's integrity with regard to funds in 2:17 becomes an important issue in later chapters (8:20–21), probably in opposition to others' doubts (12:16–18). This verse is so crucial to Paul's point in the letter that many regard it as his *propositio* (shortly after the narrative and before most of the proofs). (Others identify it as 1:12, but because letters were not handbook-style speeches, we need not be overly particular on this point.)

3:1–18: REVEALING THE GREATER COVENANT'S GLORY

3:1: Are we beginning to commend ourselves again? Or do we need, as some, letters of commendation to you or from you?

3:2: You are our letter, written in our hearts, known and read by all men;

3:3: being manifested that you are a letter of Christ, cared for by us, written not with ink, but with the Spirit of the living God, not on tablets of stone, but on tablets of human hearts.

3:4: And such confidence we have through Christ toward God.

3:5: Not that we are adequate in ourselves to consider anything as coming from ourselves, but our adequacy is from God,

3:6: who also made us adequate as servants of a new covenant, not of the letter, but of the Spirit; for the letter kills, but the Spirit gives life.

3:7: But if the ministry of death, in letters engraved on stones, came with glory, so that the sons of Israel could not look intently at the face of Moses because of the glory of his face, fading as it was,

3:8: how shall the ministry of the Spirit fail to be even more with glory?

3:9: For if the ministry of condemnation has glory, much more does the ministry of righteousness abound in glory.

3:10: For indeed what had glory, in this case has no glory on account of the glory that surpasses it.

3:11: For if that which fades away was with glory, much more that which remains is in glory.

3:12: Having therefore such a hope, we use great boldness in our speech,

3:13: and are not as Moses, who used to put a veil over his face that the sons of Israel might not look intently at the end of what was fading away.

3:14: But their minds were hardened; for until this very day at the reading of the old covenant the same veil remains unlifted, because it is removed in Christ.

3:15: But to this day whenever Moses is read, a veil lies over their heart;

3:16: but whenever a man turns to the Lord, the veil is taken away.

3:17: Now the Lord is the Spirit; and where the Spirit of the Lord is, there is liberty.

3:18: But we all, with unveiled face beholding as in a mirror the glory of the Lord, are being transformed into the same image from glory to glory, just as from the Lord, the Spirit.

*A*lthough emphasizing the strategic character of his ministry (2:14–17), Paul insists that he is not commending himself or boasting (3:1).[15] Self-commendation was viewed as inappropriate except under particular circumstances, such as those that Paul finally uses to indulge in the practice in 10:12–12:11 (see comment on 10:12). But if Paul cannot commend himself, does he then need others' recommendations on his behalf, as "some" others produced (3:1)? (Refusing to name opponents was often a way to refuse to dignify them.) These others are probably the "peddlers . . . like so many" in 2:17.

A CLOSER LOOK: LETTERS OF RECOMMENDATION[16]

Because the central value of hospitality was subject to abuse, travelers often carried letters of recommendation from people their hosts might respect, such as synagogue representatives in another town. More generally, people of higher rank petitioned peers for favors on behalf of friends or clients; such letters (typically carried by the bearer) obligated the author to the benefactor, and the beneficiary to both. Sometimes letters employed such formulas as, "Do to him as you would to me" (cf. *P.Oxy.* 32; Phlm 17). Cicero once insisted that he would stop dwelling on the merits of the case, lest anyone suppose that justice rather than Cicero's friendship had persuaded the benefactor; "any favor" the beneficiary receives should be seen as a favor to Cicero by virtue of friendship (*Fam.* 13.5.3).

Cicero was a master at writing such letters, somehow managing to avoid the impression of sending form letters while obligating many younger men to

---

[15] A person could write a letter of recommendation while claiming that the beneficiary does not need one (e.g., Cic. *Fam.* 13.16.3–4).

[16] On such letters see, e.g., C.-H. Kim, *Form and Structure of the Familiar Greek Letter of Recommendation* (SBLDS 4; Missoula, MT, 1972); more briefly, S. Stowers, *Letter Writing*, 153–65.

himself politically. Still, Cicero could be formulaic, and rather often offered statements like, "There is none like him" (e.g., *Fam.* 13.1.5, 18.2, 26.1; cf. Phil 2:20) or "This recommendation is more special than the others" (*Fam.* 13.32.2, 34.1, 35.1). He frequently asks the benefactor to prove what a good letter of recommendation he has written on the beneficiary's behalf (e.g., *Fam.* 3.1.3; 13.19.3, 20.1, 26.4).

Many philosophers rejected the value of others' endorsements (Diogenes *Ep.* 9; Epictetus *Diatr.* 1.9.27, 33–34; 2.3.1–2). Had Paul depended on Corinthian letters, he could have appeared to be their client (see comment on 12:13–14). Self-commendation (as indicated in 3:1) was often more problematic, limited by social convention to "justifiable" circumstances (see comment on 10:12).

Paul needs no external letters of reference to the Corinthians, whose own existence as a church testifies to his ministry as a life-giving aroma (3:2; cf. 2:15–16; Paul elsewhere appeals to the church's own experience, e.g., 1 Cor 2:4–5). Although everyone would understand the idea of letters or laws written in human hearts,[17] Paul's language in 3:3 alludes especially to two biblical promises he regards as fulfilled in his day (cf. 1:20). First, in Ezek 36:26 (cf. 11:19), God's Spirit would give his people hearts of flesh instead of hearts of stone, so they would keep his commandments (36:27; cf. 11:20).[18] (This explains Paul's unusually *positive* use of "*fleshly* hearts" here, which the NRSV obscures by translating "*human* hearts.") Whereas God's finger had written the law in the stone tablets (Ex 31:18; 34:1, 4), God's Spirit (Ezek 36:27) now inscribed divine life in their hearts (cf. Rom 8:2). Although "living God" is a common title, Paul wishes here to connect the Spirit of the "living God" with the giving of life (cf. 6:16; Deut 5:26).

Second, he alludes to Jeremiah: in contrast to the disobedience of God's people in history, the new covenant would write the law in their hearts (Jer 31:32–33; on that new era, cf. Jer 3:15–16; 16:14–15; 23:7–8). This text explains Paul's introduction of the new covenant in 3:6. Paul must have already explained these promises to the Corinthians (cf. 1 Cor 11:23, 25; cf. Rom 7:6).[19] Now their existence as people of the new covenant functioned as proof of Paul's ministry (3:2–3; also 1 Cor 9:2).

Careful not to boast in himself (3:1), Paul notes that the competence comes not from himself but from God (2:16; 3:5). Continuing the new covenant image

[17] E.g., Diogenes Laertius 6.1.5; laws in Josephus *Ag. Ap.* 2.178; Plutarch *Uneducated Ruler* 3, *Mor.* 780CD; Maximus of Tyre 6.5–6.

[18] Paul links texts by wordplay: stone was used to preserve laws (Livy 39.37.16), but in Greek stony hearts were considered hard, that is, unfeeling (Hom. *Od.* 23.103).

[19] Note similarly the Spirit's fruit as fulfilling the law (Gal 5:22–23; cf. 5:14; 6:2; cf. sharing the divine moral character in 2 Pet 1:4; 1 Jn 3:9). Internalizing Torah was already a Jewish ideal (Ps 40:8; Philo *Leg.* 210).

of the Spirit writing the law on the heart in 3:3, Paul notes that he is a minister of the new covenant (3:6). The "letter," what is merely written on stone or with ink (cf. 3:3; Rom 7:6), cannot give life, but only sentence transgressors to death (cf. Rom 7:5, 10; 8:2; 1 Cor 15:56; Gal 3:21); the glory that accompanies it could kill (Ex 33:20). The law that the Spirit writes on human hearts, however, brings life, enabling fulfillment (Rom 8:2–11). At the giving of the law from Sinai, Moses's experience with God rather than Israel's violation of it (and inability to endure Moses's experience) modeled what new covenant life would be like (2 Cor 3:7–18; cf. Ex 32–34).

In 3:7–11, Paul infers logically that a promised new covenant ministry's glory must exceed that of Moses's day.[20] Paul dwells on the point at length, as rhetoricians sometimes did when emphasizing a matter.[21] In his argument he employs the rhetorical devices of antithesis and repetition, as well as the conventional logical argument (used by both Jews and Gentiles) of "how much more" (cf. Rom 5:15–17). First, the Spirit must reveal greater glory than the law. God revealed glory when he gave the written law (Ex 33:18–19; 34:4–7), which could not bring life. Therefore the ministry of the Spirit today (cf. 3:17), which does give life (3:6), must reveal greater glory (3:7–8). Moses saw only part of God's glory, because no one could see God and live (Ex 33:10);[22] the new covenant reveals all God's glory without killing. This is because the new covenant transforms from the inside (cf. 3:3; 4:6, 16–18; Jer 31:31–34) rather than the outside (like Moses's glory). For the same reason, however, it is concealed to those who lack the Spirit's insight (2 Cor 4:3–4, 11; 5:7).

Second, the ministry that brings righteousness (hence life) rather than condemnation (hence death) must be more glorious (3:9). Paul already alluded in 3:3 to the text that indicates that the new covenant's law in hearts enables obedience (Jer 31:31–34). Third, Moses's glory was transient, destined to be replaced by the greater glory of Jeremiah's promised "new covenant," a glory and covenant that would never pass (3:10–11; cf. Jer 32:39–40; 33:20–26). (Contrary to subsequent Christian usage, by "old covenant" Paul refers to the Sinai covenant recorded in a portion of the Pentateuch, not to Hebrew Scripture per se; the "new covenant" refers to the new arrangement by Christ's death [1 Cor 11:25], not to Scripture written after Jesus's coming.)

Paul now contrasts the public character of new covenant glory with the visible, yet concealed, character of Moses's glory (3:12–18). Moses was "glorified" (*doxazein*, Ex 34:29–30, 35). Nevertheless, for the sake of the Israelites, who could

---

[20] Among the many helpful sources on this section, see L. L. Belleville, *Reflections of Glory: Paul's Polemical Use of the Moses-Doxa Tradition in 2 Corinthians 3.1–18* (JSNTS 52; Sheffield: Sheffield Academic Press, 1991); R. B. Hays, *Echoes of Scripture in the Letters of Paul* (New Haven, CT: Yale, 1989), 123–53.

[21] See R. Anderson, *Glossary* (2000), 53, on *epimonē*.

[22] A later Christian text develops this theme in greater detail (Jn 1:14–18; see C. Keener, *John* [2003], 405–19).

not endure the glory, Moses had to hide the glory on his face, though it was impermanent (3:13; cf. 5:13; Ex 34:30, 33–35).[23] As a new covenant minister of life, however, Paul can take courage to speak frankly (3:12; cf. 2:17; 4:2, 13; for taking courage to speak, cf. 3:4; 4:1, 16; 5:6, 11) – even if it appears too bold to some (3:1; 5:12; 10:1–2, 10–12; 11:21). Apostles are transfigured as Moses was, but in a way that does not harm their viewers. (Some think that Paul compares his opponents [2:17; 11:22] with Moses, or even that they used Moses as a paradigm of glory that Paul in his weakness could not match. This is possible, but Paul is not denigrating Moses, who was forced by old covenant circumstances to act this way. The new covenant format of the law in the heart has surpassed the old covenant format on stones, but it was always God's good gift; cf. Rom 7:12–14.)

Although the new covenant had come in Christ, Moses's followers who do not receive Christ remain under the old covenant, still unable to perceive God's full glory (3:13–16). Their minds were hardened (3:14; cf. Rom 11:7, 25; Is 63:17), like the blinded minds of all who do not believe in Christ (4:3–4; cf. both blindness and hardness in Is 6:10, as rendered in Jn 12:40). Most of verse 14 is parallel with verse 15, although verse 15 probably adds exegetical support for it: the veil remained over their minds (3:14–15), but was removed in Christ (3:14), just as Moses removed his own veil when he spoke with the Lord himself (3:15).

Paul climaxes his contrast by commenting midrashically on "the Lord" of the Exodus narrative in 3:17–18: Moses saw the partial glory of "the Lord" (Ex 33:9, 11, 19; 34:5–6, 34), but this corresponds to the greater new covenant experience of God's Spirit. In the context of this passage, this is the Spirit that comes through the new covenant and writes the full glory of God's word on his people's hearts (3:3, 6). For Paul, those who have the Spirit have "freedom" from the external covenant (Gal 2:4; 5:1, 13; Rom 7:6; 8:2), although perhaps here Paul emphasizes "freedom" to reveal the glory fully (cf. 3:12–13; or, possibly but not likely, freedom from being captives led to death, 2:14).[24]

Paul likewise climaxes his emphasis on the transforming power of the message of life in 3:18. Whereas the glory of the first covenant was limited, transient, and deadly, those who "turn to the Lord" receive the Spirit, hence the glory of the internalized, new covenant law (3:3, 6–11, 16–17). For them the veil is removed, as it was for Moses when he was before the Lord (3:16). All those on whose hearts the Spirit inscribes the new covenant message are transformed to keep God's covenant, as they continue to behold God's glory and know God (cf. 3:3; Jer 31:32–34).

Paul here presupposes two ideas his audience would share: first, God stamped his image on people through his *logos*, or wisdom, which was his archetypal

---

23 Some traditions associate this concealment with Israel's sin (e.g., *Sipre Num.* 1.10.3; cf. *L.A.B.* 12:7). Coverings also obscure "glory" and "image" in 1 Cor 11:7, although only applied there to women.

24 On spiritual "freedom" in antiquity, see C. Keener, *John* (2003), 750–51.

image; for early Christians, this image is Christ (4:4; see comment on 1 Cor 15:45–49). Greek-speaking Jews spoke of divine Wisdom as a mirror perfectly reflecting God's glory (Wis 7:26); Christ as divine Wisdom may be the "mirror" of 2 Corinthians 3:18. What was lost of God's glory and image in Adam is restored in Christ (cf. Col 3:10; Eph 4:24; see comment at 1 Cor 15:49). (The "mirror" might also imply divine glory placed in the heart; 3:3, 6; cf. 13:3–5.)[25]

Second, mentally beholding the supreme deity transformed one into that deity's likeness. Although the idea became prominent in Middle Platonism (and Paul freely borrows Platonic language; cf. 4:16–5:1), Paul found this experience in Moses's transformation in Exodus, as noted earlier (perhaps by way of Jesus; cf. Mk 9:2).

Believers' continual, Spirit-empowered encounter with God in the gospel would transform their hearts to reflect his image and glory (for divine image as glory, see 1 Cor 11:7). Moses reflected God's glory in his face; new covenant ministers and those who embrace their message reflect it in their hearts and lives (4:6), sharing Christ's resurrection power as they share his sufferings (4:10–12, 16). Paul beholds not the passionless deity of Platonism, but the God of the cross who embraced human brokenness and mortality.

Of course, the Corinthians (and some Christians since then) may have reasonably questioned whether their characters noticeably reflected Christ's image; but Paul insisted that they recognize that his own ministry did so (cf. 13:5–6). He apparently believed that Christians could choose to be transformed into Christ's image by thinking rightly (Rom 12:2; cf. Col 3:1–11; Eph 4:22–24); such meditation also may have offered a setting for his own visions of Christ (2 Cor 12:1–4). However, although Paul stresses full unveiling here, elsewhere he acknowledges that in some sense God's glory would continue to be perceived only partially, as in a mirror, until the end of the age (1 Cor 13:10–12); only at Christ's coming would believers behold fully (1 Cor 13:12) and be fully glorified and transformed into his image (1 Cor 15:49; Rom 8:29–30).

A CLOSER LOOK: DIVINE TRANSFORMATION THROUGH AN IMAGE

Although the ultimate beatific vision awaited the soul's liberation from earthly matter at death, many philosophers urged preparation for that state in the present. Middle Platonists believed that their intellects, by focusing on what was divine and heavenly, could envision the divine (Maximus of Tyre 11.9–12) or gain a heavenly perspective (Philo *Spec. Laws* 3.1–2), a view shared with

---

[25] Any concept of "divinity" involved in self-knowledge (e.g., Plato *Alc.* 1.132E–133C; Cicero *Tusc.* 1.22.52; *Leg.* 1.22.58–59), however, is more remote culturally than Wisdom theology (though later combined, *Sent. Sext.* 445–50; *Odes Sol.* 13.1–4).

Stoics.[26] Jewish mystics also sought vision of the divine, focusing on the heavenly throne-chariot (see comment on 12:2–4).

Pauline theology focused "heavenly vision" (4:18) on Christ himself (4:4; 12:1, 8–9; Col 3:1–2, 10; cf. Eph 2:6). Johannine Christians later affirmed present, past, and future transformation through vision of God (1 Jn 3:2–3, 6), although like Paul, they grounded it in OT examples (Jn 1:14–18, echoing Ex 33–34; Jn 8:56; 12:40).

BRIDGING THE HORIZONS

Many early Christian interpreters used Paul's comments about "letter" and "Spirit" to justify allegory. In its most blatant forms, allegory derived from Greek philosophers trying to salvage principles of ethical value from old myths, by way of Hellenistic Judaism (especially evident in Philo). Paul himself more often drew analogies (e.g., 1 Cor 10:1–11) rather than what we usually call allegories (the ancient term could be stretched to cover both).

Even these analogies suggest that Paul's contrast between "letter" and "Spirit" has hermeneutical implications. Most modern scholars recognize, however, that Paul's focus here is moral or ontological more than hermeneutical. The letter of ink or on stone had its place in salvation history, but only the Spirit could write the letter in the heart; the letter could only inform, whereas the Spirit came to transform.

Of course, Paul still regarded the written law as morally authoritative in content, if rightly understood; he shared Judaism's view that the Spirit inspired the written code (Rom 1:2; 3:21). He was no antinomian; though the Christian faith's marginal status in his day made merely nominal assent to it a reckless act, he would not have regarded nominal assent without transformation as true to his message. Legalism merely seeks to preserve past experience of the Spirit in the letter, attending to regulations or prepositional claims. The Spirit renews a fresh experience with God and conscious submission to God's will. God grants the Spirit in response to faith.

For Paul, transformation through faithful meditation on Christ (cf. also Col 3:1–11; 1 Jn 3:2–3, 6) or, better yet, sharing his sufferings (2 Cor 4:10–11; Phil 3:10) builds a living relationship with God. Various traditions have historically appropriated different elements of this perspective, for example, meditation on the divine in the Eastern Orthodox monastic tradition (familiar with Platonic imagery); Roman Catholic meditation on the cross; and evangelical or charismatic emphasis on a personal intimacy with God.

---

[26] They also might accept other soul travel (Lucian *Men.*; Maximus of Tyre 26.1; 38.3; cf. apocalyptic tours of heaven) or pagan rituals to induce it (Maximus of Tyre 8.2; *PGM* 4.934; 77.1–5).

4:1–15: GOD'S GLORY IN WEAK VESSELS

4:1: Therefore, since it is by God's mercy that we are engaged in this ministry, we do not lose heart.

4:2: We have renounced the shameful things that one hides; we refuse to practice cunning or to falsify God's word; but by the open statement of the truth we commend ourselves to the conscience of everyone in the sight of God.

4:3: And even if our gospel is veiled, it is veiled to those who are perishing.

4:4: In their case the god of this world has blinded the minds of the unbelievers, to keep them from seeing the light of the gospel of the glory of Christ, who is the image of God.

4:5: For we do not proclaim ourselves; we proclaim Jesus Christ as Lord and ourselves as your slaves for Jesus' sake.

4:6: For it is the God who said, "Let light shine out of darkness," who has shone in our hearts to give the light of the knowledge of the glory of God in the face of Jesus Christ.

4:7: But we have this treasure in clay jars, so that it may be made clear that this extraordinary power belongs to God and does not come from us.

4:8: We are afflicted in every way, but not crushed; perplexed, but not driven to despair;

4:9: persecuted, but not forsaken; struck down, but not destroyed;

4:10: always carrying in the body the death of Jesus, so that the life of Jesus may also be made visible in our bodies.

4:11: For while we live, we are always being given up to death for Jesus' sake, so that the life of Jesus may be made visible in our mortal flesh.

4:12: So death is at work in us, but life in you.

4:13: But just as we have the same spirit of faith that is in accordance with scripture – "I believed, and so I spoke" – we also believe, and so we speak,

4:14: because we know that the one who raised the Lord Jesus will raise us also with Jesus, and will bring us with you into his presence.

4:15: Yes, everything is for your sake, so that grace, as it extends to more and more people, may increase thanksgiving, to the glory of God.

In the face of the Corinthians' suspicions about his character and message (1:15–22), Paul continues to emphasize that what matters is not himself, but Christ working in him (4:5–15; 13:3). In 4:1, Paul and colleagues have the "ministry" of the new covenant (3:6–9), hence need not "lose heart" (also 4:16; cf. 3:4, 12), regardless of the personal cost (4:7–16).[27] (Stoics also affirmed that the sage

---

27 Although verbs of "having" (*echein*) are not unusual, their repetition in this section seems deliberate (3:4, 12; 4:1, 7, 13; 5:1). Paul's expressions of self-confidence may perform

should remain courageous in the face of adversity, though they did not credit this courage to God's help; e.g., Seneca *Lucil.* 67.16; *Dial.* 7.8.2–3; cf. 4 Macc 18:2–3.) Although the ministers are frail, the glory they reveal is God's own image, Christ (4:5–7; cf. 3:18). Preferring truth to falsehood (like the honorable stereotype of sages versus sophists; cf. 1:12; 2:17), they do not need to commend themselves, for their very character commends them to the Corinthians' consciences (4:2; cf. 3:1; 5:11–12). Paul's denial of "falsifying" God's message (4:2; the verb means something like "adulterate") recalls 2:17 and probably alludes to his rivals by way of contrast. In contrast to Moses who hid God's glory (albeit not for shame, 3:13), Paul's openness (3:12; versus what "one hides" here) should remove any suspicion.

Not everyone, however, recognized the apostles' sincerity; to some they were merely the odor of death for death (2:16). Just as a veil (*kalumma*) obscured Israel's vision of divine glory (3:13–16), so the gospel's glory was veiled (*kaluptō*) to all who were perishing, those blinded by the god of this age (4:3–4). Paul's wording in 4:4 and 4:6 underlines the contrast between the spiritually blind and the enlightened:[28]

4:4	4:6
The god	God
Of this age	Who shines light from darkness
Has blinded	Has shined
The minds of unbelievers	Our hearts
Lest should shine	For (*pros*)
The light of the gospel	The light of the knowledge
Of Christ's glory	Of God's glory
Who is God's image	In the face of Jesus Christ

Who is the "god of this age" who blinded unbelievers? Some early interpreters, combating dualists, inferred that Paul meant God (Chrysostom *Hom. Cor.* 8.2); other, like most modern scholars, inferred the devil (Pelagius *Comm. 2 Cor.* 4). Jewish texts use similar expressions for God (*Jub.* 25:23), but some early Christians used such language for the devil (Jn 12:31; 14:30; 16:11). Paul's own usage proves decisive: he elsewhere can speak of unbelievers' false "god" (Phil 3:19; cf. Euripides *Cycl.* 336–38). Granted, God also hardened Israel in Paul's theology (Rom 11:7); but apocalyptic Jewish thought accepted both God's sovereignty and Satan's wicked activity. God brings light, but Satan, darkness and spiritual blindness (6:14–15).

---

a summary function (cf. S. N. Olson, "Epistolary Uses of Expressions of Self-Confidence," *JBL* 103 [1984]: 585–97).

[28] T. B. Savage, *Power through Weakness: Paul's Understanding of the Christian Ministry in 2 Corinthians* (SNTSM 86; Cambridge: Cambridge University, 1996), 127. For texts regarding spiritual blindness, see C. Keener, *John* (2003), 796.

The glory Paul reveals, which the world rejects, is Christ, God's image (4:4). Popular Jewish thought assigned this role of God's image to Wisdom (Wis 7:26). Many thinkers argued that the supreme deity had stamped his image on creation through his *logos* or divine Wisdom (articulated most forcefully by the Jewish Platonist Philo); early Christians found in biblical personifications of Wisdom a bridge to understanding Christ as God's image (cf. Col 1:15; Jn 14:9).[29]

The God who revealed glory at creation has now revealed his full glory in Christ (4:6);[30] those transformed through trusting this once-crucified divine image (3:18) would reveal his glory by their own suffering (4:7–11). (By using the language of Is 9:1–2 to express the thought of God creating light in Gen 1:3, Paul also may evoke his Gentile mission in 4:6. According to Luke, Paul himself had been blinded and enlightened; Acts 9:8.)

Paul preached Christ's glory, not himself, who was weak (4:5, 7). In 4:7 he notes that he embraces his own weakness, identifying with the cross to share Christ's resurrection power (12:9–10; 13:4). This "treasure" contrasts with the falsified merchandise (4:2) Paul's rivals "hawk" (2:17). Paul's humble image in 4:7 would certainly have been intelligible, even if uncomfortable to the elite among his audience.[31] Scholars note that Corinth produced many cheap, frail pottery lamps. Clay vessels were easily broken and virtually disposable (cf. Ps 31:12; Is 30:14; Jer 19:11), hence frail mortals appear thus in some texts (e.g., 1QS 11.22; 1QH 3.23–24).[32] Many ancients compared the body to a vessel (cf. 1 Thess 4:4); a great person who appeared otherwise could also be compared to greatness in a small vessel (cf. Ps.-Callisthenes *Alex.* 2.15). Some stored great treasures in cheap vessels; some sages emphasized that cheap and simple vessels were as useful as expensive ones (Musonius Rufus 20, p. 124.17–31). The figurative use of treasures for wisdom or other intangible assets was still more widespread.[33]

Still, a cracked and leaking vessel was reckoned worthless (Ahiqar 109, saying 27), as were people so depicted (Heraclitus *Ep.* 8). Paul's thought is closer to later rabbis who emphasized that Torah resides only in scholars who are like the humblest vessels (*Sipre Deut.* 48.2.7), and that God prefers broken vessels because he is nearest the broken (*Pesiq. R. Kah.* 24:5; cf. Is 66:2).

Paul illustrates God's hidden glory and power in his weakness in 4:8–11. Sages sometimes used catalogues of hardships to demonstrate their integrity or ability to transcend such trials (see comment on 1 Cor 4:9–13). Paul can use such lists to emphasize his endurance (11:23–33), but his point here is God's power in his

---

[29] See C. Keener, *John* (2003), 343–60, 944–45.

[30] On the primeval light at creation, see C. Keener, *John*, 383–84.

[31] As in 2:14–16, Paul emphasizes God's greatness at his own expense; for this use of "vessels," cf. Rom 9:20–21; Is 29:16; 45:9; Sir 33:10–13.

[32] "Baked clay" pots do not necessarily evoke creation from dust (Gen 2:7), but they fit the notion of "earthly" bodies (5:1; 1Cor 15:40).

[33] E.g., Prov 2:4; Wis 7:14; Xenophon *Mem.* 4.2.9; Philo *Cher.* 48.

weakness (4:7; cf. 12:9; 13:3–4); sharing the life of the cross, Paul depends on the power of the resurrection, hence is "not crushed . . . not destroyed" (4:8–9). (The coupling of antonyms here, as in 6:8–10, was rhetorically significant; cf. Marcus Aurelius 2.11.)[34] For Stoics, nature warned against being overwhelmed (Seneca *Dial.* 6.7.3); for Paul, the help was resurrection power.

Transformation into Christ's image came not only through meditating on Christ and his death (3:18), but in sharing his sufferings while proclaiming the cross (4:10–12; cf. also Rom 8:18, 26–30).[35] If in the passion tradition disciples before the resurrection failed to follow Jesus to the cross (Mk 8:31–38; 14:50; 15:21), Paul wants postresurrection disciples to follow more faithfully. Paul experiences Christ's resurrection power concretely in testings, deliverances, and inward strength (cf. 1:9–10).

In 4:13 Paul speaks of the faith by which he meets his testing, faith that prepares him to die, if need be, without fear (5:7–8). He quotes LXX Ps 115:1 (NRSV Ps 116:10).[36] Because Jews and Christians sang or recited psalms, perhaps both he and his audience recognized that the verse's context was a psalm about the righteous sufferer's afflictions, offered to praise God for deliverance. Scholars debate what exactly Paul means by the "spirit" of faith. On the one hand, *pneuma* in such a construction can mean, "attitude" or "disposition" (e.g., Num 5:14; Is 61:3; Hos 5:4; 2 Tim 1:7; "spirit of the world" in 1 Cor 2:12). On the other, the context does suggest that God's Spirit generates faith for such endurance (5:5).[37]

The object of Paul's faith is the resurrection (4:13–14; cf. Rom 10:9–10; Col 2:12; 1 Thess 4:14; 1 Pet 1:21). Sharing Christ's resurrection life is both a present, internal experience (4:10–11, 16) and a future hope (4:14; 5:1–4); both enable Paul to face hardship confidently (4:16; 5:6). (Paul's language in 1 Thess 4:14 parallels verse 14 here.) Paul's sharing the cross brings his hearers the message of life (4:12). As Christ's life is exalted in Paul's sufferings, more receive Christ, despite the many who do not (4:15; cf. 2:14–16). In antiquity, benefactors received honor, so that both they and their beneficiaries profited from their benefactions; likewise, Paul celebrates the growth of recipients of God's grace yielding more praises to God (4:15; see comment on 9:11–15).

---

[34] For an even lengthier, analogous coupling of trials with God's deliverances, see *T. Jos.* 1:4–7, probably not influenced by Paul (in contrast to *Ep. Diognetus* 5.11–16).

[35] Scholars debate whether *nekrōsis* in 4:10 connotes deadness (Rom 4:19) or the process of dying; the term encompasses both. Rather than distinguishing between the two nuances, Paul may focus on the revolting character of the image the term conveys (cf. J. Fitzgerald, *Cracks* [1988], 177–79).

[36] The verse sounds more faithful in the LXX, and attributes some of the psalmist's complaint to *ekstasis* (115:2), the ambiguous sense of which proves useful to Paul in 5:13.

[37] Cf. the same question with "spirit of gentleness" (1 Cor 4:21; Gal 6:1); at least in the latter context, however, it is probably God's Spirit (see Gal 5:22–23). A survey of uses shows that the article is not decisive.

4:16–5:10: THE INNER PERSON'S FUTURE HOPE

4:16: So we do not lose heart. Even though our outer nature is wasting away, our inner nature is being renewed day by day.
4:17: For this slight momentary affliction is preparing us for an eternal weight of glory beyond all measure,
4:18: because we look not at what can be seen but at what cannot be seen; for what can be seen is temporary, but what cannot be seen is eternal.
5:1: For we know that if the earthly tent we live in is destroyed, we have a building from God, a house not made with hands, eternal in the heavens.
5:2: For in this tent we groan, longing to be clothed with our heavenly dwelling –
5:3: if indeed, when we have taken it off we will not be found naked.
5:4: For while we are still in this tent, we groan under our burden, because we wish not to be unclothed but to be further clothed, so that what is mortal may be swallowed up by life.
5:5: He who has prepared us for this very thing is God, who has given us the Spirit as a guarantee.
5:6: So we are always confident; even though we know that while we are at home in the body we are away from the Lord –
5:7: for we walk by faith, not by sight.
5:8: Yes, we do have confidence, and we would rather be away from the body and at home with the Lord.
5:9: So whether we are at home or away, we make it our aim to please him.
5:10: For all of us must appear before the judgment seat of Christ, so that each may receive recompense for what has been done in the body, whether good or evil.

*I*n 4:16, Paul's "inner person" experiences Christ's resurrection power even while his outer person is suffering for the gospel (4:7–15); his outer person would be "wasting away" (*diaphtheirein*) in any case because the present body is perishable (*phthartos*; cf. 1 Cor 15:42, 50–54). The "renewing" here involves spiritual transformation into Christ's image (3:18; cf. similar language in Rom 12:2; Col 3:10; Tit 3:5; cf. also Is 40:31).

Many intellectuals expected earthly passions to "weigh down" the soul, making difficult its postmortem ascent to the pure and perfect heavens (cf. Wis 9:15–16);[38] in 5:4, Paul might employ "burden," a cognate to "weigh down," comparably. In 4:17, however, Paul simply indicates that future glory will far surpass what he now suffers for it (cf. Rom 8:18), an idea intelligible to pagan and especially Jewish contemporaries.[39] "Weightier" matters were those that

---

[38] E.g., Porphyry *Marc.* 7.115–18; Augustine *C. Jul.* 70; cf. Musonius Rufus 18A, p. 112.27–28.
[39] Cf. *1 En.* 103:9–15; Wis 3:5; *4 Ezra* 7:14–16; *2 Bar.* 15:8; 48:50; *Sib. Or.* 5.269–70; *m. Abot* 5:23; Seneca *Dial.* 1.3.9.

were more important (Epictetus *Diatr.* 1.1.27), and that the Hebrew term for "glory" also means "weight" might be at least in the back of Paul's mind.

The eternality of this inner person in 4:18 echoes common Greek intellectual language for the eternality of the unseen, changeless nature in the heavens (see 5:1) versus the perishable earthly world. For many philosophers, what was unseen was intrinsically superior (e.g., Diodorus Siculus 10.7.3) and eternal (Plutarch *Isis* 78, *Mor.* 382F-383A), like Plato's ideal forms; only the intellect could perceive it (Plato *Rep.* 6.484B). For Paul, however, the basis is not the *intrinsic* eternality of the unseen world; it is participation in Christ's resurrection life (4:7–11), that will eventually affect the body as well (4:14; 5:1–4). (As most commentators note, Paul's concepts in this context are much closer to dominant forms of Jewish eschatology than to Platonism.)[40] Believers envision not an abstract, untouchable heavenly realm, but Jesus, God's image, who is enthroned there (3:18; 4:4; cf. Col 3:1–2). What is temporal and seen is the perishing outer person sharing Christ's sufferings (4:10–11, 16); faith beholds the invisible resurrection life in its midst (2:16; 4:4–16; 5:7).

A CLOSER LOOK: SOULS AND HEAVENS

Most Greeks would apply Paul's "inner person" (Rom 7:22; Eph 3:16) to the soul, which many considered eternal and heavenly.[41] The specific expression is rare in Plato, but circulated in Paul's day, most relevantly in the Jewish Platonist Philo.[42] Stoics and some others regarded externals as mostly a challenge or matter of indifference.[43] Some compared the externals of life, for a soul unenlightened by philosophy, with a squalid prison the soul will be glad to escape (Maximus of Tyre 7.5; 36.4–5); or viewed the soul as an exile imprisoned in the earthly body (Plutarch *Exile* 17, *Mor.* 607D, following Plato *Phaedrus* 250c). Even harsher was the longstanding tradition that the body (*sōma*) was a tomb (*sēma*; e.g., Philo *Alleg. Interp.* 1.108).

Many would have shared Paul's preference for what was eternal (cf. *T. Dan* 4:5; *T. Benj.* 6:2; Seneca *Lucil.* 66.31), which many identified with what was unchangeable (Seneca *Lucil.* 66.32). Many intellectuals believed that the soul was eternal but the body mortal (Porphyry *Marc.* 12.212–15; Philo *Creation* 135); Platonists specifically grounded this belief in the preexistence and unchangeableness of souls (e.g., Maximus of Tyre 10.5); see discussion at 1 Cor 15:1–11. Stoics, more

---

[40] E.g., A. D. Nock, *St. Paul* (New York: Harper & Row, 1963), 205. Cf. analogously the presently unseen future hope of Jewish apocalyptic (4 *Ezra* 7:26; 2 *Bar.* 51:8).

[41] See discussion in C. Keener, *John* (2003), 554.

[42] Cf. D. E. Aune, "Anthropological Duality in the Eschatology of 2 Cor 4:16–5:10," 215–39 in *Paul Beyond the Divide*, ed. T. Engberg-Pedersen (2001), 220–22; Cicero *Resp.* 6.24.26. Some considered the "inner nature" divine (Cicero *Leg.* 1.22.58–59).

[43] E.g., Epictetus *Diatr.* 1.4.27; 1.9; 1.11.37; 2.2.10–12; 2.16.11; 4.10; Marcus Aurelius 7.14; Crates *Ep.* 3.

common in this period, traditionally affirmed the eternality of reason more than the persistence of individual minds, but some spoke of the soul's survival (Seneca *Lucil.* 57.9) until the cosmic renewal (*Dial.* 12.11.7).

Later thinkers urged removal from passions, which fix one's soul to the body, and turning instead to "the divine."[44] Some even viewed the body as a prison and already dead, yearning for the soul's release (e.g., Heraclitus *Ep.* 5; Maximus of Tyre 7.5).[45] Even Stoics regarded the body as dispensable (e.g., Epictetus *Diatr.* 1.1.24); for Philo, wise people know that they merely sojourn in bodies (*Her.* 265).

Many believed that the heavens were purer than the earth, hence were the natural home of the soul, freed from the body by death or by philosophic discipline that prepared one for death.[46] By contemplating the divine, the intellect could rise above earthly concerns toward the divine beyond the heavens, so preparing for afterlife (Philo *Spec.* 3.1; Maximus of Tyre 11.10). In such views, immortal souls would "fly" to heaven to join the gods (Heraclitus *Ep.* 5); those who turned from mortal concerns in this life would ascend to their native heavens more quickly (Cicero *Tusc.* 1.31.75). Paul also notes the limits of "earthly" bodies (5:1; 1 Cor 15:40; Col 3:5) and their interests (Phil 3:19), although his substitution of a "heavenly" body would have shocked most Greeks (5:2; 1 Cor 15:40, 47–48).

As earlier in the letter, Paul continues to adapt the eclectic language of popular philosophy (which mixed insights from various schools even more than the schools themselves did); such philosophy was disseminated widely on urban street corners. The church's elite members would be especially familiar with his model of the enduring sage. Educated elites might respect such sages even when eschewing their lifestyle. Paul's language in 4:16–5:4 especially recalls Wisdom 9:15: "for a perishable body weighs down the soul, and this earthy tent burdens the thoughtful mind" (NRSV); 9:16 goes on to speak of what is heavenly (cf. 2 Cor 5:1). Like Diaspora Judaism in the centuries before him, however, Paul was ready to adapt philosophic language in the service of his faith. He suffers bodily hardship and death for the gospel he preaches, in hope of future reward. But also like many fellow-Jews,[47] Paul saw no conflict between the soul's survival and future bodily resurrection.

In 5:1–4, Paul moves from focusing on his present experience of Christ's resurrection power during his sufferings (4:7, 10–11, 16) to the future consummation of this experience (as in 4:14). Others also could move from depicting an ideal sage enduring hardships (4:8–11) to a discussion of readiness to depart life

---

44   E.g., Porphyry *Marc.* 6.103–8; 7.131–34; 16.265–67; 32.494–97; Iamblichus *Pyth. Life* 32.228.
45   To later Platonists, the body was like a membrane to an embryo, only briefly necessary (Porphyry *Marc.* 32.489–93); a diseased beast from which the soul desired freedom (Maximus of Tyre 7.5); or a chariot to the charioteer (41.5).
46   Plato *Phaedrus* 248A–249A; Cicero *Tusc.* 1.19.43; Plutarch *Isis* 78, *Mor.* 382F.
47   E.g., *1 En.* 22:3, 13; 39:4; *4 Ezra* 7:37, 88–101; *2 Bar.* 21:33; 30:2; 50:2; cf. further W. Davies, *Paul* (1980), 311–15. In some texts, present and future eschatologies of paradise overlap.

(cf. Seneca *Lucil.* 120.12–15).[48] For Paul, however, the basis for his moral fortitude is the present foretaste of resurrection life by the Spirit (5:5).

The outer person is decaying, but the inner person is eternal, like the Greek view of the soul in the heavens (4:18). But Paul's hope, unlike Greek cosmology, is bodily (5:4); and the "glorified" (1 Cor 15:43; cf. 2 Cor 4:17) body awaits a future moment (1 Cor 15:23–26, 52). Why does Paul say, "we *have* a building," using the present tense? He cannot refer only to his eternal "inner person" (4:16–18), because a new house replaces the tent "we live in" (5:1), the "outer person" of 4:16. The new house must be a body suited to eternity like the "inner person" it bears (4:18–5:1), that is, a "heavenly" and imperishable body (1 Cor 15:40, 48–54).

But is the heavenly body received at the believer's death rather than together with other believers at Christ's coming, as many think? It is unlikely that Paul would have changed his view from 1 Corinthians 15:51–54 without pointing this out; such a move toward the Corinthians' eschatology should have required further explanation! Indeed, the language of 4:14 suggests that Paul retains his earliest attested view of corporate resurrection in 1 Thess 4:14–17.[49] Paul's language in 2 Cor 5:1–4 is that of the corporate resurrection: groaning (Rom 8:23); being clothed (1 Cor 15:53–54); death swallowed by life (1 Cor 15:54). Perhaps the likeliest change is simply that the dangers of the preceding year had made Paul more conscious that he might not live till Christ's coming (1:8; 1 Cor 15:51–52).

1 Cor 15	2 Cor 5:2–5
Earthly vs. heavenly, 15:49	Earthly (5:1) vs. heavenly (5:1–2)
Perishable vs. imperishable, 15:42, 50, 52f	(Eternal vs. temporal, 4:16–5:1)
Mortal puts on immortality, 15:53	Mortal (swallowed up by life), 5:4
"Putting on," 15:53f	Clothed with heavenly, 5:2–4
Death swallowed up, 15:54	Mortal swallowed up by life, 5:4
Spirit characterizes resurrected life, 15:44–46	Spirit as down payment, 5:5
(Groaning for future redemption, Rom 8:23, 26)	Groaning for heavenly dwelling, 5:2, 4

Why then does Paul presently "have" such a house? By the Spirit, Paul has already begun to partake of that glory (3:18) in his inner person (4:16), sharing Christ's resurrection life in the face of death (4:10–12). The Spirit is the "guarantee," the "first installment" that guarantees the rest (5:5; cf. 1:22; Rom 8:11); therefore although Paul walks by faith (5:7), he trusts that the body is already his, even in the face of his apostolic sufferings and likely martyrdom.

---

[48] With J. Fitzgerald, *Cracks* (1988), 182.

[49] If Philippians is a unity, as is likely, Paul could hold future and realized eschatology simultaneously (Phil 1:23; 3:18–21). Just as most Jews who affirmed the resurrection also accepted the soul's immortality in the intermediate state, Jewish apocalyptic also blended the present in heaven with the future (see A. T. Lincoln, *Paradise Now and Not Yet: Studies in the Role of the Heavenly Dimension in Paul's Thought with Special Reference to his Eschatology* [SNTSMS 43; Cambridge: Cambridge University, 1981]).

In 5:1 the present "tent" recalls Wisdom 9:15, in which the body as an "earthly" tent "weighs down" the soul. Paul describes the resurrection body in language normally reserved for a temple,[50] perhaps because he views not only the church as a whole as God's temple (1 Cor 3:16), but also the bodies of its individual members (1 Cor 6:19).[51] Even more than present bodies, resurrection bodies will be receptacles of the Spirit (1 Cor 15:44–46).

Many thinkers described the body as mere "clothing,"[52] so that death was disrobing (Philo *Alleg. Interp.* 2.56; Porphyry *Marc.* 33.501–505). Some contemporary or later Jewish texts may also adapt this clothing image for the resurrection body (*1 En.* 62:15; *3 En.* 18:22).[53] Greeks celebrated exercise in the nude, though even they regarded nakedness as shameful in some situations (Polybius 14.5.11). Although Romans favored nakedness less than Greeks (Juvenal *Sat.* 1.71), they had adopted the custom of nude bathing from Greeks (Plutarch *Marcus Cato* 20.5–6; *Roman Q.* 40, *Mor.* 274A), and Corinth had notable public baths (as well as public latrines). For most Jews, however, nudity remained scandalous.[54]

Philosophers and other intellectuals sometimes emphasized using reason to decide whether it was better to remain alive, though suffering, or depart.[55] That death brought an end to toils and hardship was a commonplace;[56] some who emphasized seeking eternal and heavenly realities also expected vision of the divine at that time (e.g., Maximus of Tyre 10.3). Paul was not eager for martyrdom (contrast Ignatius *Trall.* 10.1; *Rom.* 3–8), but he welcomed it as a rest from suffering (5:6, 8). The present experience and future promise of resurrection life (5:1–5; cf. 4:10–18) is the basis for Paul's courage in the face of potentially deadly apostolic sufferings (5:6–8). Between death and the resurrection, Paul would continue to experience the resurrection life of the Spirit (5:5), and to do so undistracted from present worldly concerns. This is desirable enough for Paul to describe it as being "at home with the Lord," a foretaste of the future dwellings (5:1–2).

To be with the Lord undistracted by present sufferings was thus desirable (Phil 1:21–25), although the ultimate goal was resurrection (2 Cor 5:2–4). The present "burden" (5:4) alludes to Paul's sufferings in 1:8 (which employs the same Greek term), but also may play (by way of contrast) on the greater "weight" of glory in 4:17 (using the term's noun cognate; cf. comment there; Wis 9:15).

---

50 "Not made with hands" (Mk 14:58; Heb 9:11, 24); a "house" superior to a temporary "tent" (1 Chron 6:32).

51 Most Jews expected an eschatological temple and often a heavenly temple (e.g., *1 En.* 90:28–29; Tob. 13:10; 14:5; 11QTemple cols. 30–45; 4Q174, 3.2; 4Q509, 4.2, 12; 4Q511, frg. 35, line 3; see E. P. Sanders, *Jesus and Judaism* [Philadelphia: Fortress, 1985], 77–90).

52 E.g., Seneca *Lucil.* 66.3; Epictetus *Diatr.* 1.25.21; Marcus Aurelius 10.1.

53 For texts with likely Christian influence, see *2 Esd.* 2.39, 45; *Ode Sol.* 25:8; *Asc. Is.* 9:9.

54 See texts in C. Keener, *John* (2003), 1229.

55 E.g., Cicero *Quint.* 1.3.1–2; Pliny *Ep.* 1.22.9–10.

56 E.g., Menander Rhetor 2.9, 413.28–29; 414.9–10; Tacitus *Agricola* 44–45; Libanius *Declamation* 3; Sir 30:17; Rev 14:13.

Despite his preference for death over continued suffering (5:8),[57] Paul's ultimate desire is not for death per se, which is unclothing; rather, his goal is to be "clothed" with the resurrection body (5:2–4; 1 Cor 15:53–54). Paul wants to conclude his mortality not with death but with mortality being transformed into immortality, by the greater power of life (5:4). But it is the certain hope of the resurrection body, which he now "has" (5:1), that gives him courage to face death for the sake of his ministry of life (5:6–8). In 5:5, Paul notes that his present experience of resurrection power (4:10–11, 16) guarantees its future consummation (4:14; 5:1–4); the present experience of the Spirit is a foretaste of its future fullness (1 Cor 2:9–10; 15:44).

Paul sandwiches an affirmation of faith between two denials of his fear to die (5:6, 8). In the midst of his mortal suffering, Paul walks "by faith" rather than "by sight" (5:7), preferring unseen, eternal reality (4:18), which assures "the spirit of faith" that he will be raised like Jesus (4:13–14).

Whether living or dying, Paul's goal was purely pleasing the Lord in light of the judgment at the resurrection; what would matter in that day would be not how long one lived in the body (5:6–8) but one's works in the body (5:9–10; cf. 1 Cor 4:5).[58] Such ideas might challenge the Corinthians (cf. 1 Cor 6:13–14; 15:12, 32), but motivated Paul, whose body now suffered (4:10–11). Ultimately he, like others, would account for what he did in the body (5:10) when he was in it (5:6–8). The term for "judgment seat" (5:10) is a normal one for the raised platforms from which governors could issue decrees or judgments, including the particularly impressive one excavated in Corinth (Acts 18:12).[59] More significantly for Paul's Christology, Christ assumes the role normally reserved for God in Jewish depictions of the day of judgment (Rom 14:10).[60] In light of this reality, Paul recognizes the urgency of his mission to offer God's message of reconciliation to the world (5:11–6:2).

5:11–6:10: PERSEVERING AMBASSADORS OF RECONCILIATION

5:11: Therefore, knowing the fear of the Lord, we try to persuade others; but we ourselves are well known to God, and I hope that we are also well known to your consciences.

5:12: We are not commending ourselves to you again, but giving you an opportunity to boast about us, so that you may be able to answer those who boast in outward appearance and not in the heart.

---

[57] A commonly expressed preference (e.g., Pliny *Ep.* 1.22.1).

[58] Judgment of works could apply even to those already deemed righteous (*1 En.* 43:2).

[59] O. Broneer, "Corinth: Center of Paul's Missionary Work in Greece," *BA* 14 (4, Dec. 1951): 78–96, here, 91–92.

[60] See discussion in C. Keener, *Matthew* (1999), 602–3.

5:13: For if we are beside ourselves, it is for God; if we are in our right mind, it is for you.

5:14: For the love of Christ urges us on, because we are convinced that one has died for all; therefore all have died.

5:15: And he died for all, so that those who live might live no longer for themselves, but for him who died and was raised for them.

5:16: From now on, therefore, we regard no one from a human point of view; even though we once knew Christ from a human point of view, we know him no longer in that way.

5:17: So if anyone is in Christ, there is a new creation: everything old has passed away; see, everything has become new!

5:18: All this is from God, who reconciled us to himself through Christ, and has given us the ministry of reconciliation;

5:19: that is, in Christ God was reconciling the world to himself, not counting their trespasses against them, and entrusting the message of reconciliation to us.

5:20: So we are ambassadors for Christ, since God is making his appeal through us; we entreat you on behalf of Christ, be reconciled to God.

5:21: For our sake he made him to be sin who knew no sin, so that in him we might become the righteousness of God.

6:1: As we work together with him, we urge you also not to accept the grace of God in vain.

6:2: For he says,

> "At an acceptable time I have listened to you,
> and on a day of salvation I have helped you."

See, now is the acceptable time; see, now is the day of salvation!

6:3: We are putting no obstacle in anyone's way, so that no fault may be found with our ministry,

6:4: but as servants of God we have commended ourselves in every way: through great endurance, in afflictions, hardships, calamities,

6:5: beatings, imprisonments, riots, labors, sleepless nights, hunger;

6:6: by purity, knowledge, patience, kindness, holiness of spirit, genuine love,

6:7: truthful speech, and the power of God; with the weapons of righteousness for the right hand and for the left;

6:8: in honor and dishonor, in ill repute and good repute. We are treated as impostors, and yet are true;

6:9: as unknown, and yet are well known; as dying, and see – we are alive; as punished, and yet not killed;

6:10: as sorrowful, yet always rejoicing; as poor, yet making many rich; as having nothing, and yet possessing everything.

The knowledge of future judgment (5:10) provided the fear of the Lord to carry out his apostolic mission (5:11), perhaps for the sake of others as well as themselves (5:14). (Fearing God is a prominent OT basis for ethics.) Because they knew him, he had no need to boast (5:11–12). The Lord who would judge them already knew their hearts (5:11b), and it was that invisible heart rather than the appearance that mattered (5:12; cf. 4:18); the Corinthians, too, should know Paul's heart (5:11b; 4:2), for it is open wide to them (6:11; 7:3). (Paul apparently knows that their memory of his heart is a strong part of his case; orators would dwell on a particularly strong point; see *Rhet. Her.* 4.45.58.)

Paul quickly explains that his description of his confidence in ministry is not self-commendation (5:12). Some Corinthian Christians had apparently objected to his previous explanations (cf. 3:1; perhaps 1 Cor 4:16; 11:1), although accepting boasting from his opponents (11:17–20). To reduce the offensiveness of self-boasting, orators followed various conventions, such as denying that they were doing it (as here; 3:1; although he is: 4:2; 6:4); complaining that it was necessary (12:1) or that their audiences had forced them to do it (12:11); that one needed to silence opponents' arrogance (11:12) or respond to charges (10:10). Paul emphasizes that he is not boasting but merely giving his audience opportunity to boast about their founder, just as he boasts about them (1:14; 7:14; 9:2–3). Had they defended his honor as they should have, he would not be compelled to do so (12:11)! If he boasts, then, it is for their good only (10:8), and only within limits (10:13–17; 11:30; 12:5–6).[61]

Obviously Paul believes that his rivals have been boasting (11:12, 18) and commending themselves (10:12, 18). Probably this includes worldly criteria like social status and rhetorical impressiveness (10:10–12; 11:6). (That Paul leaves his rivals anonymous, although he likely knows their names, may follow a convention of refusing to dignify opponents by naming them.)[62] Paul points out that his rivals commend themselves on the basis of outward attributes rather than the heart; he borrows the key terms of 1 Sam 16:7 LXX, in which God chose David over his brothers (and perhaps most tellingly for Paul here, over Saul).

Many thinkers emphasized the inadequacy of appearance.[63] Nevertheless, it might be more than coincidence that Paul's term for "outward appearance," *prosōpon*, is "face," and Paul has just been contrasting the mere glory on Moses's face with the new covenant glory on the heart (3:3, 7, 13, 18; cf. 4:6).[64] Like Moses, however, Paul has more freedom for his heart when speaking with the Lord, and (despite his "uncovered face," 3:12, 18) uses more restraint with the Corinthians (5:13). The point is that the heart is less obvious than outward appearance.

Whether Paul was serving God or the Corinthians (5:13), he was clearly not living for self (5:15) as his rivals did (5:12). Stoics considered all folly to be

---

[61] On proper grounds for self-praise (including encouraging friends and responding to slanders), see P. Marshall, *Enmity* (1987), 353–57.

[62] See P. Marshall, *Enmity* (1987), 341–48 (although his examples in *Res Gestae* may also remain anonymous because Augustus's rivals still had some honor among partisans).

[63] See, e.g., Jn 7:24; 8:15; Plato *Phaedo* 83A; Seneca *Lucil.* 14.1; 94.13.

[64] "Heart" counts more than "face" (1 Thess 2:17).

"madness,"[65] but Paul is not yet parodying folly (as in 11:23; though cf. 1 Cor 1:25; 4:10), because he is "beside himself" only for God (and parallels this with "heart" rather than appearance in 5:12). More relevantly, many associated prophecy and divine possession with temporary *mania* (insanity; as in 1 Cor 14:23),[66] a charge sometimes leveled against prophets (2 Kgs 9:11; Jer 29:26; Hos 9:7; *Sib. Or.* 1.172) or philosophers (Diogenes Laertius 6.3.82). Such insanity could be contrasted with sobriety ("our right mind"), as here (cf. Acts 26:25; many cite, e.g., Philo *Cher.* 69; Plato *Phaedrus* 244A).[67]

Because Paul wanted everything to edify others, he had kept most of his deep spiritual experiences (12:2–4) to himself rather than sharing them with the Corinthians (cf. 1 Cor 14:18). Perhaps bringing into question how well they had appropriated new covenant life, the Corinthians could not accommodate Paul's personal experience of God any more than the Israelites had been able to endure Moses's (3:13; Ex 34:34–35). (Ideally God's glory should not have been covered; 1 Cor 11:4, 7.)

In 5:14–15, we learn that not only "the fear of the Lord," that is, recognition of coming judgment (5:10–11; cf. 7:1), but also "Christ's love" motivated Paul (5:14).[68] "Christ's love" probably means "Christ's love" for whomever Paul means here by "us" (Rom 5:5; 8:35; Gal 2:20; Eph 3:19), especially as demonstrated in his death on behalf of "us" (Rom 5:8; 8:32; 1 Cor 15:3; Gal 3:13).[69] It might also offer an example of sacrificial service (5:14–15); or here may mean "love for Christ" expressed in serving him (5:14–15); or a combination of these. Paul is ready in any case to lay down his life as Jesus did to spread his message (2:14–16; 4:15), because sharing the suffering of the cross also welcomes resurrection power (4:7–14). Dying and rising with Christ (5:14–15) reshaped the identity of all those in him,[70] so that they could not be evaluated by fleshly, external appearance (5:12, 16) but by the new creation. (Living for the Lord, as in Rom 14:8, includes living to please him, as in 2 Cor 5:9.)

The merely human perspective (also translatable, "according to the flesh") Paul envisions in 5:16 boasts "in outward appearance" (also translatable, "in face"; 5:12). His rivals apparently boasted in their rhetoric and status higher than

---

[65] Cicero *Parad.* 27–32; Musonius Rufus 20, p. 126.2–3; Diogenes Laertius 7.1.124.

[66] E.g., possession in Plutarch *Roman Q.* 112, *Mor.* 291AB; Artemidorus *Onir.* 2.37; see further C. Keener, *The Spirit in the Gospels and Acts* (Peabody: Hendrickson, 1997), 23–26.

[67] The application of terms to rhetoric is also plausible (M. Hubbard, "Was Paul out of his Mind? Re-reading 2 Corinthians 5.13," *JSNT* 70 [1998]: 39–64), but less likely in the immediate context.

[68] Although Jewish teachers valued both love for and fear of God as motivations, love was greater (*m. Soṭa* 5:5).

[69] Laying down one's life was a special expression of love in Greek texts (see C. Keener, *John* [2003], 1004–06).

[70] For this theme, see R. C. Tannehill, *Dying and Rising with Christ: A Study in Pauline Theology* (Berlin: Töpelmann, 1967).

Paul's (10:10), rather than in the heart.[71] The view that Paul rejected interest in the historical Jesus here (articulated by Bultmann, Conzelmann and others) reads twentieth-century existential notions into Paul, who clearly did value historical information about Jesus (cf. 1 Cor 7:10; 9:14; 11:1, 23–25; 15:3–8). (The genre of Paul's letters naturally did not dispose him to report as much about the historical Jesus as a Gospel would, but this does not mean he repudiated historical interest.)[72]

Paul more likely simply rejected his preconversion understanding of Jesus (perhaps of his apparent inadequacy by high-status standards) or (just possibly) of the Messiah (cf. 1 Cor 15:9). Most significantly, the cross, like Christ's suffering apostles, was meaningless to those who saw it merely outwardly, unaware of Jesus's resurrection (and the Spirit of life working in his agents; 2:15–16; 1 Cor 1:18). Paul's point is that Jesus's resurrection provides a new, eschatological framework of faith for seeing Christ and all who are in him (5:14–15); anyone in Christ already belongs to the eschatological order (5:17), although this new existence is perceivable only in the heart, not in appearance (5:12; cf. 3:3).

In 5:17, Paul continues his thought by emphasizing newness: he rejected appearance in favor of heart (5:12); therefore, he was not interested in a fleshly perspective on Christ or Christians (5:16), but the hidden, eschatological reality of resurrection life that had begun in Christ's resurrection.

Jewish texts often refer to an eschatological new creation (Is 65:17; 66:22; *1 En.* 72:1; *Jub.* 1:29; 4:26; *2 Bar.* 44:12). Jewish teachers later apply such language to personal renewal, probably to proselytes (cf. *Sipre Deut.* 32.2.1) and to Israel experiencing God's forgiveness on the New Year's festival or the Day of Atonement.[73] Although Paul does think of conversion in the context and of new hearts in general (cf. 3:3; Gal 6:15; Ezek 36:26; *Jub.* 5:12), the newness he means is that of realized eschatology, the vanguard of a new world. Jesus's resurrection has inaugurated a new creation (cf. 4:6), as its first fruits (1 Cor 15:20, 23). Those who hope to share Christ's resurrection fully (4:14; 5:1–4) have a present foretaste in the Spirit (4:10–11; 5:5). In this new creation, the image and glory of God partly lost in Adam (cf. Rom 5:12–21; 1 Cor 11:7) are being restored in Christ (cf. 2 Cor 3:18; 4:4; 1 Cor 15:49; Rom 8:29).

In 5:18, Paul begins to transition to his appeal to the Corinthians. "All of this" new creation (5:17) comes from God, and is the result of a reconciliation effected by Christ's death (5:14–15; Rom 5:10) and actualized by embracing the apostolic proclamation. The "ministry" of reconciliation is the life-giving "ministry" of the new covenant (3:6–9; 6:3). Reconciliation involves enemies making peace

---

[71] Some suggest that the rivals claimed a connection with the historical Jesus; although possible, their Hellenistic rhetorical competence makes that suggestion unlikely.

[72] With M. D. Hooker, *A Preface to Paul* (New York: Oxford, 1980), 19, comparing 1 Jn and its relationship to the Fourth Gospel.

[73] Cf. other sources in C. Keener, *John* (2003), 542–43.

or becoming friends (Rom 5:10; Eph 2:14–16),[74] and Paul was not the first to apply the term to relationship with God or deities (2 Macc 1:5; 5:20; 7:33; 8:29).[75] But in Roman politics and ancient Mediterranean culture in general, friendship included accepting the friend's friends as one's friends and his enemies as one's enemies (e.g., Iamblichus *Pyth. Life* 35.248–49). How then can the Corinthians be reconciled with God if they mistrust his agent (cf. 6:14–16; Matt 10:40; Ex 16:8)?

If the realized eschatology of 5:17 continues in 5:18, it may be relevant that for Paul, Adam's sin alienated humanity and the first creation from God; the new creation in Christ (5:17) is reconciled to him (cf. Rom 5:10–15; 8:20–22; Col 1:20–22). Likewise, God promised Israel "peace" with him in the time of their restoration (Is 52:7; 54:10), the new creation era (Is 65:17–18); see comment on 6:2. Although Paul writes in 5:19 that God in principle reconciled the world to himself in Christ (who died for all, 5:14–15; cf. Ps 32:2 in Rom 4:8), the world has not yet become completely a new creation (5:17). The principle is effected through the apostolic ministry of reconciliation, hence is available only to those who accept the message and its agents (5:17–20). Christ's agents bring the good news of peace offered by the divine benefactor (Is 52:7; Eph 6:15, 19–20).

Paul's concept of apostleship suits well the image of an ambassador or legate in 5:20; the treatment of such agents revealed their receivers' attitudes toward those who sent them.[76] One's response to Jesus's agents is one's response to their message, hence to Jesus himself (Matt 10:40; Lk 10:16; cf. Ex 4:16; 7:1). In a more general way, many recognized the value of agents of concord, mediators who reconciled parties at enmity (e.g., Phil 4:3).[77] (One such speaker reconciled opposing factions by pointing out that although he and his wife were both obese, their bed could hold both of them when they agreed, but not even the house could hold them when they disagreed; Philostratus *Vit. soph.* 1.485.)

Pleas of various sorts were conventional in persuasion (Quintilian 4.1.33); ancient literature sometimes reports the pleas used to invite reconciliation, although often these were pleas for forgiveness from the offenders. We could translate the plea to be reconciled to God as a quotation summarizing the message of the ambassadors' entreaty to the world (5:19–20). It seems clear, however, that Paul is summoning these Christians to be reconciled to God (6:1;

---

[74] See further J. T. Fitzgerald, "Paul and Paradigm Shifts: Reconciliation and Its Linkage Group," 241–62 in *Paul Beyond Divide* (2001), 242–52.

[75] See J. Fitzgerald, "Shifts" (2001), 252–55; in Paul, cf. I. H. Marshall, "The Meaning of 'Reconciliation,'" 117–32 in *Unity and Diversity in NT Theology: Essays in honor of George E. Ladd*, ed. R. A. Guelich (Grand Rapids, MI: Eerdmans, 1978); R. P. Martin, *Reconciliation: A Study of Paul's Theology* (Atlanta: John Knox, 1981).

[76] See C. Keener, *John* (2003), 313–14. Cf. agents reconciling hearers to deities' ways (cf. Seneca *Dial.* 1.1.5) and prophets as ambassadors (*'Abot R. Nat.* 34 A).

[77] See e.g., Homer *Od.* 1.369–371; Cicero *Att.* 1.3; also 1.5; 1.10; Tacitus *Hist.* 2.5.

13:5) – a graphic way of reminding them that they cannot straddle the fence between the world and God's agent (6:14–7:1). This would not be the only place where Paul warns Christians to attend to their salvation (Rom 8:13; 11:22; Gal 5:4; Phil 2:12; cf. 1 Thess 3:4–5), but like a good rhetorician, Paul clearly intends to jolt his audience to attention. Rhetoricians sometimes employed a sudden shock to seize attention; on a rhetorical level, the claims of 3:3 and 5:20 are no more inconsistent than the tension between ethical ideals and behavior implied in 1 Corinthians 6:9–11.

Presumably the Corinthians were familiar with Paul's teaching that Christ's death appeased God's wrath, hence reconciled humanity to God (Rom 5:9–11). In the becoming sin of one who "knew no sin" (5:21; cf. Rom 3:20; 7:7), Paul may combine the notion of unblemished sacrifices with the scapegoat that came to represent or embody Israel's sin (Lev 1:3; 16:21–22).[78] Because Paul is about to quote a servant passage from Isaiah in 6:2, he may also think of the servant whose death would bring Israel "peace" (Is 53:5–6).

But because the Corinthians (according to Paul's rhetorical shock attack) are not yet reconciled to God, the "we" in 5:21 refers, as in most of the context, to Paul and his apostolic associates. As Christ, bearing humanity's judgment, became sin's representative on the cross, so ministers of the new covenant represent God's righteousness to those they exhort (cf. the "ministry of righteousness" in 3:9; 11:15).[79] Although Paul would no doubt apply the principle to any believers who shared the gospel with others, they are "God's righteousness" not as "the justified" but as agents of the message of God being reconciled with the world.

That God's ambassadors are agents of his righteousness leads Paul to repeat the plea of 5:20 in 6:1: They must not receive grace in vain, a typical Pauline warning against failure to persevere (1 Cor 15:2, 10; Gal 4:11; Phil 2:16).

In 6:2 he underlines the urgency of his plea with the language of scripture. (Some other ancient appeals for reconciliation also expressed urgency, sometimes to display affection and the consequent pain of separation. Philosophers often discussed the question of appropriate times for frank speech.) Paul quotes Is 49:8, referring to the time of salvation, the restoration and reconciliation when God makes peace with his people (Is 52:7). Paul very likely construes the servant in part of the context (Is 49:5–7) as Jesus (cf. 5:21), so the expected eschatological moment of reconciliation has obviously come (cf. 5:17).

Far from being unreliable in his promises (1:17) or regarding money (12:17–18), Paul avoids giving cause for offense in anything (cf. 1 Cor 10:32–33), to avoid

---

[78] Cf. J. D. G. Dunn, *The Theology of Paul the Apostle* (Grand Rapids: Eerdmans, 1998), 217–19.

[79] For "interchange," cf. Valerius Maximus 2.4.5; here, see M. D. Hooker, *Interchange and Atonement* (Manchester: John Rylands University of Manchester, 1978), 462–63, though she unnecessarily rules out substitution.

the new covenant ministry being reproached (6:3; cf. esp. 8:20, referring to avoiding discrediting the ministry of the collection). This is vital because Paul's "ministry" is the service of God ("servants" in 6:4 NRSV translates a cognate of "ministry" in the Greek of 6:3); the Corinthians mistrust him wrongly.

Paul's list in 6:4–10 is worthy of any orator of his day; writers often listed several elements with one parallel form; then several others with another; and so forth.[80] After endurance, Paul lists nine sufferings (6:4–5, all introduced in Greek by *en*); then eight virtues (6:6–7, again all introduced by *en*); then ten antitheses displaying divine triumph in his weakness or dishonor (6:7–10; cf. 4:8–10), three of which are introduced in Greek by *dia* ("through," 6:7–8), then seven by *hōs . . . kai* ("as . . . and [yet]," 6:8–10).[81] Whether Paul piles up three synonyms (6:4) or lists diverse kinds of trials (6:5), his amplification of the subject fits rhetorical models. The closing contrasts of 6:8–10 resemble the balanced antitheses of other rhetorical catalogues (cf. 4:8–10; *Rhet. Alex.* 26, 1435b.25–39);[82] Cicero was particularly fond of these in his forensic rhetoric.[83] Many sages were also fond of paradox or shocking oxymorons, such as Paul displays in these verses (e.g., Musonius Rufus 9, p. 74.10–12).

Although not "commending" himself through boasting (3:1; 5:12), Paul does so by his sufferings (6:4). Orators emphasized the importance of establishing one's *ēthos*, or character, for carrying conviction (e.g., *Rhet. Alex.* 38, 1445b.30–34). Writers often used affliction lists to emphasize their integrity[84] (although, unlike Paul, Stoics also used them to underline their impassivity); sufferings were tests of character (Seneca *Dial.* 1.4.5). The rhetorical emphasis in such lists is not so much on the individual components (inviting a modern lexical focus) but the total effect.

In this list of sufferings (6:4–10), Paul makes clear that the world sees him differently than God does; but Paul, in contrast to his rivals, seeks to impress only God and those who share his wisdom, not those who are perishing because they cannot understand (2:15–17; 4:2–6; 5:11–13). How can Paul avoid offense or his life "commend" him (6:3–4) when he is often subject to dishonorable treatment (6:5) and slander (6:8)? A bad reputation was particularly painful in a society that emphasized honor, status, and shame (Prov 10:7; 22:1; Diodorus Siculus 9.33.1; 14.1.3). In such a society, jealousy also inflamed more accusations (e.g.,

---

80 E.g., Cicero *Pro Sestio* 1.1; Valerius Maximus 7.1.1; Maximus of Tyre 3.2; cf. R. Anderson, *Glossary* (2000), 78–79, 111–12.

81 Because "through the weapons" is transitional, one also can count three sets of nine elements, a number Paul uses in some other lists (11:23–25, 26; 1 Cor 12:8–10; Gal 5:22–23), although not always (1 Cor 12:28–30; Gal 5:19–21).

82 E.g., Seneca *Lucil.* 95.58; Marcus Aurelius, 2.11; Maximus of Tyre 3.4; 36.2; see further comment on 4:8–10.

83 *In Catil.* 2.10.25; *Pro Scauro* 16.37; *Pro Caelio* 22.55; *Phil.* 3.11.28; 8.5.16.

84 E.g., Sallust *Letter of Gnaeus Pompeius* 1; for Stoics, Epictetus *Diatr.* 1.1.22; Musonius 6, p. 54.12–14.

Josephus *Life* 423). Whereas those who cannot understand (hence will perish) dishonor him, those who receive his message honor him (2:15–16; 4:3–4). Many radical philosophers discounted others' opinions,[85] or even valued ill repute (Antisthenes in Diogenes Laertius 6.1.11); but others took opinions into account enough to try to protect their mission.[86] Some philosophers also spoke of sages being unknown to people but known to God (Porphyry *Marc.* 13.232–33).

"Blows" (NRSV "beatings") invited shame in antiquity (e.g., 1 Thess 2:2; Diogenes *Ep.* 20), as did imprisonments (e.g., 2 Tim 1:8);[87] for "labors" (6:5), see 1 Cor 4:12; for "sleepless nights," 2 Cor 11:27; "holiness of spirit" (NRSV) is better translated "Holy Spirit." Like vice-lists (see comment on 1 Cor 5:10–11; 6:9–10), virtue-lists (6:6–7a) were a frequent literary form (e.g., Gal 5:22–23; Phil 4:8);[88] some texts also list advantages distinct from virtue (cf. 6:8–9).[89]

In view of his earlier argument (1:9–10; 4:10–17), "dying yet behold we live" (6:9) evokes sharing Christ's sufferings and the deliverances that foreshadow sharing his resurrection. Paul adapts language from Ps 118:17 (LXX 117:17): "I shall not die but live, and recount the deeds of the Lord," a context that seems fresh on his mind (Ps 116 in 2 Cor 4:13; perhaps Ps 119:32 in 2 Cor 6:11).[90] (Judeans and Jews who made pilgrimage would know Psalms 113–118 well from the Hallel, used at Passover and Tabernacles.) He applies the verse by making the tense present (cf. 4:10; 6:2).

For Paul, continual joy and sorrow were compatible (6:10; Rom 9:2; 12:12, 15; Phil 4:4); if Paul's various trials brought him sorrow, the perseverance of his spiritual children brought him joy (2:3; 7:4, 7, 9, 13, 16).[91] The apostles' sacrificial poverty that makes many rich by the gospel (6:10; cf. 1 Cor 4:8) emulates Jesus, who became poor to make others rich (2 Cor 8:9). Despite the low status of the poor, ancients could view as a great benefactor one who remained poor to make others rich (Plutarch *Lysander* 2.4; 30.2). Their "having nothing, yet possessing everything" (6:10) resembles Cynics' claims to have access to all they needed while owning nothing (cf. Crates *Ep.* 7; also Stoics, Seneca *Lucil.* 66.22); the Corinthians already understood Paul's meaning (1 Cor 3:21–23). Some Corinthians apparently were suspicious of Paul's collection (12:16–18), but it would be widely agreed that someone who remained poor did not exploit public funds (Nepos 3.3.2).

---

85 E.g., Diogenes the Cynic in Diogenes Laertius 6.2.58; Crates *Ep.* 16.
86 See Iamblichus *Pyth. Life* 31.200; at length J. Fitzgerald, *Vessels*, 189–90, 196; C. Keener, *John* (2003), 885–86.
87 See B. Rapske, *Custody* (1994), 288–97.
88 E.g., *Rhet. Alex.* 36, 1442a.11–12; *Rhet. Her.* 3.2.3; Theon *Progymn.* 9.21–24.
89 E.g., Plutarch *Educ.* 8, *Mor.* 5DE; Menander Rhetor 2.11, 420.29–31.
90 F. Young and D. Ford, *Meaning* (1987), 66.
91 Stoics also spoke of rejoicing in all hardships but preferably not when "sorrowing"; they valued impassivity.

6:11–7:4: PLEA TO JOIN GOD'S AND HIS AMBASSADORS' SIDE

6:11: We have spoken frankly to you Corinthians; our heart is wide open to you.

6:12: There is no restriction in our affections, but only in yours.

6:13: In return – I speak as to children – open wide your hearts also.

6:14: Do not be mismatched with unbelievers. For what partnership is there between righteousness and lawlessness? Or what fellowship is there between light and darkness?

6:15: What agreement does Christ have with Beliar? Or what does a believer share with an unbeliever?

6:16: What agreement has the temple of God with idols? For we are the temple of the living God; as God said,

> "I will live in them and walk among them,
>   and I will be their God,
>   and they shall be my people.
> **6:17:** Therefore come out from them,
>   and be separate from them, says the Lord,
>   and touch nothing unclean;
>   then I will welcome you,
> **6:18:** and I will be your father,
>   and you shall be my sons and daughters,
>   says the Lord Almighty."

7:1: Since we have these promises, beloved, let us cleanse ourselves from every defilement of body and of spirit, making holiness perfect in the fear of God.

7:2: Make room in your hearts for us; we have wronged no one, we have corrupted no one, we have taken advantage of no one.

7:3: I do not say this to condemn you, for I said before that you are in our hearts, to die together and to live together.

7:4: I often boast about you; I have great pride in you; I am filled with consolation; I am overjoyed in all our affliction.

Centuries of speechmaking had taught ancients the value of an emotional appeal (*pathos*) at the climax of arguments; Paul likewise clinches his appeal to be reconciled in 6:11–7:4, emphasizing both affection (6:11–13; 7:2–4) and indignation (6:14–7:1).[92] Letters were not speeches, but their very informality invited even more natural expressions of emotion (Seneca *Lucil.* 75.1–3; Demetrius *On*

---

[92] In invective rhetoric, Quintilian defines the term *pathos* with respect to harsher emotions (6.2.20); but appeals to sympathy also were effective (e.g., *Rhet. Alex.* 34, 1439b.15–1440b.3; 36, 1444b.35–1445a.12; Cicero *Sest.* 69.144; *Font.* 21.46–47; Valerius Maximus 8.1. acquittals 2; Plutarch *Cicero* 39.6) and recommended (Cicero *Brut.* 93.322).

Style 4.227). Many ancient letter-writers offer repeated expressions of affection;[93] for example, Cicero assures an addressee that there is no one dearer to Cicero than this man (*Fam.* 2.3.2); to another, he urges him to write often to help Cicero endure his longing for him (*Fam.* 15.20.2; 15.21.1). One Plancus writes that his love for Cicero grows daily (*Fam.* 10.23.7). Later, a youthful Marcus Aurelius melodramatically insists that nothing could ever hinder his love for his tutor (Fronto *Ep. Graecae* 7.1–2). Writers invoked readers' love for them as a basis for writers appealing to readers to follow a course of action to the readers' benefit (Fronto *Ad M. Caes.* 5.1).

Paul's sacrificial ministry (6:4–10) demonstrates the sincerity of his affection, providing the groundwork for his pleas in 5:20–6:1 and especially 6:11–13: the Corinthians should be reconciled to God and to his agent. Paul emphasizes in 6:11–13 that the obstacles to reconciliation are not in Paul's heart but in theirs (also 7:2–3; cf. the similar plea and use of *pathos* in Gal 4:12–20). The protests of a wronged leader, like other protests, used *pathos* (e.g., 1 Sam 12:3; Dionysius of Halicarnassus 4.33.1–4.36.3). Writers sometimes worded intensely affectionate appeals as protests merely to underline their affectionate feeling (Fronto *Ad Verum Imp.* 1.3–4; 2.2); although this letter reveals genuine conflict, it should not be overemphasized.

An "opened mouth" (NRSV, "spoken frankly") is a common LXX idiom for speech; Paul's open mouth corresponds to his enlarged heart (NRSV: "wide open"), and here he speaks frankly what is in his heart (which fits 3:12; 4:2; 5:12). The enlarging of Paul's heart to them is to make room in his heart for them (cf. 7:3); to have another in one's heart was a deep expression of affection (3:2; Phil 1:7; 1 Thess 2:17).[94] Generosity normally invited reciprocity (at least of honor); that affection should be reciprocated was understood (Matt 5:46–47; Xenophon *Cyr.* 6.1.47).[95] Nevertheless, Paul makes explicit the reciprocity his affection demands by employing the verb *platunō* in both 6:11 and 6:13, although nowhere else in his extant writings (frequently in the LXX; with the heart most clearly in Deut 11:16; Ps 119 [LXX 118]:32; cf. 1QS 11.15–16; Acts 16:14).

In 6:14–7:1, Paul emphasizes separation, holiness, and God's sanctuary; what was sacred to the one God was utterly incongruous with shrines sacred to pagan deities (Dan 1:2; 1 Esd 2:7; cf. 1 Macc 1:47–48). The choice between God and idols reflects an early form of the Jewish "two ways" tradition (Josh 24:15; cf. Deut 30:19). The series of rhetorical questions in 6:14–16 reinforce the passage's rhetorical force (see comment on 1 Cor 9:1–13). Everyone recognized the incompatibility of some values, attested in a Greek proverb using *koinōneō* (Epictetus

---

93 E.g., Cicero *Fam.* 1.9.1; 2.1.1; 2.1.2; 2.2.1; 12.12.1; Fronto *Ad M. Caes.* 1.3; 4.1–2.

94 "Affections" (6:12; "heart" in 7:15) is *splagchna*, a strong expression (Phil 1:8; 2:1; Col 3:12; Phlm 7, 12, 20; 1 Jn 3:17).

95 Affectionate letters sometimes make the expectation explicit (e.g., Cicero *Fam.* 6.15.1; 7.14.2; 12.30.3; 15.21.3).

Diatr. 4.6.30; 4.10.24)[96] and a Jewish text using the same verb and illustrated by incompatible animals (Sir 13:16–19; cf. "yoked" here).

A CLOSER LOOK: AN INTERPOLATION IN 6:14–7:1?

Especially because 7:2–4 completes the appeal of 6:11–13, many scholars plausibly view 6:14–7:1 as an interpolation. Why would Paul shift the topic suddenly to avoiding pagan worship? Yet a digression makes better sense here than an interpolation, at least on the working assumption that any text is probably a unity unless we find compelling evidence to the contrary.[97] Structurally, Paul frequently uses framing devices around his digressions (e.g., 1 Cor 11:2, 17; 12:31; 14:1; perhaps Gal 5:2–12 in 5:1–15; *adikos* in 1 Cor 6:1, 9). The rhetorical intensity of 6:14–7:1 (and more generally of 6:11–7:4) is not surprising, because Paul is climaxing his arguments of 2:14–7:4.

Digressions had to be relevant to the context, and 6:14–7:1 fits this criterion. The passage offers not a sudden shift in topic but an emotional appeal that confronts the underlying issue of previous chapters: The Corinthians' openness to Paul's rivals has forced him to defend his ministry, but now he summons them to choose. If the analogy with idolatry that dominates this section sounds too harsh to us to apply to Paul's rivals, it is no harsher than "ministers of Satan" in the passage where he becomes most explicit against his opponents (11:14–15). Paul denies the salvation of purveyors of any false gospel (11:4; Gal 1:6–8; 5:4, 12; Phil 3:2, 18–19), although he appears gentler toward merely personal rivals (1 Cor 1:12; Phil 1:14–18). Indeed, breaking contact with "unbelievers" might prove especially applicable to those who claimed to be Christians (1 Cor 5:9–13; 15:33).[98]

Some who envision an interpolation doubt that Paul is even its author; despite some Pauline elements, the passage includes language unusual in Paul's letters. (Given its dualism, some think it a specifically Essene passage; however, although Judean parallels are instructive here if the author is Judean, the suggestion of direct borrowing fails to reckon with the geographic, linguistic, and intersectarian difficulties of such a mixup.) Digressions could reuse earlier sources, however, so, as many commentators point out, Paul may have placed it here even if the vocabulary is non-Pauline. (This must be the case at least in his quotations in 6:16–18.) More important, writers also sometimes chose more

---

[96] Cf. Maximus of Tyre 33.2. Some thought *koinōnia* possible only among the good (Musonius 13B, p. 90.6–20).

[97] For more detailed arguments, see, e.g., J. Amador, "Revisiting" (2000), 100–05; D. deSilva, *Credentials* (1998), 14–29; M. E. Thrall, "The Problem of II Cor. VI.14–VII.1 In Some Recent Discussion," *NTS* 24 (1977), 132–48; J. Murphy-O'Connor, "Relating 2 Corinthians 6.14–7.1 to its Context," *NTS* 33 (2, 1987), 272–75.

[98] Alternatively, Paul warns against making "common cause with the unbelievers, who reject the apostle" (N. A. Dahl, *Studies in Paul: Theology for the Early Christian Mission* [Minneapolis: Augsburg, 1977], 65).

striking vocabulary to underline a point (and this digression is certainly emphatic).[99] Furthermore, the parallelism requires the author to find synonyms;
some undisputed passages in Paul have an equal concentration of hapaxes;[100]
and some of the vocabulary, as well as the contrast between God's temple and
idols, is Pauline and even present in the Corinthian correspondence. If Paul uses
a source here, it is one he has freely reworked for his purposes.

Although Paul has been using antithesis to depict the paradox of the cross in
the context (6:8–10), this passage climaxes instead the soteriological antitheses
of preceding chapters. Whereas God enlightened his people, Satan blinded the
world (4:4–6); the Corinthian Christians as God's people must choose between
these options (6:14–15). They must either be like the perishing world, which
rejected Paul's message (2:15–16; 3:14–15; 4:3), or must be reconciled with Paul,
trusting him and his teaching (5:20–6:13; cf. 1:15–22).

It is not difficult to envision Paul's conflict with his rivals here; if the Corinthians must be reconciled to Paul to be reconciled to God (5:20–6:13), they also
must reject his rivals for their affection (cf. Gal 4:15–18; Demosthenes *Letter*
2.26). Urban Roman colonies understood quite well the custom that one could
not be friends with a friend's or patron's enemies. The choice between righteousness and lawlessness could be a choice between true and false ministers of
righteousness (3:9; 5:21; 6:7; 11:15). The rift between the blind world and those
who see Christ's glory and light (4:4–6) epitomizes the conflict between light
and darkness noted here; Paul's rivals bear a false "light" in 11:14–15. "Unbelievers" are plainly the lost (4:4; 1 Cor 6:6; 7:12–15; 10:27; 14:22–24), but Paul does
not have a higher opinion of his rivals (11:13–15), and they contrast with Paul's
model of ministry by faith during suffering (4:13–14; 5:7). The conflict between
Christ and Belial (6:15) appears in the conflict between Christ's ambassadors
(4:5–6; 5:20) and servants of Satan (11:14–15).

Warnings against "fellowship" or "partnership" with idolatry sound like Paul's
earlier warnings against idol food (1 Cor 10:16, 20), but probably carry the
principle further. Were Paul's Diaspora Jewish rivals more liberal than he on
the elite eating sacrificial meats (cf. 1 Cor 5:11)? Or is it just an illustration,
comparing his Jewish Christian rivals (11:22) to idolaters (as he can link them
also with Satan in 11:14–15)?

In any case, Paul's language of being "mismatched" (*heterozugeō*, "mismated"
or "yoked with another species") goes further than idol foods, although it
must include it.[101] Jews who adopted Greek culture and became uncircumcised

---

[99] See information in F. W. Danker, *II Corinthians* (Minneapolis: Augsburg, 1989), 18; B.
Witherington, *Corinthians* (1995), 335 n. 27, 402.

[100] So G. D. Fee, "II Corinthians VI.14–VII.1 and Food Offered to Idols," *NTS* 23 (1977):
140–61, p. 144.

[101] Israel "yoked itself" to paganism by immorality and idol food in Num 25:3, though the
LXX translates differently. Cf. "yoke fellow" (NRSV, "companion") as fellow-worker in
Phil 4:3; Plutarch *Cimon* 16.8.

"joined themselves" (a term also used for "yoking") to Gentiles (1 Macc 1:15). In one text, Esau could no more befriend Jacob than an ox and lion could be safely yoked (*Jub.* 37:22). Complete separation from Gentiles was not possible in the Diaspora, and even rabbis were very selective in their restrictions (e.g., *t. 'Abod. Zar.* 1:1–3; *Shab.* 2:7); practical considerations also limited restrictions in avoiding less scrupulous Jews (*t. Demai* 2:19; 3:9). But strict Jews (and Christians) would forbid compromise of one's faith and heritage.

Warning against being "mismatched" would at least include marital unions. The only related term in Scripture appears in Leviticus 19:19, warning against interbreeding (4Q418 103.2.7–8; cf. a sexual application to humans in Philo *Spec. Laws* 3.46; perhaps 4Q271 1.1.9–10); even plowing with ox and donkey together apparently risked interspecies copulation (Deut 22:9–11, esp. 22:10; although among Greeks it simply connoted insanity – Philostratus *Hrk.* 33.4!) Greek often uses words that could mean "yoking" with reference to marriage[102] or sexual unions.[103] Latin expressions cognate to "yoke" also were used for marriage, although relevant to some other close partnerships as well (Valerius Maximus 2.9.6a). Judaism clearly objected to mixed marriages (e.g., Deut 7:3; 1 Esd 8:68–96; 9:7–9; *Jub.* 30:7–11; 2 *Bar.* 42:4), though they happened. Although Paul insists on remaining in marriages with unbelievers (1 Cor 7:10–16), all new marriages should be "in the Lord" (1 Cor 7:39; cf. 9:5). But again Paul is thinking of the rivals; as Paul wishes to deliver them still virgin to Christ, Satan's agents threaten to corrupt them with their deceptive gospel (2 Cor 11:2–4).

A CLOSER LOOK: BELIAL

Early Judaism may have concocted "Belial" as a title for Satan by conflating an OT term for "worthlessness" with the pagan deity Baal (Josephus *Ant.* 8.318). The Qumran scrolls warn against his counsel (4QMMT C 29) and snares (4Q171 frg. 1–2.2.9–10).[104] They also lament his oppression (1QH 2.16–17; 3.27–32; 4.9–14; 4Q176; 4Q390 2.1.4); followers of Belial seek to hurt the righteous (1QH 2.22; 7.3–4; 1QM 1.1–13; 11.8; 4Q174 3.7–9). Belial rules evil spirits (11Q13 2.12–25) and the nations (1QM 15.2–3) but will be judged (1QM 13.11).

In some other texts, "Beliar" (a common variant)[105] sought to make people stumble (*T. Reub.* 4:7; cf. 4:11; 6:3) but would face eschatological judgment (*T. Jud.* 25:3; *T. Zeb.* 9:8; *T. Dan* 5:10). As here, some texts demanded a choice between God and Beliar (*T. Naph.* 2:6; 3:1).

---

[102] E.g., Xenophon *Oec.* 7.18; Aristotle *Pol.* 1.2.2, 1253b; Musonius 13A, p. 88.26; Ps–Dionysius *Epideictic* 2.262;

[103] E.g., *Alexandrian Erotic Frg.* col. 1.

[104] See further 1QS 1.23–24; 10.18, 21; 2.19; 1QM 13.2–6; 18.1; CD 4.13–15; 5.18–19; 8.2; 12.2.

[105] See *Jub.* 1:20; *T. Levi* 18:12; 19:1; *T. Iss.* 6:1; 7:7; *T. Dan* 1:7; 4:7; *T. Asher* 1:8; 3:2; 6:4; *T. Jos.* 7:4; *T. Ben.* 3:4; 6:1; 7:1; *Sib. Or.* 3.63. The frequent OT "sons of Belial" (also 4Q174 3.8; 4Q386 1.2.3–4) becomes "sons of Beliar" in *Jub.* 15:33.

In a context that summons God's own people to be reconciled to him (5:20–6:1), biblical texts inviting God's people to separate hence to be welcomed as his people and children (6:16–18) were appropriate. Although believers are already set apart in principle in Paul's theology (1 Cor 1:2; 6:11), he can acknowledge the need to implement this sanctification behaviorally (1 Thess 3:13; 5:23). Probably the primary midrashic principle justifying the blending of texts is their eschatological fulfillment (6:2) for God's set-apart dwelling (6:16). (Some argue that the free paraphrase and blending of texts, distinct from Paul's usual way of citing the LXX, may indicate Paul's use of a preexisting catena.)

In 6:16 Paul appeals to Leviticus 26:11–12. If Israel rejected idols (26:1), God would make his dwelling among them,[106] walk among them,[107] and he would be their God and they his people. Even those who did not catch Paul's exact allusion would be familiar with his themes. God promised to dwell among his people in his sanctuary (Ex 25:8) and be their God if they put away their idols (Ezek 14:11; 37:23; 43:9). The promise that God would be his people's God and they his people is a central covenant motif in the OT (e.g., Ex 6:7), conditional on obedience to his covenant (Jer 7:23; 11:4), including eschatologically, in the new covenant of which Paul has been writing (Jer 24:7; 31:1, 33; 32:38–40; Ezek 11:20; 36:28). Some texts involve resettling in the land (Zech 8:8); in one, much of the language of Leviticus 26:11–12 becomes eschatological in the context of a new covenant (Ezek 37:26–27); God would "sanctify" Israel and place his dwelling among them forever (37:28).

Although adapting the word order, 6:17 clearly refers to Isaiah 52:11 LXX, addressed to Levites who carry the vessels of the sanctuary back to Zion in the time of restoration. "I will welcome you" reflects another theme of restoration from exile, using a Septuagint term that translates "I will gather" (cf. Jer 23:3; Mic 4:6; Zeph 3:19–20; Zech 10:8–10), probably especially Ezekial 20:34, 41 (cf. 11:17), in which God displays his holiness by gathering Israel from the nations.

More curious is the blending of allusions in 6:18. God declared Israel his children (Ex 4:22; Jer 31:9), his sons and daughters (Deut 32:19; in the restoration, Is 43:6); but Paul borrows the specific language of a promise to David's line, that God would be their father and they his sons (2 Sam 7:14; cf. 1 Chron 17:13; 22:10; 28:6). Why apply to believers a Davidic text, probably viewed as messianic (Heb 1:5; 4QFlor)? Its context fortuitously speaks of building a temple (2 Sam 7:13); Paul also views Jesus (the messiah) as refracting Israel's promises for all his followers (who as subjects of Israel's king are heirs of the promises; 1:20; Gal 3:16, 29). "Says the Lord Almighty" is a common LXX phrase (some seventy

---

106 The LXX has, "place my covenant among them," which would have suited Paul's argument (3:3, 6); Paul's citation reverts to the Hebrew at this point, perhaps to retain the eschatological link to Ezekiel 37:27.

107 Because walking with God entailed fellowship with him (e.g., Gen 5:22–24; 6:9), many Jewish people expected God to walk among his people in the end-time (*Sipra Behuq.* pq. 3.263.1.5; cf. 1QM 10.4).

times, translating "Lord of Hosts" with one of the terms suitable for a Diaspora audience);[108] most relevantly, it appears in the context of the Davidic promise (2 Sam 7:8; 1 Chron 17:7), its only use (with "says") outside the prophets.

This catena of verses, similar to collections of quotations at Qumran and elsewhere, emphasizes that God is holy, hence his people must be separate from what is unclean, that is, idolatry (6:14–15), to be in fellowship with him. Separating themselves from what is unclean, hence cleansing themselves from what was defiling, would allow them to perfect holiness, that is, their status of being set apart to the holy God (7:1). For Paul, however, this separation involves not physical withdrawal from the people, as at Qumran (4QMMT C.7–16).

Although "unclean" applied to any ritual impurity in the Septuagint, it included contamination from idolatry (1 Macc 1:47–48; 4:43; Zech 13:2), as in the present context (6:14–15). Paul elsewhere uses the cognate of "defilement" (7:1) to refer to idolatry contaminating one's conscience (1 Cor 8:7). The Septuagint sometimes applies it to defiling God's holy temple (1 Macc 1:37; Jer 23:11 LXX), sometimes by idolatry (2 Macc 5:27; 6:2; 14:3; cf. Jer 44:3–5 LXX).

Separation or holiness (7:1) characterized temples and other sacred space (6:16), and they are clearly the temple of God (6:16), as probably in 5:1. Paul's audience may well remember Paul's warning that God would judge anyone destroying the unity of this temple (1 Cor 3:16–17).

The "promises" (7:1) refer especially to God's promises that those separating themselves from what defiled them would be God's people and his children (6:16–18). Such were the promises that were now confirmed in Christ (1:20; cf. 6:2). Paul elsewhere speaks of holiness of "body and spirit" (1 Cor 7:34; cf. 1 Thess 5:23; Heb 10:22; 1QM 7.4–5); if prostitutes defiled their bodies (1 Cor 6:20), Paul's rivals are the spiritual equivalent.[109] Holiness in the fear of God in 7:1 probably implies holiness in view of the day of judgment (an idea other Jews shared), since it likely echoes 5:11.

After his digression, Paul returns to the point in 7:2; writers could explicitly note that they were returning to a point or could signal it by verbal cues recalling their text before the digression.[110] In view of this call to choose sides (6:14–7:1), Paul urges them to "make room" in their hearts for him in 7:2, just as he already has them in his heart (7:3; echoing 6:11–13).[111] Unwilling to

---

[108] E.g., *CIJ* 1:500, §690; for sample texts on the use of *pantokratōr* and its more common Latin equivalent in paganism, see, e.g., C. Keener, *John* (2003), 371.

[109] Moral texts emphasize purity of spirit (*Let. Aris.* 234; *1 En.* 108:9; Seneca *Lucil.* 98.14; Porphyry *Marc.* 13.233; cf. C. Keener, *John* [2003], 996); purity of body was often understood in ritual terms.

[110] Explicitly, Polybius 3.9.6; Dionysius of Halicarnassus *Lysias* 13; Cicero *Orator* 43.148; *Att.* 7.2; Valerius Maximus 4.8.1; Musonius 1, p. 34.34; Arrian *Indica* 6.1; Maximus of Tyre 19.1.

[111] If Paul still thinks of "sanctity" (6:14–7:1), it may be relevant that sacred priests did not defile themselves with unclean food, for which their stomachs had no "room" (the same term, 4 Macc 7:6), a text that also mentions cleansing and *koinoō*. But Paul probably did not know this tradition.

defend his "appearance," Paul has been emphasizing the purity and affection of his heart (3:2; 5:12). The caveat that one was writing something not to stir negative emotion but to demonstrate affection (7:3; cf. 1 Cor 4:14) was an appropriate way of showing love (Cicero *Fam.* 2.4.2). That Paul was willing to die for the Corinthians (7:3) reflects a common friendship theme in ancient texts (cf. 1 Thess 2:8).[112] Because friendship was the goal of reconciliation (5:20) and a basis for rejecting a friend's enemies (6:14–16), the theme is particularly appropriate here.

Paul can address the Corinthians frankly (7:4; cf. 3:12) because of his relationship with them (*parrēsia* was especially appropriate with friends or others to whom one was close).[113] He boasts of them (cf. 1:14) – which prepares for his appeal (7:14; 8:24; 9:2) – and their affection brings him joy (cf. 1:24; 2:3; 7:7, 13, 16), despite his affliction (see 7:5). This claim rhetorically softens the appeal of 6:11–7:2 and indications of Paul's concern about their relationship with him; it also may soften their complaints about his boasting (3:1; 5:12; 11:10).

Paul also defends his actions, however, in 7:2 using threefold *anaphora* (beginning three clauses with the same word, though in English we translate "no one" at the end of the clauses) and *homoioptoton* (using verbs with the same endings, here *-amen*). That he "wronged no one" might contrast with the "offender" (using the same verb in 7:12), or with Paul's opponents countered in 6:14–16. That Paul "corrupted" no one contrasts more obviously with his rivals (11:2–4; the only other use of the same term in 2 Cor is at 11:3; cf. 1 Cor 3:17; 15:33). Paul has used the verb for "take advantage of" with reference to Satan's strategy of unforgiveness among Christians in 2:11; but it probably especially implies the offering (12:17–18), perhaps in contrast to the greed of Paul's opponents (cf. 2:17; 11:4–7, 20). Anticipating and answering expected charges was good rhetoric (some professionals called it *prokatalepsis*).

7:5–16: REPENTANT RESPONSE TO PAUL'S LETTER

7:5: For even when we came into Macedonia, our bodies had no rest, but we were afflicted in every way – disputes without and fears within.
7:6: But God, who consoles the downcast, consoled us by the arrival of Titus,
7:7: and not only by his coming, but also by the consolation with which he was consoled about you, as he told us of your longing, your mourning, your zeal for me, so that I rejoiced still more.
7:8: For even if I made you sorry with my letter, I do not regret it (though I did regret it, for I see that I grieved you with that letter, though only briefly).

---

[112] E.g., Musonius 7, p. 58.23; Epictetus *Diatr.* 2.7.3; V. Furnish, *II Corinthians* (1984), 367; C. Keener, *John* (2003), 1004–06.
[113] E.g., Alciphron *Farmers* 37.3.39; Plutarch *Profit by Enemies* 6, *Mor.* 89B; *Flatterer* 17–37, *Mor.* 59A–74E; C. Keener, *John* (2003), 705–06.

7:9: Now I rejoice, not because you were grieved, but because your grief led to repentance; for you felt a godly grief, so that you were not harmed in any way by us.
7:10: For godly grief produces a repentance that leads to salvation and brings no regret, but worldly grief produces death.
7:11: For see what earnestness this godly grief has produced in you, what eagerness to clear yourselves, what indignation, what alarm, what longing, what zeal, what punishment! At every point you have proved yourselves guiltless in the matter.
7:12: So although I wrote to you, it was not on account of the one who did the wrong, nor on account of the one who was wronged, but in order that your zeal for us might be made known to you before God.
7:13: In this we find comfort. In addition to our own consolation, we rejoiced still more at the joy of Titus, because his mind has been set at rest by all of you.
7:14: For if I have been somewhat boastful about you to him, I was not disgraced; but just as everything we said to you was true, so our boasting to Titus has proved true as well.
7:15: And his heart goes out all the more to you, as he remembers the obedience of all of you, and how you welcomed him with fear and trembling.
7:16: I rejoice, because I have complete confidence in you.

*P*aul now resumes the brief *narratio* he broke off at 2:13; although one normally used the entire *narratio* earlier in a speech, it could occur at various points when circumstances warranted.[114] Some have suggested that 2:14–7:4 is a later interpolation of Pauline material into his original narrative, but this is unlikely. In addition to our comments at 2:14, we should note that pages would be more easily mixed in later codices than in first-century papyri, but by that later period the order of the letter would be too widely known for a mistake, particularly one leaving no trace in the manuscript tradition (or protests from Christians in touch with Corinth). Some also point to stylistic arguments for unity: thus, the first-person plural in 7:5 contrasts with the singular of 2:12–13 (and 7:4) but fits 6:11–13; 7:2–3. Others find in 7:5–16 some echoes of language in 6:12 ("affection"); 7:2 (wrongdoing); and 7:4 (boasting, comfort, joy, affliction).[115] The intensity of emotional language in 6:11–7:4 certainly continues in 7:5–16 (esp. the lists in 7:7, 11); longing, friendship, and consolation were common topics in letters.

After mentioning that they are his joy and comfort in his affliction (7:4), Paul explains in more detail how Titus's news about their obedience brought him comfort (7:6) and joy (7:7) in his affliction (7:5). His afflictions in Ephesus included persecution (1:8–10), and the same could be true in Macedonia (Phil 1:28–30; 1 Thess 2:18; 3:4). In Macedonia, however, he is also concerned for

---

[114]   See F. Hughes, "Rhetoric" (1991), 252–53; B. Witherington, *Corinthians* (1995), 407 (citing esp. Quintilian 4.2.5, 79; *Rhet. Alex.* 1438b.15–25).
[115]   E.g., J. Lambrecht, *Second Corinthians* (1999), 133.

how the Corinthians have responded to the letter he sent with Titus (2:13) – an example of his anxiety for the churches (11:28). (Letters often expressed affection by displaying grief over being apart; e.g., *P. Oxy.* 528.6–9.) God comforts in affliction (7:6), as Paul had already emphasized (1:3–4); his consoling the downcast may recall Is 49:13; 54:11 LXX. (This might be part of the object of Paul's praise in 2:13–14, if he leaves its thought partly unfinished.) Paul's comfort is learning of the Corinthians' affection.

Paul had been concerned that the Corinthians had not received favorably his letter insisting that they discipline the offender. Others also could be concerned how important recipients took their letters (Cicero *Quint. fratr.* 2.16.5). Writers sometimes had to apologize when their letter caused the recipient pain accidentally;[116] here, however, Paul does not regret the pain. His goal in inflicting temporary sorrow was long-term restoration and joy (2:3–5; 7:8–10); the alternative response of death that he mentions would come by letter rather than the Spirit (3:6). Ancient moralists often compared themselves with physicians inflicting pain and opening wounds only to heal them.[117] They would not regret it if good came from it (Fronto *Ad Verum Imp.* 1.4.1); some who trusted their teachers even expressed gratitude for correction (e.g., Fronto *Ad M. Caes.* 3.12).

Respectable people were not supposed to revile, but their frankness (cf. 7:4) could bring repentance (Plutarch *Statecraft* 14, *Mor.* 810C). Orators noted that when gentler warnings (like 1 Corinthians) failed, rebuke might be necessary to produce shame (or fear; 2 Cor 7:11) and the pain (*lupē*, grief, 7:8–11) of repentance (7:9–10); Paul's tearful letter had accomplished this goal (7:8–10).[118] That Paul had done this by letter rather than in person he attributes to his affection for them (2:1–3), although some attributed it to cowardice (10:9–11; despite his emphasis here on their obedience, not everyone appreciated his letter).

Once the Corinthians realized their wrongdoing, they proved zealous to avenge it (7:11), an idea Paul picks up later (10:6). The sixfold repetition of "what . . ." in 7:11 NRSV reflects the strong Greek adversative *alla*, as if Paul repeatedly corrects himself; this allows him to heap up synonyms in a way that emotively underlines his point (cf. rhetoricians' use of *epimonē* or *synonymia*).[119] Ancient converts could understand zeal to make up for what had been lost (Polemo in Diogenes Laertius 4.16), or zealous repentance once it was too late (5.66); or that repentance destroys disobedience (*T. Gad* 5:7).[120] True repentance normally involved remorse (not, as some have wrongly taken *metanoia*, simply a change of mind).

---

[116] F. Danker, *II Corinthians* (1989), 107.
[117] See sources, e.g., in C. Keener, *Matthew* (1999), 298.
[118] See S. Stowers, *Letter Writing* (1986), 133–34, noting clear parallels in Cicero and Plutarch.
[119] For anaphora with similar patterns, see, e.g., Fronto *Ad Antoninum Imp.* 2.6.2; *Ad M. Caes.* 2.3.1; *Ad Verum Imp.* 2.1.4.
[120] "Disobedience" is missing in some MS of *T. Gad*, but some form of evil is mentioned in all of them.

Paul's joy in meeting Titus was not only in Titus's safety,[121] but in learning that his mission had gone well: The Corinthians had received Paul's agent; sorrowed; repented; and set the matter with the offender straight (7:6–12). How they received Titus revealed how they felt toward his sender (see comment on agents in 5:20). Paul is comforted to know of their affection; letter-writers sometimes expressed affection by noting that all was well with them so long as it was well with their addressees (1 Thess 3:8; Cicero *Fam.* 12.12.1; 12.13.1; 13.6a.1). He rejoices that the Corinthians demonstrated obedience and notes that testing it was more important than merely disciplining the offender (2:9), so they might realize their own loyalty to Paul (7:12; cf. Phil 4:10). Asking someone to prove their affection for one by granting a favor was a way to demonstrate confidence in the friendship (Cicero *Att.* 12.18).

He recounts Titus's appreciation of the way they had received him (7:15), and repeatedly emphasizes his boasting or confidence in them (7:4, 14–16). Such expressions of confidence were sometimes used to "butter up" hearers before an offering or other request;[122] one might emphasize confidence even when repeating a request (Cicero *Fam.* 13.44.1). Indeed, he is counting on the Corinthians' zeal for him (7:7, 11) translating into continued zeal for the collection (9:2). Still, some of his expressions of "confidence" use terms elsewhere involving frank speech (7:4; cf. 3:12) or boldness in the face of hardship (7:16; 5:6–8; 10:1–2). Although not embarrassed by this boasting (7:12), he at least pretends to be anxious about his boast about the collection (9:4).

Despite the repentance and reconciliation effected in 7:9–16, Paul is looking for more reconciliation (5:20–6:1). It is helpful to preface his "offering" request (Chs. 8–9) with such positive words, but Paul seems at least slightly anxious even that some Corinthians will not honor their promise of benefaction for the Jerusalem church, jeopardizing the momentum of Paul's collection among the Diaspora churches (9:3–4).

8:1–15: EXAMPLES OF SACRIFICIAL GIVING

8:1: We want you to know, brothers and sisters, about the grace of God that has been granted to the churches of Macedonia;
8:2: for during a severe ordeal of affliction, their abundant joy and their extreme poverty have overflowed in a wealth of generosity on their part.

---

[121] Travel was dangerous (11:26) and the Corinthians' hospitality was, despite 7:13–15, in question (cf. 1 Cor 16:10). Joy characterized safe arrivals and arrival speeches (Menander Rhetor 2.3, 385.7–8).
[122] See S. N. Olson, "Pauline Expressions of Confidence in His Addressees," *CBQ* 47 (1985), 282–95; cf. e.g., Cicero *Fam.* 2.4.2; 13.44.1.

8:3: For, as I can testify, they voluntarily gave according to their means, and even beyond their means,

8:4: begging us earnestly for the privilege of sharing in this ministry to the saints –

8:5: and this, not merely as we expected; they gave themselves first to the Lord and, by the will of God, to us,

8:6: so that we might urge Titus that, as he had already made a beginning, so he should also complete this generous undertaking among you.

8:7: Now as you excel in everything – in faith, in speech, in knowledge, in utmost eagerness, and in our love for you – so we want you to excel also in this generous undertaking.

8:8: I do not say this as a command, but I am testing the genuineness of your love against the earnestness of others.

8:9: For you know the generous act of our Lord Jesus Christ, that though he was rich, yet for your sakes he became poor, so that by his poverty you might become rich.

8:10: And in this matter I am giving my advice: it is appropriate for you who began last year not only to do something but even to desire to do something –

8:11: now finish doing it, so that your eagerness may be matched by completing it according to your means.

8:12: For if the eagerness is there, the gift is acceptable according to what one has – not according to what one does not have.

8:13: I do not mean that there should be relief for others and pressure on you, but it is a question of a fair balance between

8:14: your present abundance and their need, so that their abundance may be for your need, in order that there may be a fair balance.

8:15: As it is written,

> "The one who had much did not have too much,
> and the one who had little did not have too little."

A minority of scholars have argued that Chapters 8–9, or at least Chapter 9, represent separate letters from Chapters 1–7; Hans Dieter Betz has articulated this thesis most forcefully.[123] The burden of proof must always rest on the more complex thesis, however, and it is easier (as we have argued at other supposed breaks) to account for the letter's current unity (excepting possibly Chs. 10–13) if it were written as such.[124] Given recent conflicts between Paul and the Corinthians, Paul's defense of his ministry and affectionate language

---

[123] H. D. Betz, *2 Corinthians 8 and 9* (Philadelphia: Fortress, 1985). See ibid., 3–36, for a history of interpretation of Chapters 8–9.

[124] Favoring the original connection between Chapters 8 and 1–7, see, e.g., M. Thrall, *2 Corinthians* (1994), 36–38.

in Chapters 1–7 form a necessary prologue to his revisiting the subject of the collection. The collection, meanwhile, offers an opportunity to demonstrate their newfound zeal for reconciliation with him (7:7, 11; 9:2). His discussion of Titus's previous mission (7:5–15) paves the way for his next one (8:16–9:5), and his confidence in 7:16 recurs in 8:7. Nevertheless, many of Betz's insights from administrative letters prove almost equally relevant to an administrative section of a fuller letter; business was a common topic in ancient letters.

The fit with Chapters 10–13 is more difficult, but if we argue for the unity of our current 2 Corinthians, the collection retains a somewhat climactic role, although in this case only a penultimate one. The rivals he addresses in Chapters 10–13 either challenged his economic lifestyle or at least exacerbated the Corinthians' uneasiness with it (11:4–12; 12:14–19); Paul must defend his integrity and that of his agents (8:20–22; 12:17–18).[125] Despite Paul's complimentary wording in Chapters 8–9 (appropriate given his interest in their benefaction), his gently probing their loyalty regarding the collection (8:6, 11; 9:3–4) paves the way for Paul's frontal assault on his rivals and, thereby, the Corinthians' imperfect loyalty to him (10–13).

Paul is eager to avoid the charge of charlatanry (2:17; 4:2), and has refused to take money for himself (11:7–9; 12:16–18). Some of the Corinthians want to be his patrons or benefactors; but Paul is their benefactor (6:10; 12:14), and will allow them to be benefactors only for the needy of the Jerusalem church (9:12–13). Given the recent conflicts with the church, Paul is extremely cautious and gentle (cf. 10:1) in how he raises support for the collection in chs. 8–9.[126]

He thus avoids direct references to "money," while offering a wide variety of terms that function as synonyms in Greco-Roman administrative documents, or terms that define the collection in terms of ministry.[127] The collection is "grace" (*charis*, 8:1, 4, 6–7, 19; 9:14), modeled on that of Jesus (8:9) and the Father (9:8, 15). (Greco-Roman administrative texts also use *charis* for benefactors' generosity,[128] as well as for the gift itself and the beneficiary's gratitude; cf. 8:16; 9:15.) It is also "this case" (literally, "part"; 9:3); "this undertaking" (cf. business documents in BDAG; 9:4); "this bountiful gift" (a term usually meaning, "blessing"; 9:5). His use of *leitourgia* (9:12; cf. Rom 15:27; Phil 2:25, 30) is striking; although this can refer to priestly or analogous service (Rom 15:16; Phil 2:17; Lk 1:23; Heb 10:11; scores of times in the LXX), ancients also used the term for annual offices of public benefaction (often levied on the wealthy).[129] He speaks of *haplotēs*,

---

[125] Some suggest that other rivals in Galatia may have charged Paul's subordination to Jerusalem based on a levy view of the collection (cf. Gal 2:10; L. W. Hurtado, "The Jerusalem Collection and the Book of Galatians," *JSNT* 1 (5, 1979): 46–62, here pp. 48–52).

[126] Knowing the audience was essential when giving advice about funds (B. Witherington, *Corinthians* [1995], 411, cites Quintilian 3.8.14).

[127] Cf. N. Dahl, *Studies* (1977), 37–38; F. Matera, *II Corinthians* (2003), 181.

[128] F. Danker, *II Corinthians* (1989), 117–18, citing *OGIS* 383.9; 666.22; 669.29.

[129] See S. R. Llewelyn with R. A. Kearsley, *New Documents Illustrating Early Christianity* 7 (North Ryde: Ancient History Documentary Research Centre, 1994), §5, pp. 93–111

generosity (8:2; 9:11, 13; Rom 12:8)[130] and terms for "abundance" (8:2, 7, 14; 9:8, 12; used in business documents for profit margins). In short, Paul can use the same language for proclaiming his message (e.g., *diakonia* in 3:3, 7–9; 4:1; 5:18; 6:3; 11:8) and for social ministry (*diakonia* in 8:19–20; 9:1, 12–13). For further discussion of Paul's collection, see the "Closer Look" on the collection at 1 Corinthians 16:1–12.

Paul uses the conventional rhetorical strategy of comparison (*synkrisis*), in this case competition, to spur the Corinthians to action (8:1–8, esp. 8:8). The proximity between Macedonia and Achaia made them natural rivals, and civic pride and rivalry were endemic in the Empire (cf. Acts 21:39).[131] In this period such competition usually involved more friendly banter than hostility. Leaders who appealed to rivalry did so to provoke action, not to divide enemies (e.g., Xenophon *Cyr.* 2.1.22; 7.1.18).[132] (Even when the rivalry was with enemies, Leaders often exploited it to produce action; Plutarch *Them.* 4.2.) Paul notes the sacrificial giving of the impoverished Macedonians (8:1–5) and invites Achaia to do likewise (8:6–8). Apparently before the conflict between Paul and the Corinthian church, he also boasted of Achaian zeal for the collection to the Macedonians (8:24–9:2); now he is anxious to ensure that the Corinthians follow through, lest he and they be embarrassed by the Macedonian delegation (9:3–4; cf. 8:11). Thus, he sends Titus back to make sure everything is in order (8:6; 9:5; cf. 8:16–23). (He also may prepare for 11:7–9, in which he counters the Corinthians' charge that he allowed the Macedonians a privilege he prohibited to them.)

Although Philippi was relatively prosperous and Macedonia's economy had been growing, the prosperity failed to affect most of the poor, many of whom were unemployed. Much of the urban proletariat depended on benefactors' generosity for the grain dole.[133] Whether the Macedonian Christians' poverty (8:2) is related to their persecution is unclear, but we know that they did face persecution (1 Thess 2:14; 3:4; Phil 1:29–30); their "affliction" is described much like Paul's (cf. 1:8; 4:17; 6:4). Whatever its cause, it provides a useful foil to the Corinthians' own situation: they are not persecuted, and some are wealthy enough that their city would expect them to be benefactors at least on a small scale (see esp. Rom 16:23).

The Macedonians' giving according to their ability recalls Israel's contributions to the tabernacle (e.g., Ex 35:24); giving "according to their means" and

---

(though preferring a background in the LXX); N. Lewis, *Life in Egypt Under Roman Rule* (Oxford: Clarendon, 1983), 177–84.

[130] H. Betz, *2 Corinthians 8 and 9* (1985), 44–45, connects both senses of the term in ancient texts.

[131] E.g., Plutarch *Alc.* 12.1; Babrius 15.5–9; Herodian 3.2.7–8.

[132] Whereas *synkrisis* could denigrate one party, it often did not (see Menander Rhetor 2.1–10 passim; sources in C. Keener, *John* [2003], 916–17, 1183–84).

[133] R. Riesner, *Paul's Early Period: Chronology, Mission Strategy, Theology*, trans. D. Stott (Grand Rapids, MI: Eerdmans, 1998), 376–77 (noting also the habit of dependence in 1 Thess 4:10–12).

"beyond their means" (in this case, because they were poor) reflect conventional language for benefaction (8:3).[134] "Privilege" (*charis*), "sharing" (*koinōnia*, partnership), and "ministry" (*diakonia*; 8:4) were all common terms in Greek business documents (adopted by Jewish as well as Gentile Greek-speakers; though note that here the privilege is the benefactors'). That they donated themselves first of all (8:5) reflects one way of praising particularly dedicated benefactors, and imitates Jesus (8:9).[135]

Although the Corinthians committed themselves to this offering before the Macedonians did (some time in the past eighteen months, 8:10), after his conflict with them Paul has some reason for anxiety as to whether they are ready (8:6, 11; 9:3). Because he has Titus's verbal report, his anxiety probably in fact indicates knowledge that they are not yet ready, though Titus must believe that they can still be prepared if encouraged (8:16–17). Many inscriptions honor benefactors for not merely pledging but "completing" an obligation.[136]

In 8:7, Paul softens his concern and comparison with an assurance of his confidence (wise rhetoric, e.g., Fronto *Ad M. Caes.* 5.36 [51]). Paul has elsewhere praised the Corinthians' zeal for gifts like speech and knowledge (1 Cor 1:5); the term translated "earnestness" often appears in inscriptions honoring benefactors. Expressing superlative love for a letter's recipients, as Paul may be doing in 8:7 (if one translates with the NRSV), was a conventional way to express affection (sometimes offered by the same author to different addressees).[137] Praising one's superiority over others was also an accepted means of encouraging noble actions (Menander Rhetor 2.3, 380.21–22).

Yet he is not done with the competition he has set up with Macedonia; in 8:8 he compares the Corinthians again with their friendly rivals. "Commanding" was inappropriate for deliberative rhetoric asking a favor, so Paul takes a more strategic approach here. Here he "tests" the genuineness of their love, as he "tested" them in 2:9 (cf. 8:24). Writers often invited their addressees to prove their love for them by some particular favor the writer needed, often on behalf of a third party (Cicero *Fam.* 13.41.2; *Att.* 12.18).

Example was one tool that persuaders used to advance a case, and Paul produces the most authoritative example of all. If the impoverished Macedonians gave themselves by giving beyond their means (8:3, 5), wealthy Jesus did so even more, impoverishing himself in a manner no one expected benefactors to do (8:9; cf. Lk 2:7; similar use of Jesus's self-humbling in Phil 2:5–11). Jesus made others rich, as Paul does (6:10; cf. 1 Cor 4:8). Greek philosophers sometimes spoke of philosophy revealing the true wealth; for radical philosophers, this meant living without property because all things belong to them (an idea Paul

---

[134] F. Danker, *II Corinthians* (1989), 119, citing esp. *SIG*³ 569.32–33; Livy 34.4.15.
[135] See ibid., 122 (citing *OGIS* 339.19–20; *SIG*³ 495.125); cf. Rom 12:1.
[136] Ibid., 122 (citing e.g., *SIG*³ 613.17).
[137] See Cicero *Fam.* 2.3.2; and esp. Bk 13 (13.1.5, 18.2, 19.1, 26.1, 36.1, 45.1, 51.1).

uses in a much less economically radical way in 1 Cor 3:21–23). Another means of persuasion (common in deliberative rhetoric) was an appeal to what was expedient or profitable (NRSV "appropriate," 8:10) for the hearer.[138] Paul offers merely his "opinion" in 8:10, a term he elsewhere contrasts with a "command" (1 Cor 7:25, 40; Phlm 14), as here (8:8).

Although complimentary statements about the Corinthians here (8:11; 9:2) might seem to conflict with the rhetoric of 12:16–18, the same contexts show that some things are not quite well with the offering (8:6, 11; 9:3), and Paul is already on guard against accusations about it (8:20–21).

Remaining conciliatory, Paul repeatedly praises their "eagerness" (*prothumia*; 8:11–12; 9:2; cf. his own in 8:19), a term naturally linked with generosity in Greek and found in willing sacrifices in the LXX (1 Chron 28:21; 2 Chron 29:31, 34); another term for "eagerness" (*spoudē*) also is frequent here (8:7–8, 16; cf. 7:11–12; Rom 12:8, 11) and often was linked with the first term.

Paul wants them to give based on their eagerness, to follow others' examples, and not to feel like he is abusing his authority or exploiting them. Giving "according to what one has" (8:12; cf. 1 Cor 16:2) was all that could be expected (Tob 4:8, 16; Sir 14:13; *m. Pe'ah* 7:8).[139] Although Paul's term in 8:12 for "acceptable" is not limited to sacral contexts, it often applied to offerings (Rom 15:16, 31; 1 Pet 2:5), fitting in a context that will describe the collection as *leitourgia* (9:12).

Paul's goal is not their impoverishment (despite Jesus's example in 8:9), but the widespread ideal of equality.[140]

A CLOSER LOOK: EQUALITY

Equality was one of the central Greek characteristics of true friendship;[141] the ideal carried over into Greek-speaking Judaism (*Let. Aris.* 228, 257, 263, 282). Many of the Corinthians preferred the fictitious equality of patronal reciprocity, also called "friendship"; this view of friendship was common in Roman circles, and naturally appealed to the upwardly mobile of Roman Corinth.[142] Although some applied the ideal of equality even as far as table fellowship, many of the Corinthian Christians had been undermining it especially at that point (see comment on 1 Cor 11:21–22).

---

[138] E.g., Plato *Alc.* 1.114–27; Aristotle *Rhet.* 1.7.1, 1363b; Sextus Empiricus *Against the Ethicists* 2.22 (on Stoics); see comment on 1 Corinthians 6:12.

[139] Many prorated fees based on property (Philostratus *Lives* 1.21.519), and everyone (except perhaps tax collectors exploiting peasants) understood that offerings based on one's ability were acceptable (Dionysius of Halicarnassus *Ant. rom.* 11.27.7).

[140] For this ideal, see, e.g., Musonius Rufus 4, p. 48.9.

[141] E.g., Plato *Laws* 8.837AB; Aristotle *E.E.* 7.9.1, 1241b; Arrian *Alex.* 7.14.6; for sources, see C. Keener, *John* (2003), 1008–09.

[142] See sources in ibid., 1007–08.

In ethics, many viewed "equality" as a principle of justice (Dionysius of Hali-carnassus *Ant. rom.* 10.1.2). For some philosophers (like the legendary Pythagoras and his followers), "equality" was a principle of justice and demanded sharing things in common (Iamblichus *Pyth. Life* 30.167–68; Diogenes Laertius 8.1.10, 33; 8.2.65). Others applied it less strictly, but valued the ideal (Marcus Aurelius 1.14). Aristotle felt that equality (by which he meant equity) in justice was only proportionate to merit, but equality in friendship required equal quantity (*N.E.* 8.7.3, 1158b).[143]

Avoiding Jesus's Middle Eastern hyperbole but retaining his economic ideal (cf. Lk 3:11; 12:33; 14:33; 18:22), Paul balances Jerusalem's dramatic need with the voluntary character of the collection. Although "present" (literally, "in the now, or present, time") could refer to the present era (6:2; Rom 8:18; 11:5), it was good Greek for noting times of crisis (cf. 1 Cor 7:26).[144] Jerusalem's famine was an urgent crisis, not a regular levy on Corinthian Christians' resources. In Paul's application of "equality," the person with more than what is needed to live on shares with those who have less, and can expect reciprocation if the roles are reversed. (Reciprocity was at the heart of the ancient ideal of benefaction,[145] although usually it involved the beneficiaries bestowing honor on the benefactors.) The Corinthians might well never imagine the roles being reversed (except perhaps as part of end-time distress; 1 Cor 7:29–31; or wise foresight, Sir 18:25), but in principle probably accepted the ideals of friendship, "equality," and reciprocity.[146]

Although the language of "equality" was Greek, Paul illustrates the principle from Scripture. The manna narrative to which Exodus 16:18 belongs empha-sizes depending on God rather than hoarding.[147] Other Greek-speaking Jewish intellectuals like Philo drew on the same text to emphasize equality (*Heir* 191); Josephus emphasizes that the Israelites were to gather the manna "equally" (*Ant.* 3.29–30).[148] During the brief period in Israel's history when God provided for all his people directly, no one had more or less than what they needed, but only the right amount. This economy depicted God's ideal for his people.

BRIDGING THE HORIZONS

Why was Paul so concerned about this collection, when he had scrupulously avoided taking money for himself (11:7–9; 12:17–18)? Unlike many Christians

---

[143] See further *Pol.* 3.7.2, 1282b; 5.1.7, 1301b. The equality ideal of democracy (e.g., Xenophon *Cyr.* 1.3.18) never affected slaves or women.

[144] For sources, see F. Danker, *II Corinthians* (1989), 128–29.

[145] E.g., Xenophon *Cyr.* 6.1.47; Statius *Silvae* 4.9 (an equal gift); Cicero *Fam.* 12.30.3.

[146] Although the values were more widespread, someone who actually practiced equal sharing might be thought a philosopher (Philostratus *Hrk.* 2.1–6).

[147] See more fully R. Hays, *Echoes* (1989), 88–90.

[148] Diodorus Siculus 40.3.7 preserves a somewhat modified biblical tradition that Moses divided the land equally (*isous*) among citizens; cf., e.g., Lev 25.

today, Paul lived simply and sacrificially, completely committed to the needs of others; he hoped to teach by example (1 Cor 4:9–16). We also should note that, in contrast to much use of Scripture for fundraising today, Paul's emphasis here (and in most fundraising in his letters) involves care for the *poor*. In my country, some of the churches most insistent on believing the Bible give the least heed to biblical teachings concerning economic justice. With some good reason, Paul's emphasis on equality appeals to modern egalitarian sentiments; it does not, however, lend itself well to the ardent sponsorship of laissez-faire capitalism or social Darwinism that has often accompanied it.

Paul's principle of "equality" is a dramatic challenge to Christians today. It takes Jesus's teachings on care for the poor (e.g., Matt 6:19–21; Mk 10:21; Lk 12:13–33), which might otherwise be limited to local needs known firsthand, to an international level through networks of churches. If God has blessed some countries with more than what we need to live on, he will call us to account if we squander those resources selfishly rather than sharing with the desperately needy (through development, healthcare, peace-keeping, and other means). My country rightly expressed horror when terrorists murdered some three thousand people in New York in September 2001. Yet many people remain oblivious to the fact that ten times that number of people, mostly children, die daily from malnutrition and preventable diseases. Tens of millions of children are destitute, lacking clean drinking water or a place to live; others are drafted to fight in ethnic wars, enslaved for lives of prostitution, or orphaned through AIDS.

Christians in my own Western nation tend to follow our consumer-driven media in looking the other way in the face of unbearable pain. After the Nazi holocaust and Pol Pot's genocide, the world protested, "We did not know." In fact, the gatekeepers of public information simply did not believe the on-the-ground reports available to them. After half a million died in a few weeks of genocide in Rwanda, the world said, "We must never let it happen again" – all the while ignoring the fact that it had never stopped. The region was destabilized, and, over the next decade, over three million people died in Central Africa. Although 1 percent of that many deaths in the West would have made front page news in the United States, Central Africa was not "strategic" enough to merit so much attention.

My friend Médine Moussounga, after completing her Ph.D. at the University of Paris, returned to her Central African country. She wrote me her concerns after war came to her region, but none of the media sources I read here even mentioned her country, much less that a war was occurring there. By the time I received her last letter, her town had been burned to the ground. Unknown to me, she, her sisters, her mother, and an aged relative had fled into the forest, pushing her disabled father in a wheelbarrow. Médine often walked many hours per day, through snake-infested swamps and fields of army ants, to secure food for her family. They remained refugees for a year and a half, often sick and sometimes close to death. Today Médine is my wife, but the plight of the desperately needy can never be far from our hearts. Even if the world looks the other way, Christians do not have the right to ignore the pain of our brothers and sisters, with whom we have become one body.

8:16–9:5: THE DELEGATIONS

8:16: But thanks be to God who put in the heart of Titus the same eagerness for you that I myself have.

8:17: For he not only accepted our appeal, but since he is more eager than ever, he is going to you of his own accord.

8:18: With him we are sending the brother who is famous among all the churches for his proclaiming the good news;

8:19: and not only that, but he has also been appointed by the churches to travel with us while we are administering this generous undertaking for the glory of the Lord himself and to show our goodwill.

8:20: We intend that no one should blame us about this generous gift that we are administering,

8:21: for we intend to do what is right not only in the Lord's sight but also in the sight of others.

8:22: And with them we are sending our brother whom we have often tested and found eager in many matters, but who is now more eager than ever because of his great confidence in you.

8:23: As for Titus, he is my partner and co-worker in your service; as for our brothers, they are messengers of the churches, the glory of Christ.

8:24: Therefore openly before the churches, show them the proof of your love and of our reason for boasting about you.

9:1: Now it is not necessary for me to write you about the ministry to the saints,

9:2: for I know your eagerness, which is the subject of my boasting about you to the people of Macedonia, saying that Achaia has been ready since last year; and your zeal has stirred up most of them.

9:3: But I am sending the brothers in order that our boasting about you may not prove to have been empty in this case, so that you may be ready, as I said you would be;

9:4: otherwise, if some Macedonians come with me and find that you are not ready, we would be humiliated – to say nothing of you – in this undertaking.

9:5: So I thought it necessary to urge the brothers to go on ahead to you, and arrange in advance for this bountiful gift that you have promised, so that it may be ready as a voluntary gift and not as an extortion.

I n 8:16–23, Paul turns to the subject of the advance delegation who will help prepare the collection (introduced in 8:6, and continued after a brief caveat in 9:3–5). He is sending them to ensure that the Corinthians will be prepared before he comes with representatives of the Macedonian delegation (9:3–5). Paul's thanks to God in 8:16 and 9:15 may bracket this section (although most outlines break units between Chs. 8 and 9). Paul hopes for representatives from each of the churches to accompany the collection to Jerusalem (1 Cor 16:3; cf. Acts 20:4–5); as with the temple tax in Judaism, such delegates could be called "commissioned ones" (*apostoloi*, NRSV, "messengers," 8:23; cf. Phil 2:25). Titus is Paul's personal agent, and the others are agents of the churches (8:23), with the implication that the Corinthians must treat the agents as respectfully as their senders.

Titus, encouraged by the Corinthians' hospitality (7:13–15), is eager to return to help them prepare (8:16–17). Paul treats Titus (8:16–17, 23) and "the brother" (8:18–19, 22) in chiastic fashion. For the other delegates Paul provides a "recommendation" (see comment on 3:1), although his recommendation is unusual in not naming them (8:18–23). Most regarded a good reputation as an important qualification for leadership (cf. Ex 18:21; Acts 6:3; 1 Tim 3:2, 7, 10).[149] Messengers often traveled in pairs (8:22), and delegations of three or more (8:23) were not unusual for important matters.

Commentators' primary question here is the identity of "the brother" (8:18, 22; 12:18). The need for an independent witness rules out a genetic brother. The title applies to Sosthenes (1 Cor 1:1) or Timothy (2 Cor 1:1), but also to any Christian. Based on "we" material in Acts, some suggest Luke; but Luke may have joined the delegation in Macedonia (Acts 20:5–6). Others plausibly suggest the non-Macedonian delegates of Acts 20:4. Apollos would have been a pleasant surprise (1 Cor 16:12), but the "brother's" anonymity is not for surprise; the Corinthians would know his identity when they heard the letter, because it arrived with Titus and the "brothers." Whatever their identity, Paul did not omit their names to weaken their authority, as some have suggested; 8:18, 22 can hardly be classified as "damning with faint praise." If the person was well known, Paul could substitute an epithet for his proper name (*Rhet. Her.* 4.31.42); furthermore, inscriptions do not always include the members of delegations.[150]

As a precaution to avoid scandal (8:20–21), churches appointed their own delegates to supervise the funds (8:19; 1 Cor 16:3), just as cities chose envoys of virtuous reputation to carry gifts for the temple (Philo *Special Laws* 1.78; cf. *Embassy* 216).[151] Paul's precautions probably suggest that some in the church mistrust him (cf. 12:16–18), a mistrust that Paul believes more suitable for his opponents (2:17). In fact, Paul echoes his defense of his ministry from an earlier context, where he pleaded with the Corinthians to be reconciled to him: *mōmaomai* ("blame") appears elsewhere in the NT only at 6:3, and the term the

---

[149] E.g., Dionysius of Halicarnassus *Dem.* 18; Plutarch *Caesar* 10.6.

[150] F. Danker, *II Corinthians* (1989), 130, cites as an example *SIG*³ 370.42–46.

[151] The term translated "appointed" in 8:19 probably implies elections (Menander Rhetor 1.3, 364.1–2), although it does not always carry this sense (Acts 14:23).

NRSV renders "administering" is a cognate of Paul's term for ministry in that verse.

"We intend" (from *proneō*) in 8:21 fits the language of financial propriety; ancient inscriptions use the term to honor benefactors' forethought, including for their sending good representatives. The verse also echoes Proverbs 3:4 LXX, although Greeks also liked to pair statements about God and people, including for doing what was acceptable in their sight (Chariton *Chaer.* 1.10.3). Paul attests the character of the brother by noting that he has "tested" him (8:22) and found him eager, perhaps by pretending to dissuade him (e.g., 2 Kgs 2:2–6; Caesar *C.W.* 2.32–33). Many valued leaders who had first been successfully tested.[152] Paul is concerned about propriety especially because it is not his own honor that is at stake, but the Lord's "glory" or honor (8:19, 23) as the great benefactor.[153] (Paul's own reputation was significant only as his agent; 1:17–22; 5:20; 6:3.) Calling someone the "glory" of an institution meant that they brought glory to it (Fronto *Ad M. Caes.* 2.3.2; 2.7; 5.3).

Traditional Cynics and Stoics did not regard reputation as important, but some philosophers, like virtually all politicians, recognized the importance of leaders avoiding giving cause for suspicion (cf. Rom 12:17).[154] Being above reproach with respect to financial impropriety was particularly important, as it remains today.[155] This was important to Jewish people and other minorities,[156] given the public attention accorded financial scandals in which any of their number were involved.[157] This would be especially the case with the temple tax from the Diaspora (see *m. Sheq.* 3:2, also citing Prov 3:4; *t. Sheq.* 2:2).

As Paul had tested the brother, so now he requests evidence of their love (8:24; cf. 8:8) and to make good his boast about them (8:24; cf. 1:14; 7:4). (Others could affectionately request proofs of love, e.g., Fronto *Ep. Graecae* 6; *Ad M. Caes.* 3.2.) They had already proved true his boasts to Titus (7:14); but now his boasting to the Macedonians about Corinth's zeal for the collection is at stake (9:2–3).

A CLOSER LOOK: CHAPTER 9 A SEPARATE LETTER?

More scholars argue for separating Chapter 9 from Chapters 1–8 than for separating Chapter 8 from Chapters 1–7,[158] but their arguments are still not

---

152 E.g., 1 Tim 3:10; *Let. Aris.* 264; Columella *Rust.* 1.8.2.
153 Honor and shame were dominant values (see, e.g., B. Williams, *Shame and Necessity* [Berkeley: University of California, 1993]); on reputation, see, e.g., sources in C. Keener, *John* (2003), 885–86.
154 E.g., Isocrates *Demon.* 17; *Nic.* 54; Quintilian 2.2.14; Nepos 25.6.4 (although cf. 25.9.7).
155 E.g., Aeschines *Timarchus* 56; Iamblichus *V.P.* 27.129; commentators often cite Cicero *Off.* 2.21.75.
156 E.g., *Sipre Deut.* 79.1.1; *m. Abot* 2:1; 3:10; *t. Ber.* 3:3; *b. B. Bat.* 8b, bar.
157 Josephus *Ant.* 18.81–84; Juvenal *Sat.* 6.542–47; Artemidorus *Onir.* 3.53.
158 E.g., J. Héring, *The Second Epistle of Saint Paul to the Corinthians* (London: Epworth, 1967), xiii; first proposed by J. Semler in 1776.

compelling.[159] Some think 9:1 mentions the collection as if for the first time, but in context it merely assures the Corinthians that Paul is not sending the advance delegation out of any lack of confidence in them (although in fact that is likely why he is sending it; cf. e.g., Heb 6:9). It may thus be related to *paraleipsis*, the rhetorical figure in which one ironically broaches a matter while claiming not to mention it (cf. e.g., Phlm 19; Heb 11:32);[160] compare also similar phrasing in 1 Thessalonians 5:1. The sentence's opening *peri men gar* regularly alludes to what precedes it in the phrase's many occurrences in Greek literature.[161]

More importantly, Paul addresses the delegation in 8:16–23 and 9:3–5, pausing in 9:1–2 to assure the Corinthians that he is confident of them. He has been boasting about them (8:24), and is sending the advance delegates to assure that his boast will not embarrass him when the Macedonians come (9:2–3). The subject has barely changed between Chapters 8 and 9, so a seam between two letters here is extremely unlikely.[162] As Frank Matera notes, "Apart from 8:16–24 Paul's reference to 'the brothers' in 9:3 would make little sense, and without 9:1–5 one would not understand what he means in 8:24 about his boasting on behalf of the Corinthians."[163]

After discussing the advance delegation under Titus and the "brother" (8:16–23; 9:3), he explains that he sends it not because of any lack of confidence in the Corinthians (9:1–2a). Paul wishes to express his confidence in them while at the same time urging them to be ready – that is, he politely covers his anxiety, stemming from incomplete confidence. Similarly, Cicero notes in a letter of recommendation that a petitioner is already confident, but hopes that Cicero's letter will make matters even more likely; Cicero entreats the benefactor not to let this hope be disappointed (*Fam.* 3.1.3; cf. also 1.3.1–2). Paul has sent the advance delegation to ensure that the Corinthian offering will be ready before the Macedonian representatives come with Paul to Corinth (9:4–5), so Paul's confidence in them will not prove unfounded (9:2–3). He has acted from "necessity" (9:5; cf. 12:11), a standard defense for why one chose a particular course of action.[164]

Paul is counting on the Corinthians' zeal for him (7:7) translating into continued zeal for the collection (9:2). He reminds the Corinthians of their promise (9:5), depending on the importance of promises in his milieu (cf. 1:20); honorary

---

[159] In favor of unity here, see those who hold to only two letters (e.g., C. H. Talbert, *Reading Corinthians: A Literary and Theological Commentary on 1 and 2 Corinthians* [New York: Crossroad, 1987], 181–82) or one in 2 Corinthians.

[160] J. Amador, "Revisiting" (2000), 107; cf. *Rhet. Her.* 4.27.37; R. Anderson, *Glossary* (2000), 88–89; for examples, see, e.g., Cicero *Verr.* 2.4.52.116; 2.5.8.20–21.

[161] S. K. Stowers, "*Peri men gar* and the Integrity of 2 Cor. 8 and 9," *NovT* 32 (4, 1990), 340–48.

[162] With, e.g., J. Lambrecht, "Paul's Boasting about the Corinthians. A Study of 2 Cor. 8:24–9:5," *NovT* 40 (4, 1998), 352–68.

[163] F. Matera, *II Corinthians* (2003), 203 (cf. ibid., 32).

[164] See, e.g., Hermogenes *Issues* 77.6–19; R. Anderson, *Glossary* (2000), 17. He will not, however, impose "necessity" on them (9:7).

inscriptions praised those who kept their promises and called to account political opportunists who broke theirs.[165] The NRSV interprets the final clause
of 9:5 as a contrast between a "voluntary gift" (*eulogia*, blessing) and "extortion" (*pleonexia*, greed), that is, the funds being forced from them. Although
Paul would accept this contrast (9:7), and later Jewish texts do warn charity
collectors not to oppress the poor who cannot give (*b. B. Bat.* 8b; *Pesiq. R.* 51:1),
this might not be the point here. God's purpose is equality, rather than having
too much (*pleonazō* in 8:15), so Paul's warning against *pleonexia* in 9:15 may be
against the Corinthians accumulating more than what they need. Ancient texts
condemn greed for (among other things) being against the public interest. The
phrase translated "voluntary gift" could apply to benefactions (and also applied
to the honor that responded to such gifts).

9:6–15: SOWING GOD'S GIFTS, REAPING GOD'S PRAISE

9:6: The point is this: the one who sows sparingly will also reap sparingly, and the
one who sows bountifully will also reap bountifully.

9:7: Each of you must give as you have made up your mind, not reluctantly or
under compulsion, for God loves a cheerful giver.

9:8: And God is able to provide you with every blessing in abundance, so that
by always having enough of everything, you may share abundantly in every good
work.

9:9: As it is written,

"He scatters abroad, he gives to the poor;
his righteousness endures forever."

9:10: He who supplies seed to the sower and bread for food will supply and multiply
your seed for sowing and increase the harvest of your righteousness.

9:11: You will be enriched in every way for your great generosity, which will produce
thanksgiving to God through us;

9:12: for the rendering of this ministry not only supplies the needs of the saints
but also overflows with many thanksgivings to God.

9:13: Through the testing of this ministry you glorify God by your obedience to
the confession of the gospel of Christ and by the generosity of your sharing with
them and with all others,

9:14: while they long for you and pray for you because of the surpassing grace of
God that he has given you.

9:15: Thanks be to God for his indescribable gift!

---

[165] For sources, see F. Danker, *II Corinthians* (1989), 137.

*P*aul uses a widespread agricultural principle to make his point in 9:6, 9–10, which he applies to their nonagrarian wealth in 9:7–8, 11. That God rewards the generous (9:6–11) is a frequent affirmation of Jewish wisdom (Prov 11:25; 22:9). Reaping what one sows was an agricultural commonplace with a ready moralistic application (e.g., Job 4:8; Prov 22:8; Hos 8:7; Sir 7:3); "fruit" commonly meant "profit." Many Gentiles as well as Jews used sowing and reaping figuratively, often to describe benefaction and reciprocity.[166] Proverbs described generosity as sowing, with the expectation of God's blessing as increase, in contrast to the ultimate need of the stingy person (Prov 11:21 LXX; 11:24–26). Whereas people praised generosity (Aristotle *N.E.* 4.1.6–14, 1120a), they ridiculed the stingy person (Prov 11:26; Theophrastus *Char.* 10; 22). Paul structures the saying in rhetorically appealing fashion: x ... y/x ... y (whoever sows ... reaps ... whoever sows ... reaps), a device that rhetoricians called *symploche* or *koinotēs*.

Their willing heart (9:7; cf. also 8:3) recalls the voluntary contributions to the tabernacle (Ex 25:2; 35:5, 21–22, 26, 29), which proved more than sufficient (Ex 36:5–7); perhaps also the later temple (1 Chron 29:6–9; Ezra 2:68). "Not reluctantly" echoes Deuteronomy 15:10 LXX. Gentiles also supported "willing" contributions (e.g., Musonius 19, p. 122.30, employing a cognate of "eagerness" in 8:11–12, 19; 9:2; Hesiod *Op.* 353); Cicero urged an addressee not to grant him a favor unless he had already convinced himself to act willingly (*Fam.* 13.1.2).[167] Giving "freely" without compulsion was also the mark of an honorable benefactor. God's love for a cheerful giver closely echoes Proverbs 22:8 in the LXX, which adds to the Hebrew that God blesses a cheerful giver (same terms; cf. Sir 35:8 LXX; *T. Job* 12:1).

Paul's promise in 9:8 would appeal to his audience; the fivefold repetition of "all" cognates in Greek (plus two other *p*-words) was rhetorically effective (cf. p-alliteration in Heb 1:1), and "contentment" (*autarcheia*) was a virtue accepted by not only Stoics (e.g., Epictetus *Diatr.* 1.1.27; Marcus Aurelius 3.11.2) but also many others (cf. Prov 30:8 LXX; *Ps. Sol.* 5:16; Ps.-Phoc. 6). For some philosophers, it meant learning to live without external resources; others, like Paul, thought of contentment with basic resources (Phil 4:11).[168]

In 9:9–10 Paul views Scripture in light of Scripture, following good midrashic procedure. In 9:9, he quotes Psalms 112:9, which in context refers to the generosity and vindication of the righteous; having given to the poor, their righteousness endures. Yet God is the supreme benefactor on whom these generous benefactors also must depend; thus in 9:10 Paul recalls Isaiah 55:10, which speaks of God as the one who gives seed to the sower (i.e., to those who scatter in 9:9) and

---

[166] For sources, see, e.g., M. Thrall, *2 Corinthians* (2000), 575; H. Betz, *2 Corinthians 8 and 9* (1985), 102; D. deSilva, *Honor* (2000), 150–51.

[167] For different texts, see F. Danker, *II Corinthians* (1989), 139.

[168] Cf. H. Betz, *2 Corinthians 8 and 9* (1985), 110; J. N. Sevenster, *Paul and Seneca* (NovTSup 4; Leiden: Brill, 1961), 113–14.

bread for food. As they kept giving, God would keep multiplying their seed so they could give more and multiply their harvest of righteousness (the enduring righteousness of 9:9; cf. Prov 3:9 LXX; 11:30; Is 61:11; esp. Hos 10:12 LXX). Later rabbis told stories of God blessing the resources of the generous (*b. Shab.* 119a; *Lev. Rab.* 5:4; *Deut. Rab.* 4:10).

Paul draws heavily on ancient conceptions of benefaction in 9:11–15. Beneficiaries regularly reciprocated benefactors' gifts by honoring them; their honorary inscriptions and words of thanks repaid the benefactors with what they valued much in a political culture based on honor (see Seneca *Ben.* passim). For centuries, well-to-do citizens who supported works for the public benefit were deemed honorable, whereas those who failed to do so were dishonorable.[169]

In 9:11–15, however, God is the object of honor. Paul has already established that God is the ultimate benefactor who supplies even for those who give (9:8–11); thus when human benefactors dependent on him spread gifts in his name, both the givers and the receivers honor God their ultimate benefactor. (Paul elsewhere addresses people giving God more thanks when he delivers and uses his servants, in answer to many prayers; 1:11; 4:15.) The human agents of benefaction also receive the tangible benefit of beneficiaries' prayers (9:14; cf. also *Hermas* 51.5–7). Some Jewish people also affirmed that God, answering the gratitude of the poor, would reward the generosity of landowners, more than making up for their small sacrifice (Josephus *Ant.* 4.232; Deut 15:9; 24:15). Clement of Rome continued this major adaptation of the patronage system: when the rich supply for the poor, the latter thank God (*1 Clem.* 38.2).[170]

Paul employs the language of benefaction and honor throughout. The term *leitourgia* (9:12) applied to priestly ministries but also duties of benefaction volunteered for by or (often) imposed on the well-to-do. For Paul the gifts must be voluntary (9:7), but they generated honor just as civic "liturgies" did.[171] Their "obedience to the confession of the gospel" by giving (9:13) does reflect fidelity to the message of Christ, but it is no coincidence that the terminology was precisely that used in inscriptions for fulfilling contractual obligations ("confession" as "contract").[172]

Paul's exclamation of thanks (9:15) fits other such exclamations in this letter (common also in the papyri); though some begin new paragraphs (2:14; 8:16),

---

[169] E.g., Lysias *Or.* 19.58, §157; Isaeus *Apollodorus* 37–38; *Dicaeogenes* 36; *Nicostratus* 27; *Philoctemon* 60–61.

[170] Both terms Clement employs here for "supply" appear in this context in Paul (*epichorēgeō* in 9:10 and a cognate of *anaplēroō* in 9:12).

[171] For civic liturgies, see, e.g., H. I. Bell, "Egypt Under the Early Principate," 10:284–315 in *CAH* (1966), 300–01 (and Egypt's eventual economic collapse partly in consequence, 315); S. R. Llewelyn with R. A. Kearsley, *New Documents Illustrating Early Chrisianity* 7 (North Ryde: Ancient History Documentary Research Centre, 1994), §5, pp. 93–105, though it concludes (105–11) that the NT and Fathers drew only on the cultic LXX usage.

[172] See H. Betz, *2 Corinthians 8 and 9* (1985), 122; F. Danker, *II Corinthians* (1989), 145.

Paul could also use them in closing summaries (Rom 7:25; 1 Cor 15:57). God's "gift" may be his gift in Christ (8:9; Rom 5:15–17), but in the immediate context also God's provision for all, including for the destitute through the endowed. This had always been God's way – not only providing enough for everyone, but offering some the privilege of sharing in his generosity (Deut 15:4–11). Although Paul's language here explicitly involves only reconciling rich and poor, he also viewed the offering as reconciling Jew and Gentile (Rom 15:27; Gal 2:9–10).

10:1–18: THE MEEK LETTER-WRITER VERSUS HIS CHALLENGERS

10:1: I myself, Paul, appeal to you by the meekness and gentleness of Christ – I who am humble when face to face with you, but bold toward you when I am away! –

10:2: I ask that when I am present I need not show boldness by daring to oppose those who think we are acting according to human standards.

10:3: Indeed, we live as human beings, but we do not wage war according to human standards;

10:4: for the weapons of our warfare are not merely human, but they have divine power to destroy strongholds. We destroy arguments

10:5: and every proud obstacle raised up against the knowledge of God, and we take every thought captive to obey Christ.

10:6: We are ready to punish every disobedience when your obedience is complete.

10:7: Look at what is before your eyes. If you are confident that you belong to Christ, remind yourself of this, that just as you belong to Christ, so also do we.

10:8: Now, even if I boast a little too much of our authority, which the Lord gave for building you up and not for tearing you down, I will not be ashamed of it.

10:9: I do not want to seem as though I am trying to frighten you with my letters.

10:10: For they say, "His letters are weighty and strong, but his bodily presence is weak, and his speech contemptible."

10:11: Let such people understand that what we say by letter when absent, we will also do when present.

10:12: We do not dare to classify or compare ourselves with some of those who commend themselves. But when they measure themselves by one another, and compare themselves with one another, they do not show good sense.

10:13: We, however, will not boast beyond limits, but will keep within the field that God has assigned to us, to reach out even as far as you.

10:14: For we were not overstepping our limits when we reached you; we were the first to come all the way to you with the good news of Christ.

10:15: We do not boast beyond limits, that is, in the labors of others; but our hope is that, as your faith increases, our sphere of action among you may be greatly enlarged,

10:16: so that we may proclaim the good news in lands beyond you, without boasting of work already done in someone else's sphere of action.
10:17: "Let the one who boasts, boast in the Lord."
10:18: For it is not those who commend themselves that are approved, but those whom the Lord commends.

Whether or not the final part of 2 Corinthians (Chs. 10–13) was originally part of the same letter (see our introduction to 2 Corinthians), the break here is the most abrupt in the letter. Granted, Paul nowhere else begins a discrete section with "and I" (elsewhere such a phrase normally picks up in the middle of a thought); but Paul introduces a new train of thought here with no transition. He presupposes here an assault on his meekness when present, that is, his failure to carry through on his discipline threatened in letters (1 Cor 4:18–21; cf. 2 Cor 10:1–2, 10; 13:2–3; or other promises, cf. 1:17). That is, the reason for the new subject (as in 1 Cor 7:1; 12:1; 15:1) lies primarily in the situation rather than in Paul's logic.

Going on the offensive was a standard part of defense speeches, pervasive in forensic rhetoric.[173] Only portions of this section, however (those directed against the opponents, not the Corinthians), are pure invective rhetoric, the emotions of which were mostly hostile (Quintilian 6.2.20).

Paul reserves the expression "I, Paul" (10:1) for emphatic remarks (Gal 5:2; 1 Thess 2:18; 2 Thess 3:17; Phlm 19; Col 1:23; Eph 3:1);[174] the reflexive pronoun "myself" underlines it all the more. Paul is gentle toward them, and sent them a firm letter rather than disciplining them more harshly in person, only because he loves them (10:1–2, 9–11; cf. 1:23–2:1; 13:2–3, 10). They, however, view such gentleness as weak by the leadership criteria of their culture;[175] in Paul's language, they evaluate him by purely human standards (cf. 5:12, 16; 1 Cor 2:14–16; 4:3–5). Introductory exordia often mentioned an opponent's charge, and this paragraph fulfills an analogous function for Section 10–13.[176] Meekness was despicable in some settings (*tapeinos* also could mean "base" or "servile"; cf. 11:7), and this is probably how some applied the designation to Paul.[177] A "meek ruler" meant a merciful one, however, and Paul could expect his audience to know this.[178]

Paul's meekness is characteristic of Christ, who became poor (8:9) and would not boast (11:17; cf. Phil 2:8; Matt 11:29). (Paul could have also appealed to the

---

[173] E.g., *Rhet. Alex.* 36, 1442b.6–9; Cic. *Orator* 40.137; *De Orat.* 3.204; see C. Keener, *John* (2003), 753.
[174] Cf. similar language in, e.g., Tob 1:3; *Apoc. Mos.* 34:1.
[175] See esp. T. Savage, *Power* (1996), 65–69; Pliny *Ep.* 1.23.2.
[176] B. Peterson, *Eloquence* (1998), 84, citing Quintilian 4.1.54; Cicero *De Inv.* 1.17.25.
[177] E.g., Epictetus *Diatr.* 1.9.33; 3.24.75; Marcus Aurelius 9.40; Iamblichus *Pyth. Life* 32.226; 33.234; see P. Marshall, *Enmity* (1987), 323–24.
[178] See esp. D. J. Good, *Jesus the Meek King* (Harrisburg, PA: Trinity, 1999); Xenophon *Cyr.* 2.1.30; Tacitus *Hist.* 2.5; additional sources in C. Keener, *John* (2003), 870, 906.

example of Moses as in 3:7–13; he was known for meekness.)[179] One who trusted God to raise the dead also would trust the God who exalts the humble (cf. 7:6; Phil 2:8–9; 3:21; esp. Ezek 17:24; 21:26; Matt 23:12; Lk 1:52; 14:11; 18:14; Jms 4:10; 1 Pet 5:6). Paul's appeal in 10:1–2 recalls that in 5:20, in which as Christ's agent he urges them (using the same two verbs, *deomai* and *parakaleō*) to be reconciled to God (and to God's agent). Such entreaties could add pathos (e.g., Isaeus *Menecles* 44, 47).

Paul's reference to "human standards" (10:2–3) probably responds to Corinthian charges about his unreliability. Paul did not make his plans "according to human standards" (1:17; cf. 5:16); if he chose to spare them a harsh visit for their sake (1:23–2:1), this did not make him timid (10:1)! By contrast, his accusers *do* boast according to human values, as he will demonstrate (11:18).

Far from being weak as alleged (cf. 10:1–2), Paul is powerful, but for fighting the Corinthians' false ideas, rather than for being harsh with the Corinthians themselves (10:4–6); his authority was only to build them up (10:8). Paul's weapons and warfare are not human (cf. 10:2–3), but divinely powerful (though *tō theō* may well reflect the dative of advantage, i.e., "for God"). Philosophers and orators often used military imagery to describe their battle against rival ideologies.[180] For example, some spoke of waging war against human passions (cf. Rom 7:23; 1 Pet 2:11).[181] Many also spoke, as here, of warring against false opinions (Diogenes *Ep.* 10; Philo *Sacr.* 130; *Conf.* 128–33). Philosophers fought the "arguments" (*logismoi*) of sophists; Paul may well include philosophic arguments as well (cf. Col 2:8; Chrysostom *Hom. Cor.* 22.5). Fronto claimed rhetorical devices as an orator's "weapons" (*Eloquence* 1.16); the best weapons, said Cicero, were those of intelligence and debate (*de Or.* 3.14.55; *Brut.* 2.7; *Fam.* 4.7.2).

This is not Paul's first use of military imagery in his Corinthian correspondence (2:14; 6:7; 1 Cor 9:7); he used it often (Rom 13:12; 1 Thess 5:8; cf. Phil 2:25; Phlm 2; Eph 6:10–20). Because the obstacles oppose "the knowledge of God" that also appears in God's (military) triumphal procession (2:14) through the gospel (4:6), Paul may be thinking about knowing God's character through the message of the cross. The "proud" obstacles contrast with the meekness characteristic of Christ (10:1); these obstacles display the attitude of Paul's rivals (10:2).

Vengeance ("punish," 10:6) suggests the image of a ruler subduing a revolting city or province, destroying their walls, and then enslaving the inhabitants

---

[179] Num 12:3; Sir 45:4. Cf. Hillel in *b. Shab.* 31a.

[180] For philosophers, see, e.g., Seneca *Lucil.* 109.8–9;117.7, 25; Diogenes Laertius 6.1.13; A. J. Malherbe, "Antisthenes and Odysseus, and Paul at War," *HTR* 76 (1983): 143–73. For orators, see Seneca *Controv.* 9, pref.4; Tacitus *Dial.* 32, 34, 37; Philostratus *Lives* 2.1.563.

[181] Xenophon *Mem.* 1.2.24; *Oec.* 1.22–23; Valerius Maximus 4.1. ext. 2; Diogenes *Ep.* 5; 12; Iamblichus *Pyth. Life* 17.78; in Judaism, *T. Levi* 2:3; *Num. Rab.* 14:11.

(cf. Matt 22:7; Lk 21:24). (Many commentators focus on Proverbs 21:22 as background, but siege imagery was so common we need not narrow it to that source; cf. 1 Macc 8:10.)[182] The Corinthians had already established their "obedience" regarding the offender in 2:9; 7:15, and even executed vengeance in 7:11; but their obedience was not yet complete so long as they entertained his rivals. Once their obedience was complete, Paul would be in position to punish disobedience. Paul is here God's general (contrast 2:14), perhaps ready to take them captive for their rebellion against him (really he wants reconciliation, 5:18–6:1). But in 10:8 Paul desires to build them up rather than to tear them down (they themselves are not the strongholds of 10:4). Although he could refer to other areas of the Corinthians' disobedience (cf. 12:20; 1 Cor 4:21), in the immediate context Paul may well think of the disobedience of his rivals (though "obedience" may fit better his children; 12:14; 1 Cor 4:14–15).

Paul's accusers claim to be Christ's servants (10:7); Paul asserts that he is also, and later asserts that he is more so (11:23), and they are in fact Satan's servants (11:13–15). As he goes on to point out (and do), if required to boast more, he could (10:8; cf. Phil 3:4). Paul reemphasizes his affection when he notes that whereas a prophet to God's people might both build up and tear down (Jer 1:10), the Lord authorized Paul only to build them up (10:8; 13:10; cf. 12:19).

Scholars debate whether his terms in 10:10 (e.g., "weighty") are technical rhetorical terms,[183] but Paul's speaking ability is certainly one subject of Corinthian criticism (11:6). Urban audiences developed the conventional skills of comparing and evaluating speakers, and would intuitively apply these to Paul, Apollos, and the new missionaries.

A CLOSER LOOK: RHETORICAL EXPECTATIONS

People of status demanded appropriate appearance, gestures, and voice intonation as important components of good oratory.[184] It was effective delivery that made sound reasoning rhetorically effective (Pliny *Ep.* 2.3.9; 2.19.2–6). The ideal was a strong, pleasant voice and graceful movements (Cicero *Brut.* 55.203), although a voice both strong and pleasant was a rare combination (Seneca *Controv.* 3.pref.3). Skilled argument was inadequate for politics without delivery (Cicero *Brut.* 31.117); some even made up with delivery what they lacked in content (Cicero *Brut.* 66.234). Deficiency in any of these factors led to mockery.[185] Demosthenes had to discipline himself at length to make his delivery acceptable (Plutarch *Dem.* 7.2–3; 11.1–2); because Cicero was initially weak in delivery, he

---

[182] See A. Malherbe, *Paul and Philosophers* (1989), 91–93.

[183] Positively, P. Marshall, *Enmity* (1987), 385–86; negatively, R. Anderson, *Rhetorical Theory* (1999), 278.

[184] See, e.g., Dionysius *Dem.* 54; *Comp.* 11; Valerius Maximus 8.10; Suetonius *Claud.* 30; Plutarch *Dem.* 6.3; 7.2–3; 11.1–3; *Cic.* 3.5; 4.3.

[185] See P. Marshall, *Enmity* (1987), 62–66.

studied with actors (Plutarch *Cic.* 4.3) and trained his voice (Cicero *Brut.* 91.316). For Demosthenes, the greatest (or only!) factor in oratory was acting (Valerius Maximus 8.11.ext. 1).

Gestures were part of rhetoric. Exaggerated movements were appropriate to a forceful subject (Cicero *Rosc. Amer.* 32.89), and one orator's movements drew crowds as much as his speech (Valerius Maximus 8.10.2). One renowned orator's theatrical effects included jumping up and stamping the ground after he had reached an excited stage (Philostratus *Vit. soph.* 1.25.537–38).[186] Because not all of Caesar's army could hear him at once, his exaggerated gestures communicated some of his thought (albeit inaccurately in Suetonius *Julius* 33). One teacher of rhetoric complained that modern cloaks inhibited the free movement necessary to oratory (Tacitus *Dial.* 39). To get gestures wrong invited ridicule (Philostratus *Vit. soph.* 1.25.541–42).

Some compared correct tone and rhythm with music (Dionysius of Halicarnassus *Lit. Comp.* 11), although this applied to only some forms of rhetoric (Cicero *Orator* 23.77). Correct tone was critical (Plutarch *Dem.* 11.2–3), including appropriate indignation (Dionysius of Halicarnassus *Dem.* 54). Some spoke more forcefully when angry, so that audiences sought to provoke them (Seneca *Controv.* 3.pref.4–5); other speakers lost gracefulness when angry (Suetonius *Claud.* 30).

Appearance and garb could predispose an audience to listen (Philostratus *Vit. soph.* 2.5.572), and some suggest that Paul's appearance is at issue here.[187] But by "presence" Paul means not his appearance only but the totality of his personal ministry, in contrast to his letters (cf. Phil 2:12). Athenians demanded a pure Attic accent, and Romans pure Latin. Foreigners rarely achieved even precise command of Attic grammar (Philostratus *Vit. soph.* 1.8.490; 2.31.624). Greek was likely Paul's first language (esp. if we credit Luke's account that he spent his earliest years in Tarsus and grew up, as is likely from his own letters, among the urban elite in Jerusalem); but we cannot tell whether he retained a "foreign" accent (cf. Acts 21:37).

The greatest problem of Paul's personal addresses to them, however, goes beyond accent, appearance, or gestures: it is that he apparently wrote bold letters from a safe distance but avoided "frankness" when present (10:11; cf. 3:12; 7:4; 10:1–2). (The likelihood that Paul had never been a father may have left him less experienced in offering firm discipline than some others were.) The compatibility of word and deed (10:11) is a pervasive topic in ancient literature.[188] Critics of oratory often demanded the ability to speak (or at least

186 Such behavior dismayed more dignified observers (Cicero *Brut.* 43.158; Seneca *Lucil.* 75.1–3; Musonius frg. 36, p. 134.14–16).
187 See F. Danker, *II Corinthians* (1989), 155, with sources (though the portrait in *Acts of Paul and Thecla* 3 may be meant as flattering; see A. Malherbe, *Paul and Philosophers* [1989], 165–70).
188 See sources in C. Keener, *Matthew* (1999), 255, 540.

appear to speak) well extemporaneously,[189] though others preferred prepared speeches.

Evaluation by means of comparison (*synkrisis*; cf. 10:12) was a standard rhetorical exercise, pervasive in speeches and literature.[190] Comparing oneself with others was often a means to exalt oneself at their expense, as Cicero did (*Brut.* 93.321–322; *Pis.* 22.51). Such comparisons played well to the already factious Corinthian church (see comment on 1 Cor 1:12). Some, however, recognized that the rare individuals of prominence who did not exalt themselves (e.g., Socrates) were the wisest (Plutarch *Plat. Q.* 1.2, *Mor.* 1000B).

As in 10:2 ("daring"), that Paul would not "dare" to act as boldly as his rivals (10:12) is pure irony. ("Mock modesty" was one of the most common senses of *eirōneia*.)[191] Mock praise was a rhetorically sophisticated form of denunciation; thus Cicero declares of one whom he believes wronged both Cicero and the state, "What a sterling character! What a peerless patriot!" (*Fam.* 5.2.8; LCL 1:331). Josephus mocks a rival as "the most clever of historians, as you boast yourself to be" (*Life* 340). They have accused him of writing boldly when he is personally cowardly (10:1–2). It violated all conventions to compare oneself with members of a higher class to which one did not belong;[192] to take on one's betters was considered not only "daring" but shameless.[193] Yet Paul goes on to emphasize that in any contest with him his rivals have nothing genuine to boast about (10:14–15); it is they who have engaged in comparison out of their class! He finally "dares" to boast in 11:21 and even enters a point-by-point comparison in 11:22–23. Paul's vague title for them, "some," "certain persons," may follow an ancient convention of damning enemies with anonymity, that is, not deigning to even acknowledge them by name (cf. also 2:17; 5:12; 10:18; 11:4, 12).[194]

Some commentators also take Paul's rejection of rhetoric here as ironic, given his careful balance of sounds even in the immediate context. But although Paul is ready to display his ability to use a measure of rhetoric, he clearly prefers dependence on content (11:6; cf. 1 Cor 1:18–2:6). At the same time, his parody of self-praise throughout his "fool's boast" defies and critiques the entire enterprise of self-promotion central to Greco-Roman masculine culture.[195] Like some philosophers, he also can ridicule those who simply exchanged compliments among themselves (cf. Epictetus *Diatr.* 2.17.35–38).

---

[189] B. Winter, *Philo and Paul* (1997), 205–06. Orators varied in their preference (Philostratus *Vit. soph.* passim).

[190] For surveys of sources, see C. Keener, *John* (2003), 916–17, 966–69, 1183–84.

[191] See R. Anderson, *Glossary* (2000), 39.

[192] E.g., Homer *Il.* 1.280–81; Fronto *Ad Antoninum Imp.* 1.2.4; *Syr. Men. Sent.* 340–44.

[193] Cf. the rhetorical figure of "removal" (R. Anderson, *Glossary* [2000], 121).

[194] See P. Marshall, *Enmity* (1987), 341–48.

[195] See esp. C. Forbes, "Comparison, Self-Praise and Irony: Paul's Boasting and the Conventions of Hellenistic Rhetoric," *NTS* 32 (1, 1986): 1–30; idem, "Paul and Rhetorical Comparison," 134–71 in *Paul in the Greco-Roman World: A Handbook*, ed. J. P. Sampley (Harrisburg, PA: Trinity, 2003).

A CLOSER LOOK: SELF-BOASTING

Quintilian warns against self-praise, which tends to annoy audiences (11.1.15). Plutarch complains that for all his fame, Cicero invited censure by excessive self-praise (*Cic.* 24.1–2); various other public figures exhibited the same flaw, such as Alexander (*Alex.* 23.4) or Cato (*Marcus Cato* 14.2; 19.5). One guilty of self-commendation provided an opening for enemies' criticisms;[196] one who wished to amplify his greatness did best to find another to praise him (as, e.g., in Fronto *Ad Verum Imp.* 2.3). Some praised the rare sophist (Philostratus *Lives* 2.27.616) or other person (Valerius Maximus 4.1.6a) who managed to avoid self-praise. Jewish sages likewise discouraged self-praise (Prov 27:2; '*Abot R. Nat.* 22, §46 B).

Apologies for needing to discuss oneself were thus common (Isocrates *Nic.* 46; Dionysius of Halicarnassus 1.1.1). One could justify self-boasting under some kinds of circumstances. As scholars often note, Plutarch provides the most extensive list of justifications for self-praise. Although offensive in principle, self-praise could be acceptable in practice (*Praising Oneself Inoffensively* 1, *Mor.* 539AC). One could, for example, praise oneself "purely" to provide a moral example and invite imitation (*Praising Oneself Inoffensively* 15, *Mor.* 544D). Self-praise is acceptable if it can be used to invite imitation, to counter the praise of evildoers, to refute slander, to serve the audience, and so forth. Crediting God or chance, and mentioning one's minor flaws, could also reduce offense.[197]

Plutarch's views reflect wider conventions. One could appeal to one's deeds to answer criticisms (e.g., Demosthenes *Cor.* 299–300), that is, to engage in *apologetic* self-commendation. One could use it to discredit adversaries (Demothenes *Embassy* 174). One could use it for a greater purpose, such as reconciling rivals (Dio Chrysostom *Fifth Disc.* 3–9) or serving others (Pliny *Ep.* 1.8.13). One could boast if forced to do so (Cicero *Fam.* 5.12.8, claiming that he had precedent from others); to be forced by adversaries was most understandable (Quintilian 11.1.19, on Cicero). Cicero also boasted in passing when sharing news (*Att.* 1.14; *Quint. fratr.* 1.1.9.26), as others also noted (Quintilian 11.1.21).

Thus, a boaster avoiding the appearance of boasting had to feign subtlety. Noting that vanity about greatness was inappropriate, Cicero declined to comment on his greatness (Cicero *Against Caecilius* 11.36); his rival, however, was clearly unfit (12.37), and if Cicero, who had spent his entire life developing the requisite skills appeared inadequate, his rival must be less equipped (12.40)! One orator had many examples of his greatness read, dismissing each in succession

---

196 E.g., Thucydides 3.61.1; Publilius Syrus 597; Josephus *Ag. Ap.* 2.135–36.

197 See also P. Marshall, *Enmity* (1987), 353–57; further, G. Lyons, *Pauline Autobiography: Toward a New Understanding* (SBLDS 73; Atlanta: Scholars, 1985), 53–59, 68–69; D. E. Aune, *The Westminster Dictionary of NT & Early Christian Literature & Rhetoric* (Louisville, KY: Westminster John Knox, 2003), 81–84.

by noting that no one would want to hear them (Fronto *Ad Antoninum Imp.* 1.2.9).

Paul also used self-praise to answer criticisms (10:10–16) and because "forced" to do so (11:30; 12:11). He countered his rivals lest evil be praised (11:18), and to silence them (11:12); ultimately, he acted for the Corinthians' good (12:19).[198] Paul also credits God (10:13; 1 Cor 15:10) and is lavish with his flaws (11:6), even if perhaps ironically. Although Paul follows established conventions for self-praise, the subject of many of his boasts (tribulation lists without including triumphs earned or character displayed) becomes a parody of Greco-Roman elite values (11:24–33). Paul is a servant who honors his master Christ, not himself, apparently in contrast to some who preach themselves (4:5). For a discussion of commendation in general, see "A Closer Look" on 2 Corinthians 3:1–2.

Paul can boast more than his rivals because his ministry reached even to the Corinthians (10:12–16) – that is, they are the proof (3:2). Paul's implied charge that his adversaries "boast beyond limits" (10:13) suggests that they act "immoderately," violating a central tenet of Greek ethics.[199] "Moderation" was emphasized by Aristotle (*Eth. eud.* 2.3.1–5.11, 1220b–1222b; *Eth. nic.* 2.7.1–9.9, 1107a–1109b) but more widespread,[200] even in Judaism (e.g., *Let. Aris.* 221–23; Ps.-Phoc. 36, 59–69, 98).[201] The Greek behind the NRSV's accurate "comparing themselves with one another" is ambiguous enough to allow the interpretation, "with themselves." Perhaps they thought like those who strove for such excellence that they would rival themselves alone (Cicero *Quint. fratr.* 1.1.1.3), but for Paul they have made themselves the standard! They were the sort of arrogant self-boasters the culture despised.

But the "limits" in view probably also specifically involve spheres of authority, perhaps reflecting the ethnic comity agreement of Galatians 2:7–9 (cf. Rom 11:13). The term translated "sphere" (*kanōn*) usually meant "standard," but could extend to a specifically geographic sphere, as a first-century governor's edict attests.[202] Here the "standard" is probably ministers' particular callings, in this case with implications for jurisdiction. Spheres of ministry (whether geographic or not) were assigned by God, not by his agents. This notion of divine assignment comports with Stoic dependence on providence (see comment on 1 Cor 7:17–24) and expresses biblical trust in God's sovereignty (including for ministry offices,

---

[198] Chrysostom noticed most of the same justifications cited by modern scholars (see M. Mitchell, "A Patristic Perspective on Pauline περιαυτολογία," *NTS* 47 [2001]: 354–371).

[199] See P. Marshall, *Enmity* (1987), 199–202; e.g., Musonius 18B, p. 116.12.

[200] E.g., Cicero *Fin.* 3.22.73; Plutarch *Dinner of Wise Men* 20, 21, *Mor.* 163D, 164B; Diogenes Laertius 1.93.

[201] For Philo, see H. A. Wolfson, *Philo: Foundations of Religious Philosophy in Judaism, Christianity, and Islam* (4th rev. ed.; Cambridge, MA: Harvard University Press, 1968), 2:236, 277.

[202] G. H. R. Horsley, *New Documents Illustrating Early Christianity* 1 (North Ryde: Ancient History Documentary Research Centre, 1981), §9, pp. 36–45, esp. 44–45. It also might refer to the architect's "rule" (cf. Rom 15:20).

e.g., Num 16–17). Paul maintained his appropriate, God-appointed lot; in an attitude of hubris against God, his opponents did not. By classing themselves beyond their God-ordained role, these boasters are "without understanding" (10:12); failure to "know oneself," that is, one's human limits, was considered immoderate and the epitome of exceeding proper limits (cf. Plutarch *E at Delphi* 2, *Mor.* 385D; *Oracles at Delphi* 29, *Mor.* 408E).[203]

By the "jurisdiction" criterion, Paul's rivals fare poorly. Paul fathered the church (cf. 1 Cor 4:15); by contrast, his rivals are boasting in another's (i.e., Paul's) labors (2 Cor 10:15), in another's sphere (10:16). Paul does allow that spheres are not static, hoping that his will be expanded, with their help (10:15–16); but this would be accomplished in new territory (Paul thinks here of Spain, Rom 15:24, 28), not stealing another apostle's work (Rom 15:18–21).

The only appropriate boasting, Paul reminds them, is in the Lord (10:17); here he recalls Jer 9:23–24 (LXX 9:22–23), as he had in an earlier letter (1 Cor 1:26–31). Thus, human commendation or honors (such as in Jer 9:23) were worthless; only divine commendation mattered (10:18; Rom 2:29), and that would be rendered at the judgment (2 Cor 5:10–12; 1 Cor 4:5).

11:1–21a: FORCED TO FOLLY

11:1: I wish you would bear with me in a little foolishness. Do bear with me!

11:2: I feel a divine jealousy for you, for I promised you in marriage to one husband, to present you as a chaste virgin to Christ.

11:3: But I am afraid that as the serpent deceived Eve by its cunning, your thoughts will be led astray from a sincere and pure devotion to Christ.

11:4: For if someone comes and proclaims another Jesus than the one we proclaimed, or if you receive a different spirit from the one you received, or a different gospel from the one you accepted, you submit to it readily enough.

11:5: I think that I am not in the least inferior to these super-apostles.

11:6: I may be untrained in speech, but not in knowledge; certainly in every way and in all things we have made this evident to you.

11:7: Did I commit a sin by humbling myself so that you might be exalted, because I proclaimed God's good news to you free of charge?

11:8: I robbed other churches by accepting support from them in order to serve you.

11:9: And when I was with you and was in need, I did not burden anyone, for my needs were supplied by the friends who came from Macedonia. So I refrained and will continue to refrain from burdening you in any way.

---

[203] P. Marshall, *Enmity* (1987), 369–73. This might imply the supreme hubris of self-deification; but many applied self-knowledge to innate divinity (see C. Keener, *John* [2003], 236–37).

11:10: As the truth of Christ is in me, this boast of mine will not be silenced in the regions of Achaia.

11:11: And why? Because I do not love you? God knows I do!

11:12: And what I do I will also continue to do, in order to deny an opportunity to those who want an opportunity to be recognized as our equals in what they boast about.

11:13: For such boasters are false apostles, deceitful workers, disguising themselves as apostles of Christ.

11:14: And no wonder! Even Satan disguises himself as an angel of light.

11:15: So it is not strange if his ministers also disguise themselves as ministers of righteousness. Their end will match their deeds.

11:16: I repeat, let no one think that I am a fool; but if you do, then accept me as a fool, so that I too may boast a little.

11:17: What I am saying in regard to this boastful confidence, I am saying not with the Lord's authority, but as a fool;

11:18: since many boast according to human standards, I will also boast.

11:19: For you gladly put up with fools, being wise yourselves!

11:20: For you put up with it when someone makes slaves of you, or preys upon you, or takes advantage of you, or puts on airs, or gives you a slap in the face.

11:21a: To my shame, I must say, we were too weak for that!

*I*n 11:1–21a, Paul justifies his reasons for apologetic self-commendation, all of them accepted among his contemporaries (see "A Closer Look" on 10:12–18): concern for them (11:1–4); self-defense (11:5–6); and undercutting his rivals' pernicious boasts (11:7–21). He also reminds his audience of what they should already know, namely that boasting is normally foolish (11:16, 19, 21), thereby denigrating the rhetorical technique of his opponents (*synkrisis*, 10:12) as folly (11:19–21). (Some suggest that Paul ironically presents himself in the role of the "foolish boaster," a character type known in ancient texts.) He will continue in the same vein afterward: Necessity (12:1) "forced" him to join the fray of worldly boasts and comparisons (12:11).

In short, his opponents have forced him to "answer fools according to their folly," yet he endeavors to do so without making himself like them (Prov 26:4–5). Excessive self-denigration was viewed as negatively as self-praise was, sometimes as false humility (Valerius Maximus 7.2. ext. 11b);[204] Paul portrays his boasting as foolish purely ironically, to denigrate the boasting of his rivals.

Paul calls his argument foolish. One could, as in 11:23, even decry one's line of argument (adopted merely for a *reductio ad absurdum*) as "insane" (Aelius

---

[204] See P. Marshall, *Enmity* (1987), 356–65; Chrysostom *Hom. Cor.* 23.3. For exceptions, see comment on 1 Cor 2:1–3.

Aristides *Defense of Oratory* 339, §112D).[205] Accepting excessive praise could inspire the insanity of pride (Philostratus *Love Letters* 69, 15). The only genuine basis for Paul appearing "insane," however, would be outsiders' failure to appreciate his experience with God (5:13; 12:2–4). The Corinthians ought to "put up with" him acting foolishly, since they offer the same favor to his more dangerous rivals (see the same term in 11:4, 19–20).

Although boasting is foolish (cf. 10:17–18), Paul will need them to withstand him engaging in this foolishness (11:1, 16–17). Having already disavowed voluntary boasting, he now provides preliminary arguments justifying his forthcoming boast (11:2–15), just as he will continue defending himself after he has finished boasting (12:11, 19). Such preliminary justification for shocking statements was a standard rhetorical technique (which academic rhetoricians called prodiorthosis).[206] Orators often had to request pardon for something they were compelled to say (Aeschines *Tim.* 37–38).

As a father figure (12:14; 1 Cor 4:15), Paul has arranged for his children's betrothal (11:2; see comment on 1 Cor 7:36–38).[207] Fathers were responsible for protecting their daughters' virginity from sexual predators (Deut 22:15–21), sometimes a matter of grave concern as here (Sir 42:9–12). Likewise, Paul is concerned lest they be spiritually corrupted into unfaithfulness to the true Christ (cf. 1 Cor 6:15–17). Paul's "divine jealousy" (11:2) reflects God's biblical character, focusing biblical monotheism for fidelity to Christ (cf. contrast Rom 10:2). Although "jealousy" could negatively characterize pagan deities,[208] it also described Israel's one God who made a marriage covenant with Israel (Ex 20:5; 34:14; Deut 4:24; 5:9; 6:15; Josh 24:19).[209]

Paul compares the Corinthians with Eve and their corrupters, his opponents, with the serpent and Satan (11:3, 13–15). The serpent deceived Eve in Genesis 3:1–7; in some traditions, Satan approached her then and on subsequent occasions as something like an angel of light (hence Paul's development of the comparison in 11:14).

A CLOSER LOOK: CORRUPTING EVE (11:2–3)

Betrothal could be ended only by death or divorce. Some compare Paul's role here to that of an agent in betrothal, like Moses for Israel in some later Jewish

---

[205] For philosophers, human ignorance was madness (Musonius 20, p. 126.2–3). An insanity defense could also be used to evade or reduce punishment for a crime (e.g., Hermogenes *Issues* 58.19–59.3).

[206] See G. O. Rowe, "Style," 121–57 in *Handbook of Classical Rhetoric*, ed. S. Porter (1997), 142.

[207] For further details on betrothal, see also C. Keener, *Matthew* (1999), 89–91.

[208] E.g., Pindar *Hymns* frg. 37.

[209] Later interpreters clarified the positive character of this jealousy (*Mekilta Bahodesh* 6.100–06, in Lauterbach 2:244).

traditions;[210] but the father figure better fits the context and the mention of "jealousy." Others suggest that the analogy between the church and Eve presupposes Paul's portrait of Jesus as the new Adam (1 Cor 15:22, 45);[211] although this is plausible, it is not clear that Paul's use of Eve is premised on his new Adam theology (cf. 1 Cor 11:8–9).

In the OT, God's people were married to the Lord (e.g., Hos 2:19–20; Is 54:6; Jer 3:1–2) and would ultimately be restored to him (cf. Is 49:18; 62:5; Hos 2:14–20; 3:1–5).[212] It was only natural for Paul to reapply the image to a future marriage to Christ (cf. Rev 19:7; realized eschatology in Eph 5:25–27). Just as infidelity to God remained a consistent danger in the OT (Jer 2:32; 3:1; Ezek 16:31–42; Hos 1:2; 2:1–13), so it does for God's people in the interim eschatological era.

Some traditions had amplified Eve's deception[213] or blamed primarily her for humanity's fall.[214] Greek stories about Pandora may have influenced the development of such traditions (Hesiod *Op.* 90–95). Many men thought women too susceptible to sexual temptation.[215] The most obvious allusion beyond Genesis (if the text was early and widespread enough for Paul to have known it), is 4 Maccabees 18:7–8, where a pious mother insists that she remained a "pure virgin" (the same expression as in 11:2) in her father's house, in contrast to Eve's defilement through the deceitful serpent.

Many traditions connected the serpent or Eve's deception with Satan (Wis 2:24; Rev 12:9).[216] Although the fullest picture of the story to which Paul may allude is first attested as a later composite, many individual elements are early and had probably already coalesced in tradition. The devil acted because he was jealous of Adam or refused to worship him at God's command;[217] in some traditions, he desired to marry Eve (*t. Sota* 4:17; *Gen. Rab.* 20:4) and impregnated her (*b. Yeb.* 103b; *Shab.* 146a).[218] (That some later rabbis associated the serpent with slandering God might be relevant to Paul's accusers,[219] but because the tradition is late it is probably only coincidental.) See further comment at 11:14.

---

[210] R. A. Batey, *New Testament Nuptial Imagery* (Leiden: Brill, 1971), 16–17; cf. Augustine *Converts and the Creed* 213.7. On this role, see C. Keener, *John* (2003), 311, 579–80.

[211] P. Minear, *Images* (1960), 55.

[212] In subsequent Jewish sources, see, e.g., *Sipre Deut.* 1.11.1; 43.16.1; *Sipra* Shemini Mekhilta de Miluim 99.2.2.

[213] *Sib. Or.* 1.40–45; *L.A.E.* 10:1; 18:1; 25; *Apoc. Mos.* 9; 29:17.

[214] E.g., *L.A.E.* 25:35; 38:1–2; 44:1–5; *Apoc. Mos.* 9; 11:1–2; 14; 21:6; 31–32; *p. Shab.* 2:6; *Gen. Rab.* 17:8. But Eve was not always negative (e.g., Tob 8:6).

[215] Cf. 2 Tim 3:6; Chariton 1.4.1–2; C. Delaney, "Seeds of Honor, Fields of Shame," 35–48 in *Honor and Shame and the Unity of the Mediterranean,* ed. D. D. Gilmore (Washington, DC: American Anthropological Association, 1987), 41.

[216] E.g., *3 Bar.* 9:7; *2 En.* 31:6 J; *Apoc. Mos.* 17; *Apoc. Ab.* 23:1, 11; *Tg. Ps.-Jon.* on Gen 4:1; an angel in *1 En.* 69:6.

[217] Wis 2:23–24; Josephus *Ant.* 1.41; *L.A.E.* 13:1–16:4; *'Abot R. Nat.* 1 A; *b. Sanh.* 59b; *Apoc. Sedr.* 5.

[218] For other demons' involvement, see *b. Erub.* 18b; *Gen. Rab.* 24:6.

[219] *Gen. Rab.* 19:4; *Num. Rab.* 19:2; *Qoh. Rab.* 10:11, §1.

Paul most often paints his opponents as personal rivals for the Corinthians' affection, but it is clear in 11:4 that he regards them as leading the Corinthians away from Christ (cf. Gal 1:6–9). In what way did they misrepresent Christ? Paul emphasizes that he, unlike them, has suffered (11:23), and bases most of the defense of his ministry in 2:14–6:10 on his own sharing in Christ's sufferings. Apparently he views his opponents as playing down the offense of the cross both for Christ and for themselves, a compromise some other early Christian sources count as Satanic (Mk 8:31–38, reproving Peter himself). This need not mean that they denied Jesus's death and resurrection; only that they offered a costless, overcontextualized version of Christian faith. It is possible that it resembled much of Christianity currently practiced in the Western world, which, apart from some doctrines and rituals, often leads to behavior virtually indistinguishable from that of non-Christians.

Hinting at the more thorough rhetorical comparison (*synkrisis*) to come in 11:22–23, a competition he accuses his opponents of having begun (10:12–15), Paul emphasizes that he is not their inferior (11:5).[220] He applies to them the ironic label, "superlative apostles" (11:5; 12:11), but elsewhere denigrates as arrogant the use of superlative labels (*hyper-* prepositions in 10:14, 16; 12:6–7; cf. 11:23). Despite some similarities to Paul's less forceful challenge to the hegemony of Jerusalem's "pillars" in Galatians 2:6–10, most scholars agree that Paul refers to his opponents in Corinth here, not (pace a smaller number of careful exegetes, including Barrett and Bruce) the Jerusalem apostles.[221] Especially given the moderate rhetorical polish apparent in Paul's letters, it is almost impossible that the Jerusalem apostles would be competing rhetorically with Paul (11:6)! Furthermore, Paul has been referring to opponents (11:4) and uses the same title to summarize his opposition in 12:11.

"Untrained in speech" (11:6) may imply one not proficient in rhetoric, and certainly not a professional speaker (cf. 10:10). Paul's letters demonstrate that even if he lacked tertiary training in rhetoric he must have had the basic training in rhetoric available to highly educated individuals in Greco-Roman cities. Paul's presentation may have been imperfect (10:10), but even if his concession involves rhetorical humility (1 Cor 2:1–4),[222] it does show where Paul's emphasis lies. Scholars note that the famous orator Dio Chrysostom contrasts himself with the sophists, ironically claiming to be unskilled (*Or.* 12.15). Paul likewise concedes, perhaps ironically, "I am just an *amateur* speaker compared to the splendid apostles" of 11:5 – but I am sound on what matters.

---

220 Rhetorical protests that one was "not inferior" were common (e.g., Menander Rhetor 1.2, 353, lines 9–10; Philostratus *Hrk.* 27.4; 29.2; 37.2).

221 See esp. M. Thrall, *2 Corinthians* (2000), 671–76 (in contrast to her 1980 article); F. Matera, *II Corinthians* (2003), 246–47; R. Bultmann, *The Second Letter to the Corinthians*, trans. R. A. Harrisville (Minneapolis: Augsburg, 1985), 208, 215.

222 B. Winter, *Philo and Paul* (1997), 213–15, shows that *idiōtēs* applies even to graduates of rhetorical schools so long as they were not professors, that is, not professionals.

Like a good ancient debater, Paul is ready to concede an inconsequential point to gain credibility for an essential one.[223] "Not inferior" could be rhetorical litotes; such understatement was useful as a technique to diminish possible hints of arrogance (*Rhet. Her.* 4.38.50). Paul paints his conflict with his rivals the way philosophers painted their conflicts with the sophists (cf. comment on 1 Cor 2:1–5).[224] Sophists prided themselves in being able to argue either side of a debate equally well, behavior that philosophers, emphasizing truth, rejected. Even if more aristocrats paid attention (and money) to rhetoricians, their education invited them to respect philosophers. Even some great orators emphasized moral content over form (Maximus of Tyre 25); one needed logic as well as verbal eloquence (Cicero *Orator* 32.113). Claiming knowledge rather than speaking ability "is an argument of the same order: Paul rhetorically boasts that he is no mere sophist."[225]

Paul defends his "volunteer" status in 11:7–9. Just as sophists emphasized rhetorical form over content, they charged fees from their students; Paul is truly an "amateur" rather than a professional (11:6) in this regard. Scholars often quote a sophistic criticism of Socrates: though he admittedly avoids avarice, he could not be wise, because his knowledge is not worth wages (Xenophon *Mem.* 1.6.12). The Jesus tradition emphasizes the need for apostles to depend on local hospitality (Mk 6:10; Lk 10:5–8). This commission was for a relatively short-term mission, however, and hospitality rarely extended beyond several weeks.[226] Paul maintained the simplicity and sacrifice of the tradition, and simply added more sacrifice by laboring, while depending only on already established churches. This practice apparently raised the question, however, why he failed to accept support from the Corinthian church even once it was established.

Paul did not wish to be seen as an exploitive charlatan (2:17) or as some sage dependent on a local patron's support (see "A Closer Look" at 1 Cor 9:1–27); he was no "employee" of the Corinthian church. A long tradition of Greek thinkers before Paul had rejected the role of paid teacher (esp. the role of sophists), although most did not "humiliate" themselves (in the elite's perspective) so far as to work a manual trade. In Roman Corinth, accepting benefaction required reciprocity; one had to honor one's patron or benefactor.[227] Some gifts might appear too great to accept (Pliny *Ep.* 6.32.2). If the church was divided into factions (1 Cor 1:10–12), accepting support from any faction brought Paul into a relationship of hostility with their rivals; ancient enmity networks made such an outcome inevitable.

---

[223] Cf., e.g., Xenophon *Hell.* 1.7.16–17; Cicero *Sest.* 69.145–46; Josephus *Life* 139–43. Thus, although Aeneas was weaker than Hector, he was smarter (Philostratus *Hrk.* 38.1).

[224] Cf. H. D. Betz, *Der Apostel Paulus und die sokratische Tradition* (Tübingen: Mohr/Siebeck, 1985), 66; closer to Paul's era, see B. Winter, *Philo and Paul* (1997), passim.

[225] W. A. Meeks, *The First Urban Christians: The Social World of the Apostle Paul* (New Haven, CT: Yale, 1983), 72.

[226] See, in some detail, R. Hock, *Social Context* (1980), 29–31.

[227] For these and other factors, see P. Marshall, *Enmity* (1987), 242–45 (cf. 7–12).

Rejecting benefactions, however, was tantamount to rejecting an offer of friendship, an act that normally produced an enmity relationship instead.[228] What may have been merely a point of disagreement in 1 Corinthians 9 has thus become a major point of contention since Paul's rivals arrived and accepted such support. Those who rejected gifts had to mount a strong case why this was acceptable (e.g., Fronto *Ep. Graec.* 5). Paul must now explain that he acted on the Corinthians' behalf, countering his rivals' negative spin on his "ingratitude" with his own positive spin by inverting traditional roles (12:14).[229]

Paul's "Did I commit a sin by" accepting humiliation for your good, by refusing to "burden" you (11:7), is irony, probably harsh enough to count as sarcasm.[230] Benefactors contributed to others "free of charge" (11:7), expecting only honor in return; by portraying himself as their benefactor, Paul shames them for their ingratitude. Commentators note that refusing to be a "burden" (11:9) is also familiar language from benefaction texts (inscriptions; Seneca *Ben.* 2.21.3) and appears even in depictions of sages dependent on patrons (some cite Lucian *Salaried Posts* 20). The image's force is graphic: prosecutors and moralists elsewhere used "robbery" figuratively for exploitation.[231] Far from dishonoring the Corinthians by accepting other churches' gifts, Paul "sinned" by "exploiting" other churches to serve them! But Paul's crimes are ironic, just as Cicero ironically jibes that surely if the wicked Catiline committed crimes, they could not have taken place without Sulla (whom he is defending; *Sulla* 24.67).

The Corinthians were embarrassed by Paul's boasting about Macedonian support (11:9–10), although a receiver of benefaction was obligated to honor a benefactor. But Paul had boasted about the Corinthians, too (9:2), and claims here that he received gifts from Macedonian Christians precisely to serve the Corinthian Christians. As in 11:11, good writers and speakers included reminders or protests of continuing love (7:3; Cicero *Fam.* 2.4.2).

Paul now provides a justification for this boast: he offers it to silence his rivals, who falsely claim to be his peers (11:12); silencing such competitors was accepted grounds for boasting in antiquity (see "A Closer Look" at 10:12). One also could justify boasting by claiming that one did it to remove any excuses for failing to do as one advised (Isocrates *Nic.* 47); likewise Paul denies an "opportunity" to his opponents in 11:12. They claim to be his "equals" in what they boast about (undoubtedly apostleship, 11:13), but do not sacrifice and suffer as he does. One category of fool in Greek literature was the boaster oblivious to his own limitations.

---

[228] See P. Marshall, *Enmity* (1987), 13–18, 245–46, 257 (cf. 175–77); Cicero *Fam.* 14.3.1.

[229] Debaters could deny charges, or could admit them but show that their action was justified (cf., e.g., Hermogenes *Issues* 48.15–23).

[230] For irony, see, e.g., Cicero *Orator* 40.137; Dio Chrysostom *Or.* 31.9–10; Josephus *Ag. Ap.* 1.295; *Life* 340; comment on 1 Cor 4:8.

[231] Cicero *Verr.* 1.1.2; 2.3.20.50; *m. Pe'ah* 5:6.

Their claims to be his equals invite comparison (see 11:21–23), and comparisons with hostile rivals typically impugned them (as Paul does in 11:13–15). An angry tone was rhetorically appropriate when responding to, hence returning, charges.[232] The countercharge of deception (11:13) was standard when responding to opponents' charges.[233] Many also acknowledged that vices could imitate virtues, seeking to pass for them (Cicero *Part. or.* 23.81). Like "apostle," "worker" could be positive (Lk 10:7), but also could be negative (Phil 3:2; *Let. Aris.* 231).

Stories of supernatural beings transforming themselves were familiar in ancient lore (e.g., Achilles Tatius 2.15.4).[234] In later Jewish sources, Death disguises himself as a glorious angel (*T. Ab.* 16.4–18.2 A; 13.2–4 B); Satan disguised himself as mortals (*T.* Job 6:4; 17:1–2; 23:1); a demon disguised himself as King Solomon (*Pesiq. Rab Kah.* 26:2). Most relevantly here, however, Satan disguises himself with angelic brightness to seduce Eve (*L.A.E.* 9:1–2; *Apoc. Mos.* 17:1–2), fitting Paul's comparison between the serpent and the false teachers (11:3–4).[235] Paul suggests that their "end" (11:15) will be destruction (cf. Phil 3:19).

BRIDGING THE HORIZONS

In parts of the world where Christians are not a persecuted minority, some people use churches primarily as places to make business contacts or to display social status. Such people miss the point of what the gospel is about, just as the Corinthians did. Christendom has redefined "church" as a meeting hall for religious services; Paul thought of God's eschatological people, exemplified in house churches where believers met to encourage each other's faith and together to honor God alone.

Some churches of a particular status expect their ministers to display trappings of the status in which they take pride. Experiences in one drug-infested, low-income neighborhood where I lived, worked, and ministered brought this home to me: One neighbor was convinced that I was not a minister because I wore jeans when telling children Bible stories and did not own a car, much less an expensive one. Granted, many poor people there deliberately sacrificed to give their ministers the best, as symbols for their community. But we too often define "ministry" differently than the NT defines the terms so translated. Different cultures and churches indeed require different gifts, but Paul always kept serving people with God's message at the center of his definition.

If Paul counters false apostles' boasts initially in 11:1–15, he provides an apology for boasting in 11:16–21, directly before boasting in sufferings (11:22–33).[236]

---

[232] E.g., Aeschines *Fals. leg.* 146; Cicero *De or.* 2.45.189.

[233] E.g., Cicero *Quinct.* 6.22; *Cael.* 29.69; see C. Keener, *John* (2003), 762.

[234] See further C. Keener, *John* (2003), 1189–90.

[235] For Satan's "servants" (which the NRSV renders "ministers" in 11:15), cf. also *1 En.* 54:6.

[236] Augustine *Doct.* 4.7.11 found 11:16–30 to be rhetorically sophisticated (R. Anderson, *Rhetorical Theory* [1999], 17–18).

Have his opponents characterized him as weak or uneducated (10:10; 11:6)? Then he is justified in adopting the assigned posture of a fool (using the rhetorical exercise of *prosopopoiia*, writing speeches in an assumed character). Although assuming the role assigned by one's opponents was, when attempted, rarely developed at such length,[237] the Corinthians should recognize that Paul constructs a caricature that assails his opponents rather than himself; he adopted this "foolish" character of boasting from the behavior of his opponents (10:12). Thus, he creatively returns the charge of folly. (Returning charges was one of the most conventional exercises in ancient defense speeches.)

That the Corinthians "put up with fools" because they are wise (11:19)[238] is pure irony, obviously meaning the opposite of what it says, just as when Paul said that he was a fool but they were wise (1 Cor 4:10). Others also ridiculed someone who would allow himself to be exploited as either (sarcastically) a great example of patience or (literally) a fool (Dionysius of Halicarnassus *Demosth.* 3). (Mock respect was not unusual in Greco-Roman rhetoric.)[239] The point is that they are allowing others to exploit them; such a claim constituted an invitation to action. Slaves do not put up with unfair treatment, one speaker charged; why should you Romans do so (Sallust *Jug.* 31.11)?

In one blow Paul calls his opponents fools, challenges the Corinthians' course of action as unwise, and offers a reason why they ought to be patient with his own boasting: In contrast to the opponents who exploit them, Paul at least is harmless (11:20–21a). In fact, Paul was too "weak" to abuse them (11:21a);[240] he is reducing to the absurd their characterization of him as weak because he was too merciful to want to punish them harshly in person (1:23; 10:1–2, 9–10; 13:2–3). Although Paul allegedly says this "to my shame" (11:21), he means it to theirs (cf. 1 Cor 6:5; 15:34). It was good rhetoric to remind an audience that one had done favors for them, or for others who now sought the speaker's hurt (*Rhet. Alex.* 36, 1444b.35–1445a.12).

One should focus on the behavior of one's opponents that would most offend one's audience (*Rhet. Alex.* 36, 1442a.13–14). Paul's anaphora in 11:20, like repetition in general, stirs emotion; five times Paul repeats, "if someone," and lists the offense against the Corinthians. The exploitation in view probably is partly financial (2:17; 11:7–9). "Preys upon you" is literally "devours you"; it was a common but graphic image for hostility (Gal 5:15).[241] A blow to the face

---

237   P. Marshall, *Enmity* (1987), 356–64, may overstate its rarity. Qualifications like the *hōs* in 11:17 slightly limit the harshness.

238   Taking *ontes* as a causal participle; it also could be concessive, but "though you are wise" reduces the irony.

239   Aelius Aristides *Fifth Leuctrian Oration* 4; Libanius *Declamation* 36.12.

240   Some rightly compare Demosthenes' "confession" of weakness, which he uses to emphasize all the more his loyalty to Athens (*Cor.* 320).

241   E.g., Musonius 10, p. 78.26–28; Diogenes Laertius 6.1.4; *1 En.* 103:11, 15; *m. 'Abot* 3:2; *T. Gad* 2:2.

constituted a deliberate insult and an offense punishable under some ancient law codes.[242]

11:21b–33: THE FOOL'S BOAST IN SUFFERINGS

11:21b: But whatever anyone dares to boast of – I am speaking as a fool – I also dare to boast of that.

11:22: Are they Hebrews? So am I. Are they Israelites? So am I. Are they descendants of Abraham? So am I.

11:23: Are they ministers of Christ? I am talking like a madman – I am a better one: with far greater labors, far more imprisonments, with countless floggings, and often near death.

11:24: Five times I have received from the Jews the forty lashes minus one.

11:25: Three times I was beaten with rods. Once I received a stoning. Three times I was shipwrecked; for a night and a day I was adrift at sea;

11:26: on frequent journeys, in danger from rivers, danger from bandits, danger from my own people, danger from Gentiles, danger in the city, danger in the wilderness, danger at sea, danger from false brothers and sisters;

11:27: in toil and hardship, through many a sleepless night, hungry and thirsty, often without food, cold and naked.

11:28: And, besides other things, I am under daily pressure because of my anxiety for all the churches.

11:29: Who is weak, and I am not weak? Who is made to stumble, and I am not indignant?

11:30: If I must boast, I will boast of the things that show my weakness.

11:31: The God and Father of the Lord Jesus (blessed be he forever!) knows that I do not lie.

11:32: In Damascus, the governor under King Aretas guarded the city of Damascus in order to seize me,

11:33: but I was let down in a basket through a window in the wall, and escaped from his hands.

Paul's "Fool's Boast" runs from 11:22 through 12:9, although we treat 12:1–10 separately from this first section. Although Paul ironically eschewed "daring" to compare himself with his rivals in 10:12, he indicates in 11:21b that he can match them on every point in which they boast. He therefore begins with a point-by-point comparison in 11:22, where he matches them, before proceeding to areas where they cannot hope to be in his league (11:23–12:9). Rhetoricians valued point-by-point comparisons, comparing individuals, cities, and heroes

---

[242] See sources in C. Keener, *Matthew* (1999), 197–98.

of the past virtue by virtue (Menander Rhetor 2.3, 381.31–32; 386.10–13; 2.10, 416.2–4; 417.5–9). Such comparison can include not only deeds (2.3, 379.5), but the person's home city and country (2.3, 379.6–8), as here (11:22).

Many have compared the form of Paul's list to Augustus's *Res Gestae*, a self-encomium posted throughout the empire as imperial propaganda. It sometimes even enumerates boasts (like Paul in 11:24–25): Augustus gave three gladiatorial shows in his own name and five in the name of his sons or grandsons (*Res Gestae* 22.1). But Augustus did not emphasize his setbacks, although a later writer did so for him, balancing his own list of exploits.[243] (Paul implies a sort of "achievement" in 10:13–18, although crediting it to God's will; but instead of listing churches planted, he mentions only his anxiety for them, in 11:28–29.)

Paul's focus on sufferings distinguishes him from usual lists of achievements, including those of his competitors[244] but was not unheard of. Many heroes of the past would not be remembered apart from their sufferings (Maximus of Tyre 34.8); those who idealized philosophers sometimes emphasized what they suffered for their teachings (Maximus of Tyre 15.9; 34.9). Generals and states-men who sacrificed for the state often boasted in what they had suffered on its behalf;[245] these also appear in summaries of past exploits.[246] Some would face dangers to win honor (Xenophon *Cyr.* 1.2.1). Stoics provided their endurance in sufferings as a moral example and proof of their genuineness. Lovers like-wise could list afflictions as signs of devotion (Achilles Tatius 5.18.3–6). Closest are texts that emphasize the greater rewards for the virtuous who sacrifice or are despised in the present (Maximus of Tyre 39.5 on Socrates). Contrary to those who claim that Paul's adventures in Acts must be Luke's fiction because they are intriguing, Paul's list here reveals that Luke omits far more than he includes.

Paul matches his opponents on all their hereditary criteria in 11:22; despite technical differences, he probably employs the three designations synonymously. The rhetorical pattern of three rhetorical questions with answers was a conve-nient one (Cicero *Rosc. Amer.* 1.2). Josephus's opponents pointed out that if Josephus claimed to be from Jerusalem, so were they; if he knew the law, so did they; if he was a priest, so were some of them (*Life* 198).

In 11:23, Paul transitions from answering his own questions with equality to his opponents to a longer list where he surpasses them. He denies that they can match him as Christ's "ministers" (*diakonoi*, as in 3:6; 6:4; more harshly, 11:15), because he defines this "ministry" (3:7–9; 4:1; 5:18; 6:3; 11:8) in terms of sufferings for Christ, sharing the way of his cross. (On his parenthetical insanity claim, see 11:1, 16–21; 12:6, 11; comment on 5:13.) Before elaborating more

---

[243] See Pliny *N.H.* 7.45.147–50 (P. Marshall, *Enmity* [1987], 558–60).

[244] Some think that his opponents even expected faith to prevent suffering (Pelagius *Comm.* 2 *Cor.* 4).

[245] E.g., Aeschines *Fals. leg.* 168–69; Cicero *Cat.* 4.1.2; Sallust *Letter of Gnaeus Pompeius* 1; Arrian *Alex.* 7.10.1–2; others cite Demosthenes *Cor.* 173, 249.

[246] Valerius Maximus 3.2.6b; Plutarch *Alex.* 45.3–4; cf. *T. Jos.* 2:3.

narrowly occasions of particular sufferings (11:24–25), he summarizes many "imprisonments, countless floggings, and often near death" in 11:23. Prison (cf. Acts 16:23) was merely detention until trial or execution, but having been in prison and bonds were matters of grave shame in the culture – not a typical subject of boasting![247]

In later accounts, beatings (11:23) endorse the credibility of some radical philosophers (Crates in Diogenes Laertius 6.5.91), prophets (Jos. *Ant.* 6.302–4, 307), or martyrs (2 Macc 6:3). Paul expands on this category of "countless floggings" in 11:24–25a. Renouncing ties with his people would have freed him from synagogue beatings (limited to thirty-nine lashes, Deut 25:3; *m. Mak.* 3:10–12); the record here demonstrates that Paul continued to identify with and preach to his people (as in the accounts in Acts, though Acts never recounts these beatings).[248] It was considered terrible for Roman citizens to be beaten with rods, but it happened occasionally in the provinces,[249] and if Acts is accepted as a source here, Paul may have allowed it for the sake of legal advantage after the fact (Acts 16:37–39). As most scholars note, this report cannot count against Luke's claim about Paul's Roman citizenship (Acts 16:37), especially given his name, a fairly respectable Roman cognomen rare in the Greek East.[250] Ancient sources suggest that shipwreck was a common experience for those who spent much time on the sea (cf. Ps.-Phoc. 25), especially if they traveled even during the more dangerous seasons. Some would view surviving them (especially multiple times), however, as divine protection or even vindication.

If 11:24–25a expand on "beatings" in 11:23, the eightfold anaphora (initial repetition) of "dangers" in 11:26 expands on the "frequent journeys"; travel was difficult in antiquity (see Sir 34:12–13).[251] Dangers from robbers, Jews, Gentiles, and false siblings encompass the human dimension; rivers, the city, wilderness, and sea the environmental dimension. Robbers could be found on land, sea, and rivers (1 Esd 4:23–24) as well as in cities; although less than before Rome suppressed naval piracy, they remained a grave danger (cf. Lk 10:30).[252] Rivers swollen in rainy season were difficult to cross, and in winter and early spring often overflowed onto roads; the interior of Asia Minor probably provided special hazards and difficulties. Even inns were often unsafe (and, for Jews, generally unsavory, used only from necessity). Corinthians (who had more coin types

---

[247] See B. Rapske, *Custody* (1994), 288–97.

[248] On synagogue floggings, see C. Keener, *Matthew* (1999), 322–23. The later and specifically rabbinic rules of *m. Mak.* 3:1–9 are informative but cannot count against Paul's firsthand claim.

[249] E.g., Cicero *Verr.* 2.5.54.142; Josephus *War* 2.308; Quintilian 4.2.113. It also happened, again illegally, to allies (Cicero *Fam.* 10.32.2). For degrees of severity, see B. Rapske, *Custody* (1994), 124–25.

[250] Cf. B. Rapske, *Custody* (1994), 86.

[251] See esp. B. Rapske, "Travel and Trade," 1245–50 in *DNTB*; L. Casson, *Travel in the Ancient World* (London: George Allen & Unwin, 1974).

[252] See C. Keener, *John* [2003], 803–04.

related to Poseidon than to any other deity) knew well the potential hazards for sea travel. The false siblings (cf. Gal 2:4) are the climactic final "danger" because they recall his current conflict (11:13).

Soldiers respected leaders who had endured their rugged lifestyle, such as hunger, temperature extremes, and sleeping on the ground (Sallust *Cat.* 54.4; *Jug.* 85.33).[253] Such sacrifices, also, however, characterized radical philosophers,[254] and sometimes God's servants (Oxford Geniza Text Col. A + 1Q21; Lk 9:58). Some of these tests plainly concerned Paul beyond this passage: sleepless nights (11:27), perhaps caused by ministry, danger, or anxiety for the churches,[255] appear in 6:5; hunger, thirst, and nakedness in 1 Corinthians 4:11 (cf. Rom 8:35); labor in 1 Corinthians 4:12. He also displays anxiety for the churches (11:28) beyond his affliction lists (e.g., 1 Thess 3:5).

He has been displaying his anxiety over the Corinthians (11:28) already throughout this letter (e.g., 9:3–4). It was honorable to suffer with others' hardships;[256] boasting of concern over one's audience displayed affection. As in 11:29, if Paul is genuinely "weak" (10:10; 11:21), it is partly through identifying with the weak (1 Cor 9:22), out of compassion for them; he anguishes over each weak individual who stumbles (cf. 1 Cor 8:9). (Paul's "indignant" is literally, "burn," a description Paul reserves for the most disturbing emotions; cf. 1 Cor 7:9; Rom 1:27.)[257] Paul concludes his summaries of sufferings by summarizing his agenda: he will boast in his sufferings, or what involves his weakness (11:30; cf. 12:5, 9). Sometimes, as in 11:31, Paul calls God to witness to underline that he is not lying in statements about himself (Gal 1:20), possibly before recounting them (cf. Rom 9:1–2).

It is probably not from forgetfulness (cf. 1 Cor 1:16) that Paul positions his specific anecdote of danger (his escape through a window in Damascus' wall, 11:31–33) after the summary in 11:23–29 and its conclusion in 11:30. Paul is hardly finished with his fool's boast (12:1–10), but is increasing the emotional intensity with a specific example of danger (an intriguing one, which Paul perhaps often retold; cf. Acts 9:24–25), a descent perhaps paired with the story of his ascent in 12:2–4.

As many scholars note, the people of Roman Corinth would know that Rome awarded a special wreath (the *corona muralis*) to the brave first soldier to scale an enemy wall; here Paul follows the reverse course. Paul probably intends his escape from a window more as a dramatic example of danger

---

253 These were privations expected in military life (e.g., Xenophon *Anab.* 3.1.23; *Cyr.* 1.2.10; Cicero *Fam.* 8.17.2; Suetonius *Tib.* 18.1–2; Philostratus *Hrk.* 33.41).

254 Musonius 14, p. 92.1–4; Crates *Ep.* 19; Maximus of Tyre 34.9; 36.5; appropriate for others in Musonius 6, p. 54.12–15.

255 See C. Keener, *John* (2003), 841.

256 Cicero *Fam.* 14.3.1; Seneca *Nat. Q.* 4.pref. 15. Cicero uses a rhetorical question similar to Paul's for sharing joys (*Quint. fratr.* 1.3.3).

257 It often applies to anger (Sir 28:10–12; Josephus *Life* 263; Plutarch *Cor.* 21.1–2).

than as humiliation, however, given his positive biblical precedent (Josh 2:15; 1 Sam 19:12).[258]

Although few of Corinth's citizens in the 50s would have known or cared about Aretas, they may well have heard a fuller version of this story from Paul before. Aretas IV was king of the Nabatean Arabs from 9 B.C.E. to 39 C.E., and inaugurated a period of prosperity and massive building. Although once nomadic, the Nabateans by this period had cities and a Hellenized ruling class.

Many think that a Nabatean *ethnarch* in Damascus indicates that Aretas controlled Damascus as he did the surrounding territory, a possibility especially between 37 and 39 C.E. (because Gaius favored local client rulers). Some push his control as early as 34 (Roman coins are so far conspicuously absent from Damascus for 34–62), in view of Pauline chronology. But it is no less possible, in our current state of knowledge, that the ethnarch ruled only the Nabatean population in Damascus, analogous to the Jewish ethnarch in Alexandria (Josephus *Ant.* 14.117), and exercised considerable freedom under a weak local governor. Nabateans had trading colonies elsewhere in the region, and a quarter in Damascus.[259] Interestingly, the traditional site for Ananias' house (cf. Acts 9:10) abuts the Hellenistic-Roman wall in the Nabatean quarter.[260]

Luke's most significant divergence from Paul's account here is that he envisions Paul's enemies as local Jews; this portrayal fits Luke's emphasis, but may also provide an explanation for Nabatean hostility. Whatever Paul was doing in Nabatea for many months ("Arabia," Gal 1:17), he probably at least started in connection with Jews there. A Nabatean ethnarch ruling only Nabateans might have little authority over Paul unless local Jewish leaders consented; and we know that Paul sometimes faced local Jewish hostility (11:24).[261] Both Jews and Nabateans had a strong presence in the city and Nabateans controlled the surrounding countryside. If Jews and Nabateans cooperated against Paul in Damascus, it was to the local governor's advantage to remain uninformed or look the other way, and Paul's situation there was dire indeed.

12:1–10: THE FOOL'S BOAST IN VISIONS

12:1: It is necessary to boast; nothing is to be gained by it, but I will go on to visions and revelations of the Lord.

12:2: I know a person in Christ who fourteen years ago was caught up to the third heaven – whether in the body or out of the body I do not know; God knows.

---

[258] To sneak away by night might appear shameful for an army (Polybius 1.23.4; Josephus *War* 2.551) but not necessarily for an individual.

[259] See R. Riesner, *Early Period* (1998), 75–87, 262.

[260] Ibid., 86–87.

[261] Given recent hostilities between Aretas and Herod Antipas and their overlapping constituencies (*Ant.* 18.109), such cooperation would be politically savvy.

12:3: And I know that such a person – whether in the body or out of the body I do not know; God knows –

12:4: was caught up into Paradise and heard things that are not to be told, that no mortal is permitted to repeat.

12:5: On behalf of such a one I will boast, but on my own behalf I will not boast, except of my weaknesses.

12:6: But if I wish to boast, I will not be a fool, for I will be speaking the truth. But I refrain from it, so that no one may think better of me than what is seen in me or heard from me,

12:7: even considering the exceptional character of the revelations. Therefore, to keep me from being too elated, a thorn was given me in the flesh, a messenger of Satan to torment me, to keep me from being too elated.

12:8: Three times I appealed to the Lord about this, that it would leave me,

12:9: but he said to me, "My grace is sufficient for you, for power is made perfect in weakness." So, I will boast all the more gladly of my weaknesses, so that the power of Christ may dwell in me.

12:10: Therefore I am content with weaknesses, insults, hardships, persecutions, and calamities for the sake of Christ; for whenever I am weak, then I am strong.

*B*y reminding them that boasting is "necessary" (12:1), Paul reminds them that it is not his own choice (12:11). Self-boasting was despised unless properly justified (see A Closer Look at 10:12), but "necessity" was a major justification for deeds otherwise considered inappropriate (Hermogenes 77.6–19). "Nothing is to be gained by it" (NRSV), however, reflects another ancient moral criterion, that of what is "useful" (see comment on 1 Cor 6:12; with regard to boasting, Plutarch *Praising Inoffensively* 15, *Mor.* 544D). After providing this warning, Paul shifts (12:1b) from sufferings (11:23–33) to his most dramatic boast, in revelations (12:1–9); yet the only specific revelation he articulates invites Paul to embrace his weakness (12:7–9). Even here, Paul boasts only in his weakness (12:5, 9–10), as before (11:21, 29–30). He frames his climax (12:5–10) with weakness (12:5, 9–10); possibly weakness also frames 11:30–12:5, if Paul pairs his "embarrassing" descent in 11:33 with his ecstatic ascent in 12:2–4. But whereas the Corinthians may have heard Paul's Damascus story before, Paul may be sharing this vision report for the first time, though the occasion he specifies occurred circa 42 C.E., nearly a decade before Paul's first visit to Corinth.

Against some, Paul does not "parody" an ascension narrative; he parodies only boasting. Although most scholars believe that Paul counters his rivals' boasts in charismatic phenomena, most of Paul's boasts have differed from his rivals' criteria (11:23–33), and perhaps not all the rivals appreciated aspects of Paul's spiritual experience (5:12–13). At the very least, however, Paul's visions are analogous to their boasts, as something powerful and desirable; Paul thus focuses on the thorn and his weakness. Still, he is more charismatic and prophetic than his rivals could hope to be (1 Cor 14:18, 37–38).

Like many biblical prophets, Paul regularly experienced visions (e.g., Ezek 1:1; Dan 7:1); this also was a dominant mode of discourse in the apocalyptic tradition (cf., e.g., *1 En.* 1:2; 13:8–10; *2 Bar.* 81:4). The term for "revelations" (12:1, 7) does not come from the LXX but Paul elsewhere uses it for divine disclosures (1 Cor 14:6, 26; Gal 1:12; 2:2; cf. Eph 3:3; Rev 1:1); in apocalypses angels sometimes mediated these (e.g., *1 En.* 72:1; 74:2; *4 Ezra* 4:1).

Although visions "of the Lord" may specify simply their source (cf. Ezek 1:1; 8:3; 40:2; perhaps Rev 1:1), they may well be visions whose object is the Lord (cf. 3:18; Gal 1:12, 16; Is 6:1; Ezek 1:26), as in the example in 12:8–9. Some Greeks sought mystical vision of God through contemplating the divine or rituals (see comment on 3:18); Jewish mystics also sought visions of God's throne chariot, through secret knowledge, fasting and other means. (On the soul's ascent in death or visionary experiences in both Greek and Jewish sources, see comment on 3:18; 4:18–5:1.)[262] Although Paul sought intimacy with Christ (3:18; 5:13), he may not have "sought" visions per se; he was "caught up" (cf. Ezek 8:1–3). Jewish writers also spoke of being "caught up" (Wis 4:10–11; *1 En.* 39:3; 52:1). Sometimes they emphasized the dangers or adventures of the ascent (later rabbis told that of four rabbis who beheld paradise, only one escaped unscathed); Paul himself received a "thorn" (12:7).[263]

Paul's "person in Christ" could be someone else, but is presumably Paul, who is here boasting in visions (12:1). Luke also claims that Paul had multiple visions (e.g., Acts 9:12; 16:9), many of these involving the Lord himself (9:3–6; 18:9; 22:17). Furthermore, Paul would hardly need a thorn to compensate for excessive revelations (12:7) if he had no significant ones. One could speak of oneself or another as "that person,"[264] and some groups even reverently described their founder in such language (Iamblichus *Pyth. Life* 18.88). Some suggest that Jewish apocalyptists sometimes transferred their own visionary experiences to the pseudonymous characters in whose names they wrote; apart from Philo (and perhaps 4Q491), the Jewish reports before Paul's time are pseudonymous. Some Greek writers allowed one to describe one's experience as another's if one were ashamed to describe it openly (Isocrates *Demon.* 34). Most relevantly, one could reduce the offense of boasting by attributing the claim to another (while transparently speaking of oneself; Danker cites Demosthenes *Cor.* 321).

Not knowing whether he was in the body or out of it (12:2–3) might be rhetorical *aporia* (feigned uncertainty), but Paul has already contrasted being at home in the body with the afterlife of being away from the body and at home with the Lord (5:6–8). Although in some Jewish texts only the souls were

---

[262] See also sources in C. Keener, *John* (2003), 538.

[263] Visionary dangers may earlier echo Egyptian postmortem travel (e.g., *Book of Dead* Spells 7, 145–46).

[264] E.g., Ps–Plato *Hippias* passim; *y. Hag.* 2:1, §9; Taan. 1:4, §1; Suk. 5:1, §7; Ket. 4:14, §1; Shebiit 6:1, §9.

caught up to see heaven (*1 En.* 71:1–6),[265] sometimes the experience sounds as if it involves the entire body (Ezek 2:2; 3:14, 24; 8:3; 11:1, 24; Wis 4:11; *1 En.* 39:3).

A CLOSER LOOK: PARADISE AND THE THIRD HEAVEN

Because the Persian loanword "paradise" meant "garden," it applied well to the garden in Eden (Gen 2:8–3:24 LXX; Josephus *Ant.* 1.37). Jewish people spoke of paradise as in heaven (*T. Ab.* 20:14 A; *3 Bar.* 4:6) and expected a new paradise or Eden in the future (*4 Ezra* 7:36; 8:52; *2 Bar.* 51:11).[266] Jewish texts placed paradise, the new Eden, on earth in the coming age, but in heaven at the present. Jewish texts ranged from 3 to 365 in the number of heavens they imagined; the most common numbers were three (*T. Levi* 2–3) and seven. Texts often placed paradise in one of these (in the third in *2 En.* 8:1; *Apoc. Mos.* 37:5; 40:1); the lowest of "heavens" was the lower atmosphere. Paul presumably envisions paradise as in the third of three heavens.

Visions of paradise appear commonly in apocalyptic texts (*L.A.E.* 25:3). Later rabbis often retold the story of the four rabbis who achieved a vision of paradise, in which only Akiba escaped unharmed (*t. Hag.* 2:3–4; *b. Hag.* 14b–15b).

Instead of boasting in the content of his revelation, however, Paul boasts that it was something too sacred to be discussed (12:4) – again mocking boasting. (He will recount a revelation – but one that boasts in his weakness – in the following verses.) Greeks recognized such mysteries in some philosophers;[267] religious secrets;[268] magical formulas and rites; and most commonly in their mystery cults.[269] Jewish sages also recognized some categories of mysteries inappropriate for public dissemination.[270] Yet even in the mysteries, the secret could be shared with initiates! Perhaps most relevantly, some mysteries were simply too sublime for description in words (Plutarch *Isis* 78, *Mor.* 383A), as Paul seems to have agreed (Rom 8:26; perhaps 1 Cor 14:2). (In a later era, some think that St. Thomas Aquinas eventually withdrew from his earlier scholastic career partly because of such experiences.)

Only to the extent that he embraces his human weakness (12:5, 10) does he fully depend on and qualify for God's power (12:9; 13:3–4; cf. 1 Cor 2:3–5; 15:56) – not the sort of values the status-conscious Corinthians would appreciate. Rather than boasting, he wishes not to appeal to anything others cannot already see in him (12:6), an acceptable claim (Cicero *Caecin.* 11.36). (To claim that one will

---

[265] Closer to Greek models (e.g., Maximus of Tyre 10.2–3; 38.3; Porphyry *Marc.* 9.172–83).

[266] Pervasive in rabbinic texts, e.g., *Sipre Behuq.* pq. 3.263.1.5; *Sipre Deut.* 357.6.6.

[267] E.g., Philo *Worse* 175–76; Menander Rhetor 2.17, 442.28–29; Iamblichus *Pyth. Life* 31.193–94; 34.246.

[268] *PGM* 4.2474–90; Philostratus *Hrk.* 2.10–11; 44.2–4; 58.2.

[269] E.g., Lysias *Or.* 6.51, §107; Callimachus *Aetia* 3.75.8–9; Aelian *Farmers* 1; Apuleius *Metam.* 11.23.

[270] See sources in C. Keener, *Matthew* (1999), 378–79.

not say something, while incidentally saying it, also was a frequent rhetorical move.)[271] Paul reinforces his weakness by recounting only one revelation he received from the Lord – a revelation that endorsed the suffering that would compensate for his other revelations (12:7–9).

Ancient healing shrines, including the famous Epidauros sanctuary near Corinth, promoted themselves with epigraphic testimonies of healings there. Ironically, however, Paul's prayer for deliverance is not granted; the Lord offers grace instead, and that is better than deliverance. (Many see here a parody of the genre of healing stories, as Paul parodies the wall crown in 11:32–33 and the secret revelation in 12:4.) Some parallel Paul's three prayers with threefold Jewish or Greek prayers, but the number may simply recollect how many times Paul prayed before the Lord spoke. Some also think that Paul's threefold prayer recalls Jesus's own threefold prayer at Gethsemane, with an analogous result (Mk 14:32–41).

Scholars debate the precise identity of Paul's "thorn in the flesh." Some opt for moral or psychological temptations (more popular among Medieval interpreters and Reformers); others for a physical ailment (popular today); still others (including many today; Chrysostom; Theodoret; Severian) for Paul's opponents, whether persecutions or the opponents he has been challenging (or both).[272] In favor of the physical ailment is Paul's use of "flesh," but this cannot be decisive (see below). Paul also had an ailment in Galatians 4:13 (although not of the eyes, against some interpretations of 4:15).[273]

Opposition is more likely. The expression undoubtedly alludes to the ancient thorn in the "side" or the "eyes" (Num 33:55, Josh 23:13), where God leaves some of Israel's enemies to test them. Paul has just rehearsed his sufferings for the gospel (11:23–33), and earlier used the same term for "torment" (*kolaphizō*, "beat," 12:7) for physical abuse against himself (1 Cor 4:11). It is not difficult to envision "an angel of Satan" stirring crowds to persecute Paul; it is also possible that the opposition includes the agents of Satan against whom Paul has been railing (11:13–15). If Paul knew that earlier writers used a cognate of his term for "thorn" (*skolops*) for Persian crucifixion, the image is also appropriate for one sharing Christ's sufferings. "Was given me" is the "divine passive"; Paul asks the Lord to remove the thorn because the Lord was sovereign over it (12:7–9). That God is sovereign over Satan and uses him fits OT and mainstream Jewish perspectives (see analogously Job 1:6–2:6).

Whatever the thorn, Paul embraces any weakness on the human level if in it he may find Christ's grace and power more fully (12:9–10).[274] This is the same

---

271 E.g., Demosth. *Cor.* §268; Cicero *Fam.* 13.5.3; Men. Rhet. 2.14, 429.1–4 ; Phlm 19.

272 For a thorough survey, see M. Thrall, *2 Corinthians* (2000), 809–18.

273 Treating another as dearer than one's eyes was a figure of speech (e.g., Catullus 3.5; 14.1–3; 82.1–4; *Sipre Deut.* 313.1.4).

274 Scholars compare Philo *Mos.* 1.67–69, in which those oppressed were not destroyed, and their weakness (what sought their destruction) was their power (when they would shine with the greatest glory).

theology he articulates throughout the letter (4:7–17), the theology he finds most clearly in the message of the cross (13:4).

12:11–18: CONCLUDING APPEAL AND SUMMARY

12:11: I have been a fool! You forced me to it. Indeed you should have been the ones commending me, for I am not at all inferior to these super-apostles, even though I am nothing.

12:12 The signs of a true apostle were performed among you with utmost patience, signs and wonders and mighty works.

12:13: How have you been worse off than the other churches, except that I myself did not burden you? Forgive me this wrong!

12:14: Here I am, ready to come to you this third time. And I will not be a burden, because I do not want what is yours but you; for children ought not to lay up for their parents, but parents for their children.

12:15: I will most gladly spend and be spent for you. If I love you more, am I to be loved less?

12:16: Let it be assumed that I did not burden you. Nevertheless (you say) since I was crafty, I took you in by deceit.

12:17: Did I take advantage of you through any of those whom I sent to you?

12:18: I urged Titus to go, and sent the brother with him. Titus did not take advantage of you, did he? Did we not conduct ourselves with the same spirit? Did we not take the same steps?

*I*f Paul prepared for his fool's boast with the requisite explanations and apologies in 11:16–21, he follows it with the same in his conclusion in 12:11–13 (which I have not assigned a separate section only because of its brevity). (Either 12:11–13 or 12:11 are epidiorthosis, a rhetorical justification following what one has already written.) Boasting was justifiable if others "forced" one to do it,[275] as in 12:11. Paul was forced to do it by comparison with his opponents (10:10–12; 11:5–6), and because those who should have defended him failed to do so (12:11). (On the "super-apostles," see discussion at 11:5.) Toward the end of a speech, one might revisit the charges one had answered. It also was natural to remind one's audience of one's benefactions, thereby arousing their friendly feelings toward oneself and hostile feelings toward one's accusers.[276]

Some think Paul's claim to be a "nobody" (12:11) echoes his opponents' derision of him; the claim naturally tended to denigrate.[277] Paul's use of the concept

---

[275] E.g., Quintilian 11.1.17–19; Cicero *Fam.* 5.12.8; Pliny *Ep.* 1.8.6.

[276] Cf. *Rhet. Alex.* 34, 1439b.15–1440b.3; 36, 1443b.16–21; 1444.35–1445a.26.

[277] Cf. Philostratus *Love Letters* 66 (8). Aeschylus *Suppliant Maidens* 749, applies it to powerless women.

is not, however, limited to apologetic contexts (1 Cor 13:2). It also serves as an emphatic way of disavowing his former boasting, however: Having aired the evidence in his favor, he now refuses to claim honor. A Stoic could apply the title to all mortals (Seneca *Lucil.* 101.1); to those without understanding (Epictetus *Diatr.* 2.24.19); or to himself if he depends on others (Epictetus *Diatr.* 4.8.25).

The Corinthians themselves were witnesses of Paul's "signs and wonders," hence did not require his testimony; these should have been concrete enough to have invited their defense of his apostleship (12:11–12). That "sign" in rhetoric was a secure foundation for certainty might underline Paul's point for any aware of this technical usage. Despite some scholars' skepticism about Paul's meaning, however, he is drawing on language for miracles familiar in the LXX and early Christianity (e.g., Deut 6:22; 7:19). He elsewhere claims such miracles (Rom 15:19) and sometimes his audience's experience of them (Gal 3:5; cf. 1 Cor 12:28). Whether Paul's rivals claimed signs[278] or he is again outclassing even their categories (as in 11:23–33 and perhaps 12:1–4), he writes as if his opponents cannot rival his signs.

The position and importance of funds in 12:13–18 suggests that it was prominent in the conflict between Paul and the Corinthians (and made him more vulnerable regarding the collection, Chs. 8–9). Paul revisits his refusal to "burden" the church (see 11:7–9) with biting irony. "Forgive me [for sacrificing to avoid your hardship]!" is ironic; orators could say one thing when expecting the audience to construe the opposite (Cicero *Or. Brut.* 40.137).

Some Corinthian patrons wanted to sponsor Paul, in effect making him their client; to reject their gifts was offensive (cf. 11:7). Paul argues that he is no mere household sage, but instead the congregation's spiritual patron and father (12:14; cf. 1 Cor 4:14–21).[279] Given this relationship, it is appropriate for him to provide for them rather than the reverse; they are in *his* debt. Paul has thus spent even himself on their behalf (12:15), the way of the greatest possible benefactors (many cite Seneca *Providence* 5.4), especially in Christian teaching (8:9; Phil 2:4–11, 17).[280] He loves them for themselves and not for what he could acquire from them, a compelling affectionate plea (commentators compare Cicero *Fin.* 2.26.85).

Paul draws on a vast reservoir of cultural understanding. A benefactor would accept honor (they failed to grant Paul this, 12:11), but not money (e.g., *Apoll. K. Tyre* 10). A teacher who sacrificed for his student's sake was considered honorable indeed (Plutarch *Alc.* 7.3), but this role was more often attributed to parents

---

278 Cf. perhaps some of his Jewish contemporaries (Juvenal *Sat.* 6.542–47; Acts 19:13; magical papyri suggest that Jewish formulas were highly valued).

279 Commentaries cite numerous parallels to 12:14 (see, e.g., F. Danker, *II Corinthians* [1989], 201). Associations could call patrons "fathers," a practice followed by many synagogues.

280 Sacrificing oneself in battle or other conflict was praiseworthy (Livy 10.28.12–29.1), especially for leaders (Cicero *Cat.* 4.2.3).

(e.g., *Let. Aris.* 248). Parents were children's benefactors, in a sense (cf. Seneca *Ben.* 3.11.2), and children were hard-pressed to fulfill a parent's role (Fronto *Ad Verum Imp.* 2.10). (Children might reciprocate parents' gifts in the parents' old age;[281] Paul does not press the analogy that far.) An ideal ruler provides wisdom like a father provides his children's needs (Xenophon *Cyr.* 8.1.1). The bond between parents and children was one of the closest offered by nature.[282] Gratitude to parents (what they here neglect) was thus an essential obligation, and ingratitude to them a serious offense (Xenophon *Mem.* 2.2.3, 13–14).

Paul then exposes their inconsistency, reducing their arguments to the absurd. Although they complain that he (as he puts it) rejected personal gain, they also mistrust his motives regarding the collection, requiring his defense (12:15–18). So although he did not want to burden them, he simultaneously desired to exploit them deceitfully! That Paul's opponents had criticized his plans for the collection is likely; charlatans often exploited people (2:17), and speakers (whether philosophers, moralists, or orators) often charged other leaders as greedy and exploitive. Paul's "craftiness" in 12:16 echoes language in 4:2 and 11:3 (generally rare in Paul); this may suggest that Paul did not originate the issue.

Speeches often invited an audience to point to any wrongdoing or failure of benefaction of the speaker's, as in 12:17–18 (cf. comment on 1 Cor 9:1–13).[283] Although the Corinthians had received Titus well at least once (7:13–15), Paul wants to ensure that they will treat favorably the collection, which remains outstanding (cf. 9:3–5). That Paul asks the question without offering evidence indicates that he expects the Corinthians to agree that Titus did not exploit them (although he possibly knew that some sophists had received payment deposited with a third party).[284]

The expected answer regarding Titus's exploitation (12:18) is "No" (cf. 7:15; 8:16–17). Paul's reference to "the brother" with Titus could refer to any traveling companion (even during his first journey, it is unlikely that Titus would have traveled alone), but more likely refers to "the brother" of 8:18, 22, whom Paul was sending along with the letter that included Chapter 8. This is one of the strongest arguments for viewing 2 Corinthians 10–13 as later than the rest of 2 Corinthians, although it is not sufficient to carry the weight of the case by itself if, as we have argued, strong arguments support the letter's unity. The verbs for sending are aorist in both 8:18, 22, and 12:18, and if the former are epistolary aorists (the action completed from the standpoint of the Corinthians receiving the letter), there is no reason that the aorist cannot be epistolary in

---

[281] E.g., Hesiod *Op.* 188–89; Hierocles *On Duties. Parents* 4.25.53; Tob 4:3–4; Josephus *Ag. Ap.* 2.206; 1 Tim 5:4.

[282] Cicero *De Officiis* 1.17.54; Stoics in *Fin.* 3.19.62.

[283] E.g., 1 Sam 12:3–5; Lysias *Or.* 8.3, §112; 24.24–25, §170; Aeschines *Embassy* 160; Dion. Hal. *R.A.* 4.33.1–36.3; Cicero *Sest.* 21.47.

[284] Cf. B. Winter, *Philo and Paul* (1997), 218 (although he views 12:16 as responding to a real rather than a hypothetical charge).

12:18. Titus not having exploited them could then refer either to his first visit or again represent an epistolary aorist (although this is more difficult).

12:19–13:10: PAUL'S VISIT

12:19: Have you been thinking all along that we have been defending ourselves before you? We are speaking in Christ before God. Everything we do, beloved, is for the sake of building you up.

12:20: For I fear that when I come, I may find you not as I wish, and that you may find me not as you wish; I fear that there may perhaps be quarreling, jealousy, anger, selfishness, slander, gossip, conceit, and disorder.

12:21: I fear that when I come again, my God may humble me before you, and that I may have to mourn over many who previously sinned and have not repented of the impurity, sexual immorality, and licentiousness that they have practiced.

13:1: This is the third time I am coming to you. "Any charge must be sustained by the evidence of two or three witnesses."

13:2: I warned those who sinned previously and all the others, and I warn them now while absent, as I did when present on my second visit, that if I come again, I will not be lenient –

13:3: since you desire proof that Christ is speaking in me. He is not weak in dealing with you, but is powerful in you.

13:4: For he was crucified in weakness, but lives by the power of God. For we are weak in him, but in dealing with you we will live with him by the power of God.

13:5: Examine yourselves to see whether you are living in the faith. Test yourselves. Do you not realize that Jesus Christ is in you? – unless, indeed, you fail to meet the test!

13:6: I hope you will find out that we have not failed.

13:7: But we pray to God that you may not do anything wrong – not that we may appear to have met the test, but that you may do what is right, though we may seem to have failed.

13:8: For we cannot do anything against the truth, but only for the truth.

13:9: For we rejoice when we are weak and you are strong. This is what we pray for, that you may become perfect.

13:10: So I write these things while I am away from you, so that when I come, I may not have to be severe in using the authority that the Lord has given me for building up and not for tearing down.

When Paul comes, he will not depend on them financially (12:14; cf. 11:9–10), because he will come as their parent. Like their parent (cf. 1 Cor 4:15, 21), he will also execute discipline when he comes (12:20–13:1), because they are dissatisfied with his gentle demeanor (10:1–2, 10–11).[285] They should prepare themselves for his coming by testing themselves (13:5) – hopefully sparing Paul the pain of needing to exercise the threatened discipline (13:10), as in an earlier case (cf. 1:23–2:3).

Paul's apparent self-defense (esp. 2:14–7:4; 10:1–12:18) has been for their sakes, not his own (12:19; cf. 1:19–22; 5:20–6:1); he is called only to build them up (cf. 10:8; 13:10). Leaders sometimes emphasized that they had acted only for the good of their hearers, not for their own interests (cf. 1 Cor 10:33). This was especially important in the case of self-praise (see A Closer Look at 10:12).[286] Yet just as defense speeches typically shifted to offensive prosecution at the end, so Paul now begins to convict the Corinthians, warning that he must soon act as their judge (13:1–3).

Paul repeats his fear of needing to confront the Corinthians both regarding their divisiveness (12:20) and sexual sin (12:21), both major issues in 1 Corinthians. Unless Chapters 10–13 are earlier than 1–7 (which is unlikely; see 12:18), Paul's concern that they have not repented indicates that his diplomatic praise of their repentance in 7:9–11 involves only the specifically mentioned issue of the offender (7:12). Paul has diplomatically disposed of the offender, the collection, and opponents; now he must address the church members' behavior.

Paul previously avoided coming lest he need to exercise discipline regarding the offender, sending a warning letter instead (1:23–2:4). Now he is offering a more general warning, aware that he may need to exercise discipline (13:1–3), hoping that they will repent and spare him the need to discipline them (13:10). If they do not, Paul will suspend his gentle approach, which they took as non-confrontational weakness (10:1–11). Whether the three witnesses of 13:1 refer to observations from Paul's three visits, to literal witnesses, or simply evoke forensic imagery, Paul uses the language of prosecution in a church court (cf. 1 Cor 5:4–6:8), following biblical and early Jewish judicial procedure (Deut 17:6; 19:15; 1 Tim 5:19; Josephus *Ant.* 4.219).[287]

Paul has spoken much of "proof" (*dokimē*) in this letter (2:9; 8:2; 9:13; elsewhere in the NT only Rom 5:4; Phil 2:22; cf. cognates in 2 Cor 8:8, 22), perhaps in response to the sense that the Corinthians want "proof" that Paul is superior to his rivals (13:3). Here, as elsewhere, he turns the demand for proof back on the Corinthians (13:5; cf. 2:9; 8:8; the opponents in 10:18), not so he may appear "proved" but for their sake (13:7, *dokimos*). Like Jesus who yielded to the cross but was raised by God's power, Paul embraces the weakness God places in his way, depending on God's power to more than compensate, to fulfill his calling (13:4) and live with him (4:10–13).

---

[285] Chapter 13 recalls many motifs in Chapter 10, framing Chapters 11–12 (for details, see J. Lambrecht, *Second Corinthians* [1999], 158–59).

[286] See, e.g., F. Danker, *II Corinthians* (1989), 204.

[287] See early Jewish procedures in C. Keener, *Matthew* (1999), 454.

Have the Corinthians sought to evaluate Paul (cf. 11:5–6; 1 Cor 2:14–15)? In his conclusion (as in any ancient apologetic speech or work), Paul turns the tables, and challenges them to evaluate themselves (13:5; cf. 1 Cor 11:28; Gal 6:4). Paul often emphasizes "approval" or having passed the test (Rom 5:4; 14:18; 16:10); failing the test is a serious shortcoming (Rom 1:28).[288] Passing the test in the present prepared one to pass it eschatologically (1 Cor 3:13). Some philosophers stressed self-evaluation based on reason (Epictetus *Diatr.* 1.4); but the thought of "approval," including divine approval, is widespread (e.g., *Sib. Or.* 3.824; *T. Jos.* 2:6–7), and some later epistolary theorists called letters of praise "approval" letters.[289] The test here is whether Jesus is in them (13:5), as he is in Paul (13:3), and Paul is united with him (13:4); this was an essential mark of the Christian life (e.g., Gal 2:20; Rom 8:9). If they as the fruit of Paul's ministry are genuinely converted, then they ought to recognize the genuineness of Paul as well. A leader might remind his followers that he proposed something favorable for them not to gain more honor, but for their sake (13:7; *FIRA* 1.78). Honoring truth (13:8) also was an acclaimed virtue.[290]

13:11–13: CLOSING GREETINGS

13:11: Finally, brothers and sisters, farewell. Put things in order, listen to my appeal, agree with one another, live in peace; and the God of love and peace will be with you.

13:12: Greet one another with a holy kiss. All the saints greet you.

13:13: The grace of the Lord Jesus Christ, the love of God, and the communion of the Holy Spirit be with all of you.

*P*aul closes with one summary exhortation, greetings, and a blessing. "Agree with one another" reflects language often directed against factions; the Corinthians still are divided (12:20; cf. 1 Cor 1:10–12). For the kiss and greetings, see comment on 1 Corinthians 16:20.

Scholars often have called the blessing in 13:13 proto-trinitarian, although many argue that in Paul's day this was a matter of Christian experience more than specific articulation. We might not make so much of the linkage of Jesus, God, and Holy Spirit here except for two factors: Paul portrays Jesus as a divine Lord (cf. comment on 1 Cor 1:3), probably related to wisdom (1 Cor 1:30; 8:6), and he parallels Jesus, God, and the Spirit elsewhere (1 Cor 12:4–6). That Paul

---

[288] "Examination" is also the language of ethical criteria (Rom 2:18; 12:2; Phil 1:10; 1 Thess 5:21) and those proved in ministry (2 Cor 8:22; Phil 2:22; 1 Thess 2:4).

[289] S. Stowers, *Letter Writing* (1986), 78.

[290] See, e.g., 2 Thess 2:10; 1Q27 I.9–11; Jos. *War* 2.141; *Let. Aris.* 206; Maximus of Tyre 18.5.

uses such language is no more difficult to believe than the notion held by some that the linkage occurred spontaneously a generation later (Matt 28:19; Jn 1:1; 14:16–17).

The phrase "communion of the Holy Spirit" can be taken as "fellowship with the Spirit"; "fellowship created by the Spirit" (relevant also to 13:11; Phil 2:1); or both (unless Paul had explained the phrase, he might not expect his audience to differentiate various uses of the genitive; cf. 1 Cor 1:9). "Love of God" can mean "love for God"; "love authored by God"; or "God's love for you." Given the nature of blessings and "wish-prayers" (see comment on 1 Cor 1:3), Paul is praying for God to accomplish these works among them.

Author Index

Scripture and Apocrypha Index

Note: This index excludes 1 and 2 Corinthians.

4 Maccabees (*cont.*)
Sirach

Tobit
Wisdom of Solomon

NEW TESTAMENT

Matthew

Index of Extrabiblical Jewish and Christian Sources

Note: Use of attributions is for identification, not passing judgment on authenticity.

269

Other Greco-Roman Sources

Note: Use of attributions is for identification, not passing judgment on authenticity.

Subject Index

CPSIA information can be obtained at www.ICGtesting.com
Printed in the USA
LVOW08s1817070115

421884LV00004B/879/P